THE

DARTMOUTH COLLEGE

CAUSES

AND THE

SUPREME COURT OF THE UNITED STATES.

By JOHN M. SHIRLEY.

THE LAWBOOK EXCHANGE, LTD.
Clark, New Jersey

ISBN 9781584773375 (hardcover)
ISBN 9781616192716 (paperback)

Lawbook Exchange edition 2003, 2012

The quality of this reprint is equivalent to the quality of the original work.

THE LAWBOOK EXCHANGE, LTD.
33 Terminal Avenue
Clark, New Jersey 07066-1321

*Please see our website for a selection of our other publications
and fine facsimile reprints of classic works of legal history:*
www.lawbookexchange.com

Library of Congress Cataloging-in-Publication Data

Shirley, John M. (John Major), 1831-1887.
 The Dartmouth College causes and the Supreme Court of the United States
/by John M. Shirley.
   p. cm.
 Originally published: Chicago: G. Jones, 1895.
 Includes bibliographical references and index.
 ISBN 1-58477-337-5 (cloth: alk. paper)
   1.Dartmouth College—Trials, litigation, etc. 2. Dartmouth College—
Charters. 3.
Possessory actions—New Hampshire—Hanover. 4. United States. Supreme
Court. I. Title.

KFN1321 .S53 2003
378.742'3—dc21   2002041359

Printed in the United States of America on acid-free paper

THE

DARTMOUTH COLLEGE

CAUSES

AND THE

SUPREME COURT OF THE UNITED STATES.

By JOHN M. SHIRLEY.

CHICAGO:
G. I. JONES, PUBLISHER.
1895.

My aim has been to put the reader in the place of the great actors in these controversies. These pages were penned in the fierce gallopade of a busy life, within earshot, as it were, of the paternal homes of the Websters and Bartletts, those of Thomas W. Thompson, Worcester, and their compeers, within the shadow of the lone mountain they loved so well, upon the historic ground so often trodden by them, and in the midst of the traditions relating to these causes and their origin. Besides those referred to in text and notes, I am indebted to Jeremiah Smith, late one of the justices of the Supreme Judicial Court of New Hampshire, and son of the late Chief Justice Smith, for a mass of valuable papers; James Barrett, of the Supreme Court of Vermont, for the use of copies of letters of Kent to Marsh, Hopkinson to Marsh, and others to which no special reference has been made; Charles H. Bell, President of the New Hampshire Historical Society; and the late Robert Means Mason, for verifying copies of the "Harvey-Webster Papers" and "Mason Papers;" Professor Edwin D. Sanborn, of Dartmouth College, for Webster's original notes of the arguments at Exeter and Washington, his MS. argument, the brief of Hopkinson as written out for publication by Webster, and letters of Hopkinson and President Brown to Webster; the New Hampshire Historical Society, for placing their treasures, and particularly the "Farrar Papers," at my service; and William H. Duncan, for the use of the "Olcott Papers."

J. M. S.

ANDOVER, N. H., Oct. 1, 1879.

CHAPTER I.

THE CAUSES SUMMARIZED — WEBSTER'S REASONS FOR BRING-
ING SUITS IN THE FEDERAL COURTS — CHANGES IN THE
CHARTER PROPOSED BY TRUSTEES AND OTHERS — EFFECT
OF THE DECISION — THE SUPREME COURT OF THE UNITED
STATES.

THERE were five civil causes. Four were brought to test
the validity of the act of the Legislature of New Hampshire of June 27, 1816, "to amend the charter, and enlarge
and improve the corporation of Dartmouth College," and
the supplementary acts of December 18 and 26, 1816.

The College was located upon the Connecticut River, at
Hanover, in the county of Grafton. Haverhill on the Connecticut, and Plymouth on the Pemigewasset, were then, as
now, the half shire-towns of that county. The Court of
Common Pleas sat at Haverhill on February 25, and at
Plymouth on September 9, 1817; and the Superior Court
sat at the same places respectively on May 20 and November 4, 1817.

The first action was "trespass on the case," brought by
"The Trustees of Dartmouth College," in the Common
Pleas, against William H. Woodward, chief justice of that
court, for converting, etc., on October 7, 1816, "divers
books & records in writing, containing the doings & transactions of sd. trustees from the time of their first meeting
as a corporation until sd. seventh day of October, & also
of the original charter of sd. college and the common seal
of sd. college, & also of all the books of account containing
charges in favor of sd. trustees, & all the leases, bonds, notes
& other assurances in writing," etc. The mandate was, to
attach the defendant's goods to the value of $50,000, " and

(1)

for want thereof," to arrest his body. The writ was dated February 8, and served February 10, 1817, by "attaching a chair," "valued at one dollar," and giving "him a summons for his appearance at court." The case was entered at the February term, 1817.

The defendant filed the formal plea of "not guilty," "reserving liberty to waive this plea & plead anew, as well in abatement as in bar, at the Superior Court." The plaintiffs, "agreeing to the reservation aforesaid, & reserving liberty to waive this replication & reply anew at the Superior Court," replied "that the plea aforesaid, in manner & form aforesaid pleaded, & the matters therein contained, are not sufficient in law to bar the plfs.," etc., and prayed "judgment for their damages and costs."

The cause could not properly be tried before the defendant, and these formal pleadings were filed by an arrangement between the counsel, for the purpose of taking the cause directly to the highest court of the State. Accordingly it was entered at the May term, 1817, of the Superior Court. The plaintiffs amended their writ by striking out the declaration and substituting a new one. It was twice argued. The report states that "the cause was submitted to the decision of the court upon a statement of facts, * * * and it was agreed that if either party should desire it, the statement of facts should be turned into a special verdict, in order that the case might be carried to the Supreme Court of the United States." (1 N. H. 111.) The precise facts will appear hereafter.

This case is reported in 1 N. H. 111–138, and in 1 Wheat. 518–715. (4 Curtis's Dec. 463–534.) The case in both courts is also reported at length in a volume of about four hundred pages, by Timothy Farrar, the son of one of the plaintiffs, the former partner of Mr. Webster, and one of the counsel in the cause, from whose report that of Wheaton was taken.

The United States Circuit Court, in which three of these

cases were brought, sat in the extreme south-eastern corner of the State, at Portsmouth and Exeter, on May 1 and October 1, 1818, respectively.

The second was a suit in ejectment (for $3,000), brought in this court by Horace Hatch, of Norwich, Vermont, against Richard Lang, of Hanover, for a lot of land about one mile east of the College. This writ was dated March 9, 1818. In form, a special verdict about twenty pages in length was rendered at the October term, 1818, and the case went, upon a certificate of the division of opinion between the judges, to the Supreme Court of the United States.

The third was a similar suit of ejectment in the same court (for $2,000), brought by David Pierce, of Woodstock, Vermont, *ex dem.* Job Lyman, on March 27, 1818, against Benjamin Gilbert, of Hanover. The trustees of the University were vouched in at the October term, 1818, and made defendants, and the cause went to the Supreme Court on a similar verdict.

The fourth was a similar suit (for $3,000), brought by Charles Marsh, also of Woodstock, one of the trustees, and one of the plaintiffs in the first suit in the State court, against William Allen (afterwards the plaintiff in the Bowdoin College case, and the son-in-law of Dr. John Wheelock, the former president of the College and University), Henry Hutchinson, and Ahimaz B. Simpson, on March 27, 1818, in the same court, with a like result.

Mr. Mason advised the bringing of another suit, to test the right to the libraries, etc., but the clerks fail to find any trace of it upon the files of the courts.

The criminal prosecutions instituted in the name of the State, which grew out of these troubles, were fruitless, and seemingly had no influence upon the current of the others.

The fifth was instituted on September 23, 1819, by " William Allen, clerk, & Maria Wheelock, widow," " executors of the last will & testament of John Wheelock," against the College for $10,000, for the services, etc., of Wheelock as president of the College. It was entered at the November term, 1819, of the Superior Court, at Plymouth. At the May term, 1820, judgment was rendered for the plaintiffs for $7,886.41 damages, and for their costs. This case was supposed to involve, upon one point, the same question as the others.

The suits in the United States Circuit Court were instituted by the special direction of Mr. Webster. His reasons were twofold. The first suit was not instituted by him, but by Mills Olcott, of Hanover, secretary, etc., of the board of trustees. Webster came into it " at the eleventh hour."

The writ of error in this case was brought as a " forlorn hope." It raised but " a single point," —whether the legislative acts impaired the obligation of contracts. Upon the whole case, Webster had but little faith in that point.

Webster was not a learned man, much less a learned lawyer; but he was a great man. A sort of half justice has been done to his purely intellectual gifts; a century hence ample justice may be done them. Few gave him credit for tact and management; but no American equalled him in his knowledge of men, and his power to overawe and persuade judges as well as others. No skilled performer ever handled the keys of his instrument with any thing like the consummate skill and art with which Webster, when hard pressed, played upon the prejudices, passions, and sympathies, as well as the understanding, of men. He turned his knowledge of genealogy into a system of philosophy. He knew Judge Marshall, his court, their prejudices, and their antecedents.

His conviction was that Marshall would set aside these acts, upon the ground taken by Mason in his argument at Exeter, that they were " not within the general scope of legislative power," if that point could be got before the court.

The first reason Mr. Webster confided to those who were

close to his heart, as he afterwards did to Choate. We copy the following letter *verbatim :—*

BOSTON, Dec. 8, 1817.

Charles Marsh, Esq.

DEAR SIR, — You are aware that in the college cause, the only question that can be argued at Washington, is whether the recent acts of the Legislature of N. Hampshire do not violate the Constitution of the U. S. This point, tho. we trust a strong one, is not perhaps stronger than that derived from the character of these acts, compared with the Constitution of N. Hampshire. It has occurred to me whether it would not be well to bring an action, which should present both and all our points to the Supreme Court. This could be done by bringing the action originally in the Circuit Court. I am a good deal inclined to favor the proposition of bringing such a suit. Altho. I now mention it only for consideration. Suppose the trustees should sue for the Wheelock lands in Vermont? Or suppose they should lease portions of the N. Hampshire lands to a citizen in Vermont? In either of these cases an action might be brought in the courts of U. S. in which all the questions could be considered. I have suggested this idea to Mr. Mason & Judge Smith (& nobody else). If they should think the hint worth considering I shall probably hear from them, and in that case I write you again. Such a suit would not of course at all interfere with our present proceedings.

I am dear sir, with great respect,

Yours,

D. WEBSTER.

This letter was sent, not to Marsh, but to Francis Brown, president of the College, with a note thereon, saying, "I have written the above for the consideration of yourself and Mr. Marsh."

Webster, in his letter of December 8, 1817, to Judge Smith, says : "It is our misfortune that our cause goes to Washington on a single point. I wish we had it in such shape as to raise all the other objections, as well as the repugnancy of these acts to the Constitution of the United States. I have been thinking whether it would not be advisable to bring a suit, if we can get such parties as will give jurisdiction, in the Circuit Court of New Hampshire. I have thought of this the more from hearing of sundry sayings of a great personage. Suppose the corporation of Dartmouth College should lease to some man of Vermont (*e.g.*, C. Marsh) one of their New Hampshire farms, and that the lessee should bring ejectment for it. Or suppose the trustees of Dartmouth College should bring ejectment in the Circuit Court for some of the Wheelock lands. In either of these modes the whole question might get before the court at Washington." (1 Webster's Priv. Cor. 267, 268.) In his letter of the same date to Jeremiah Mason, Webster says: " I am sorry our college cause goes to Washington on *one* point only. What do you think of an action in some court of the U. States that shall raise all the objections to the act in question? Such a suit could easily be brought; that is, jurisdiction could easily be given to the court of the U. States by bringing in a Vermont party." In his letter from Washington, of March 11, 1818, to Mr. Brown, Webster says: " Yours of the 28th Feb. I received this morning. I am glad a suit is to be brought. I am very much inclined to think the court *will not* give a judgment this term. It is therefore most essential to have an action in which all the questions arise. Pray therefore take care that a *proper* action be *properly* commenced, and in the earliest season, in the Circuit Court of N. H." (Mason's Papers.) In his letter to Mr. Mason, of March 22, 1818, Webster says: " I believe it is fully expected that a case raising the question in the amplest form will be presented at the Circuit Court. I have given some reason to expect this, and, unless for good causes, should be mortified if it were not so." (1 Webster's Priv. Cor. 278.) In his letter to Mr. Brown, of March 30, 1818, he says: " I am glad an action is brought, and hope it will come on regularly at the May term." (1 Webster's Priv. Cor. 279.) In his letter to Mason, of April 28, 1818, he says: " I saw Judge Story as I came along. He is evidently expecting a case which shall present all the questions. It is not of great consequence whether the actions or action go up at this term, except that it would give it an earlier standing on the docket next winter. The question which we must raise in one of these actions, is whether by the general principles of our governments the State Legislatures be not restrained from divesting vested rights. This, of course, independent of the constitutional provision respecting contracts. On this question I have great confidence in a decision on the right side. This is the proposition with which you began your argument at Exeter, and which I endeavored to state from your minutes, at Washington. The particular provisions in the New Hampshire Constitution no doubt strengthen this general proposition in our case; but, on general principles, I am very confident the court at Washington would be with us. If so, then nothing will remain but this: ' Are the powers, privileges, or authorities of the trustees under this charter, rights within the meaning of the proposition? Are they franchises, liberties, or privileges such as the law protects, or are they merely disinterested duties or official services?'' I cannot state this question very accurately, but this is the general idea. If we get up one of these cases in due form, we shall defeat our adversaries.'' (1 Webster's Priv. Cor. 282, 283.)

It is to be observed that the last letter was written nearly two months after Mr. Webster had made his celebrated effort at Washington in Judge Woodward's case. It shows most distinctly the ground upon which he relied, — and that not the obligation clause.

The policy of legislative interference did not originate with the acts in question, nor has it been confined to them. Contrary to the almost universal understanding, based mainly upon the argument put by counsel to intensify a point, the necessity and propriety of amending this college charter have been conceded by the leading trustees from a very early period.

John Wheelock came from Yale, was a student there, and was familiar with the troubles of President Clap which grew out of the attempt to secure the passage by the Legislature of Connecticut, in 1763, of an act providing for the government of Yale, and for the appointment of a "Commission of Visitation," to rectify abuses in the College, or report thereon to the General Assembly. In 1791, before the troubles which resulted in the exclusion of Wheelock from the board had arisen, its controlling minds, with Wheelock and Olcott at their head, of their own accord, adopted a plan by which the Senate and the House were to have "some" share in the government of Dartmouth College.

On February 5, 1789, the State granted to the College a township eight miles square, with the following proviso:

"And be it further enacted, that the President and Council of the State for the time being shall be, and they are hereby incorporated with the Trustees of said College, so far as that they shall have a right to act with them, as one board, in regard to the expenditures and applications of this grant & all others which have been, or may hereafter be made by New Hampshire."

This grant was a substitute for the Landaff grant, which had failed, and was duly accepted by the corporation.

The trustees, on June 5, 1805, addressed a memorial to the Legislature, praying for "aid;" setting forth that the College was a matter of "common concern to the citizens" of the State; and that "Your memorialists would with deference suggest whether, as the Trustees, actuated by no personal interest, consider themselves bound to attend to the concerns of the Seminary only as it is an object of public importance," etc. Whereupon the Legislature, on June 15, 1805, granted them $900.

On June 18, 1807, the Legislature made a grant of a township six miles square, with the proviso that the members of the Council, president of the Senate, and the chief justice of the highest court should be, " *ex officio*, members of the Board of Trustees in respect to this and any future grant to said College."

Threats that the legislative authority would be invoked were apparently bandied about and openly discussed in the board, from 1805, till it came in 1816. The charter created the first Board of Trustees, made them the corporation, and gave them and their successors the power of filling all vacancies. It fixed their number, " forever," at " twelve and no more," and made the board a species of " Council of Ten."

On June 19, 1816, while the act subsequently passed was pending before the Legislature, Thompson, Paine, and McFarland, three of the leading trustees, addressed to that body a remonstrance against its passage, covering nearly eight pages in print. As might have been expected from the ability of the draughtsman, the objections to the bill were stated with great force and clearness. Among other things, they said : —

" Whilst the undersigned deem it their indispensable duty to remonstrate in the most respectful terms against the passage of the bill referred to, they have no objection, and they have no reason to believe their fellow-trustees have any objection, to the passage of a law connecting the government of the State with that of the College, and creating every salutary .check and restraint upon the official conduct of the trustees and their successors that can be reasonably required ; and, with respectful deference, they would propose the following outlines of a plan for that purpose :

" The councillors and senators of New Hampshire, together with the speaker of the House of Representatives for the time being, shall constitute a Board of Overseers of Dartmouth College, any ten of whom shall be a quorum for transacting business. The overseers shall meet annually at the College, on the day preceding commencement. They shall have an independent right to organize their own body, and to form their own rules ; but as soon as they shall have organized themselves, they shall give information thereof to the trustees. Whenever any vote shall have been passed by the trustees, it shall be communicated to the overseers, and shall not have effect until it shall have the concurrence of the overseers; *provided*, nevertheless, that if at any meeting a quorum of the overseers shall not be formed, the trustees shall have full power to confer degrees in the same manner as though there were no overseers, and also to appoint trustees or other officers (not a president or professor), and to enact such laws as the interests of the institution shall indispensably require; but no law passed by the trustees shall in such case have force longer then until the next annual meeting of the boards, unless it shall then be approved by the overseers. Neither of the boards shall adjourn, except from day to day, without the consent of the other. It shall be the duty of the president of the College, whenever in his opinion the interests of the institution shall require it, or whenever requested thereto by three trustees or three overseers, to call special meetings of both boards, causing notice to be given in writing, to each trustee and overseer, of the time and place; but no meeting of one board shall ever be called except at the same time and place with the other. It shall be the duty of the president of the College, annually, in the month of May, to transmit to his excellency the governor a full and particular account of the state of the funds, the number of students and their progress, and generally the state and condition of the College.''

The truth is, the trustees were willing that almost any amendment should be made to the charter, if so framed that they could exclude Wheelock and his friends from any share in the government of the College, and could retain possession for themselves and their friends.

Soon after the decision, in 1819, some of the trustees, who so stoutly resisted all similar attempts on the part of the State, proposed to make material changes in this " inviolable " contract, by creating a Board of Overseers, etc.; and these attempts have continued till the present day. It is unnecessary to inquire now what would have become of the corporation in the possible, but improbable, event of the death of a quorum of the trustees, or their neglect or refusal to choose successors. Under the charter, the alumni have no rights, but for years they have been knocking at the door of the corporation, and asking recognition and representation in the Board of Trustees. As they had given, or were expected to contribute, liberally to the aid of their *alma mater*, the demand was in itself reasonable. The trustees were inclined to grant it, if it could be done. There was the "rub." The "successors" of those who denied all legislative power in the premises in 1816–17, gravely considered the proposition to ask the Legislature to amend the charter so that the alumni could elect a portion of the trustees; but they had not forgotten that a step somewhat akin to this, proposed by Olcott and others, who had denied the power in 1816–19, was under consideration in 1821, nor that Daniel Webster (see his letter to his brother Ezekiel, of June 17, 1821), probably having in mind the argument of Parsons on that point, to which we shall hereafter advert, advised against the scheme as one "not without danger," and said: "It would be injurious, I think, to propose to take this important alteration in the charter, before the ground was well explored."

In his letter to Webster, of June 13, 1821, Mills Olcott says: "Some of the friends of old D. College who are here have thought that her real interest might be subserved by some legislative arrangements at this time, whereby not only State patronage, but State funds, should be obtained. They have thought of a board of overseers, say of 20, — to include the president of the Senate, the speaker of the House, the others to be appointed by the Governer & Council, — to have a veto upon the appointment, &c., of the trustees, & afterwards fill up their own vacancies themselves, & to be somewhat on the footing of Cambridge. A tax is expected to be raised for the State treasury this session from banks, & from this fund have say $5,000 annually for ten years appropriated for D. C. There is no **real** college man in the Legis., except Bro. Ez. & my humble self, & we cannot have the benefit of consulting with trustees.

"I therefore take the liberty to ask your advice as to the policy of attempting this or any thing of the kind, more especially of the best way to bring Mason's giant abilities & influence into hearty & strenuous exercise. He can do here (as he can almost everywhere) what he chooses to set himself about in earnest. He has been consulted, & I believe is sincerely well disposed ; but unless he is the prime mover, so that it acquires its momentum from him in the first instance, I should hardly expect success in effecting any thing. Some influential republicans profess to be pleas'd with a reconciliation, though it has only been whispered to a few.

"Will you take the trouble to give me your views of what is advisable on this subject as early as may be. You may rely on its being most strictly confidential, if you wish it."

This letter was written from Concord, while the Legislature was in session, Olcott being a member of the House from Hanover, and Ezekiel Webster, who was as gifted in his way as his famous brother, representing Boscawen, as he did for many years

Webster, in his reply, writing from Boston, under date of June 17, 1821, says: " I wish I had more hope of good than I have to the College from the Legislature. Of course you know best the feeling on such subjects at present existing, but for myself I do not believe the College could get a dollar from the Genl. Court. They would be very likely to accept the proposition *to appoint overseers*, but as to the money part of the bargain I do not think they would give a cent. Besides, I do not think the present a favorable moment to create a board of overseers by executive appointment, with power afterwards of filling their own vacancies. It is easy to see what sort of men would be first appointed,

& what sort of men they would perpetuate. All would be *political* & nothing literary. My own impression is, that if the College must *die*, it is better that it should die a natural death. A board of overseers, such as would probably be appointed, would *negative every important nomination of the trustees.* Of this I have no sort of doubt. There are reasons not applicable to D. College, & to such a board as you would create, which alone prevented elsewhere the utmost embarrassment.

"I have given my *opinion*, as you request, & beg you to treat it as entirely confidential. I have no room to state reasons at large. At any rate, I should not think it expedient to move in the matter without much circumspection, & a previously arranged plan, which should have recd. the approbation of the trustees. Is there any *reliance* to be placed in the quarter from which the first appointments would proceed? My own judgment & opinion do not answer that question favorably.

"I had hoped to be in Concord before you leave it, & still intend so to be, but our Sup. Court is still in session & may last too long for my purpose. Mr. Blake, with Mrs. B. & George, are gone to Newport on a little excursion, partly to attend the Circuit Court and partly for pleasure."

In this letter, probably Mr. Webster did not intend to reflect upon his personal friend and client, the governor, but upon other influences that might control the appointing power through the Council.

This project was recently abandoned as "too hazardous." The proposition lately under consideration by the trustees was, in substance, to adopt regulations whereby the alumni should "nominate" a certain number of the trustees, with the understanding that the trustees should "confirm" that "nomination," by going through the forms of an election. It is understood that a majority of the trustees were in favor of the plan stated.

The following, issued April 21, 1878, shows what steps were ultimately taken : —

Nomination of Trustees by the Alumni of Dartmouth College. — On the 12th of August, 1875, the trustees of Dartmouth College voted to submit to the Association of Alumni the following plan:

I. On the occurrence of the next three vacancies in the Board of Trustees, including one outside of New Hampshire, the trustees will request the alumni to make nominations in the following manner : —

[1.] Information of each vacancy shall be given by the secretary, as soon as it occurs, to the secretary of the Alumni Association, and he shall give timely notice to the alumni, in such manner as the association shall determine, requesting the graduates in course, of four years' standing, both of the academic and scientific departments, to send to him, before the next meeting of the board, a nomination under their own signature, of four eligible candidates for said vacant place. And the secretary shall state in said notice the limitations, if any, imposed by the charter, as to the class or locality from which the vacant place is to be filled.

[2.] The four names receiving the largest number of votes shall be reported by the secretary of the alumni to the board. While there are certain legal objections to any positive and formal agreement on the subject, it is understood that ordinarily, and in all probability, invariably some one of the persons nominated will be elected to the vacant place.

[3.] When any of the places so filled shall become vacant, by death or otherwise, it shall be refilled in the manner aforenamed.

II. [1.] If either the Association of the Alumni or the Board of Trustees shall hereafter desire any modification of the arrangement, it may be signified to the other party, and become the subject of conference between them.

[2.] This arrangement may be terminated, by vote of either the association or the board, if at any future time it shall be deemed desirable by either.

The above plan was presented to the Alumni Association at their meeting in June, 1876, and was unanimously adopted, and the curators of the association were appointed a committee with powers to attend to any details, on the part of the association, necessary to carry out the plan; and the secretary of the association duly certified said action to the Board of Trustees.

S. C. BARTLETT,
President.

This arrangement has been carried into execution. It is difficult to understand how trustees charged, as claimed, in the most solemn manner with the execution of great trusts, by the very instrument to which they owed their own existence and their powers, could, of their own motion, lawfully divert or annihilate the one, and change the legal effect of the other. If one step like this can be taken, another may; and this "inviolable" charter would be virtually abolished by the trustees.

The Legislature seemingly had some "color" of authority for these enactments. Before and since the Revolution, the legislative bodies in New Hampshire were its "General Court." That court was accustomed to set aside fraudulent conveyances, order specific performance, revive rules of reference, blot out levies, cancel executions, open, annul, and relieve against judgments, and grant new trials, and in general to give relief where justice had not been done by the ordinary legal tribunals. This was sometimes, though rarely, done upon the ground that there was "no remedy at common law." These powers were exercised, not as a court of chancery, *eo nomine*, but subject to a few theoretical restraints, upon the ground of legislative or parliamentary omnipotence. From 1692 to 1821, New Hampshire had no court of chancery. In 1821, two years after the final decision in this cause, Mason, one of the leading counsel in it, as chairman of the committee on the judiciary, reported a bill, which became a law, conferring chancery powers in relation to trusts upon the highest court of the State.

The act of June 19, 1817, granting a new trial to Dolly Merrill, as administratrix of the estate of Benjamin Mer-

rill, for which a petition had been pending before the Legislature for years, was carried by one of Mr. Webster's most
memorable efforts. Mason defended the constitutionality
of this act, which was before the court at the same time as
Trustees v. Wooodward. The positions necessarily taken
by Webster and Mason in these cases were, in some
respects, antagonistic. This act was set aside in Merrill v.
Sherburne (1 N. H. 199–217), upon the ground that "an
act of the Legislature awarding a new trial in an action
which has been decided in a court of law is an exercise of
judicial power. It is also in its operation retrospective ;
and, for these two reasons, is unconstitutional."

If, as Webster and Mason contended, the acts amending
the charter of the College were the exercise of a judicial and
not of a legislative power, it was doubly clear that the act
granting a new trial, which the one had carried through the
Legislature and the other defended before the court, was
unconstitutional. To this may be added the doubts, to call
them by their mildest name, of Judge Smith, and the
adverse opinion of Mason, to say nothing of that afterwards
given by Chancellor Kent.

The practical results of the final judgment in Trustees v.
Woodward exhibit in a striking light the short-sightedness
of men. That decision was invoked by one of the warring
factions in the Board of Trustees to dethrone another. It
made, what the parties to the charter and the "laws of
England" never did, a contract which no human external
power could ever modify or change.

Judge Marshall decided, in effect, that the Revolution
blotted out the legal existence of the "party of the first
part,"—the fountain from which all its chartered blessings
flowed, — and put the State of New Hampshire in his place ;
that prior to the adoption of the Constitution of the United
States, the charter might lawfully have been so modified or
changed ; that the most vital attribute of the "contract,"
an inviolability as fixed as the laws of the Medes and Per-

sians, inhered not in the language used by the parties and
the recognized law at the time of its creation, but had been
injected into it, twenty years after it was made, by that Constitution.

But the important question for the American people is
not whether the judgment against Judge Woodward could
have been sustained upon other grounds, which the judges
of the Supreme Court could not consider without a violation
of the Constitution, the laws of the United States, and their
oaths, but whether the principle underlying that decision
is definite, tangible, and sound; whether it covers the innumerable causes which have found shelter under the wings
of the opinions popularly supposed to have been delivered
when that decision was given; and, in fact, whether the
countless and constantly increasing array of corporations
in this great country have more of sovereignty than the
power which gave them being. No questions which can
be raised involve such far-reaching consequences as these.
And their importance increases year by year, in a ratio
which has no parallel in the past, and can have none when
we have attained a population of from two to five hundred
millions.

The tide of events will force their discussion and compel
their determination. They must be brought in review. The
truth will be sought till found. It is best that this should
be done by judicial decision. The court, as now constituted, may not be able to settle them: if not, their successors must; or, if the republic endures, the people, in
the proper way, will.

The present judges are of varying, but, in general, of eminently respectable attainments. Some of them are very
eminent in special departments; but no fact is more pain-
fully apparent to those who have studied closely the course
of that great tribunal, than that its decisions lack the unity
which marked them during the dictatorship of Marshall and
under the great triumvirate of the " old bench,"—Taney,

Nelson, and Campbell.   For years it has had no commanding spirit on its quarter-deck.   It has lost its reckoning; it
has been beating about in a storm; it has relapsed into the
chaos of doubt and uncertainty which marked the earlier
years of its existence, when the politicians — or statesmen —
of that day bivouacked in the chief justiceship on their
march from one political position to another.

The territorial extent of the Union when that court was
created, as compared with the present, was but a " patch
upon the earth's surface."   The population has gone up
from four to more than forty millions, and the judicial business has increased out of proportion to both.   The country
has outgrown the court.   Laying out of the case the mass
of causes originating in the District or Circuit Courts, which
may go to the Supreme Court for final determination, it is,
as to a most important class of questions, the court of last
resort for nearly fifty States and Territories.   That the dis-
parity must increase year by year is inevitable.   It was the
remark of Judge Curtis, one of the most eminent judges of
the Supreme Court, that no lawyer could be of much assistance to a court unless he had grown up in the atmosphere
of the statutes and the practice of that jurisdiction.   It is
simply impossible for the judges to have this knowledge of
the local law, which they are so often called upon to interpret.   The result of all this has been hasty, conflicting, and
ill-considered decisions and opinions, sometimes slipshod,
and wandering in darkness, while filled with learning.

Recruited at an early period in our history by the political
department of the government, and to a great extent from
political life, and hence to a certain degree fashioned by it,
the Supreme Court has betrayed in its acts the defects of
its organization.   It has suffered from internal dissensions
and outside pressure.   It has sometimes done the things
which it ought not to have done, and much oftener omitted
to do those things which it ought to have done.

The power of taxation is generally conceded to be one of

the primary attributes of sovereignty. If corrupt legislative bodies can irrevocably auction off this power to the highest bidder by instalments, why not the whole, and at once? If one of these attributes can be constitutionally converted into merchandise under the legislative hammer, why not others? Did the Constitution, under the clause, "no State shall * * * pass any * * * law impairing the obligation of contracts," establish the doctrine of State suicide, or grant the power to destroy the "foundation idea of the government," or forever prohibit the States from so amending their respective Constitutions as to confer judicial power upon their legislative bodies?

CHAPTER II.

THE Dartmouth College causes have a history. With Coke,
as briefly as we may, let us begin at their "fountains
to trace the streams." Sorely against the will of the settlers, who numbered less than four thousand, the king, in
1680, created the province of New Hampshire, for the purpose of enabling the royal favorites to plunder them of
the fruits of their lands, which they had reclaimed in spite
of the red man's scalping-knife and fagot. For years they
suffered severely from these proconsular robbers and their
agents; but, at a later period, under the guidance of able
leaders, the province had far less occasion to complain of
the royal policy than many of her sister colonies, and often
received marked favors at the hands of the crown. Massachusetts had long claimed dominion over the heart of the
province, by an alleged boundary-line running from "Endi-
cot's tree," "three miles due north of the crotch" of the
Merrimack River, through a point about four miles north
of Webster's birthplace, and due west to the South Sea.
But on April 9, 1740, the king decided against Massachusetts, and established the existing boundary-line, which was
supposed to extend to a point twenty miles east of the
Hudson River. Soon after, Benning Wentworth, governor
of New Hampshire, laid out and granted away one hundred and thirty-eight towns, containing more than half a
million acres of land, west of the Connecticut River, in what
is now the State of Vermont, ending with Bennington,

(20)

named for himself. Dunmore, governor of New York, subsequently granted away five hundred and eleven thousand
nine hundred acres of the same lands. This brought on
the controversy between New York, New Hampshire, Vermont, and the settlers in the valley, about the "New
Hampshire grants," which kept the settlers on both sides
of the river in a political ferment for years, and brought
the whole to the very verge of civil war.

In 1733, Eleazar Wheelock graduated at Yale, and in
1735 was ordained, and settled as the minister of the second (or north) society, in Lebanon, Connecticut, then called
"Lebanon Crank," and since about 1800 known as the
town of Columbia, where he remained till late in 1770.
His salary was nominally £140 ; but some years he received
only about one-third of that, partly paid in provisions.
Finding his salary inadequate, he taught a few pupils at his
house. Wheelock was a man of powerful intellect, great
tact, energy, and intense religious zeal. He stood in the
van of the great religious awakening of 1740.

In December, 1743, Wheelock took Samson Occom, a
Mohegan Indian, into his family, where he remained for
five years. Occom proved to be an excellent scholar, of
rare ability, and soon became a "preacher of distinction."

From this humble origin sprang the Charity-School. On
July 17, 1755, Joshua Moor, a farmer of Mansfield, gave
by deed a house, shop, and about two acres of land "for
the Foundation, Use, and Support of a Charity-School, for
the Education of *Indian* Youth ;" and in consequence this
school was ever after called "Moor's Indian Charity-School."

William Smith, of New York, in his letter to Wheelock,
of August 6, 1755, suggested to him that there was "no
incorporation." Soon after, Wheelock took steps to obtain
a "royal charter" for this school. He applied to Lord
Halifax. In his "Narrative," Wheelock says : —

"Sometime after those Boys came, [December 18, 1754] the
Affair appearing with an agreeable Aspect, it being then a Time of

profound Peace in this Country, I represented the Affair to Colonel *Elisha Williams, Esq.;* late Rector of *Yale-College,* and to the Rev'd Messi'rs *Samuel Moseley* of *Windham,* and *Benjamin Pomeroy* of *Hebron,* and invited them to join me; they readily accepted the Invitation; and a Gentleman learned in the Law supposed there might be such an Incorporation among ourselves as might fully answer our Purpose. And Mr. *Joshua Moor,* late of *Mansfield,* deceased, appeared to give a small Tenement in this Place, for the Foundation, Use and Support of a Charity-School, for the Education of *Indian* Youth, &c. But it pleased God to take the Good Colonel from an unthankful World soon after the Covenant was made and executed, and thus deprived us of the Benefit of his singular Learning, Piety and Zeal in the Affair. Notwithstanding, a Subscription was soon made of near £500 lawful Money, towards a Fund for the Support of it, at 6 per Cent. But several Gentlemen of the Law, doubting of the Validity and Sufficiency of such an Incorporation; several steps were taken to obtain the Royal Favour of a Charter, but none effectual.''

The result is thus stated by Wheelock in his letter to William Smith, of 1760: " We sent home some years ago for the Royal favor of a charter. Lord Halifax approved the design, but (to save expense) advised, instead of a charter, the establishment of the school by a law of Connecticut Colony, and promised that when sent there it should be ratified in council, which he supposed would be as sufficient as any act there. Hereupon I attended our Assembly in May, 1758, with a memorial. The prayer of which was granted by the House of Representatives; the governor and council negatived it upon the ground that their action would not be valid if ratified in England, *beyond this Colony,* and that a corporation within a corporation might be troublesome as Yale College had sometimes been. I am since informed that the Earl of Dartmouth has promised, if the matter shall be put into a proper channel, to undertake and go through with it at his own expense.'' (See Smith's History of Dartmouth College, etc., 41.)

In May, 1764, Wheelock without avail petitioned the

Connecticut Assembly " to incorporate " six gentlemen of
that colony, including George Willys, of Hartford, and himself, as legal guardians of this *school*.   What he desired was
a charter that would enable him to locate in *any* of the
American colonies.

While the movements to secure a charter were going on,
subscription papers were circulated throughout the colonies,
commencing in 1755, and were numerously signed, by which
the subscribers promised to pay, etc., for the sole " use and
benefit " of this " school," " as soon as the school should
become a body corporate," etc.

In December, 1765, Wheelock sent Occom to England and
Scotland to preach, and solicit funds for the school, where
he arrived early in 1766.   He aroused great enthusiasm
among the clergy and nobility, and his mission was a success.   In 1766, the king gave £200 and the Earl of Dartmouth £50 for this school.   Over £9,000 were collected in
England, and placed in the hands of a board of London
trustees, of which the Earl of Dartmouth was the head, and
John Thornton, a rich merchant of London, treasurer and
one of the principal managers.   Between £2,000 and £3,000
were collected in Scotland, and called the Scotch fund,
which was deposited with the " Scotch Society for the Propagation of Christian Knowledge," etc.   As manager of the
school, Dr. Wheelock always accounted for his disbursements to these trustees.   Occom returned, having raised
about £12,000 in all.   The Legislatures of Connecticut,
Massachusetts, and New Hampshire also granted aid.
Wheelock had thus been instrumental in securing large contributions for this purpose in England and Scotland, as well
as America.

The following is from William Smith to Wheelock's
agent : —

NEW YORK, 30 March, 1767.

Several questions proposed by Mr. Phelps relating to Mr.
Wheelock's Indian School.

1st. Which will be most for the interest of the school, the lodging of the money given to it in a bank at home, or the transfer of it to America?

Answer. The preference must be given to that country where it will produce most and be most safe. I am confident that it can be let out in the province of New York for the legal interest of seven per cent, and secured by bonds and mortgages of persons, and on lands worth ten times as much as the sums let, & that it may be let out in large sums of one, two, or three thousand pounds together. I suppose it will not raise in England above four per cent.

2d Question. Ought the school and its funds to be in the hands of a private trustee, suppose Mr. Wheelock, and he to appoint a successor by his last will, or will it induce most to its interest to have it incorporated by charter?

Answer. Beyond all doubt it would be best to have a charter. Incorporating a number of warm friends in America, near to each other to direct and govern the school, and some reputable friends in England for correspondence and protectors. This is the only way to render the project permanent, to secure wisdom and council equal to the work, to defend it against opposition, and to encourage future donations; but I refer to what I wrote upon this head to Dr. Finley, who communicated my remarks to Mr. Wheelock, and also to the suggestions contained in my letter to Mr. Wheelock last fall. I shall only add that a charter is more necessary for such an institution in this country than it can be in England. An incorporated body will not only acquire rights maintainable by law in the courts of justice, but command the favor of the officers of the government, who, without that sanction, may at such distances from the crown oppress the undertaking a thousand ways and utterly destroy it.   * * *

3d Question. By what method can a charter be obtained?

Answer. A petition should be proffered to his majesty, for a *mandamus* to the governor and council, and all subordinate officers, to pass a charter according to a form annexed *in hoc verba*, under the great seal of the province; and at the same time a standing instruction should be procured to the governor and secretary for Indian Affairs, to aid, countenance and protect the corporation in the execution of the powers and privileges granted to them by the charter, as they will answer to the * * * at their peril.

It is noticeable that the course pointed out was not taken in New Hampshire, though the common process for many years had been to induct appointees into office, and accomplish other special objects by *mandamus*. The Home Office suggested to Wheelock to go to the Legislature of Connecticut for his charter. No such suggestion was made in relation to New Hampshire, nor was any such attempt made. Why should the Colonial Legislature of Connecticut be deemed to have the power, and that of New Hampshire not?

After he ascertained that no incorporation could be had from Connecticut, plans were set on foot to remove the school to lands on the Mississippi, given to the officers of the old French War; to fix it in the Middle States; to remove it to Albany, New York; to establish it in Springfield and other places in Massachusetts; and to locate it at Landaff, Bath, Haverhill, Piermont, Lyme, Orford, Hano- ver, Lebanon, Cornish, Hinsdale, Canaan, Plymouth, Rumney, Campton, and other towns in New Hampshire. Wheelock spent over two years in fixing upon a new location, and in preparation for its removal; but after repeated conferences with the governor of New Hampshire and several of its leading men, the " Indian Charity-School " was removed to Hanover.

On July 20, 1768, Wheelock commissioned Ebenezer Cleveland, and his son, Ralph Wheelock, to explore the province with reference to the location, and, in effect, to ascertain what grant, if any, would be made. In his report, made in December, 1768, which describes the town of Landaff, sets out its situation, and that the governor was ready to make a grant, he says: " I waited upon His Excellency, John Wentworth, Esq., Governor of New Hampshire. He appeared very friendly to the design, promised to grant a township six miles square to the use of the school, provided it should be fixed in that province, and that he would use his influence that His Majesty should give the quit-rents to the school, to be free from charge of fees, except from surveying.'' (Smith's History of Dartmouth College, etc., 35, 36.) Other things no doubt contributed materially; but without this promise, upon which Wheelock relied, it is safe to say that '' the school '' never would have been removed to New Hampshire.

After Landaff had been occupied for some time, questions arose as to the validity of the judgment of forfeiture entered up by Wentworth and his council without notice, which preceded the grant, and the trustees, declining to enter into litigation, lost the grant in 1787; but in 1789 the State replaced it by that already referred to.

The rivalry between New Hampshire towns for the location was intensely bitter. As late as 1770, the trustees in New Hampshire instructed Wheelock to locate at Landaff, or within a mile of it. Situated as he was with reference to all, it became a matter of policy on the part of Wheelock to transfer the formal responsibility of fixing the location to the board of trust who held the foreign funds of the school and were responsible for their '' due application.'' Wheelock, in his '' Narrative,'' says : —

'' The determination of the site of this school now appeared to be an affair *so public* and so important, and that in which so many gentlemen of character were now interested, and therefore so delicate, that I could not think it prudent to attempt it myself, but to refer it wholly to the decision and determination of the honorable trust in England, who had condescended to patronize the institution by becoming sureties to the generous donors for the due application of the monies collected in South Britain for the only use and benefit of it; and accordingly, I faithfully represented to them the case, and all the reasons which were offered in favor of the respective places to which it was invited, in order fully to enable them understandingly to give the preference, and determined to be governed myself wholly by their determination thereon. In consequence of which, for many weighty reasons, they gave the preference to the western part of the province of New Hampshire, on Connecticut river, and determined that to be the place for it.''

Nothing can be clearer than that all this refers, not to a college, but to the charity-school.

The negotiations for a charter between Wheelock and Governor Wentworth were carried on through Wheelock's agents, and by correspondence.

For twelve years prior to this time, the clergy of the Congregationalist denomination of eastern and middle New Hampshire had in vain sought to obtain a charter for an academy or a college. They applied to Governor Benning Wentworth for it. He was friendly to the Presbyterians, but a member of the Church of England, and much attached to its interests. In his grants of townships he reserved a right for the benefit of his church. When the application was made to him for a charter, he refused to grant it unless the institution was put under the direction of the Bishop of London.

Wheelock did not ask for a charter for a college. He made no formal petition or "application" for a charter for any thing.

The board of trust were opposed to any incorporation for the school even. In his letter of April 7, 1769, to Dr. Langdon, Wheelock says, referring to the board of trust: "The affair is very delicate, and as such must be conducted, or it will disgust those who are the gentlemen, and overset all. Their sentiments of an incorporation have been differing from mine. They have insisted that I should conduct the whole affair without one, and that my successor should be nominated and appointed by my will. Experience, they think, has fully taught them that by means of an incorporation, such designs become jobs, and are soon ruined thereby. They choose to hold the moneys collected there in their own hands for this purpose, and accordingly have publicly declared their trust of the same under their hands and seals, and have disposed of it, as their wisdom directed, for the benefit of the school." (Smith's History of Dartmouth College, etc.)

In June, 1769, Wheelock wrote to Wentworth: "I have been making some attempts to form a charter in which some proper respect may be shown to those generous benefactors in England who condescended to patronize this school, and I want to be informed whether you think it consistent to make the trust in England a distinct corporation, with power to hold real estate, &c., for the uses and purposes of this school."

At least the postscript of the following letter is important: —

LEBANⁿ, Aug. 22, 1769.

SIR: — May it please y^r Excellency. A few days ago I rec'd from the Hon^{bl} Trust in England their unanimous preference of y^r Western part of y^r province for the site of my school. We had just before been advised by ye public prints of your Excellency's tour to Nova Scotia, which necessitates a delay of ye whole affair till you return, and my physician advises that I make trial of a mineral spring near Albany for the recovery of my health, which I design (D. V.) soon to attempt. As it is near the season which favors my aim and y^r design, and which will likely be at the expense of some weeks, by which means likely I shall not be able to wait upon your excellency on your return, however I shall appoint my son, or some suitable person or persons, in my name to wait upon you, if you please, to know your determination on a rough draft of a charter of incorporation for the academy which I herewith transmit and humbly submit to your Excellency's corrections. * * * And it becomes me to advise your excellency by the earliest opportunity of the so interesting determination of the Hon^l Trust. * * * Considering how far the year has advanced, and how much there is to be done in securing the donations generously made, to invite and encourage its settlement in your Province (after you have made it capable of the disposal of them) before I can with prudence or honor enter upon the performance on my part, and when these steps are taken I shall make it the object of my attention to prepare for ye removal of my family and school by next June if possible, which I think I can have no ground to expect unless the spot be fixed upon and all materials for building, &c., be provided this fall & winter, & a sufficient number of laborers be ready to enter upon the work early in the spring.

I find y^t a great number of the best sort of inhabitants in these parts are spirited, and much engaged to remove into that country and settle with me, which strengthens my hope that the affair will be owned of God, and be made eminently beneficial to that new and wide country, and that I may live to enjoy a comfortable settlement there.

That your excellency may live long to bless a people already happy under your mild and prudent administrations, and at last receive a crown of righteousness as the reward of grace at the end of your toil, is the earnest prayer of him who is with highest esteem & respect,

May it please your Excellency,

Your most obedient and most humble servant,

ELEAZAR WHEELOCK.

P. S. — Sir, if you think proper to use the word "college" instead of "academy," in the charter, I shall be well pleased with it.

To his Excell^{cy} Govr Wentworth.

Wheelock had been gathering funds for this school, by subscription and otherwise, for at least fourteen years. So far as appears, not a penny was subscribed or pledged after this postscript was written, and before the granting of the charter. Up to this time, he had never suggested to any authority supposed to have power to incorporate, that he desired a charter for a college or university.

Wheelock had many agents, but his principal ones in relation to the charter were his son-in-law, Phelps, and Rev. Dr. Whittaker.

The following correspondence clears up many things which have not hitherto been understood. Governor Wentworth, in his letter to Wheelock, of October 18, 1769, says: "Colonel Phelps has this morning show'd to me your letter 5th Oct. You are sensible, Sir, of my earnest disposition to serve the public Charity under your care. My Conduct both here and in Europe testify for me. I wish my private Abilities were more equal to support an enlarged liberality, yet what is given is with a willing heart. I am

certain there must have been an important misunderstanding
of my proposal convey'd to you. Without entering into
the accident, I wish now to be explicit, and am sure that
you nor no other catholic Christian can object. As many
insinuations have been and are yet frequently transmitting
to England, to depreciate the reputation of the intended
College, insinuating that the benevolent Charity's will be
applied *merely* and *exclusively* to the advancement of sectaries and particular opinions, with a fix'd view to discourage
the establish'd Church of England, it is not only important,
but essential that such ideas should be exterminated, therefore
I propos'd to add the present Bishop of London by name to
the Trust at Home in England, solely without any other connection than any other of the Gent[l] mentioned in London;
that thereby all the world may know our sincerity and universal good wishes to mankind; at his demise the vacancy to
be filled up by selection, as of other members. This is so
open and candid that I think it cannot be a bugbear to any
man of common sense, nor objected to unless upon party
principles, incompatible with and dishonorable to our generous plan of Education and government propos'd, and am
therefore certain that in this light you will not only see, but
approve the nomination, which, it is my opinion, will be
cordially acceptable to the respectable trust at home, who I
am convinc'd will at all times gladly accede to so respectable
a nomination, w[h] must eminently tend in that country and
in this to evince the extensive principles of the Society.
The nomination of the three provincial Officers to be of the
active, influential conducting Trust in this country, I
strongly recommend, but do not insist upon. They will be
a natural defense, honor, and security to the institution,
which perhaps may be the more eligible as they can't be supposed to be at any time other than the safest and most natural guardians of Education. However I shall not insist upon
them, yet would wish so well to the design as to be desirous
of its being avail'd of such an honorable patronage. That I

did not mention any other than the Gov' to be of the trust can by no means be preclusive, neither did I so intend it. The same reason would operate Equally against any part, every part of the Charter w^h you did not particularly mention to me. It was indeed show'd on my side that the Gov' should be one. But by no reason or considerate supposition can it be thence infer'd, the only one; for if so, all those that are mentioned by you must also be contrary to the plan — which I by no means suppose. In short, sir, I entertain a high respect for the Institution as proposed to me in England, and since in America. My promises I will sacredly make good and exceed them, influenc'd by an ardent desire to do right without discrimination of sects or names. I shall at all times seek the welfare of the College, the good of the remote part of the province, which you intimate may (be in their opinion) crossed, upon the general principles of Candor and rectitude, w^h will produce the just stability, w^h you are politely pleased to attribute to me, whatever may be the event, believe me Sir, I am hearty in the cause, and doubt not, as we profess the same, that explanations of sentiment will unite our judgment; at least I promise you that however I may have in future to blame my head, I will not leave the least self-reproach upon my heart, either for too rigid requisitions or unsupported deviating conclusions.''

Colonel Phelps, in his letter of October 19, 1769, to Wheelock, says: "I this morning had an audience ye Gov., who appears very Friendly to you personally and to ye School, and I conceive he was not understood when he made his proposal to add ye Bishop of London to the Trust. he says he did not mean that he should be of ye Trust on this side the water, but of ye Trust in England. I then asked how he could add him in the Charter, which upon considering he says he cannot, but only recommend him to ye Gentlemen of ye Trust at home to elect him, which if they would comply with, he then would be of the Trust. I then urg'd that

he could not be made non-elective, to which he consented.
I then said that he, as Bishop of London, could not I con-
ceiv'd be a member of ye trust for ye time being, and upon
ye whole ye Govr consents to make a charter, only inserting
therein a Recommendatory Clause in ye Charter to ye Trust
at Home to Elect the present Bishop to be one of the
Trust in England to act with them and them only,
and also not to recommend him as Bishop to be one,
but only considered in private character, and that his
recommendation shall not extend to his successors. I
also queried with the Govr whether ye Trust at home
could add him to their number, and he seems to think
they cannot without a vacancy, and he is willing even to
suppress ye said Bishop in s^d recommendation, and I think
he will consent to omit the addition of ye President of
the Council, as speaker of ye House, or Judge of y^e
Supreme Court. I have not had time to advise with but
two of Y^e Council and one or two others, they are wholly
averse to a Bishop in particular being concern'd in y^e
School, or any other Non-Elective member, but they whose
judg't I think you would value (Strict Dissenters) seem
to think ye Bishop of London, being only a nominal member
of ye trust in England, is but a mere matter of moon-
shine and not worthy of much consideration. Y^e Bearer is
desired to wait on you with this, and * * * ye Govr's
present purpose, as I have mentioned, should be so disagreeable that you will not comply, I pray you would write
to me by a special post, who may be here by Saturday
of next week.

"Y^e Trust at home can, if they please, choose ye Bishop
of London without the Govr's recommendation, and they
can refuse him if recommended.

"S^r, please to recommend me to my wife, to whom I
can't write if ye Bearer waits for this.

"I don't think ye Govr has any view to Clogg ye School
by recommending ye present Bishop of London to ye Trust

at home to be one of s^d Trust   *   *   *   and he can't if ye Trust at home shall see fit to elect him, have any influence on ye School; this is ye sentiment of ye best men here, who are averse to ye Church   *   *   *   Y^e Govr has given up almost every thing I asked, and will it not be a pity to break with him for a mere circumstance. if the school should be   *   *   *   I fear he will not be its benefactor, and if fixed in his province, I believe he will do everything for you, yours, & ye School. he says he abhors every thing like party, and I don't [believe] he is a Churchman.''

Wheelock replied to Wentworth as follows: "I have this minute rec'd your Excellency's Favour of 18th inst., and have read it with great pleasure and satisfaction. The bearer of it having been retarded in his Journey leaves me no time to consult a Friend in the case, and make this return to your proposal by the time fixed for it by Col. Phelps; and indeed your proposal, since you have explained it, appears so condescending, your views so catholic, your motives so great, your reasonings so strong, and your friendship, integrity, and uprightness therein so evident as scarcely leave room for hesitation, or any apprehension of any need I have of council, in order to a full compliance with what you propose, viz.   To add the present Bishop of London by name to the Trust at home in England solely; without any other connection than any other of the gentlemen mentioned in London, that thereby the world may know our sincerity and universal good wishes to Mankind, and at his demise the vacancy to be filled up by Election as of another Member. — This indeed appears to be as safe a passage thro' the straits between *Scylla* and *Charybdis* as perhaps can be tho't of; and yet I conceive the bare mention of the name of *Bishop* in this affair will give offence to numbers, tho' I cannot see at present but their offence must be groundless, and I will therefore run the venture of the consequences.   But what authority your

Excellency or any other man may have to add him to that
trust, or whether anything more can be done than to express
a desire that he might be one, is out of my Province to
determine.

"I here present you a Narrative lately printed in London,
in which your Excellency may see a copy of their declaration of their Trust, and perhaps be thereby assisted in forming your judgment in that matter. I perfectly agree with
your Excellency's sentiments of the importance of exter-
minating all Ideas that the benevolent charities are designed
to be applied merely and exclusively to the advancement of
Sectaries and particular opinions, with a fixed view to discourage the established Church of England — yet, as the
reigning Distempers & Prejudices of our Day are, and considering also the vast disadvantage of an unwieldy Body,
and more so by having the Members at a great distance, I
am glad your Excellency will not insist upon the addition
of the Provincial Officers you mentioned. And if your
Excellency shall see fit in your Wisdom & Goodness to
compleat the Charter desired, and it will be the least satisfaction to you to christian the House to be built after your
own name, it will be exceeding grateful to me, & I believe
to all concerned ; and that God may lengthen out your
important Life to bless the rising Institution, and make to
you thereby a name better than of Sons and Daughters even
to the latest Posterity, will be the fervent prayer of him
who is with the most sincere respect and esteem," etc.

In 1768, there were but eight lawyers in New Hampshire,
and apparently none of them were consulted by Wheelock
in relation to the charter. Wheelock drafted a charter
himself, — not an application for one, — with such assistance as he procured from his counsel, who were, probably,
William Smith and William Smith, Jr., of New York ;
George Willys and John Ledyard, of Hartford, Connecticut. William Parker, of Portsmouth, New Hampshire,
was apparently the sole legal adviser of Governor Went-

worth, and the changes made in the " draught of the charter," to a great extent, were undoubtedly the work of his hand.

Judge Parker was born in Portsmouth, New Hampshire, in 1703; was a tanner by trade, and after he became of age was a school-master. Later he studied law, and was admitted to the bar in 1732, and in 1737 was clerk of the commissioners to settle the line between New Hampshire and Massachusetts. Later he was register of probate; in 1765, a representative to the Assembly; and in 1771, a justice of the Superior Court. He was self-educated, and died in Portsmouth, April 29, 1781, aged seventy-seven.

Judge Parker, in his letter to Wheelock, of October 28, 1769, says: " I have had an opportunity of confering with Col. Phelps on the affair of the college proposed to be erected here.

" You will find some alterations in the scheme & draft of the charter. They are supposed to be amendments, and I think they (to say the least) will not be impediments. I cannot stay to enumerate them, the charter will show them & the Col. will be able to explain the grounds and reasons of them. I have spent some considerable time with the governor to form the plan in such a manner as will make it most beneficial, and to prevail on him to make such concessions as would suit the gentlemen with you. I am apt to think the plan will be more serviceable as it now stands than it was before. I shall be glad to serve the cause, and have persuaded Col. Phelps to communicate it before the finishing stroke tho. it will cost him another journey. I have only to add that I am with great esteem," etc.

The Wheelock draft is still in existence, and apparently in the handwriting of Sylvanus Ripley, Wheelock's relative and bosom friend. We have carefully compared this draft with the charter.

About two-thirds of a page in print was struck out of the original draft, and two pages and a half added to the

charter. Some of these changes were vital. "In this the
title is 'Dartmouth Academy,' instead of 'Dartmouth College,' and Dr. Wheelock is called the founder of the *school*,
and not of the academy. The words are: 'We appoint
our trusty and well beloved Eleazar Wheelock, doctor in
divinity, the founder of the said *school*, to be president of
said Dartmouth *academy*." (Memoir of Eleazar Wheelock,
by Dr. Allen, Am. Quar. Register, August, 1837.)

The governor struck out the names of some of the trustees inserted in the "draught," and added the names of six
Connecticut clergymen, retaining his own name and that of
one member of the Connecticut colonial government; and
contrary to the expressed wish of Wheelock, inserted the
names of four of the provincial officers of New Hampshire.
He also struck out the names of Ralph Wheelock and Samuel
Kirtland.

Wentworth, and not Dartmouth, was the chief benefactor
and patron of the institution, and it should have borne his
name; "and this, in fact, Dr. Wheelock authorized his
agent, in the negotiation about the charter, to propose to
the governor." (Memoir of Eleazar Wheelock, by Dr.
Allen.)

How the institution came to be named for Dartmouth
may never be known. Such a thing was manifestly no part
of Wheelock's original intention or purpose. It did not
originate with Dartmouth or the London trustees. They
not only knew nothing about it, but were bitterly opposed
to the charter and establishment of the College when they
found it out. The probabilities are that it was proposed
by Wheelock, to avert the storm which he must have known
would follow, and that Governor Wentworth acquiesced for
the same reason.

On March 12, 1770, Wheelock enclosed to Dartmouth a
copy of the charter, saying: "Governor Wentworth thought
best to reject that clause in my draught of the charter which
gave the honorable trust in England equal power with the

trustees here to nominate and appoint the president from time to time, apprehending it would make the body too unwieldy, but he cheerfully consented that I should express my gratitude and duty to your Lordship by christianing after your name, and as there seemed to be danger of many embarrassments in many ways in the present roughened and distempered state of the kingdom, I thought prudent to embrace the first opportunity to accomplish it."

The wishes of Governor Wentworth were disregarded in relation to the location of the College. In his letter of January 29, 1770, to Wheelock, he says: " Col. Phelps is very justly desirous to have some certain town determined on immediately for the site of Dartmouth College. It is scarcely possible to give any proper advice upon the subject, unless I know what soil was in each town, and the other interest, circumstances of reward or gratuity w^h wou'd arise from any particular people obtaining it within their district. Yet from all I can at present gather, either Bath or Haverhill have the most advantages. As to the particular spot in either of these towns, it can only be chosen by actual and intelligent survey, perhaps *cæteris paribus,* the center of either may be expedient for communications with others. I wish that the college may have the gov^t of the town wherever it stands, as is usually in England. This cannot be so easily had in Landaff, which upon all accounts is much my preference, but by no means my positive determination, which will be much inclin'd to pursue your advice in it. Upon the whole, I consent to Bath, Landaff, or Haverhill. The college to have at least one hundred acres adjoining, & to stand not less than a mile from the River. I have great pleasure in hearing, by Mr. Cushman, of your good health, and sincerely wish you every blessing."

Wheelock, in his " Narrative," after setting forth in detail the offers made if he would locate the school in other jurisdictions, and what was promised if it should be located in

New Hampshire, and stating the promised grant of land
(as by "THE King's most gracious Majesty, by advice of
his Excellency John Wentworth, Esq. ; his Majesty's Governor of the province of New Hampshire, and of his council,
a Charter of the township of Landaff, about 24,000 acres,"
which was followed by a printed list of subscriptions several
pages in length), says, in relation to the charter : —

"My next business was to secure the generous donations made
to it in said province.   And in order thereto, having consulted the
principal gentlemen of the law, in this and the neighbouring
provinces, who unanimously advised that an incorporation, if it
could be obtained, was the only course I could take that would be
safe for the institution,   *   *   *   I therefore fixed upon this as
my next and immediate object,   *   *   *   and accordingly I
employed a proper agent to solicit his Excellency *Governor Wentworth*, whom God has raised up to serve the interests of the great
Redeemer, in his province, and who appears to be unwearied in
doing good, and by him have obtained a generous charter, by the
name of DARTMOUTH COLLEGE, endowed with all the powers
and privileges of a university, with which this school is connected,
and to which it is designed to be subservient, and is by said charter invested with the donations made to it in said province, though
the school itself remains under the same jurisdiction and patronage as before.

"But as neither the honorable trust in England, nor the charter
had fixed upon the particular town or spot on which the buildings
should be erected, Wherefore to complete the matter, as soon as
the ways and streams would allow, I took the Rev. Mr. Pomeroy,
and Esq. Gilbert, (a gentleman of known ability for such a purpose,) with me to examine thoroughly, and compare the several
places proposed within the limits prescribed, for fifty or sixty
miles on, or near said river; and to hear all the reasons and arguments that could be offered in favor of each of them, in which
service we faithfully spent eight weeks, and in consequence of our
report, and representation of facts, the trustees unanimously
agreed that the southwesterly corner of Hanover, adjoining upon
Lebanon, was the place above any other to fix it in; and that for
many reasons.   *   *   *

" The charter of this school requiring the meeting of the corporation within a year from the date of it, I did therefore, as was requisite to save the forfeiture of it, call a meeting of the trustees on the 22d day of October.—At which meeting it was proposed to the trustees whether something could not be done by them to perpetuate the name and deed of Mr. Joshua Moor, late of Mansfield, in Connecticut, deceas'd; who was the first considerable benefactor to the school when it was obscure, and by many esteemed contemptible, and after taking the matter into consideration, it was resolved that they had no right by the charter to do anything in that matter, *and that the charter gives the trustees no right of jurisdiction but over the college; and that the school remains still under the same patronage, authority and jurisdiction as it was under before the charter was given.*"

One of the rules established for the government of the institution provided : —

" Lastly, That this Indian charity-school, connected with Dartmouth College, be constantly hereafter, and forever, called and known by the name of *Moor's School.* * * * And I would also take this opportunity to advise the generous subscribers, in the Colony of Connecticut, and province of Massachusetts Bay, &c., who have not yet paid their subscriptions made in the year 1755, and following, for the only use, benefit, and support of this school (the yearly interest whereof was payable on condition, and so long as the school should be continued, *and the principal to become payable as soon as the school should become a body corporate, and thereby capable of the tenure and disposal of land, &c.*), *that I suppose the said subscriptions are now become payable by this incorporation, according to the true design and intention of the pious subscribers.* * * * As to the surmises and prejudices thereby raised at a distance, that I have changed my object, and that the charitable donations made for the use of this school and missionaries are in whole or part perverted to my own, or some other English design, &c., were it not for the operation of these slanders beyond my acquaintance, I should not think it worth my pains to say a word about them. * * *

" I have invariably kept the same object in view, and there has not been a step taken, nor a stroke struck by me or my order, in the whole affair of my removing, settling and accommodating myself, family, and this seminary in this wilderness, but what has been meant, calculated, devised, and designed, to be in direct subserviency to my first object, viz., the gospelizing the Indians; *nor has there been anything done here* (excepting what I or others have done at our own expense), *but it must have been done if an English college had never been thought of. The Indians are the first object in the charter, and the first object designed by all the lands secured thereby, and of many other subscriptions and donations made to it.* And there never has been, from the first to this hour, directly or indirectly, one farthing of the money collected on either side of the water, for the use of my Indian school, or for the support of missionaries, improved for my own, or my family's support, or for any other purpose, with my knowledge or consent."

The "Narrative" further sets out the circumstances under which £500 were given by the General Assembly of the province, £200 sterling by the king, the Phillips donation, and others. On July 30, 1770, one of the trustees, referring to Dartmouth and Thornton, wrote to Dr. Wheelock: "They, as well as the other trustees, see clearly that by the affair of the charter, the trust here is meant to be annihilated. It was certainly a very wrong step for you to take without consulting us."

Dr. Wheelock, in his reply of November 9, 1770, three months after his removal to Hanover, says: "There was no design on the part of any of the trustees in Connecticut to annihilate the trust in England;" on the contrary, he says, "that the Connecticut trustees desired that the trustees in England should have not only the patronage of the school, but of the college too, so far as to have an equal share in the choice of a president, so long as they should see fit to perpetuate their board, and so the charter was drafted, when it was sent to Governor Wentworth; nor have I ever heard that one of the trustees in this province objected against it, but the governor, apprehending it would be a burden you would not be fond of, and that it would make the body too unwieldy, rejected that clause in it. The charter means to incorporate the school with the college, and give it possession of the donations and grants made in *this* province to it.   But the charter was never designed to convey the least power or control of any funds collected in Europe, nor does it convey any jurisdiction over the school to the trustees of the college.   The charter granted them jurisdiction only over the college.   If I resign my office as president of the college, I yet retain the same relation to the school and control of it as ever."   On April 25, 1771, the board wrote Wheelock the following letter : "We have lately taken into our serious consideration the affairs of your Charter, and the matter appears to us in the same light now as it did when we wrote to you the 30th of July last.   When we consider that the money collected here was given for the express purpose of ' creating, establishing, endowing and maintaining an Indian ' Charity-school and a suitable number of missionaries to be employed in the Indian Country, for the instruction of Indians in the Christian ' Religion,' and for no other purpose whatsoever, we cannot but look upon the charter you have obtained, and your intention of building a college and educating English youths, as going beyond the line by which both you and we are circumscribed.   The motives that induced the subscribers to contribute so generously to this undertaking were doubtless the hope of spreading the knowledge of the only true God and of his son Jesus Christ, that his way might be known on those dark corners of the earth, and his salvation among those unenlightened nations.   With the same views and upon the same plan we formed ourselves into a Trust and pledged ourselves to the subscribers as the guardians of their contributions to see them faithfully applied (as far as should be) to the purposes above mentioned and no other.   We think ourselves bound to adhere invariably to this original plan, and must therefore insist upon it that you do not deviate from it. We shall expect that you keep a regular and distinct account of all the monies laid out in erecting the school, educating Indian youths, and equipping and maintaining missionaries agreeable to the design of our institution, and that you do not blend them with your College, and other matters foreign to and separate from our undertaking; that you do not attempt to draw bills on us upon any other consideration, but that you keep the accounts as before mentioned, clear and separate, and annually transmit them to us, properly authenticated, with the seal of the Province annexed; and moreover, that you endeavor to compile and draw up a fresh Narrative as a continuation of that drawn up by us and printed in 1769. It is high time there should be one, and the public expect it. We have no materials by us since your unhappy division with Mr. Kirtland. His separation from you renders the accounts we have from him abortive, and we have no other, so it entirely rests with you, and if you mean to stand fair in the eye of the public, or hope for any further assistance from them, do not neglect or delay sending over such a narrative, and be as open and explicit as possible. We are desirous of strengthening your hands and furthering the design while it appears to be well executed, and no longer. With regard to Mr. Kirtland and your misunderstanding one another, as you are parted, our interfering will not avail. Dr. Whitaker has sent us a long letter in your behalf; and others have informed us as favorably on Mr. Kirtland's; all we can say of him is to wish him well, and that the Lord may own and bless his labors among the Indians, and abundantly supply his place with other missionaries in your connection. You have and will continue to have our warmest wishes for your success in the great and important work of bringing Indians to the faith of Christ, and you may depend upon having our best support in anything that comes within the limits of the design, beyond which we do not think ourselves at liberty to apply the money that has been deposited in our hands.'' This letter was signed by Dartmouth, S. S. Smythe, John Thornton, Chas. Hardy, Dan'l West, Sam'l Savage, and Rob't Keen. This letter cannot be misunderstood. Wheelock obeyed its mandate.

CHAPTER II.—Continued.

Wheelock died April 24, 1779. His last will was apparently executed April 2, 1779. In it he says: "I have founded on my own tenement, and at my own expense, an Indian Charity-School, now called Moor's Charity-School;" sets out that he is the founder thereof, "and as founder and proprietor thereof, as well as by grant in said charter," undertakes "to dispose of said school, and all donations, and grants of land, and other interests any way given or granted for the benefit of said school," and appointed his son his "successor in said office of president of my Indian Charity-School and Dartmouth College," etc.

By it he gave two acres of land to the college. After referring to the Indian school, he says: "To this charity-school, I do give and bequeath the stream called Mink Brook, with mills," etc. He also gave his servant-boy, Archelaus, his freedom, upon certain conditions, when he should attain the age of twenty-five years. The bequest, etc., to the College and that to the school were as distinctive from each other as was this to the slave. On June 14, 1785, the Legislature of Vermont granted to the school and to the College, each, one-half of the township of Wheelock, Vermont, which was six miles square. The terms of the grant were distinctly to "the said Wheelock as president, and his successors in office, to have and hold the one moiety of said premises as above described solely and exclusively for the use and benefit of said school forever, and the said trustees and their successors in office to have and to hold the other moiety solely and exclusively for the use and benefit of said Dartmouth College forever."

(44)

At a regular meeting of the Board of Trustees of Dartmouth College, holden at said College, May 7, 1789, the following preamble and resolutions were adopted : —

Representations having been made to this board that apprehensions have arisen in the minds of some persons that monies collected in Great Britain by the Revd. Messrs. Whitaker and Occom for the use of Moor's Charity-School under the direction of the Revd. Dr. Wheelock have been applied by this board to the use and benefit of Dartmouth, —

Resolved that this board have never had any control or direction of said monies,. nor have they to their knowledge at any time received or applied any sum or sums thereof to the use & benefit of sd. college, but on the most critical examination relative thereto, we are convinced this board have ever considered themselves as having no concern with the application of the said monies, but that they were subject to the application of the late Rev'd. Dr. E. Wheelock & his successors in the Presidency of Moor's Charity-School, & those only; nor have they to their knowledge any interest in their hands on which revenues have arisen to them as the effect of monies laid out by Dr. Wheelock or others, which were of monies collected by Dr. Whitaker and Mr. Occom in Great Britain as aforesaid; and should any such in future arise, it is the sense and intention of this board that such revenues be applied by Dr. Wheelock's successors solely to the objects for which those donations in Great Britain were made.

On June 10, 1807, the Legislature of New Hampshire passed the following act, entitled " An act more effectually to define and improve the charitable establishment known by the name of the President of Moor's Charity-School, and the powers and duties of the President thereof, and to constitute a board to assist in directing the expenditures of the funds of said school " : —

WHEREAS a school was a long time since founded by the late Rev. Eleazer Wheelock, S. T. D., who was President or director thereof, and also President of Dartmouth College, which was formerly and still is known by the name of Moor's Charity-School, as well as Moor's Indian Charity-School, and has since the death of said Eleazer been kept up and continued at Hanover in this State, by the Hon. John Wheelock, LL.D., President thereof and of Dartmouth College, as the successor of said Eleazer, as President of said College and said school, —

AND WHEREAS money and valuable donations and grants have been made of property in America for the benefit of said school, not only to the said Eleazer, but to the said John, the successor of said Eleazer in the office of President or director thereof, considered as being distinct in its objects from Dartmouth College, —

AND WHEREAS it has always been considered that Dartmouth College and Moor's Charity-School are different branches of the same institution, and that the President of said college ever has been and ever should be President of said school; and as the trustees of said college have not considered that they had any official right to be concerned in the application of the funds of said school, and as it is the desire of the President and deemed by the friends of the INSTITUTION advisable that the President in the application of the funds of said SCHOOL should act by and with the advice and concurrence of other persons, —

THEREFORE, Be it enacted by the Senate and House of Representatives in General Court convened, that the said John Wheelock, President of Dartmouth College, and his successors in Office for the time being, appointed agreeably to the Charter of said College, whether by the last will of the President preceding or otherwise, shall forever hereafter be, and hereby is declared to be the President of Moor's Charity School, and the Board of Trustees of Dartmouth College for the time being shall forever hereafter be and hereby is declared to be the Trustees of said School; and that said School as a Corporation, and as heretofore considered for the purposes aforesaid may and shall be known and called hereafter by the name of the President of Moor's Charity-School; and that said President with the advice and consent of said Trustees may and shall expend the issues and avails of all the funds and property of said school for the uses intended by the donors. *Provided nevertheless* that the funds of said College and School, and their proceeds, shall be distinct and separate ; and that nothing herein contained shall be considered as having any concern with the funds in the care of the Hon. Society in Scotland for propagating Christian Knowledge, or as interfering with their rights of inspection, or as affecting any other property belonging to said School, than such as has been or may be here-after granted in America for the use and benefit of said school.

And the funds of the school have been so kept and administered to this day. All these important grants, commencing with that of the town of Wheelock, besides large donations, were secured through the exertions of the second Wheelock.

A protest against the act of June 27, 1816, was prepared by the trustees, signed by most of the minority, and spread upon the legislative records. In that, fourthly, "they protest, because if this act can have any legal operation without the consent of the trustees under the charter, it must in effect destroy the former corporation, and consequently endanger the funds belonging to the College; especially the valuable township of Wheelock, granted to the College and Moor's School by the State of Vermont. So sensible did the House of Representatives appear to be of this consequence, that they refused so to amend the act as to make the State of New Hampshire responsible for the losses the College might sustain by reason of passing the act protested against."

The charity-school from the outset was a preparatory school.

The gazetteers show that at times the school numbered between fifty and sixty scholars. The hand-books say that it ceased to exist as a separate and distinct institution in 1846. The records, however, show that Asa Weeks was the last "preceptor" of Moor's School, and that he ceased to occupy that position in 1849. The treasurer of the College has never had any thing to do with the funds of the school.

The entire management has been in the hands of the president alone. A scanty fund still exists. Indians still have the benefit of this fund, though they take the same courses, enter the same classes, and receive the same instruction as other students.

If they fail to pass examination when they apply for admission, they are sometimes sent to a neighboring academy as a "preparatory school."

We transcribe from the original draft, among the Wheelock papers, the following deed of trust: —

To all the people to whom these presents shall come, greeting.

WHEREAS Eleazar Wheelock of Lebanon in the county of Windham and Colony of Connecticut in New England, in America, doctor of divinity, hath heretofore with great zeal and diligence and of his own accord, founded a charity-school within the said town of Lebanon in the colony aforesaid, with the sole view and design of civilizing and gospelizing the Indian natives of North America, in which (with the smiles of heaven) he hath been hitherto very successful; and may in time bring about (with the same blessing) that most happy and important event; towards the encouragement of which great and laudable undertaking, there have been made to the said Eleazer Wheelock, both in Europe and America, many valuable gifts, grants, contributions and donations, and especially those of late so generously given and collected in Great Britain, upon the application and address of that worthy undertaker, the Revnd. Doctor Nathanael Whitaker commissioned and appointed for that purpose by the said Eleazer Wheelock, and by and with the advice and influence of those noble and generous friends and benefactors, the right Honble William Earl of Dartmouth, Mr. Baron Smythe, John Thornton, Samuel Roffey, Charles Hardy and Daniel West, Esquires, Mr. Samuel Savage, Mr. Josiah Robarts, and Mr. Robert Keen, all of London in Great Britain aforesaid, who voluntarily became guarantees to the public for the due application of the monies that should be there collected for and in behalf of the said Eleazer Wheelock for the design and purpose aforesaid.

And whereas by means thereof it hath pleased the Almighty, who hath the hearts of all men in his hands, to dispose many free and charitable people both in England and Scotland to give and contribute to the said Eleazer Wheelock for the establishing and promoting the institution aforesaid many large sums of money, amounting nearly to the sum of £11,000 sterling money of Great Britain aforesaid, which said monies have been received and put into the hands of the aforesaid right Honble William Earl of Dart-mouth, Mr. Baron Smythe, John Thornton, Samuel Roffey, Charles Hardy and Daniel West, Esquires, Mr. Samuel Savage, Mr. Josiah Robarts, and Mr. Robert Keen, who now hold the same for the said Eleazer Wheelock untill further advice and order necessary thereto be by him given for the better securing and improving the said monies and donations, and the interests and profits thereof for the uses and purposes aforesaid.

And whereas it may so happen that further gifts and dona-tions may hereafter be made, both in Europe and America, towards, and for the furtherance of the undertaking and purposes aforesaid, for the well being, ordering and disposing whereof, as well as of those which have been so generously contributed as aforesaid, it will be necessary that a board of trustees be nominated and appointed by me the said Eleazer Wheelock, in Europe and America, with several and distinct powers and in-structions and to several purposes; for the taking and receiving all gifts, grants, subscriptions or donations made or to be made on each side of the water; for the use, support and due regula-tion of said school, and the missionaries and officers thereof, that may or shall, from time to time, be appointed; and also to dispose of and improve the same, according to the true intent, will and meaning of the donors, and for the advancement of the great and good ends proposed thereby.

Now therefore know ye that I Eleazer Wheelock, for the considerations aforesaid, and for divers other weighty and good reasons me thereunto moving, (and committing the affair to the wise Disposer of all things,) do nominate and appoint my much honoured and worthy friends aforesaid, the Right Honble William Earl of Dartmouth, Mr. Baron Smythe, John Thornton, Samuel Roffey, Charles Hardy and Daniel West, Esquires, Mr. Samuel Savage, Mr. Josiah Robarts and Mr. Robert Keen to be trustees as aforesaid. And I do also by these presents give, grant and make over unto them the Right Honble William Earl of Dartmouth, Mr. Baron Smythe, John Thornton, Samuel Roffey, Charles Hardy and Daniel West, Esquires, Mr. Samuel Savage, Mr. Josiah Rob-arts and Mr. Robert Keen, and to their successors in trust, and for the sole use and purpose aforesaid, all such grants, gifts, sub-scriptions or donations, as have been or may hereafter be made or given, of any kind or in any way whatsoever thro' their hands means or influence, and also all such monies, gifts or grants, already collected and by them received, or to be received in any parts or places in Europe for the uses and benefits aforesaid, for them and their successors, to have, hold, dispose of and improve in the best way and manner, only for the uses aforesaid under such limitations and regulations as shall hereafter be mentioned; and to do whatsoever they shall judge proper and necessary to be done on that side the water, for the security, well-being, prosperity, success, and increase of the whole design in view. And in case of the death or resignation of any of the aforesaid nine gentlemen, such vacancy be declared and others chosen by a majority of the remaining trustees to fill up such vacancy or vacancies, of such men as are of the Protestant Reformed religion, and who believe the Scriptures according to the publick standards of the Protestant churches.

I do also nominate and appoint one (whom I have named in my last will) to be my successor in the immediate care, oversight, guidance and direction of this whole affair, reserving to him all the power, privilege, jurisdiction, and authority which I now have or may have, in and about the premises, so long and under such limitations and restrictions, as shall hereafter be mentioned.

I do also nominate and appoint my faithful and trusty friends Col. William Pitkin, Esqr. of Hartford, the Revnd. Benjamin Pomeroy of Hebron, the Revnd. James Lockwood of Weathersfield, the Revnd. Timothy Pitkin of Farmington, the Revnd. Nathaniel Whitaker, D.D. of Norwich, the Revnd. William Patten of Hartford, and my son Ralph Wheelock, all of the Colony of Connecticut, and the Revnd. Samuel Kirtland missionary, or any others whom I shall think fit in my last will to· add to their number or appoint in their stead to be trustees of all the donations that have been, or shall hereafter be made, in the American colonies for the use, support, and benefit of the school and missionaries as aforesaid; and to them the trustees last mentioned I give, grant, and make over a lot of land or tenement in the second society in Lebanon aforesaid given originally by Mr. Joshua Moore of Mansfield in said colony, and since confirmed to me by a deed from his widow for the use and support of said school; together with the subscriptions made by diverse well disposed persons in these colonies for the support and benefit of the same; and any, and all other real or personal estate that has been or shall be given or any way conveyed or made over to this school and missionaries, or to me for the use and benefit of the same; to them the trustees last mentioned and to their successors, to have and to hold, or alienate and dispose of, as they, or the major part of them shall judge best, only for the uses aforesaid. And that they or any five of them the whole being duly notified (by letters from my successor or otherwise,) of the time and place of meeting, shall have full power to choose another trustee if they shall think fit, and then to confirm the appointment I have made of my successor, or to chuse another of their number in his stead; and that the same so chosen to be my successor, be approved by the right honorable, noble and worthy gentlemen of the trust in England, otherwise that a new nomination be made by either set of trustees, till one be found on which all may unite, and that the one appointed by the trust on this side of the water, shall officiate as my successor till that matter be settled.

And I do further order and appoint, that my successor be from time to time appointed by will, with the advice or approbation both of the trustees here and in England, forever, or untill a legal incorporation shall be obtained; and that he be approved by each of the boards of trustees, or that another be by them chosen, as aforesaid. And in case my successor or successors shall be without will, that one be chosen by both sets of trustees as aforesaid, and that he who shall be appointed by the trustees in America, officiate till that matter be settled as aforesaid. And in case of any vacancy by the death or resignation of any of the trustees here, that such vacancy or vacancies be supplied by others chosen by the major part of the remaining trustees.

And it shall be the duty of the American trustees to examine and authorize missionaries and school masters and appoint them to their respective services and judge of their skill and fidelity in performing the same; and accordingly to place and continue, or displace and remove them, as they shall judge fit; and do anything for the help and assistance of my said successor, in the vigorous prosecution of the said great design. And to appoint determine and fix upon laws rules and orders, for the due government, edification, decency and good economy of the whole affair

on this side of the water, as they shall from time to time judge
necessary submitting the same to the correction and approbation
of the trustees in England.

Also that my successors keep a faithful and fair account of
all the expenses and disbursements in this whole affair, and transmit the same twice a year with an account of all successes and
remarkable occurrences, to the trust in England. And also that
he shall do the same with respect to any new plan which he or the
trust here shall think fit to introduce in the prosecution of this
design, when and as soon as there is an opportunity for it, and if
it may be, before he enters upon the execution of it, in order for
the approbation of the trust in England. And the account being
thus kept and transmitted, my successor or successors shall have
power to draw for monies as occasion shall require, and the trust
in England shall not have right to protest any bill or draughts
made upon their treasurer to pay any expenses, made before my
successor shall have received notice of their disapprobation of
the measures he is pursuing. And I hope in God, who hath
hitherto so marvellously appeared to maintain and promote this
cause, which is his own, that he will yet take care of it and perform the highest wishes and hopes of his saints concerning it;
and particularly that he will yet further open the hearts of such as
he hath endowed with ability to provide a lasting fund for the support, not only of the school, but of the president, instructors,
and other officers necessary for the same.

And I do by these presents bind myself, &c., that the plan
aforesaid shall not by me be altered, without the consent and
approbation of the trust in England, but shall remain and be the
form and manner of the school, only reserving to myself the liberty to change my successor or to nominate another instead of
him who is now named in my will, and also to add two trustees
more than are now named, or remove either of these, and appoint
another or others in their stead, if I shall think it expedient.

The College charter, in the form of "Letters Patent,
under the publick seal of the Province," issued on December 13, 1769. It was recorded in the office of the Secretary of the Province, December 18, 1769, and the corporation was duly organized under it, October 22, 1770. The

charter, *in theory*, was granted by George III., the same as all writs in the province were issued in his name ; but *in fact* it was granted by John Wentworth, governor of the province, without the knowledge of the king or the Home Office.

The royal commission to Governor John Wentworth is a very elaborate document, covering nine long pages in print, and details the powers conferred upon him with great minuteness ; yet nowhere in terms, or by any reasonable implication, does it confer upon him the power of chartering colleges, or any other form of what are termed private corporations.

The charter declared Dr. Wheelock the founder, made him the first president of the College, and authorized him, by his last will, to appoint his successor.

The following grant was made by Governor Wentworth, months before the acceptance of the charter by the trustees :

PROVINCE OF NEW HAMPSHIRE.

George the third by grace of God of Great Britain, France and Ireland King, Defender of the faith, & so forth.

To all people to whom these presents come, greeting.

Whereas many liberal & pious Donations both in Europe & America have been made for the purpose of civilizing & educating Indians, & for the furtherance of christian knowledge, — and whereas the most extensive good will undoubtedly result from such a wise & generous design both to the cause of christianity & knowledge and also to our service & the permanent security of our Colonies by reclaiming the savages to virtuous knowledge & social subordination to the Laws and also enabling our good subjects in those remote parts of our dominions to acquire learning and thereby preventing their insensibly & unavoidably sinking into an illiterate and savage state unhappy to themselves & dangerously dishonorable to good government, and whereas a College hath by us been incorporated & erected by the name of Dartmouth College under the great seal of our said Province, for these and many other equally worthy & commendable purposes of the like nature, — Now Know ye, that for these purposes, we, of our special grace, certain knowledge & mere motion, and for the due encouragement of settling a new plantation within our said Province, by and with the advice of our trusty and well beloved John Wentworth Esquire our Governor & Commander in chief, in & over our said Province of New Hampshire in New England and of our Council of the same, Have upon the conditions and reservations hereinafter made given & granted & by these presents for us our heirs and successors do give & grant as a public donation to the Trustees of Dartmouth College (lately incorporated and erected in this our said Province) and to their successors in that trust for the use and benefit of said College and to their assigns a certain tract or parcel of land commonly called and known by the name of Landaff, situate, lying, and being within our said Province & containing by admeasurement twenty-five thousand two hundred and forty-seven acres, three roods & ten perches, out of which an allowance is to be made for highways & unimprovable lands by rocks, ponds, mountains & rivers, one thousand & forty acres free according to a plan & survey thereof exhibited by our Surveyor General of lands for our said Province by our said Governor's order & returned into the Secretary's office, a copy whereof is hereunto annexed, butted & bounded as follows, vizt: —

[Description omitted.]

To have and to hold the said tract of land as above expressed together with all the privileges & appurtenances to them the said Trustees of Dartmouth College in their said capacity & to their successors in said Trust & to their assigns for the use and benefit of said College forever by the name of Landaff upon the following terms, conditions & reservations, vizt.: First, that there shall be settled & resident on the premises sixty families by the expiration of four years, vizt., twelve families in one year from the first day of March next, also twelve families more in the next year, vizt., by the first day of March 1772, also twelve families more in the third year, vizt., by the first day of March 1773, and also twenty-four families more in the fourth year, vizt., by the first day of March which will be in the year of our Lord 1774, on penalty of the forfeiture of any & every delinquent's share & of such share or shares reverting to us, our heirs & successors, to be by us or them entered upon & regranted to such of our subjects as shall effectually settle and cultivate the same. Second, that all white and other pine trees within the said Township fit for masting our royal navy be carefully preserved for that use & none to be cut or felled without our special license for so doing first had & obtained on penalty of the Forfeiture of the right of any proprietor possessor or settler to us our heirs & successors, as well as being subject to the penalties prescribed by any present as well as future act or acts of Parliament. Third, that a site for a town plot be within one year laid out by the Trustees in such part of the said Township as they shall find best for settlement of at least one hundred and fifty families to each an acre, which town plot shall be laid out in streets parallel to each other so as to intersect at right angles, the two middle streets to be one hundred & thirty feet wide, and all other streets to be at least sixty feet wide. Fourth, that there be cut, cleared & made passable for carriages a road of four rods wide through the said tract & this to be completed in two years from the date of this grant, in failure whereof the premises to revert to us, our heirs & successors. Fifth, yielding and paying therefor to us, our heirs & successors on or before the first day of March 1779, the rent of one ear of Indian corn only if lawfully demanded. Sixth, that every proprietor settler or Inhabitant, shall yield & pay unto us, our heirs & successors yearly & every year forever from and after the expiration of one year from the above said first day of March, vizt., on the first day of March which will be in the year of our Lord Christ 1780, one shilling proclamation money for every hundred acres of land he so owns, settles or possesses & so in proportion for a greater or lesser tract of the said land, which money shall be paid by the respective persons above said their heirs & assigns in our Council Chamber in Portsmouth or to such officer or officers as shall be appointed to receive the same. Seventh, that any of the said tract appearing to be well adapted to the growth of hemp or flax, there shall be annually cultivated & improved a due proportion of the said land not less than ten acres in every thousand acres with that beneficial article of produce & these to be in lieu of all rents & services whatsoever. In testimony whereof we have caused the seal of our said Province to be hereunto affixed. Witness John Wentworth Esquire our Governor & commander in chief in & over said Province of N. H. the nineteenth day of January in the tenth year of our Reign Anno que Domini 1770.

Recorded Jan'y 22, 1770.

PROVINCE OF NEW HAMPSHIRE.

George the Second by the grace of God of Great Britain, France
[L. S.]   and Ireland King, Defender of the Faith, &c.

To all to whom these presents shall come, Greeting.

Whereas we did by our letters patent under the seal of our
Province aforesaid dated the thirteenth day of December 1769
erect & incorporate a college within our said Province by the name
of Dartmouth College for the laudable purpose of spreading
christianity among the Indians, and we did also thereby erect &
incorporate certain of our loving subjects therein named into a
body corporate & politic & their successors to have continuance
forever & to be known & distinguished as the Trustees of Dartmouth College & by that name to receive, purchase & possess &
enjoy lands, tenements, hereditaments, jurisdictions and franchises
for themselves and successors in fee simple & to erect any houses
·or buildings as they may think needful and convenient for the purposes of said college, all which will more fully appear by reference
to our said letters patent. And it being represented unto us that
the said Trustees have accordingly erected part of the buildings of the said college on a tract of land of about five hundred
acres situate in the southwesterly angle of the town of Hanover
in our said Province which tract as yet remains ungranted
by us, —

Know Ye therefore that of our special grace & favour for reclaiming the Savages to virtuous knowledge & by and with the
advice of our trusty & well beloved John Wentworth Esq. our
Govr & Commander in chief in & over our said Province & of our
Council of the same Have upon the conditions and reservations
hereinafter made given & granted & by these presents for us, our
heirs & successors to give and grant unto the Trustees of Dartmouth College & to their successors in that trust for the use &
benefit of the said College & to their assigns, three hundred acres
of land being the particular spot on which said College stands, the
same being butted & bounded as follows : —

[Description omitted.]

To have and to hold the said tract of land as above expressed
together with all the privileges & appurtenances to them the said
Trustees of Dartmouth College in their said capacity & to their

successors in that trust & their assigns for the use & benefit of said College forever, upon the terms hereafter mentioned. And in consideration of the faithful endeavours of our trusty & well beloved Eleazer Wheelock, Doctor in Divinity the present President of our said College to further & promote the general advantage & benefit of the same, particularly in his having generously made a donation of four hundred acres of land in the said Town of Hanover to the said College we have by & with the advice aforesaid & by these presents do give & grant unto the said Eleazer Wheelock & to his heirs & assigns forever two hundred acres of land being the remaining part of the aforesaid five hundred acres butted & bounded as follows: —

[Description omitted.]

To have & to hold the said two hundred acres of land to him the said Eleazer Wheelock & to his heirs & assigns forever upon the following terms, conditions & reservations, viz — First, That a road of three rods wide be cut; cleared & made passable for carriages of all kinds through each of the tracts of land aforesaid as may be hereafter directed or ordered by the Gov' & Council aforesaid. Second, That five acres for every fifty acres of land contained in the above described premises respectively be improved, cultivated & planted within two years from the date of this grant on penalty of the forfeiture of the delinquents right in these presents & of its reverting to us our heirs & successors. Third, That all white & other pine trees fit for masting our Royal Navy be carefully preserved for that use & none to be cut or felled without our special license for so doing first had & obtained on penalty of the forfeiture of the right of the grantee in the premises his heirs & assigns to us our heirs & successors as well as being subject to the penalties prescribed by any present as well as future act or acts of Parliament. Fourth, Yielding and paying therefor to us, our heirs & successors on or before the nineteenth day of December 1774 the rent of one ear of Indian corn only, if lawfully demanded. Fifth, That the said Trustees and their successors in their capacity aforesaid & the said Eleazer Wheelock his heirs & assigns shall respectively yield & pay unto us our heirs & successors yearly & every year forever from & after the expiration of five years from the date of this Grant one shilling proclamation money for every hundred acres contained in their respective rights in the premises hereby granted; which money shall be paid as above said in our Council chamber in Portsmouth or to such officer or officers as shall be appointed to receive the same & these to be in lieu of all other rents & services whatsoever. In testimony whereof we have caused the seal of our said Province to be hereunto affixed.

Witness John Wentworth Esq. our aforesaid Governor & commander in chief the nineteenth day of December in the twelfth year of our reign A. D. 1771.

J. WENTWORTH.

By his Excellency's command &c.
THEODORE ATKINSON, *Secy.*

Wheelock, in his letter from Lebanon, Connecticut, to Colonel Phelps, dated November 20, 1769, says: "For your direction in the business on which I now employ you, I need only give you some general hints, and leave you to conduct the whole affair according as your own prudence, with the advice of such as you shall see fit to consult, shall dictate. When his excellency Gov. Wentworth has given me the charter, & you have got it recorded, let the deed of lands given to the school & myself be executed, in which let your eye be upon having as much near & convenient for speedy improvement for the present support of my family & school, as may be. Bring the several offers made to induce a preference for the site of it in particular places, and have with you the estimate of judicious & impartial men relative thereto, and especially his excellency's reasons for preferring the place he shall choose to fix it in.

"Give my duty to his excellency the late Govern^r, and tell him I would humbly propose to his consideration, whether it would not be an offering well pleasing to Christ if, in addition to all his acts of piety and charity, he should settle a pension for the support of a professor, or tutor, or some needy youths in Dartmouth College, as his wisdom and goodness shall direct, and the benefited person to bear his name and so perpetuate his memory with the memory of his deed, to the latest posterity. Let the proposal be properly made to his excellency, and I am persuaded he will gladly embrace the opportunity to give such a dying testimonial of his respect to the kingdom of the great Redeemer.

" See what donations may be had by charitably disposed gentlemen of materials which shall be necessary for the buildings, such as glass, putty, coloring, papering, spikes, nails, for floors, ceiling, enclosing, shingling, clapboarding, lathing, locks, latches, * * * hinges, fire-shovels, tongs, hand-irons, &c.

" And if a good bell should be offered, don't refuse it.

" See what provision may be made most conveniently for putting seed of all kinds into the ground seasonably for the support of my family and school, & what provision for my removal, & what way my family and school may be supported there at first, &c.

" See what materials for building may be had on the spot, viz., of boards, shingles, clapboards, window frames, sashes, laths, &c., stones, limestone, brick.

" And how laborers of all kinds may be employed in the cheapest manner for the school," etc.

The reference to the late governor is to Benning Wentworth.

The distinction here drawn between the College and the school is as marked as that between himself and either.

The following explains the grant to Wheelock : " In the Memoirs of Dr. Wheelock it is stated that for his great labors, eight or nine years president of the College and school, professor of divinity, and pastor of the church in the College, he received no salary, his only compensation being a supply of provisions for his family. The Legislature of New Hampshire, after the College was established, voted him one hundred pounds.

" Governor Wentworth granted him, December 19, 1771, two hundred acres of land in Hanover, in consideration of his having made a donation of four hundred acres in Hanover to the College. The history of the affair is this : Benning

Wentworth had given five hundred acres to the College, and the proprietors of the town had given Dr. Wheelock four hundred acres. At the first meeting of the trustees, October 22, 1770, they agreed with him, at his request, to exchange two hundred acres out of the five hundred for his four hundred acres ; but this gift proving illegal, Governor John Wentworth made the grant of the two hundred acres directly to Dr. Wheelock, who allowed the College to retain the four hundred acres formerly agreed to be given for the same two hundred acres.'' (See Memoir of Wheelock, by Dr. Allen.)

It is not only apparent that Governor Wentworth intended to put the College upon the same footing as the universities at home, with which he was familiar, but, from the '' Narrative,'' from which we have already quoted, that Dr. Wheelock regarded the charter as creating a university ; that the trustees in the most solemn manner, for years even after the troubles commenced, so denominated the institution. Dr. Belknap, the unfriendly critic of Wheelock, who was familiar with the whole history, says : '' The township of Hanover, on the eastern bank of the Connecticut River, was finally determined as the most convenient situation for the school ; to which the Governor annexed a charter of incorporation for an university, which took the name of Dartmouth College, from its benefactor, the Earl of Dartmouth. Of this University Dr. Wheelock was declared the founder and president.'' (2 Belknap's History of New Hampshire, 270.)

Dr. Wheelock's views probably appear more fully than elsewhere in the following elaborate memorial to the Vermont Legislature : —

To the Honorable the General Assembly of the State of Vermont to be convened at Bennington June, 1778.

The Memorial of the Rev. Eleazer Wheelock D.D. President of Dartmouth College on Connecticut River.

Humbly showeth

That Your Memorialist did, at his own expense and upon his own inheritance above 20 years ago found a Charity-School for the

education of the Children of the native Savages of this land and
also such Youth of the English as should appear of pregnant parts
and piously disposed in the learned Languages and all the liberal
Arts and Sciences and especially in the doctrines and principles
of our holy religion in order to qualify them to spread the knowledge of the only true God and Saviour and to advance the Kingdom of the Redeemer amongst all the several Nations and Parties
of Men upon this Continent; and by the blessing of God on his
feeble endeavors many Missionaries and School-masters educated
here have been sent forth and many schools set up and children of
the savages taken into them in the Wilderness and the prospects
were so encouraging as that numbers of piously disposed Gentlemen not only in America but Gentlemen and Noblemen of first
characters in Europe have condescended to patronize and encourage the same.   And generous collections were made for the support and furtherance of it in consequence of the solicitations of
the Rev. Dr. Whitaker and the Rev. Mr. Sampson Occom whom I
sent into Europe for that purpose; that in consequence thereof
many subscriptions of landed and other interests were generously
made in the several governments of New England and parts adja-
cent to invite the settlement of it with them respectively.

The decision of which being referred to the right Honorable
and Worthy Trustees in London who gave the preference to the
place where it is now settled.   *The royal favor of a charter was
hereupon granted at the desire of your Memorialist, amply
endowing it with jurisdictions powers immunities and privileges
equal to any University within the Realm of Great Britain*, and
whereby it became a body corporate and politic as independent as
any corporation — or any other incorporate body whatsoever is or
can be; that since the commencement of the present War all
resources for its support from beyond the Seas have been wholly
cut off and suspended, whereby it has been exposed to great necessities and to require a charitable patronage and assistance from
some one or other of the United States in America.   And as it is
by the Providence of God located in your vicinity and I have
with pleasure observed in your well formed constitution the
expressions of your pious care early to lay a foundation to promote Religion, Learning and Virtue in your State, and particularly to erect a *University* in the same for the encouragement of
those pious purposes, I am encouraged to make this proposal to

you and desire you to take it into consideration whether you will or not take this School under your friendly and charitable patronage and assist and vindicate the rights, jurisdictions, immunities, powers and privileges which it is entitled to by royal Charter and which has since been ratified and confirmed by the Honorable Continental Congress and particularly that till it shall be in a capacity to appoint such Officers and Orders as it is by Charter entitled to for the safety edification and well-being of the same that you would enact that the President for the time being shall be a justice of the peace he being duly qualified therefor, and that the Corporation of said College shall have right to appoint another to that Office to be an assistant and officiate with him therein, *and this more especially for the trial of causes which concern the School or University,* that they shall have right as occasion shall require to call in a Magistrate or Magistrates a Justice or Justices of the peace of the vicinity in your State to assist as there shall appear occasion in the trial of such causes as may be before them and that the Officers of your State shall be under the same obligation to obey the precepts issued forth by the aforesaid authority, that they are to obey any other Officer or Judicatory whatsoever; that appeals from this court shall be to the superior court of your State; *that all tryals and determinations wherein those are concerned who do not belong to or are not connected with this School or University and all processes respecting such shall be according to the Laws of your State.* And moreover, that you grant unto this *University,* that there be two or three Charity-Schools or Academies besides the present erected upon the same plan and under the same jurisdiction and for the same pious purposes as the present in connexion with this *University* is, and they to be fixed in such places as your State shall judge most convenient; that the respective schools shall be endowed with landed and other interests as the charity and pious disposition of your State or any individual thereof shall induce them to liberality towards the same. — That this corporation shall have liberty as they see occasion, due respect being had to the friendship and liberality shown to them respectively by the inhabitants in the vicinity, to give the preference to either of them as the place for the *Annual Commencement to confer the honors of said University,* or to erect a principle building to accommodate the students belonging to the same; that those glebes of land which were granted in the respective Townships to the Society in Land as for the propagating of the Gospel in foreign parts shall, or such part of them as you shall judge fit, be granted and sequestered to the only benefit use behoof and support of said Schools *or of the University to which they shall be subordinate and this as being most agreeable to the original charitable and pious purpose and design of the same,* and *I submit to your consideration whether you will not esteem a grant to this University* of the Township of Kingsland which was once granted for the encouragement and building up of an Episcopal College in New York to be a reasonable and acceptable return and offering to the Lord Jesus Christ for the signal tokens of the divine favor hitherto manifested to your State; and as to what I have said respecting your charitable endowment of this Institution it is wholly submitted to your wise and prudent determination. And *as to what concerns the powers, jurisdictions and immunities of the same here expressed they do not exceed those which were granted by the royal charter.* And your own thoughts will suggest whether they are more than are necessary for the safety and well-being of an Institution of such a nature and so liberally endowed with an invaluable treasure to be defended and secured or more than will best subserve the honor and reputation of your State and render it respectable in the account of the present and of generations yet to come.

Respected Gentlemen, with my best wishes and ardent prayers that you may enjoy peace, unanimity and divine guidance and direction in all your consultations and determinations in the important matters that are before you and that the word of God in due time may have free course, run and be glorified and the Redeemer's Kingdom be built up and glory dwell in your state,

I subscribe with much affection and esteem your Honorable Assembly's most obedient and most humble servant,

ELEAZAR WHEELOCK.

DARTMO. COLLEGE, 4 JUNE, 1778."

We have italicised some of the more important passages.

The following extracts from its journals show to some extent the actions of the Continental Congress : —

July 12, 1775.

That as there is a Seminary for the instruction of Indian youth which has been established under the care of Dr. Wheelock, on

Connecticut River, and as there are nine or ten Indian youths at that school, chiefly from the tribes residing near Quebec; and as for want of a proper fund, there is danger that these youths may be sent back to their friends, which will probably excite jealousy and distrust, and be attended with bad consequences, the Commissioners for Indian Affairs in the Northern Department be authorized to receive, out of the Continental Treasury, a sum not exceeding Five Hundred Dollars, to be applied by them for the support of said Indian youths. (1 Jour. of Cont. Cong. 163.)

JAN. 10, 1776.

Resolved, That the Commissioners for Indian Affairs in the Northern Dept. be directed to pay Rev. Dr. Wheelock $500, agreeable to a resolution of Congress passed the 12th day of July last. (2 Jour. of Cont. Cong. 18.)

APRIL 10, 1776.

Resolved, That although the prosperity of Dartmouth College, in the colony of New Hampshire, is a desirable object, it is neither reasonable nor prudent to contribute towards its relief or support, out of the public Treasury. (2 Jour. of Cont. Cong. 126.)

SEPT. 19, 1776.

As it may be a means of conciliating the friendship of the Canadian Indians, or at least of preventing hostilities by them, in some measure, to assist the President of Dartmouth College in New Hampshire, in maintaining their youth, who are now there under his tuition, and whom the revenues of the College are not, at this time, sufficient to support; that for this purpose $500 be paid to the Rev. Dr. Eleazer Wheelock, President of the said College. (2 Jour. of Cont. Cong. 365.)

FRIDAY, 18 December, 1778.

A report from the Board of Treasury was read. Whereupon Congress came to the following order and resolution: —

Whereas Dr. Wheelock has incurred expense in supporting a number of Indian Youth of the Caghnawaga tribe at his school which in times past has been the means of conciliating the friendship of that tribe: —

Ordered that a warrant issue on the Treasurer in favor of Lieutenant Colonel Wheelock for nine hundred and twenty-five dollars for the use of the said Doctor Eleazer Wheelock.

When the Indian school and College were established in the wilderness at Hanover, Wheelock's religious and personal friends from Connecticut swarmed up the valley and located above and below him on both sides of the river. Fifty-two people from Connecticut settled Hanover, and eight hundred families from Connecticut gathered in a few towns on the New Hampshire side alone. In a word, he founded on the extreme western border of New Hampshire, separated from the rest of that State by a vast wilderness, a Connecticut colony which had but a mystical legal connection with it. The better to conserve his power, a district three miles square, called Dresden, was created, to be under the immediate jurisdiction of Dartmouth College, and special jurisdiction over this little empire was given to President Wheelock as its magistrate. Aside from Wheelock, the College faculty were at the bottom of the secession of the sixteen river towns from New Hampshire, and the movement to establish a new confederacy, with the College district as its capital. The church, school, and College were under the personal, or, as he termed it, the "paternal," government of the president till his death, in 1779, when they descended as an heirloom to his son John Wheelock, who was called from the army, and became by force of his father's will his dynastic successor. He retained his office until he was removed by the trustees in 1815, after a service of thirty-six years.

The second Wheelock had had the benefit of foreign travel; gathered contributions for the College in all countries; was rich, courtly, and strong-willed; had given his services, and oftentimes his money, to the College, and had proposed to give more, and make it, in effect, his heir.

CHAPTER III.

THE RELIGIOUS PHASE OF THE CONTROVERSY—DIFFER-
ENCES BETWEEN DR. WHEELOCK AND DR. BELLAMY—
CHURCH TROUBLES AT HANOVER—THE FAMILY DY-
NASTY—CORRESPONDENCE—THE STANDING ORDER—THE
CLERGY EXEMPTED FROM TAXATION—LIBERAL VIEWS
AND POLICY OF GOVERNOR PLUMER—DR. WHIPPLE'S TOL-
ERATION ACT.

A FUNDAMENTAL provision of the College charter was that
there should be no discrimination on account of religious
faith or principles.

The population of the province, at this time, was about
sixty thousand, and probably a majority of them were orthodox of the Plymouth Rock school ; but Episcopalians were
quite abundant on the sea-coast, and many of the prominent
men of the province, including the governor who granted the
charter, affiliated with that church. Presbyterian churches
were scattered along the valley of the Merrimack. Wheelock had great popularity, and, in his later years at least,
was a Presbyterian, and gathered about him churches of
that order.

There were natural and substantial reasons for Wheelock's
course. His lot was early cast in what was essentially a
Scotch settlement, to whom the faith and forms of their
fathers came by inheritance. From first to last, the Presbyterian Church cordially sustained him, and contributed with
marked liberality to forward the great enterprise which was
nearest his heart. The royal governors of New Hampshire,
though strongly attached to the Church of England, favored
the Presbyterian Church over the Congregationalist. Exceedingly strict in morals and decided in matters of faith,

(66)

he was tolerant far beyond his time of those who differed from him in opinion, as long as he felt that they were sincere and led pure lives. Unworthy persons had been brought within the fold through the half-way covenant, and otherwise; and he felt that such would be less likely to vote themselves and their fellows out of its pale than a more conservative body like the sessions.

Difficulties arose in the church at Hanover.

There was "a woman in the case." We quote the following : —

To ye Session of ye Church of Christ in Hanover.

Rev'd and Beloved. Y^e subscriber being aggrieved with Sam'l Haze, [Hayes] a member of said Church, for his browbeating and insulting me when attempting to admonish him for forbidding his family to come to my house unless of an arrand; in telling me I was doing all in my power to undo his family, and that I had been trying to do it this number of years; also for telling me I was meddling ye most of my time with that I had no business with, and that my character was, as a certain man told me, as black as Hell, he told me I knew where; also he told me I had almost broke up one school by my conduct; also for telling me when put in mind of our neighbor's settlement, that he had never settled anything with me; also by way of irony, he told me if I proceeded against him, he supposed I would get Mr. Rudd to enter ye complaint; also he told me my dealing with him was publick; and being asked how that came to be, told me that he had made it so; also that my conduct was erroneous, and far worse than Mr. Bassetts; which conduct of Said Haze I apprehend to be a breach of ye ninth command, and also a violation of his covenant engagement; and having taken ye more private steps, and being unable to recover ye brother from his error, I, in this way, tell it to ye Church, that he may be dealt with as God, in his word requires.

RACHEL MURCH.

HANOVER, APRIL 26, 1783.

Mr. Haze was tried, convicted, and censured by the sessions. He appealed to the Grafton Presbytery, which then embraced most of the churches in that region, and which, in effect, held him guilty, but not censurable. The sessions, led by the pastor, Rev. Dr. Burroughs, remonstrated, and arraigned the presbytery for its decision. The latter vacillated, but finally cited the sessions, which refused to obey until the obnoxious decision was annulled. In March, 1784, the sessions, and such of the church as adhered to them, — fifty-six persons in all, — separated from the presbytery, which, in May, 1784, cited them to appear at Orford to show cause why they should not be dealt with as rebels and covenant-breakers. On June 4, 1784, this summons was formally defied by the sessions. Four days later, the presbytery decided that Dr. Burroughs and his followers, in separating themselves from the church and presbytery, were covenant-breakers, and cut them off from fellowship with the churches connected with that presbytery ; but, as there was no synod, proposed a mutual council. The sessions promptly rejected the proposition, and the church confirmed their action. The other church at Hanover, Wheelock, the professors, and some of the trustees, were involved in the controversy until Dr. Burroughs was dismissed, in 1809, when there was a change of form in these church troubles.

From the outset, the pivot question was one of discipline, and into that the one of church government entered.

The mass of details, into which we cannot enter, have been gathered with praiseworthy industry by the Rev. Charles A. Downs, superintendent of public instruction in New Hampshire, and former pastor of the Congregationalist church at Lebanon, which is about five miles from the College.

In the Board of Trustees, Dr. John Wheelock led the Presbyterian wing, and Dr. Shurtleff, apparently, but Judge Niles really, led the other.

Judge Niles was a favorite student of and read theology with Dr. Joseph Bellamy, of Connecticut, who graduated at Yale in 1735, two years after the elder Wheelock.

Bellamy was a pungent controversialist, and there was a radical difference between him and Dr. Wheelock about church polity, etc.

Dr. Wheelock claimed that the Presbyterian, and Dr. Shurtleff that the Congregational, form of church government should prevail. The former was a government by the eldership, and the latter by major vote of the body of the church, — a pure democracy.

Many of those who are best informed believe that the subsequent troubles and the famous litigation arose in fact, as well as in form, from this apparent difference of opinion about church government. The eight trustees who removed Dr. Wheelock were manifestly of the opposite opinion. They say : " The trustees now solemnly declare that they do not feel, and never have felt, any hostility toward the Presbyterian form of church government, or toward the church of which the president is a member ; nor any wish to give the new church any advantage over the old, or in any way to interfere with their unhappy controversy. * * * They do, however, believe that the seeming attachment of the president to this particular form of church government is mere pretence."

We think this difference was only the name of the case, — the John Doe and Richard Roe of the ejectment ; or, as Judge Crosby emphatically puts it, " The second Wheelock lost his presidency by removal. True, perhaps too true. It was not caused by incompetency, nor by neglect of duty, nor change of religious opinion, but simply to rid the board and College of the family dynasty."

Mr. Adams was a professor in the College under Dr. Wheelock. He was the special, intimate, and confidential correspondent of Thomas W. Thompson, one of the hostile trustees, and one of the most active and efficient managers on the anti-Wheelock side. On September 10, 1814, he wrote a lengthy letter to the elder Farrar, another trustee, in relation to politics and the affairs of the College. In it he says : " I have heard it suggested that a project is on foot to have the president resign, the trustees first pledging themselves to appoint Mr. Allen.   This is indeed a project I have expected, but did not look for it quite so soon.   I trust, however, that the trustees are not yet prepared to give a warranty of the college to the *family dynasty*.   I hope also that they do not think they have such a set of turbulent, refractory professors that it is necessary to place over them a democratic president to punish them for their iniquities.''

Ever since the Revolution, and indeed before, the Congregationalist, the '' standing order,'' as it was often termed, had been the dominant religious sect.   It had become a species of '' State religion.''   Its ministers were nearly all Federalists, and its laymen largely so.   But a few years before this explosion, a representative man asserted, in a public address, that there were in the denomination, in the State, but two clergymen who were Anti-Federalists, and as publicly urged that they should be '' cast out '' for their irreligion in politics.

Taxation in those days was a grievous burden, and no part of it was borne by the clergy.   By a law passed in 1705 it was made the duty of the freeholder who took the account for the purposes of assessment to faithfully perform '' the trust,'' '' in going through the town,'' '' to every inhabitant thereof, to take a just and true account of each person's ratable estate.''   By the act of May, 1719, it was made the duty of the selectmen, in making their assessments, '' to make perfect lists under their hands, or the major part of them, setting down every person's name and several proportion.''   By an act of 12 Geo. II. it was provided '' that the selectmen and assessors of said towns, parishes, and precincts are hereby authorized and enabled to assess the polls and estates of the inhabitants within their respective districts, each one according to his known ability, their proportion of all province, charge and taxes yearly, upon the receipt of the

treasurer's warrant, to be directed to the selectmen as has
been usual." These acts did not exempt clergymen, or provide that they should not be deemed "persons." There
were other acts in a similar vein.

In Kelley v. Bean and others, selectmen of Warner, the
highest court in the State, at the May term, 1798, in Hillsborough County, decided "that a minister of the church
and congregation in a town" was not liable to be taxed.

In Kidder v. French, decided by the same court, in the
same county, at the April term, 1807, it was held by a
majority of the court that the estate of an ordained minister
of the gospel who is *not* settled over a corporate society was
not exempt from taxation. From this decision Wingate, J.,
dissented. Chief Justice Smith was a liberal in his religious
views and opinions. We undoubtedly owe to that fact, and
his influence with his associate, that they were not exempted
from taxation under all circumstances. The plaintiff, Kidder, failed because the pastoral relations between himself
"and the church and town of Dunstable" had been dissolved prior to the assessment of the tax. (Smith's N. H.
Rep. 155.)

In Moore v. Poole, decided by the Supreme Court, in the
same county, in December, 1815, upon a demurrer to the
declaration, the general doctrine of Kelley v. Bean was
affirmed. The demurrer was overruled, and the plaintiff
had judgment for $7.08. The court held that when an
assistant assessor of the United States direct tax enumerated
in the list of taxable property the real estate of a settled
minister, and a tax was afterwards assessed upon this list by
the principal assessor, and was collected, the minister's
land was exempt, and that he could maintain case against
the assistant assessor. The opinion was delivered by the
chief justice, and these cases are to be found in his MS.
reports.

There were other cases to the same import. All other
denominations had to support, not only their own church

organizations, but, through the " contract " system and the
tax power, were also compelled to contribute to the support
of this denomination as if they were members of it. By the
act of May, 1714, it was provided that every town, in town-
meeting, might by themselves, or by any other person
appointed, " agree with a minister or ministers for the
supply of such town, and what annual salary shall be
allowed him or them ; and the minister or ministers so made
choice of and agreed with shall be accounted the settled
minister or ministers of such town ; and the selectmen, for
the time being, shall make rates and assessments upon the
inhabitants of the town for the payment of the minister's
salary, as aforesaid, in such manner and form as they do for
defraying of other town charges. * * * *Provided*,
always, That this act do not at all interfere with her
majesty's grace and favor in allowing her subjects liberty of
conscience ; nor shall any person, under pretence of being
of a different perswasion, be excused from paying toward the
support of the settled minister or ministers of such town,
aforesaid ; but only such as are conscientiously so, and constantly attend the publick worship of God on the Lord's day
according to their own perswasion, and they only shall be
excused from paying towards the support of the ministry of
the town."

" Sec. 2. *And it is hereby further enacted and ordained*, That
for building and repairing of meeting-houses, ministers' houses,
school-houses, and allowing a salary to a school-master, of each
town within this province, the selectmen, in their respective towns,
shall raise money by an equal rate and assessment upon the inhabitants, in the same manner as in this present act directed for the
maintenance of the minister."

The act of February 8, 1791, provided " that the inhabitants of each town in this State, qualified to vote as aforesaid, at any meeting duly and legally warned and holden in
such town, may, agreeably to the Constitution, grant and
vote such sum or sums of money as they shall judge neces-

sary for the settlement, maintenance, and support of the ministry, schools, meeting-houses, school-houses, the maintenance of the poor, for laying out and repairing highways, for building and repairing bridges, and for all the necessary charges arising within the said town, to be assessed on the polls and estates in the same town, as the law directs.''

The same statute declared parishes with town privileges towns.

The law of 1791 was, in practice, treated as a reaffirmance of the prior law. Under these laws, "the Congregational clergy in the State had been originally settled by the towns or parishes where they preached, and the inhabitants were all taxed for their support. But many individuals of their congregations, having now become Baptists, Methodists, or Universalists, were no longer willing to pay for preaching they did not attend. Property had been taken, in many cases, on distraint, for taxes so assessed, and suits were commenced to ascertain the rights of the parties.'' (Life of Governor Plumer, 185.)

The Constitutions of 1784 and 1792, with the exception of the disgraceful provisions (always a dead letter) which prohibited Catholics from holding a few political offices, put all religious denominations upon the same level.

They provided, —

" That the several towns, parishes, bodies corporate, or religious societies shall at all times have the exclusive right of electing their own public teachers, and of contracting with them for their support and maintenance ; and no person of any one particular religious sect or denomination shall ever be compelled to pay toward the support of the teacher or teachers of another persuasion, sect or denomination.

" And every denomination of Christians, demeaning themselves quietly and as good subjects of the State, shall be equally under the protection of the law ; and no subordination of any one sect or denomination to another shall ever be established by law.

" And nothing herein shall be understood to affect any former contracts made for the support of the ministry, but all such contracts shall remain and be in the same state as if this Constitution had not been made.''

These provisions wrought no essential change in these settlements or the form of the contracts. As late as 1806, one of the most important towns in the State '' settled '' a clergyman, eminent for his scholarship, over the parish where the writer dwelt in his boyhood, under a '' contract '' vote '' that the town of —— pay —— $450 annually, for preaching and attending to all the duties incumbent on a settled minister of the gospel in said town, until two-thirds of that part of the town denominated Congregationalists shall wish to discontinue the salary ; and it shall be discontinued in one year after a regular notification, in writing, from the town to said ——, purporting such wish.'' He retained this charge for about forty-six years. This instance well illustrates the whole system in its best estate. Except for such purposes of taxation, the existence of those who were not Congregationalists was practically ignored. Those who would not pay such taxes were harassed with suits. Their difficulty was to satisfy courts and juries that they were not making '' pretence of being of a different persuasion,'' etc. The astute counsel for the settled ministers dragged into all these jury trials every conceivable ecclesiastical dogma and theological vagary, and the most subtle distinctions between baptism, immersion, etc., their point being to induce the juries to hold that, for the purposes of church taxation, everybody was a Congregationalist, though he might not be for any other purpose. '' In one such case, where the party resisting the tax was a Universalist, the decision was against him. Judge Wingate charged the jury that if the party claiming the exemption did not prove himself, in the words of the Constitution, to belong to ' another persuasion, sect or denomination,' he was bound to pay his tax for the support of the minister of the town ; and that, to make him such, the difference must be something more

than that which separated Calvinists from Universalists; in
other words, that a person who believed in universal salvation might, in the eye of the law, be of the same persuasion
with another who believed that not one in ten would be
saved. They agreed, said the judge, in more points than
they differed in. They were both Christians; and the inference, somewhat harshly drawn, was that they were both
bound to support the same preacher." (Life of Plumer,
186.)

Wingate was a clergyman, and one of the judges of
the highest court, whose judicial life terminated in 1809.
Judge Farrar, one of the trustees, though more discreet
in their expression, shared and enforced the same general
views of Wingate. He was a judge of the same court
for about thirteen years, ending in 1803, and chief justice of the Common Pleas for more than three years, ending
in June, 1816.

With such judges, and juries who were not likely to agree
against a church of which, in general, a majority of them
were members, or in sympathy, the people were compelled
to pay "tithes" to the dominant sect, or to be ruined by
litigation.

Acts of incorporation in the interests of the "standing
order" were granted, but similar acts in the interests of
other denominations were denied.

When the College quarrel opened the breach, the other
denominations took courage and massed together to wring
the legislation which followed — the College Acts, the laws
equalizing taxation, and "the Religious Toleration Acts" —
from the "standing order," which they succeeded in doing
in less than seven years.

The College was located on the border. The district was
the birthplace of secession; prior to the Federal Constitution, the Confederacy had denied and defied the jurisdiction
of New Hampshire; the liberals in politics and religion had
long regarded the institution as exclusive, aristocratic, and

the stronghold of Federalism and the " standing order," and the leading Federalists and their organs had given Wheelock the cold shoulder. The politicians were not slow to see the drift, and took the rising tide.

Mason, the most sagacious of men, saw the gathering of the elements, and in the circles where he moved, as in his letter to his cousin Marsh, of August 15, 1815, warned them of the consequences ; but the warning passed unheeded, and the deluge came.

The Anti-Federalists put William Plumer, Jr., "the Epping wizard," as he was termed by some of his opponents, who had been governor in 1812, again in the field.

In 1849, Webster, in a public address, said of his old opponent : " Governor Plumer is a man of learning and of talent. He has performed important service in the Congress of the United States. He has been many years governor of the state of New Hampshire. He has lived a life of study and attainment, and, I suppose, is, among the men now living, one of the best informed in matters pertaining to the history of his country. He is now more than ninety years of age." (Life of Plumer, 518, 519.)

Plumer was a strong man and an eminent lawyer. When a mere child he was a Baptist preacher, whose powers of reasoning astonished even the veterans of his day. Afterwards he relapsed into the liberalism of Jefferson, and took to the law.

In the House, in 1791, Welman, an ex-preacher, moved that any person " convicted of speaking disrespectfully of any part of the Bible should have his tongue bored through with a hot iron." (Life of Plumer, 112, 113.) Plumer, by great exertions, succeeded in defeating its passage by a small majority. In the same year, he was a member of the convention which formed the Constitution of 1792. That Constitution, which, with a single amendment, remained unchanged until 1876, was popularly termed " Plumer's Constitution." " On the subject of religion he proposed, instead. of the former provisions, an article securing to every person in the State the inestimable privilege of worshipping God in a manner agreeable to the dictates of his own conscience ; and prohibiting the Legislature from compelling any person either to attend any place of public worship, or to pay taxes for the building of churches, or for the support of religious teachers, except in pursuance of his own free act and agreement. This amendment was wide enough to embrace the Roman Catholic, on the one hand, and the Deist on the other." (Life of Plumer, 116, 117.) This was defeated. He moved to abolish the religious test for office-holders, who were required by the Constitution to be " of the Protestant religion." This provision was at first rejected, but afterwards adopted by the convention though rejected by the people. " He refused, in the church-tax cases, to be of counsel for any town or parish which sought to compel men to pay taxes, contrary to their will, for religious purposes ; but offered his services readily to those who claimed exemption from such taxes." He had defied the judges. " During the session of the Superior Court at Dover (February, 1799), Judge Livermore privately informed me," says Governor Plumer, " that his brethren, Farrar and Wingate, had expressed to him a decided disapprobation of my constancy and zeal in supporting those who claimed exemption from taxes for the maintenance of clergymen. I replied I was sorry that any of the court were so much in favor of supporting a privileged order ; but that this circumstance, instead of checking, would increase my exertions, and so long as I remained at the bar, the court would find me a persevering and determined advocate for the rights of conscience and of property, both involved in these issues." (Life of Plumer, 185, 187.)

In his message to the Legislature of June 6, 1816, Governor Plumer said : " The rights of conscience and of private judgment in religious matters are not only secured by our Constitution to all men, but are, in their nature, inalienable.

Civil and religious liberty have usually flourished and expired together. To preserve their purity requires the constant, unremitted vigilance of the people and their legislators. If any religious associations request acts of incorporation, to enable them more fully and securely to enjoy their religious privileges, it appears to be our duty to grant them. The correctness of their tenets is a subject that lies between God and their own consciences, and is one that no human tribunal has any right to decide. While, therefore, it becomes every man scrupulously to examine the foundations of his own belief, he cannot guard with too much jealousy against the encroachments of the civil power on his religious liberties.''

Emanating from almost any other source, the easy flowing words of the message in relation to religious toleration would have had little significance ; but coming from Plumer, it was otherwise.

Everybody knew that he had been assailed without measure for these opinions ; that for more than a quarter of a century he had been the unyielding, persistent, and unpaid champion of religious toleration, and that his message was the signal gun for an assault all along the line. The Legislature promptly responded by passing acts of incorporation in the interest of all denominations.

In the Senate, on June 27, 1816, an attempt was made to engraft upon the College Act the anti-toleration views so offensive to Plumer, by an amendment providing '' that the president and other executive officers of said University shall be of the Protestant religion.'' This was defeated, four of the senators, led by Bingham, — Webster's college chum and intimate friend, — voting in the affirmative, and eight in the negative.

The act amending the charter provided that '' perfect freedom of religious opinions should be enjoyed by all the students and officers of the University.''

The rule which Governor Plumer observed in the appointment of trustees and overseers of Dartmouth University is thus stated by his son : "He introduced men of both political parties, and of all the prominent religious sects. The College government had been hitherto Calvinistic in its religion and Federalist in its politics. His appointments brought both political parties into each board, without giving any one religious sect the preponderance in either. Dr. Parish having written to him, expressing the hope that a man's being a Federalist would not prevent his being elected an officer of the institution, he said, in reply : ' It has been a subject of deep regret to me that the cause of Dartmouth University has been considered a party question. My political opponents made it such, in hopes of obtaining support of their party politics. But, had I the power of appointing the officers of the University, I would select those men only for office who are best qualified, without regard to the religious sect or political party to which they are attached.' " (Life of Plumer, 439.)

On December 25, 1816, the Legislature passed an act providing —

"That the real and personal estates of all ordained ministers of the gospel, of every denomination, within this State, shall hereafter be assessed and taxed in the same way and manner as other estates are now, or hereafter may, by law, be taxed; any law, usage or custom to the contrary notwithstanding. *Provided, nevertheless,* that nothing in this act shall be so construed as to affect any contract, in writing, heretofore made between any town in this State and the minister thereof."

After a most unprecedented struggle, this movement for religious toleration culminated, in 1819, in Dr. Whipple's Toleration Act. This was so called because Dr. Whipple, the member from Wentworth, — member of Congress from 1822 to 1830, — was the author of its most vital provisions, and supported it with great ability and eloquence. Its passage marked an era in the religious and political history of the State.

On June 22, 1819, Dr. Whipple proposed the following amendment to the pending bill : —

And be it further enacted, That every religious sect or denomination of Christians in this State may associate and form societies, may admit members, may establish rules and by-laws for their regulation and government, and shall have all the corporate powers which may be necessary to assess and raise money by taxes upon the polls and ratable estate of the members of such association, and to collect and appropriate the same for the purpose of building and repairing houses for public worship, and for the support of the preaching of the gospel; and the assessors and collectors of such associations shall have the same powers in assessing and collecting said moneys, and shall be liable to the same penalties, as similar town officers now have and are liable to. *Provided,* That no person shall be compelled to join or support, nor be classed with or associated to, any congregation, church, or religious society, without his express consent first had and obtained. *Provided, also,* If any person shall choose to separate himself from such society or association to which he may belong, and shall leave a written notice thereof with the clerk of such society or association, he shall thereupon be no longer liable for any future expense which may be incurred by said society or association.

This amendment was supported by Ichabod Bartlett, counsel for Judge Woodward and others, Dr. Whipple opening and closing the debate. It was carried: yeas, 96; nays, 88. The passage of the act was treated with a storm of denunciation. Its supporters were declared to be infidels, — enemies of God and religion. It was said, " When the wicked bear rule, the people mourn," and the people were advised to burn their Bibles. But time, which tests all things, demonstrated that this sect, like others, could live, thrive, and prosper without the aid of what were virtually " forced loans."

CHAPTER IV.

ORIGIN OF THE CONTROVERSY — THE TRUSTEES — THE WAR
OF THE PAMPHLETEERS — WHEELOCK RETAINS WEBSTER,
AND APPLIES TO THE LEGISLATURE — HEARING BEFORE
THE LEGISLATIVE COMMITTEE — WEBSTER FAILS TO
APPEAR — CORRESPONDENCE — REMOVAL OF WHEELOCK,
AGAINST THE ADVICE OF MASON — BROWN PUT IN WHEE-
LOCK'S PLACE.

THE College troubles probably had their primal source
in the antagonisms, personal and otherwise, between the
elder Wheelock and Dr. Bellamy, the theological tutor of
Judge Niles. John Wheelock and Niles inherited their
views respectively from father and tutor. The rill fresh-
ened into a stream, and, gathering affluents on every hand,
finally swept all before it.

Niles became a trustee in 1793. Those who thoroughly
understood the natures of the two men must soon have
seen that it was only a question of time when one or the
other would be driven from the board.

The quarrel which resulted in the College causes came to
the surface in the Board of Trustees some twelve years
before the removal of the second Wheelock.[1] Political differences there had nothing to do with it, nor matters of faith ;

[1] Trustees of Dartmouth College : —

Name.	Trustee from — to	Died.	Age.
Nathaniel Niles	1793–1821	1828	86
Thomas W. Thompson	1802–1817	1817	51
Timothy Farrar	1804–1826	1849	101
Elijah Paine	1806–1828	1842	85
John Taylor Gilman	1807–1819	1828	74
Charles Marsh	1809–1849	1849	83
Rev. Asa McFarland	1809–1822	1827	57
Rev. Seth Payson	1813–1820	1820	62
Rev. Francis Brown	1815–1819	1820	36
Rev. John Smith	1811–1820	1831	65

(81)

for the board were nearly all rank Federalists, and differed in form, only, as to church polity.

The Board of Trustees, etc., was, and for years had been, a strange medley in composition, but as a whole the members were endowed with remarkable intellectual gifts.

Judge Niles graduated at Princeton, in 1766. He was the classmate and devoted friend of the elder Adams. In theory, he was a follower of Calvin in theology and of Jefferson in politics. He was a man of angles and opposites; a tactician, and an adept at what he termed " caucusing ;" a manager of men; one who read every thing, remembered and questioned it. He was a member of the Legislature, speaker of the House, six times a presidential elector, a representative in Congress from 1791 to 1795, and one of the judges of the Supreme Court of Vermont. He was an inventor, manufacturer, poet, lawyer, priest, physician, and metaphysician, — a man of great and varied powers. Jefferson once said of him, " He was the ablest man I ever knew."

It will be long before the people of Vermont will forget Captain Trotter's jest at his expense.

Judge Paine was born in Brooklyn, Connecticut, January 21, 1757, and graduated at Harvard, in 1781.

He was the first president of the Phi Beta Kappa Society at Harvard, and pronounced the first oration before the same.

Settling in Vermont, he was one of its pioneers, and was farmer, road-maker, manufacturer, and lawyer. In 1786, he was a member and secretary of the Convention called to revise the State Constitution; and in 1787, was elected to the State Legislature, and was a member until 1791, when he was appointed judge of the Supreme Court of Vermont. He was one of the commissioners to settle the controversy between Vermont and New York in 1789, president of the Vermont Colonization Society, and held many other responsible positions. He was a senator in Congress from 1795 to 1801, when he was appointed by President Adams judge of the District Court of Vermont, which brought him into close connection with Judge Livingston, and which office he held until his resignation in 1842.

He was a man of iron, and in physical and mental stature a giant. It is said that his voice could be heard distinct and audible three-fourths of a mile. Fair-minded, sincere, and obstinate, by nature, he was in many respects the Drouet of the board.

Judge Marsh, as he was popularly called, — he had from the most creditable motives refused to accept the position of chief justice of the Supreme Court of Vermont, — was a man of immense ability, the cousin of Jeremiah Mason, and the father of that eminent scholar and diplomatist, George P. Marsh, long one of our foreign ministers. He was endowed with an understanding of singular penetration, was tenacious, a hater of what he termed demagogues, unsparing in speech, trenchant with the pen, ever on the alert, unyielding and unfearing to the last degree, and an intense Federalist.

None of these were New Hampshire men.

Thomas W. Thompson was born in Boston; fitted for college at Dummer Academy, in Byfield, in the town of Newbury, Massachusetts, entered Harvard College in 1782, received his degree in 1786, served in Shay's Rebellion, studied theology, became a tutor in Harvard, read law at Newburyport with Chief Justice Parsons, and was admitted to the bar early in 1791. In June, 1791, he removed to Salisbury South Road, New Hampshire, and entered upon the practice of the law. About a year later, he moved near to the Webster place, in what is now Franklin, formerly known as the "Elms Farm," and now as the Orphans' Home, — Richard Fletcher, afterwards one of the justices of the Supreme Court of Massachusetts, taking Thompson's place at the South Road in 1809.

Thompson was several times a member of the State Legislature from Salisbury and Concord; was speaker of the

House in 1814. In 1805-7, he was a representative, and afterwards a senator, in Congress; in 1809, he removed from Salisbury to Concord, where he resided at the time of his death. He was an eminent lawyer; was, with Judge Webster, an influential member of Parson Worcester's church; and the leading, managing politician of the Federal party in New Hampshire. He was rich and courtly, — a gentleman of the old school. He had been the patron and legal instructor of Daniel Webster, and was one of his most intimate friends.

Judge Farrar was another. He was a leading Federalist, and the father of the second Judge Farrar, — who read law with Webster, was his partner at Portsmouth from 1812 to 1816, and one of the counsel in the case against Judge Woodward.

Mills Olcott, the father-in-law of Rufus Choate, was an eminent lawyer at Hanover. He was born at Norwich, Vermont, and was a son of General Olcott, who was a member of the Council and lieutenant-governor of that State. He read law with Judge Jacob, of Windsor, Vermont, another of the trustees; was made secretary and treasurer of the College, in place of Judge Woodward, by the old board, in 1816; and in 1821 was chosen trustee, which office he held until his death, in 1845. He was the friend and special attorney of William Smith, the famous Tory chief in New York, afterwards chief justice in Canada; was a prominent Federalist, the intimate friend of Webster, and tainted with the odor of the Hartford Convention.

Thompson and Olcott married sisters. They were men of the same type, and their family and personal intimacy was very close and confidential.

The rest were notable men.

Nothing short of divine power could control such men. Dr. Wheelock, walking in the footsteps of his father, was generally supported by a majority of the board till 1809, when death and the influence of Judge Smith, who was then

governor of New Hampshire, gave a majority to his adversaries. After that, no friend of his was elected to the board.
For years there was a struggle on the part of Wheelock to
retain, and on the part of a minority, afterwards grown to a
majority, "to put down" what they termed the "domination" of Wheelock.

Open hostilities broke out in April, 1815, by the publication of a pamphlet of eighty-eight pages, in the interest of
Wheelock, entitled, "Sketches of the History of Dartmouth
College and Moor's Charity-School, with a Particular Account of Some Late Remarkable Proceedings of the Board
of Trustees, from the Year 1779 to the Year 1815." The
"Sketches" charged the trustees with the misappropriation
of the Phillips and other funds, and with withholding from
him several thousand dollars which Wheelock had allowed
to remain in their hands, subject to his right of future
appropriation, etc., etc. The trustees charged its author-
ship upon Dr. Wheelock, Col. Josiah Dunham, a noted
Federalist politician, and secretary of state of Vermont, who
wrote the letter of October 21, 1811, to Dr. McFarland,
and was familiar with the history of the College troubles,
and Rev. Dr. Elijah Parish. This was quickly followed,
on the same side, by a like pamphlet of thirty-two pages,
by Dr. Parish, entitled, "A Candid Analytical Review of
the 'Sketches of the History of Dartmouth College and
Moor's Charity-School, with a Particular Account of Some
Late Remarkable Proceedings of the Board of Trustees,
from the Year 1779 to the Year 1815.'"

These publications created a great sensation. The newspapers took up the war, and made the most of it. Judge
Niles, the soul of the anti-Wheelock party, published a
series of elaborate articles in reply. In one of them, in a
two-column article published August 15, 1815, he says, in
reference to the facts stated in the "Sketches:" "I readily
admit that they [the trustees] have done the facts that are
charged."

In 1815, Benoni Dewey, James Wheelock, and Benjamin J. Gilbert, a committee of the Congregational Church at Hanover, replied to the " Sketches " in a pamphlet of sixty-eight pages, entitled, " A True and Concise Narrative of the Origin and Progress of the Church Difficulties in the Vicinity of Dartmouth College, in Hanover," etc. In August, 1815, the trustees published, in a pamphlet of one hundred and four pages, " A Vindication of the Official Conduct of the Trustees of Dartmouth College," etc., written by Charles Marsh. In 1816, Peyton R. Freeman, a learned lawyer of the old school, soon afterwards appointed clerk of Story's courts in New Hampshire, published, in reply, a pamphlet of thirty-two pages, entitled, " A Refutation of Sundry Aspersions in the ' Vindication ' of the Present Trustees of Dartmouth College on the Memory of their Predecessors." In 1816, Col. Dunham also replied in a pamphlet of ninety-five pages, entitled, " An Answer to the ' Vindication of the Official Conduct of the Trustees of Dartmouth College,' in Confirmation of the ' Sketches,' with Remarks on the Removal of President Wheelock." These documents contained charges and counter-charges, criminations and recriminations, in abundance.

About the time of the publication of the " Sketches," legal proceedings were threatened and seriously contemplated by Wheelock. He at once took steps to procure counsel. There were obvious reasons why he should not employ governor Plumer, Judge Smith, or Jeremiah Mason. The feeble health of Plumer had driven him out of practice ; Smith's vote, as *ex officio* trustee, in 1809, had delivered Wheelock over to his enemies ; and Mason was the relative and intimate friend of Marsh, one of the hostile majority.

Through a friend he applied to Webster, whose personal sympathies were then, as they always were, with Wheelock, for his " professional " assistance, which was promised. In June following, Wheelock personally consulted Webster with reference to his troubles with the trustees, retained him, and had paid him therefor. This, of course, was not a formal retainer in the particular litigation which followed. At the June session, 1815, the time of his consultation with Webster, Dr. Wheelock followed up his charges with the oft-threatened memorial to the Legislature, in which he set forth that the trustees had "forsaken its original principles, and left the path of their predecessors;" that they had, by improper "means and practices," "increased their number to a majority controlling the measures of the board;" "that they have applied property to purposes wholly alien from the intention of the donors;" that they have "transformed the moral and religious order of the institution by depriving many of their innocent enjoyment of rights and privileges for which they had confided in their faith; that they have broken down the barriers and violated the charter by prostrating the rights with which it expressly invests the presidential office."

He then charges misapplication of funds, and various breaches of trust; and concludes with the prayer, "that you would please, by a committee invested with competent powers, or otherwise, to look into the affairs and management of the institution, internal and external, already referred to; and, if judged expedient, in your wisdom, that you would make such organic improvements and model reforms in its systems and movements, as, under Divine Providence, will guard against the disorders and their apprehended consequences."

In a remonstrance presented to the Legislature, June 19, 1816, by Thompson, Paine, and McFarland, in behalf of the trustees, they say: —

"By a reference to the memorial, it will be seen that the trustees are charged directly or indirectly with having exercised religious intolerance; with having systematically promoted one sect or party, with political objects dangerous to government. Dr. Wheelock alleged in the said memorial that the trustees have misapplied the funds of the college; that they have invaded the rights of the

presidential office; that they used improper means in the appointment of executive officers; that they have formed an unjustifiable
connection with an academy; and improperly furnished students
thereof with aid from the college treasury; that they have ob-
structed the application of the funds of Moor's Charity-School,
according to their original destination; that they have oppressed
him in the discharge of his office as president. These are heavy
charges; and if they were founded in truth, the trustees deserve
the severest reprobation.''

In spite of the strenuous opposition of the trustees, the
House, by a vote of one hundred and twenty-three to fifty,
granted the prayer of Wheelock, and a resolution to this
effect passed the Legislature, June 28, 1815. Governor Gilman appointed Daniel A. White, Nathaniel A. Haven, both
intimate friends of Webster, and Ephraim P. Bradford, a
committee '' to investigate the concerns of Dartmouth College and Moor's Charity-School,'' etc. The hearing was
had before this committee, commencing August 16, 1815.
Before Wheelock knew that the committee had accepted, a
portion of the trustees called upon the chairman, and had
the time of hearing fixed. He first learned of it acciden-
tally. As soon as he heard officially of this hearing, he, in
consequence of his consultation with Webster, and retainer,
applied to him for assistance before this committee, in a
letter dated at Dartmouth College, August 5, 1815, in which
he says: —

I take the earliest moment to inform, that the Hon. Mr. White
has communicated by his letter, dated the 2d inst., the assignment
made by the committee of the State, to meet, here, on Wednesday, the week preceding commencement, which will be a week from
next Wednesday, on the business for which they were appointed.

It is needless to say how highly we appreciate your distinguished talents and virtues, in whatever concerns the interests of
literature, & the happiness of society. You will permit me to
express my ardent desire, that you would make it consistent to be
here in season to conduct the interesting public cause of truth and
justice, in which a sense of duty has led me to be concerned.

It would be gratifying and useful could you find it convenient to be here by next Saturday, or as long before the meeting as may be. I much regret that the period is so short, and that there was no ground for my giving you information before this instant, as I have made dependence on you as counsellor agreeably to our consultation at Concord.

The position and relations of the great object are much as when I had the pleasure of seeing you.

I entreat your goodness not to fail. You will please to consider me responsible to remunerate you honorably to your satisfaction.

With sentiments of very cordial and great respect, I am

Dear sir,

Your obliged friend,

& obedient servant,

JOHN WHEELOCK.

P. S. — I hope the enclosed will reach your hand, $20.

For a copy of this letter we are indebted to the courtesy of the officers of Kenyon College, Gambier, Ohio.

Webster failed to appear, and Wheelock, with but a day and a half in which to procure counsel and prepare for it, went on with the hearing with such assistance as he could obtain.

Webster's reasons for this course appear in Thompson's famous letter to Professor Adams, of July 13, 1815, and Webster's letter to Dunham, of August 25, 1815. Thompson says : —

I have had a long conversation with Mr. D. W——, by which it appears, that a strong desire prevails, that the *Reply*, with the *Committee's Report*, should effectually put down a CERTAIN MAN. Mr. W., Dr. McFarland and I, are very desirous that affidavits should be immediately taken, relative to such facts as will show that person's character in a just point of view. I can't name all the points to which the testimony should be directed ; but you and our friends must hold a conversation and select such points as will be productive of the greatest effect. Full and satisfactory testimony should be taken relative to the *usury*, and particularly Mr. KELLOGG's *deposition*.

It will be very useful to obtain testimony (or documents, if practicable) to show that the college had to pay Col. Kinsman $——, in consequence of the executive neglecting to enforce the laws and orders of the trustees. Testimony should be had of every trick, contrivance and management of his, to show his true character.

On the part of our friends at Hanover, great, unceasing, and systematic efforts should be made to collect evidence. It is impossible for the trustees to collect it but through our friends. *The expense must be CLUBB'D amongst us.*

I intend, *if possible*, to collect testimony here, to show that with the democrats he was a democrat — with every sect of religionists he was one of them — with federalists he was a federalist, and thus he descended to base means to make influence.

I have *a scrap of the envelope* of the communication to the Repertory, which will show the handwriting. I wish not to communicate my suspicions, until I exhibit at the commencement. I can say thus much, I think the writer is a president's man. Perhaps this ought not to be mentioned just yet.

I shall depend much upon the exertions of our friends to procure evidence, and shall be much disappointed, if it is not immediately and effectually attended to.

Your friend,
[Signed]   THO. W. THOMPSON.

No notice to the president will be necessary.

The *animus* of this letter is too obvious for comment. It is to be borne in mind that Mr. Thompson had been an eminent lawyer; that he was professedly a devoted Christian; that this letter was written by him to one of the most bitter and active of Wheelock's enemies, knowing him to be such; that he proposed to share the expense of hunting up testimony against a person upon whom he was to sit in judgment, and whom he had predetermined to "put down;" and that he was apparently the inventor of the rule that no notice should be given to Wheelock. Everybody knew that D. W. meant Daniel Webster, and that Wheelock was the man to be "put down." That this letter correctly represented Mr. Webster and his purposes, and that they were precisely the reverse of those entertained by Mason, is not open to doubt.

This letter was a bombshell in the Wheelock camp. On account of this, Dunham wrote his fiery letter to his personal and political friend Webster, giving the Wheelock view of his conduct, to which Webster replied as follows: " On the subject of the dispute between the president and the trustees, I am as little informed as any reading individual in society ; and I have not the least inclination to espouse either side, except in proceedings in which my services may be professional. It was intimated to me last spring, that the president might possibly institute process against the trustees for the recovery of money due him from them ; that proceedings might also be commenced in the courts of law, to determine whether there had been a perversion of the Phillips fund ; and that in case these events should happen, the president would be glad to engage my assistance as counsel. At Concord, the president suggested in general terms, that he might wish to obtain my professional assistance on some future occasion, which I readily promised him. After Dr. Haven had left this place for Hanover, I received the president's letter, desiring me to be at Hanover at a time which had then already elapsed. I answered it by mail, not quite so soon as I should have done if I had not expected some private conveyance, and if I had not known that an answer by any conveyance would have been wholly immaterial at that time. If I had received it earlier, I could not have attended, because the court engaged me at home ; and I ought to add here, that if I had had no other engagements at the time, and had also been seasonably notified, I should have exercised my own discretion about undertaking to act a part before the committee at Hanover. I regard that as no professional call.   *   *   *

" As to what you are pleased to say about my extricating myself from this affair, or of its being otherwise unpleasant

to me, as also what you observe of a suspicion entertained
by some that Mr. Thompson had employed me to feel of
Mr. Haven on the subject, give me leave to say that I should
know better how to answer these remarks if I were not
writing to one for whom I have the highest and warmest
esteem, and of whose sense of delicacy and propriety very
few certainly at any time have had occasion to complain.
    " I am not quite so fully convinced as you are, that the
president is altogether right, and the trustees altogether
wrong.   *   *   *   You may be well assured that in our
nomination of governor we have regarded nothing but the
political interests of the State.   I can but flatter myself
that if you were better acquainted with the circumstances
you would think less unfavorably of the conduct of your
Federal friends."   (1 Webster's Priv. Cor. 251.)
    Governor John Taylor Gilman had exceptional popularity,
and was a fast friend of Wheelock.   The political allusion
in Webster's letter refers to the well-known conviction of
Wheelock and his friends that Thompson and other leading
Federalists had determined to force Gilman into retirement,
and to put the elder Farrar, hostile to Wheelock, in his place.
    A few men, led by Webster, Thompson, and others, con-
trolled the organization of their party, and moulded its
policy to suit themselves.   In important matters they personally wrote the leaders, and directed what the editors
should say.   A mass of correspondence shows that the most
persistent efforts were made to compel Farrar to accept the
nomination, contrary to every inclination, and thus put down
Gilman, who did not desire the position, but whose friends
did not wish him driven from it.
    Putting a modest estimate upon his powers, and feeling
the infirmities of age creeping on, Farrar firmly declined.
    Webster was under great obligations to Farrar, for in one
sense he was the founder of Mr. Webster's political fortunes ;
and he could do nothing but acquiesce in the declination.
How he felt about it, in some respects, is shown in his letter

from Washington to Moody Kent, dated February 5, 1815, in which he says: " I exceedingly regret the state of things in N. Hampshire, respecting governor. It is just what I expected from the resolution taken to support Gov. Gilman again, & compel him to stay in the chair against his will. We must sometime bring forward a new candidate. When can it be probably done better than it could this year? As it is I hope Gov. G. will be chosen, & that all possible exertions will be used to reconcile those who feel dissatisfied, & to give him the undivided support of the Federalists. But it is a very bad business.

" You will see by the papers that the British army has been repulsed with great loss in an attack on Jackson's lines. Unless something signal is done by the fleet, New Orleans will be safe. At present the prospect is very favorable.

" The celebrated John Randolph of Roanoke is a lodger in this house (Crawford's). All the descriptions I had recd. of his personal appearance gave me no correct impression. I should probably fail in attempting to describe him to you. He is tall; say, a little more than six feet, legs rather long, in proportion to his body. He is slender — somewhat broad over the shoulders ; but thin, his face rather flat & broader than you have probably imagined, complexion sallow, and skin wrinkled. His eyes not large, very black & sparkling & placed a pretty good distance apart. Nose short & regular. His hair is suffered to grow long all over his head & is gathered & tied up with a ribbon behind. His countenance is older than I expected to see it. The sallow & wrinkled appearance, something such as we never or seldom see in N. E. is not unfrequent among the sedentary men of Virginia & I suppose other warm climates. So much for the person of Mr. Randolph. He is now on his return home from the northward. He is to take the field agt. Eppes in the spring, & his friends generally think he will succeed in the election. They say he would certainly if he would take unusual pains, but he seems disinclined to make much exertion for himself.

"The day after to-morrow or thereabouts I expect to leave here for home in order to be there the first day of the court when I hope to see you."

A portion of this letter is not pertinent to the matter in hand, but is so characteristic that we insert it.

That Thompson wrote the truth to Adams admits of no doubt. That Webster did not meet the issue raised by that letter squarely, is too plain for cavil. The key to this course lies in the fact that Webster's most devoted friends and political adherents were hostile to Wheelock. Their personal influence, and political complications and considerations, detached him from Wheelock, in the teeth of his sympathies and against his convictions. Webster was severely criticised for retaining the money and acting covertly, and afterwards openly, for the other side. For obvious reasons, he did not afterwards appear openly for the College in the suit brought against it by Dr. Allen and Mrs. Wheelock, for the money due his estate, and for his personal services.

This explosion ended the "professional" relations between Dr. Wheelock and Mr. Webster, and, in the belief of the writer, added by construction another provision to the Constitution of the United States, and changed the public law of the Union.

The committee of investigation made their report, a digest of facts some forty pages in length, on April 23, 1816, to Governor Gilman. On June 7, 1816, it was laid before the Legislature by Governor Plumer.

On August 15, 1815, after the letter from Thompson to Adams, Mason wrote to his cousin Marsh in relation to the proposed removal of Wheelock: "In common with many others I have felt considerable anxiety for the issue of the matter so much in public discussion relative to Dartmouth College. I do not feel either inclined or

competent to give any opinion as to the course which ought
finally to be adopted by the Board of Trustees for the
benefit of that institution. I am entirely willing to leave
that to the determination of those much better informed
on the subject and better able to judge. From certain
intimations which I have lately had, I am led to believe
an intention is entertained by some members of the board
of ending all difficulty with the President by removing him
from office. I greatly fear such a measure adopted under
present circumstances, and at the present time, would have
a very unhappy effect on the public mind. An inquiry is
now pending, instituted after considerable discussion, by
the Legislature of this State, apparently for the purpose of
granting relief for the subject-matter of complaint. The
trustees acquiesce in this inquiry; whether they appear
before the committee appointed to make it formally as a
body, or informally as individuals, the public will not
deem of much importance. The Legislature, I think, for
certain purposes, have a right to inquire into an alleged
mismanagement of such an institution, a visitorial power
rests in the State, and I do not deem it important for my
present view to determine in what department or how to be
exercised. The Legislature may on proper occasion, call it
into operation. I have never seen the President's memorial
to the Legislature, but am told it is an abstract from the
' pamphlet of sketches.' From the statements in that I
take the burthen of his complaint to be, that the trustees
have not given him a due and proper share of power and
influence in the concerns of the College, and that they have
improperly used their own power, and influence in patron-
izing and propagating in the College particular theological
opinions. The alleged misapplication of funds is stated as
an instance of such misconduct. These opinions, it would
seem, are particularly disagreeable to the President. The
whole dispute is made to have a bearing on the President
personally.

"Should the trustees, during the pendency of the inquiry in a cause in which they are supposed to be a party, take the judgment into their own hands, and summarily end the dispute by destroying the other party, they will offend and irritate at least all those who were in favor of making the inquiry. Such will not be satisfied with the answer that the trustees have the power and feel it to be their duty to exercise it. It will be said that the reasons which justify a removal (if there be any) have existed for a long time. A removal after so long forbearance, at the present time, will be attributed to recent irritations.

"That part of the President's complaint which relates to his religious grievances addresses itself pretty strongly to the prejudices and feelings of all those opposed to the sect called orthodox. This comprises all the professed friends of liberal religion, most of the Baptists and Methodists, and all the nothingarians. The Democrats will be against you, of course. All these combined would compose in this State a numerous and powerful body. Any measure adopted by the trustees with the appearance of anger, or haste, will be eagerly seized on. If the statements of the President are as incorrect as I have heard it confidently asserted, an exposure of that incorrectness will put the public opinion right. It may require time but the result must be certain. If it can be shown that his complaints are nothing but defamatory clamor, he will be reduced to that low condition that it will be the interest of no sect or party to attempt to hold him up. I see no danger in delay but fear much in too great haste. Perhaps there is no occasion at present to determine how long the trustees should delay adopting their final course. Circumstances may render that expedient at a future time which is not now. I feel much confidence that a very decisive course against the President by the trustees at the present time would create an unpleasant sensation in the public mind, and would, I fear, be attended with unpleasant consequences.

" I am sensible I have expressed my opinion very strongly on a subject in which I have only a common interest. I frankly confess I have been somewhat influenced by fears that some of the trustees will find it difficult to free themselves entirely from the effects of the severe irritation they must have lately experienced."

The trustees, disregarding the advice of Mason, and without waiting for the report of the investigating committee, on August 26, 1815, — the day after Webster's letter to Dunham, — upon the motion of Judge Paine, proceeded to carry out the programme laid down by Thompson in his letter to Adams.

The following is a record of their actions, as written down by themselves : —

A Report of a Committee· of the Board of Trustees having been accepted, stating the evidence they had received that President Wheelock had an agency in writing and publishing the pamphlet entitled " Sketches of the History of Dartmouth College," &c., and the President having presented to the Board a written representation in the nature of a plea to the jurisdiction of the court, the following Resolutions were introduced by Judge Paine, President Wheelock was served with a copy, and inquired of, at different times, if he had any communication to make to the Board on the subject, or wished time for consideration. — His answers were evasive. The truth of the allegations in the preamble to the Resolutions, *not being questioned by President Wheelock or any member of the Board*, the Resolutions were then adopted.

DARTMOUTH COLLEGE, August 26, 1815.

Cases sometimes occur, when it becomes expedient that corporate bodies, whatever confidence they may feel respecting the rectitude and propriety of their own measures, should explain the grounds of them to the public. Such an explanation becomes peculiarly important when the concerns committed to their care are dependent on public opinion for their prosperity and success. Into such a situation the Trustees of Dartmouth College consider themselves now brought. Under a sense of this duty, they have already cheerfully submitted their past acts to the inspection of a

Committee of the Legislature of the State; and from a similar view of that duty, they now proceed to state the reasons that lead them to withdraw their further assent to the nomination and appointment of Doct. John Wheelock to the Presidency of Dartmouth College.

First. He has had an agency in publishing and circulating a certain anonymous pamphlet, entitled, "Sketches of the History of Dartmouth College and Moor's Charity-School," and espoused the charges therein contained before a Committee of the Legislature. Whatever might be our views of the principles which had gained an ascendancy in the mind of President Wheelock, we could not, without the most undeniable evidence, have believed that he could have communicated sentiments so entirely repugnant to truth, or that any person who was not as destitute of discernment as of integrity, would have charged on a public body as a crime those things which notoriously received his unqualified concurrence, and some of which were done by his special recommendation. The trustees consider the above mentioned publication as a gross and unprovoked libel on the Institution; and the said Dr. Wheelock neglects to take any measures to repair an injury which is directly aimed at its reputation, and calculated to destroy its usefulness.

Secondly. He has set up and insists on claims which the charter by no fair construction does allow — claims which in their operation would deprive the corporation of all its powers. He claims the right to exercise the whole executive authority of the College, which the Charter has expressly committed to the Trustees, with the President, Tutors and Professors by them appointed. He also seems to claim a right to control the Corporation in the appointment of Executive officers, inasmuch as he has reproached them with great severity, for choosing men who do not in all respects meet his wishes, and thereby embarrasses the proceedings of the Board.

Thirdly. From a variety of circumstances the Trustees have had reason to conclude that he has embarrassed the proceedings of the executive officers by causing an impression to be made on the minds of such students as have fallen under censure for transgressions of the laws of the Institution, that if he could have had his will they would not have suffered disgrace or punishment.

Fourthly. The Trustees have obtained satisfactory evidence, that Dr. Wheelock has been guilty of manifest fraud in the application of the funds of Moor's School, by taking a youth who is not an Indian, but adopted by an Indian tribe under an Indian name, and supporting him on the Scotch fund, which is granted for the sole purpose of instructing and civilizing Indians.

Fifthly. It is manifest to the trustees that Dr. Wheelock has, in various ways, given rise and circulation to a report, that the real cause of the dissatisfaction of the Trustees with him was a diversity of religious opinions between him and them, when in truth and in fact no such diversity was known, or is now known to exist, as he has publicly acknowledged before the Committee of the Legislature appointed to investigate the affairs of the College.

The Trustees adopt this solemn measure from a full conviction that the cause of truth, the interest of this institution, and of science in general, require it. It is from a deep conviction that the College can no longer prosper under his presidency. They would gladly have avoided this painful crisis. From a respect to the honored Father of Dr. Wheelock, the Founder of this Institution, they had hoped that they might have continued him in the Presidency as long as he was competent to discharge its duties.

They feel that this measure cannot be construed into any disrespect to the Legislature of New Hampshire, whose sole object in the appointment of a committee to investigate the affairs of the College must have been to ascertain if the Trustees had forfeited their charter, and not whether they had exercised their charter powers discreetly, or indiscreetly — not whether they had treated either of the executive officers of College with propriety or impropriety. — They will ever submit to the authority of law. The Legislature have appointed a committee to examine the concerns of the College and the school generally. The Trustees met that committee with promptitude, and frankly exhibited every measure of theirs which had been a subject of complaint, and all the concerns of the institution as far as their knowledge and means would permit. They wish to have their acts made as public as possible. The committee of the legislature will report the facts, and the Trustees will cheerfully meet the issue before any tribunal competent to try them according to the principles of their charter.

They consider this crisis as a severe trial to the institution;

but they believe that in order to entertain a hope that it will flourish and be useful they must be faithful to the trust — that they must not approve of an officer who labors to destroy its reputation, and embarrass its internal concerns. They will yet hope that under the smiles of Divine Providence, this institution will continue to flourish, and be a great blessing to generations to come.

Therefore,

Resolved, That the appointment of Dr. John Wheelock to the Presidency of this College, by the last will of the Rev. Eleazar Wheelock, the Founder and first President of this College, be, and the same is hereby, by the Trustees of said College, disapproved. And it is further —

Resolved, That the said Dr. John Wheelock, for the reasons aforesaid, be, and he is hereby, displaced and removed from the office of President of said College.

Resolved, That for the reasons before stated, the said Trustees deem the said Dr. John Wheelock unfit to serve the interests of the College as a Trustee of the same, and that, therefore, he be displaced and removed from the said office of Trustee of said College; and that the Trustees will, as soon as may be, elect and appoint such Trustee as shall supply the place of the said Dr. John Wheelock as a trustee.

Resolved, That for the reasons aforesaid, the said Dr. John Wheelock be, and he is hereby, removed from the office of Professor of History in this College.

Two of the trustees, John T. Gilman, the governor of New Hampshire, and Judge Jacob, of Vermont, protested against the action of the trustees: first, because under the circumstances they had no jurisdiction; and, second, because no evidence was adduced to support any of the charges. They conclude their protest in the following pointed language: " Whatever evidence might exist in the minds of the framers of the resolutions, in proof of the allegations contained in the preamble, no evidence was laid before the board respecting the same; nor any papers whatever relating thereto; not even respecting the severe charge of ' manifest fraud ' in the application of the funds of Moor's School."

Wheelock was removed on Saturday ; and on the Monday following, Rev. Francis Brown was put in his place.

Mr. Brown was born January 11, 1784, in Chester, New Hampshire, where Judges Bell and Richardson so long resided, and made his home there till about 1810. He graduated at Dartmouth College in 1805, spent the following year in the family of Judge Paine, one of the trustees of the College, as a private tutor, and for the next three years was a tutor in Dartmouth, pursuing at the same time his theological studies.

On his twenty-sixth birthday he was ordained, and became pastor of the Congregational Church, at North Yarmouth, Maine. He was soon after chosen professor of languages at Dartmouth, a position he was compelled to decline. For five years he labored with great zeal and success at North Yarmouth. He was inaugurated president of Dartmouth, September 27, 1815, and died July 27, 1820.

He was a close student and an excellent scholar ; a man of strong intellect and firm convictions, — circumspect, courteous, patient, pertinacious ; a keen observer of men, and an astute diplomat : but the schemes with which his name is intimately connected, for attempting to overawe the State court, and manipulating the press and certain judges of the Supreme Court of the United States, probably originated in other minds than his. Made the head of the College at the early age of thirty-one, and in the midst of a tempest, he exhibited rare tact and administrative genius.

From nature, alleged personal grievances, associations, religious training, and his views as to church polity, he was an anti-Wheelock man.

CHAPTER V.

THE QUARREL BECOMES A POLITICAL ISSUE — GOVERNOR
PLUMER: HIS NOMINATION, ELECTION, AND MESSAGE —
STRUGGLE IN THE LEGISLATURE — THE BILL PASSES —
CORRESPONDENCE — MOVEMENTS TO CONTROL THE PRESS —
OLD TRUSTEES HESITATE — THEY REFUSE TO ACCEPT THE
ACT — TRUSTEES AND OVERSEERS OF THE UNIVERSITY
APPOINTED — THEIR MEETINGS FAIL FOR WANT OF A
QUORUM — PROCEEDINGS OF OLD TRUSTEES AND THE UNI-
VERSITY BOARDS — OPINION OF THE SUPERIOR COURT OF
JUDICATURE — MESSAGE OF NOVEMBER 20, 1816 — LEGISLA-
TION OF DECEMBER, 1816 — VACANCIES FILLED — ADDRESS
TO PUBLIC BY OLD TRUSTEES — WHEELOCK'S DEATH —
GIVES FORTY THOUSAND DOLLARS TO THE UNIVERSITY.

So FAR, this had been a controversy among Calvinists and
Federalists. It had originated among those professing the
same religious faith — between the Federalist trustees of a
Federalist college. A Federalist governor had appointed
an investigating committee, under the vote of a Federalist
Legislature, upon a memorial of the Federalist Wheelock.
But other forces were soon to make themselves felt. The
Anti-Federalists had again nominated Plumer for governor.
He had long been in political life, a senator in Congress,
and for many years had been one of the pillars in the great
Federal triumvirate — Smith, Mason, and Plumer — which
controlled the State. But the troubles with Great Britain
which preceded the war of 1812 carried him over to the side
of Jefferson. He lacked the affluent learning of Smith, and
the original power of Mason ; he had little of their aptitude
with the pen ; he was no orator ; but his industry, thorough-
ness of preparation, great knowledge of men, and vigor of
(102)

understanding enabled him to compete successfully with them and Webster. His private life was stainless. He possessed great moral courage and independence, and yet he was the Nestor of the politicians of his day. His sympathies were naturally, as they were openly, with Wheelock. A heated political contest came on. Under the ban in their own party, Wheelock's friends, by the hundred, voted steadily for Plumer. The strong man carried the party on his back, and was elected by a handsome majority.

Brown, Thompson, and Webster at last saw what was coming, and made ready, as best they could, to avert the storm.

Webster, in his letter of June 4, 1816, to Brown, says: "I received yours last evening. You do not feel a stronger wish than I do that nothing may take place at this session detrimental to the College, and I am willing to do anything in my power to soften the irritated feelings of Democracy towards it. I am under engagements to go to Boston to-morrow, and shall be in that town four or five days. From Boston I can go direct to Concord, if it should be thought useful. Mr. Mason will go up, I believe, the first of next week. I have some hope that the Legislature will do nothing, partly because I hope they will be satisfied in some measure with the report, and partly from the hopeless state of Dr. W.'s health. It is a favorite idea with some to create a new college. Would it not be well if this idea could be encouraged and to let the ill-humors work off in that direction? Suppose a proposition should be made for a committee to report at next session, upon the expediency of making a new college at Concord, and what donations, &c., could be obtained for such an object.

"'Resolved, That a joint committee of both Houses be appointed to take into consideration the expediency of establishing a seminary of learning, in some part of this State, to be called the University of New Hampshire, and to ascertain what endowment for such institution could be obtained from private donation, and also what grants of land or money could be properly and conveniently made to the same by the State; and also to prepare a draft of a charter for such seminary, and to report at the next session of the Legislature.'

"Perhaps if something of this sort should be brought forward by somebody who has been favorably inclined to Dr. W., but who would wish to prevent violent measures, it might do good.

"Mr. Tilton, of Exeter, I should think, might do it to advantage. Think of this; Mr. Cutts, the bearer of this, is an intelligent friend of mine, and capable of being useful at Concord. I recommend it to you to cultivate his acquaintance, while there. He is intimate with Mr. Tilton, and indeed with most other leading men in the Legislature. Anything that shall postpone the subject, will give time for the present feelings to cool and evaporate.

"N. B. The resolution might say the charter should be drawn on the following principles : —

"1. A Board of Trustees to be inserted in the bill by the Legislature, to fill up their own vacancies.

"2. A Board of Overseers, viz: Governor, Senators, Councillors, and Speaker of the House of Representatives, for the time being.

"3. An unlimited right of conscience, in officers, and students; no test, creed, or confession to be required of either, or any preference, direct or indirect, of one religion over another.

"If any thing of this sort be done it ought to be done early." (1 Webster's Priv. Cor. 259, 260.)

Mr. Webster seems to have thought that a board of overseers numbering nineteen, and religious toleration, were adapted to every institution but Dartmouth College. This adroit move had some influence for a time, but it failed "to divide and conquer."

Governor Plumer knew that corporate power too often was but another name for the uncontrolled dominion of one. or at best a few minds. With Dartmouth's Board of

Trustees he feared its tendency to "jobs" and corruption, as well as its tendency to absorb power and infringe upon individual rights, and sought to guard against it. In his message to the Legislature, of June 6, 1812, he says: "Acts of incorporation of various kinds have, within a few years, greatly increased in this State; and many of them being in the nature of grants, cannot, with propriety, be revoked without the previous consent of the grantees. Such laws ought therefore to be passed with great caution; many of them should be limited to a certain period, and contain a reservation authorizing the Legislature to repeal them, whenever they cease to answer the end for which they were made, or prove injurious to the public interest."

In his message of June 6, 1816, to which we have already referred, Governor Plumer says: —

" There is no system of government where the general diffusion of knowledge is so necessary as in a republic. It is therefore not less the duty than the interest of the State to patronize and support the cause of literature and the sciences. So sensible were our ancestors of this, that they early made provision for schools, academies and a college, the good effects of which we daily experience. But all literary establishments, like everything human, if not duly attended to, are subject to decay; permit me, therefore, to invite your consideration to the state and condition of Dartmouth College, the head of our learned institutions. As the State has contributed liberally to the establishment of its funds, and as our constituents have a deep interest in its prosperity, it has a strong claim to our attention. The charter of that college was granted December 13th, 1769, by John Wentworth, who was then Governor of New Hampshire, under the authority of the British king. As it emanated from royalty, it contained, as was natural it should, principles congenial to monarchy; among others, it established trustees, made seven a quorum, and authorized a majority of those present to remove any of its members which they might consider unfit or incapable, and the survivors *to perpetuate the board by themselves electing others to supply vacancies.* This last principle is hostile to the spirit and genius of a free government. Sound policy therefore requires that the mode of election should be changed, and that trustees, in future, should be elected by some other body of men. To increase the number of trustees would not only increase the security of the college, but be a means of interesting more men in its prosperity. If it should be made in future the duty of the President, annually in May, to report to the Governor a full and particular account of the state of the funds, their receipts and expenditures, the number of students and their progress, and generally the state and condition of the college; and the Governor to communicate this statement to the Legislature in their June session; this would form a check upon the proceedings of the trustees, excite a spirit of attention in the officers and students of the college, and give to the Legislature such information as would enable them to act with greater propriety upon whatever may relate to that institution.

"The college was formed for the public good, not for the benefit or emolument of its trustees; and the right to amend and improve acts of incorporation of this nature has been exercised by all governments, both monarchical and republican. Sir Thomas Gresham established a fund to support lectures in Gresham College in London, upon the express condition that the lecturers should be unmarried men, and, upon their being married, their interest in the fund should absolutely cease; but the British Parliament, in the year 1768, passed a law removing the college to another place, and explicitly enacted that if the lecturers were married, or should marry, they should receive their fees and stipend out of the fund, any restriction or limitation in the will of the said Gresham to the contrary notwithstanding. In this country a number of the States have passed laws that made material changes in the charters of their colleges. And in this State acts of incorporation of a similiar nature have frequently been amended and changed by the Legislature. By the several acts incorporating towns, their limits were established; but whenever the Legislature judged that the public good required a town to be made into two, they have made the division, and in some instances against the remonstrance of a majority of its inhabitants. In the charter of Dartmouth Colleges it is expressly provided that the president, trustees, professors, tutors, and other officers, shall take the oath of allegiance to the British king; but if the laws of the United States, as well as those of New Hampshire, abolished by implication that part of the charter, much more might they have done it directly and by express words. These facts show the authority of the Legislature to interfere upon this subject; and I trust you will make such further provisions as will render this important institution more useful to mankind.''

Governor Plumer communicated this message to Jefferson, who replied, in his letter of July 21, 1816: " It is replete with sound principles, and truly republican. Some articles, too, are worthy of notice. The idea that institutions established for the use of the nation cannot be touched nor modified, even to make them answer their end, because of rights gratuitously supposed in those employed to manage them in trust for the public, may perhaps be a salutary provision against the abuses of a monarch, but it is most absurd against the nation itself. Yet our lawyers and priests generally inculcate this doctrine, and suppose that preceding generations held the earth more freely than we do ; had a right to impose laws on us, unalterable by ourselves ; and that we, in like manner, can make laws and impose burdens on future generations, which they will have no right to alter ; in fine, that the earth belongs to the dead, and not to the living.'' (Life of Plumer, 440, 441.)

The committee to whom the message, etc., relating to this subject were referred did not undertake to decide in favor of either party to the controversy, but alleged that the troubles arose from certain defects in the charter, and that they would recur again, in some form, unless those defects were remedied. The case of Professor Hale, who was ousted some thirty years after on account of his Episcopal tendencies, under a charter granted by an Episcopalian governor, would seem to show that this committee had a prophetic eye. The debates upon the historical and constitutional questions involved were able. The minority were ably led, both inside and outside the Legislature, but parliamentary tactics availed them nothing.

In the remonstrance of Thompson, Paine, and McFarland, of June 19, 1816, before referred to, they say : —

"The charter of Dartmouth College vests certain rights of property for particular uses, in the trustees. The sovereign power, having once made this grant, cannot, as the trustees humbly conceive, divest them of it so long as they exercise their trust in conformity to the true intent and meaning of the charter. They respectfully call to the view of the Honorable Legislature that Dartmouth College was not founded by the then existing sovereign. It was founded and endowed by liberal individuals; and the charter was given by the sovereign to perpetuate the application of the property conformably to the design of the donors. If the property has been misapplied, if there has been any abuse of power upon the part of the trustees, they are fully sensible of their high responsibility; but they have always believed, and still believe, that a sound construction of the powers granted to the Legislature gives them, in this case, only the right to order, for good cause, a prosecution in the judicial courts. A different course effectually blends judicial and legislative powers, and constitutes the Legislature a judicial tribunal."

This remonstrance presented the Parsons view.

Apparently, the idea that no Legislature could impair or affect the charter originated with the schoolmen, the professors and doctors of divinity, and not with the legal giants in the board, or those who afterward acted as counsel. The eight trustees, in their reply to Wheelock, virtually charge him with being its author. They say: "During his troubles in the Legislature of Vermont [commencing as early as 1806] relating to the grant of the township of Wheelock, the president has been often heard to say (and if the application were from the other side, and designed to correct any of his abuses, would now say), that the charter of the College was a *royal* grant, and not under the control of the Legislature. His motive in this proceeding can be nothing either more or less than to prejudice the minds of the members of the Legislature and of the people, by inducing a belief that the trustees aim at an independence not given them by the charter."

It is quite apparent that the trustees intend to charge Dr. Wheelock with maintaining the doctrine in 1806-7 which they successfully set up years later. It is noticeable that neither Dr. Wheelock nor any of his friends denied the charge. But on June 24, 1816, Thompson and McFarland presented to the Legislature another remonstrance, setting forth that the charter was a "contract," etc.

On June 26, the bill passed to be enacted. On June 28, seventy-five of the one hundred and ninety members of the House entered their protest upon the journal, on the following grounds : —

1. Because the charter was a contract.

2. Because "the trustees have been thereby 'despoiled and deprived of their property, immunities, and privileges' as trustees of Dartmouth College as secured to them by the charter; and virtually declared guilty of the charges exhibited against them by the memorial of Doct. John Wheelock without being fully heard in their defence by themselves and counsel."

3. Because it "appears that the College is in a prosperous state and condition, and consequently that no necessity exists for any legislative interference whatever."

The fourth reason has already been set forth.

Finally, "They protest against this act, because its inevitable tendency is to make the highest seat of literature and science in the State subject to every change and revolution of party, than which nothing in their opinion can be more destructive to its welfare."

On the same day, they attempted by legislative resolution to declare the trustees innocent of Wheelock's charges.

In the Senate, a motion was made to amend the bill so that it should not take effect until approved by the trustees of the College.

A motion was then made to amend the bill by inserting a new section, providing "that if, by reason of passing this act, any of the property now belonging to said College should by judgment of court be adjudged forfeited, or should any of its funds be impaired by the operation of this act, this

State shall save harmless the trustees of said College from all losses they may sustain on account of such forfeiture, and from costs in defending any suit brought against them by reason of passing said act." These amendments were defeated by the same vote.

The recommendations of the governor became a law; the name of the College was changed to University; the number of the trustees was increased to twenty-one; a board of twenty-five overseers was created; "the president of the Senate and the speaker of the House of Representatives of New Hampshire, the governor and lieutenant-governor of Vermont, for the time being, were made members of said board, *ex officio*," and the governor and Council of New Hampshire. The president and professors of the University were required to take an oath to support the Constitution of the United States and of the State of New Hampshire.

The trustees were in a quandary, and knew not which way to turn. The following letters will explain their position better than any words of ours.

In his letter of July 5, 1816, to Judge Farrar, Thompson says: "You have doubtless seen the college act as it passed. President Brown has written me wishing for the best advice of our best friends, — and suggesting as his present opinion that the old Trustees ought not to yield. He thinks a narrative of the proceedings of the Gen. Court ought to be published, together with some of the documents. He also suggests the expediency of securing as many of the newspapers to our interest as possible, & wishes a series of numbers to be inserted in the *Oracle* exposing the outrageous conduct of the Legislature & thinks you must take hold of the business in good earnest. He wishes if practicable to secure the Keene *Sentinel*, the Dover *Sun* and *Cabinet*. Do you know of any mode? I do not. Is it practicable to secure either of the Boston papers?' If we conclude to resist the act it is absolutely necessary the public mind should be prepared in some measure for it. We think too, a good deal ought to be said in the papers & in conversation respecting a removal of the College to Concord for various reasons. He contemplates a journey to Portsmouth & on the seaboard soon to ascertain the state of public opinion. I wish you & Mr. Webster to discuss the question — what ought the old Trustees to do under existing circumstances. I have devoted much time to this unhappy business & should gladly be excused from further services, but am willing to labor as long as there is any prospect of doing any good.

"The idea of a removal of the College to Concord ought first to be started in Portsmouth papers."

Below the signature is the following list of trustees and overseers of the University : —

"*Trustees.* — Aaron Hutchinson, Josiah Bartlett, Durell, Cyrus Perkins, Joshua Darling, M. Harvey, L. Woodbury, Wm. H. Woodward, Henry Hubbard.

"*Overseers.* — Gov. Vert. [Vermont], Lieut. Gov., Pres. Senate, Speaker, Gov. Langdon, Gov. Gray, Gen. Dearborn, Doct. Baldwin, Judge Story, Ben. Crowningshield, Judge B. Green, Cyrus Perkins, Deacon Ticknor, Judge Claggett, Dudley Chase, H. A. S. Dearborn, Judge J. H. Hubbard, Geo. Sullivan, Jas. T. Austin, Clemt Stover, Levi Lincoln, Jr., Albion K. Parris, Doct. Twitchell, Rev. Mr. Sutherland, W. A. Griswold, Danville."

There was a strong and respectable following in the Federal party which was at heart with Wheelock; but they were not the men who controlled the party organization. Certain journals, to some extent, reflected their views. It was policy to silence, manipulate, or subsidize them. At a later day, the *National Intelligencer* was silenced through Marsh, Hopkinson, and others. It is obvious that the old trustees knew very early that Judge Story and Levi Woodbury were to be members of the new boards.

On July 3, 1816, the governor and council appointed five, and on the next day four more, trustees of the University ; and on July 3, they appointed nineteen overseers ; and the day following, the remaining two.

The new trustees were : Aaron Hutchinson, of Lebanon ; Josiah Bartlett, of Stratham ; Daniel M. Durell, of Dover ; Joshua Darling, of Henniker ; Matthew Harvey, of Hopkinton ; Levi Woodbury, of Francestown ; Henry Hubbard, of Charlestown ; Cyrus Perkins and William H. Woodward, of Hanover.

By the act, the governor and lieutenant-governor of Vermont and the president of the Senate and speaker of the House of Representatives of New Hampshire were members of the Board of Overseers, *ex officio*.

The other members appointed by the governor and council were : John Langdon, Portsmouth ; William Gray, Boston ; Joseph Story and Benjamin W. Crowinshield, Salem, Mass. ; Benjamin Greene, Berwick, Me. ; Cyrus King, Saco, Me. ; Clifton Claggett, Amherst ; Dudley Chase, Randolph, Vt. ; Jonathan H. Hubbard, Windsor, Vt. ; George Sullivan, Exeter ; Levi Lincoln, Jr., Worcester, Mass. ; Albion K. Parris, Paris, Me. ; William A. Griswold, Danville, Vt. ; Henry Dearborn, Roxbury, Mass. ; Henry A. S. Dearborn, Boston ; Clement Storer, Portsmouth ; Thomas Baldwin, Boston ; David Sullivan, Bath ; Amos Twitchell, Keene ; Elisha Ticknor, Boston ; James T. Austin, Boston.

By his summons, the governor promptly convened the trustees and Board of Overseers. They met at Hanover, on August 26, 1816, and remained in almost continuous session for four days.

Fourteen of the overseers were present. Of the trustees there were present on the first day Governor Plumer, Josiah Bartlett, Joshua Darling, William H. Woodward, Levi Woodbury, Cyrus Perkins, A. Hutchinson, Daniel M.

Durell, and Stephen Jacob.   Governor Plumer was made chairman, and Judge Woodward secretary.   It was —

" *Voted unanimously*, That his Excellency William Plumer be chairman of this meeting.

" *Voted*, That the Hon. William H. Woodward be clerk of this meeting.

" *Voted*, That Messrs. Plumer, Durell, and Woodbury be a committee to confer with a committee from the Board of Overseers on the business of the present meeting and the propriety and mode of proceeding thereto."

On the next day, Henry Hubbard, another of the trustees, afterwards a member of the United States Senate, appeared and acted with those heretofore named.   It was —

" *Voted*, That the chairman again notify the Rev. Francis Brown of this meeting; and request his attendance thereon, or his reasons for non-attendance."

The chairman immediately forwarded to Mr. Brown, the following notice : —

HANOVER, Aug. 27, 1816.

SIR, — A number of the trustees of Dartmouth University are convened at the treasury office of Judge Woodward.   They are authorized and prepared to proceed in the transaction of business, provided you will give your attendance as required by statute to preside over their meeting.

I am requested, therefore, by the gentlemen present to notify you of the above circumstances, in order that by repairing here as soon as possible the necessary measures may be seasonably adopted preparatory to the duties and exercises of to-morrow.

Your attendance, or reasons for non-attendance, are wished for immediately, if agreeable.

Mr. Brown replied as follows : —

TUESDAY EVENING, Aug. 27, 1816.

To his Excellency, William Plumer.

SIR, — Your note has just been received requesting my attendance at Judge Woodward's, or my reasons for non-attendance.

With respect to the act of 27th June last, referred to by your Excellency, I would remark that I have not supposed any individual of the twenty-one persons contemplated in that act, as the trustees of Dartmouth University was bound to act under it, unless with his own deliberate consent.

I have taken that act under consideration, together with the other trustees constituted according to the provisions of the charter of 1769, but no decision has as yet been taken, and until the last mentioned trustees shall conclude to abandon their charter and accept the before mentioned act, I shall probably deem it my duty not to attend. The trustees did not, as I in the morning expected they would, act upon the report of their committee. It is therefore still under consideration.

It was then "voted that Messrs. Durell, Woodward, Perkins, Hubbard and Woodbury be a committee to consider the necessary regulations for the government of Dartmouth University, and the organization of different colleges therein."

On this day the trustees of the College formally removed Judge Woodward from the office of secretary. On August 28, 1816, the trustees of the University appointed Judge Woodward secretary and treasurer *pro tem.*

They then voted that the chairman address Dr. Shurtleff and Professor Adams notices, requesting their attendance on this meeting. This was done. Both declined attending, upon the ground that a quorum of the board was not in attendance.

Forthwith Messrs. Brown, Thompson, Farrar, Paine, Marsh, McFarland, Smith, and Payson, a majority of the old trustees, formally refused to accept the provisions of the act, and expressly refused to act under the same. Mr. Brown at once gave Governor Plumer due notice of their action. The trustees of the University thereupon "voted that Messrs. Durell, Hubbard, and Woodbury draft a remonstrance against the proceedings of the above gentlemen." A lengthy remonstrance was at once adopted, and signed by all the trustees in attendance. It concludes with a " solemn protest against any and all resolves, acts, transactions, matters, and things already done by " the old trustees, " as illegal and· of none effect," and earnestly exhorts them " forthwith to desist from all and every act, matter, and thing contravening the provisions of the act aforesaid."

On August 29, 1816, the board, among other things, voted to adjourn until Tuesday, September 17, following. The meeting of the trustees of the University, owing to the illness of a single member, failed for the want of a quorum. The Board of Overseers adopted the following resolution : —

Resolved unanimously as our opinion, That we deem the measures pursued by the aforesaid trustees highly expedient, wise, and dignified, and that they meet the cordial and unqualified approbation and sanction of the members of the Board of Overseers now present.

[Signed] HENRY DEARBORN,
BENJAMIN W. CROWNINSHIELD,
PAUL BRIGHAM,
BENJAMIN GREENE,
ELISHA TICKNOR,
DUDLEY CHASE,
H. A. S. DEARBORN,
JAMES T. AUSTIN,
LEVI LINCOLN, JR.,
WILLIAM A. GRISWOLD,
ALBION K. PARIS,
AMOS TWITCHELL,
DAVID L. MORRILL,
CLEMENT STORER.

Judge Story was not present in person, but his confidential friend Crowninshield was.

CHAPTER V. — CONTINUED.

JUDGE WOODWARD had been the secretary and long the treasurer of the College. There was no whisper against him, but he was the firm friend of Wheelock. On August 27, 1816, he was removed from the office of secretary, and on September 27, 1816, from that of treasurer, and Mills Olcott put in his place.

We copy the following votes, etc., from the certificate of Mr. Olcott: —

At the annual meeting of the Trustees of Dartmouth College, holden on the Tuesday preceding the fourth Wednesday in August, being Aug. 27th, A. D. 1816.

Whereas, William H. Woodward, Esq., heretofore Secretary of the Trustees of Dartmouth College, has when repeatedly requested thereto by the President refused to attend the meeting of this Board, or to furnish the records for their use; therefore,

Resolved, That it is the pleasure of this Board that the sd. Woodward hold the sd. office of Secretary to sd. Trustees no longer & that the same is hereby considered vacant, & the said Trustees will proceed to fill the vacancy. Voted & chose by ballot unanimously, Mills Olcott, Esq., Secretary of the Trustees of Dartmouth College.

Mills Olcott appeared & accepted the office of Secretary of this Board.

THOMAS W. THOMPSON, *Secy. pro tem.*

Voted, That Mills Olcott, the present Secretary of the Trustees of Dartmouth College, be directed to call on the Hon. William H. Woodward, their late Secretary, & demand of him the original charter, records, files & other papers belonging to sd. office of Secretary, and also the former seal of the corporation now in his possession.

(116)

Voted, That Mills Olcott, Secretary to the Trustees of Dartmouth College, be empowered to take such legal measures to obtain the seal, charter, files & other papers belonging to the office of Secretary (in case of the refusal of the Hon. Wm. H. Woodward, their late Secretary, to deliver the same on request) as may be deemed advisable.

Voted, That Mills Olcott be authorized to appear for and act as agent to the Trustees of Dartmouth College in any actions hereafter to be brought in favor of or against sd. Trustees.

At a meeting of the Trustees of Dartmouth College, holden by adjournment at sd. College on the 27. day of Sept. A. D. 1816, being the last Friday of sd. month of Sept.—

Voted, That Mills Olcott, Esq., the present Treasurer of the Trustees of Dartmouth College, make a legal demand of Wm. H. Woodward, Esq., their former Treasurer, of the property & evidences of property in his hands belonging to sd. Trustees.

A copy of the foregoing, duly certified, was furnished by Mr. Olcott to Judge Woodward. On the back of the copy is the following certificate, signed by "Wm. H. Woodward" : —

I hereby certify that Mills Olcott this 7. day of October, A. D. 1816, called on me at my dwelling-house in Hanover & delivered to me the certificates on the opposite side, & demanded of me the original charter, records, files & other papers (which he claimed as) belonging to the office of Secretary of the Trustees of Dartmouth College, & also (what he styled) the former seal of the corporation, and that he also demanded of me the property & evidences of property supposed to be in my hands as Treasurer & (which he claimed as) belonging to sd. Trustees, all of which I declined to deliver to him — [because I entertained doubts of his authority to demand and receive the same of me; & because I was not satisfied of the legal corporate existence of such a board of trustees as those under whom he claims to have derived his authority, nor of the legality of their meetings or proceedings — more especially as they have refused to accede or submit to the act of the Legislature passed June 27th last, entitled an act to

amend the charter & enlarge & improve the corporation of Dartmouth College; claiming myself however to hold the books &
papers & whatever else I am possessed of as Secy. & Treas. of
the said corporation, only for the use of the rightful trustees, &
subject to their orders; my present impressions of duty leading
me to respect & submit to the provisions of the act aforesaid].

The clauses in brackets are apparently in the handwriting
of Judge Woodward, and the remainder of the certificate in
that of Mr. Olcott.

The action was trover, and the point was taken by the
counsel for the defendant that upon such a demand and refusal the form of action was misconceived.

The chief justice intimated that this objection was well
taken, but it was waived in the argument at Exeter by counsel, as other points were waived by counsel on the other
side.

The adjournment was mainly for the purpose of devising
measures for filling the vacancies in the Board of Trustees.

The original act provided " that the Governor and Council
are hereby authorized to fill all vacancies in the Board of
Overseers, whether the same be original vacancies or are
occasioned by the death, resignation, or removal of any
member; and the Governor and Council in like manner shall
by appointments, as soon as may be, complete the present
Board of Trustees to the number of twenty-one, as provided
for by this act; and shall have power also to fill all vacancies that may occur previous to or during the first meeting
of the said Board of Trustees."

On September 19, 1816, the governor and council, then
in session at Hanover, made the following application to
the judges of the Superior Court for their opinion : —

The undersigned respectfully request the opinion of the
hon^ble the Justices of the Superior Court of Judicature, upon the
following questions : —

First. Has the Legislature of this State authority to amend the charters or acts of incorporation of literary corporations, by increasing the number of Trustees, adding Boards of Overseers and prescribing modes of visitation in cases where such corporations were established by the present Government of this State, or by John Wentworth formerly Governor of the province of New Hampshire, exercising authority in the name of the British king?

Second. Have the Governor and Council of this State in virtue of an act passed June 27th, 1816, entitled " An act to amend the charter, and enlarge and improve the corporation of Dartmouth College," authority to fill any vacancies in the Board of Trustees or Overseers happening since the 26th of August last, there not having been on that day a meeting of a quorum of either of said Boards as prescribed by said act.

WILLIAM PLUMER,
ELIJAH HALL,
SAMUEL QUARLES,
B. PIERCE.

The following answer was received and recorded November 25, 1816, viz. : —

To his Excellency the Governor and the Honorable Council of the State of New Hampshire.

The undersigned, Justices of the Superior Court of Judicature, have considered the two questions proposed by your Excellency and Honors for their opinion.

As to the first question, " whether the Legislature of this State has authority to amend the charters or acts of incorporation of literary corporations, by increasing the number of Trustees, adding Boards of Overseers and prescribing modes of visitation," we have examined the Constitution of this State and also the Constitution of the United States, and have not been able even to conjecture any ground upon which such an authority in the Legislature can be questioned, unless it be that such alterations if made without the consent of the corporation may possibly be construed to be a violation of private vested rights, which are protected by those Constitutions. Not being able to see any other objection to the exercise of such an authority, it instantly occurs to us that those who may deem their rights infringed by such alterations may have recourse to our courts for the protection of their supposed privileges, and a doubt arose in our minds as to the propriety of our forming an opinion upon a question supposed to affect private rights alone, till those who may think themselves interested in the question, have had an opportunity to be heard. This doubt led us again to an examination of the Constitution, and upon the most mature reflection we are inclined to believe that the Constitution of this State did not contemplate that the opinion of the Justices of the Superior Court should be required upon a mere question of right between the Legislature and individuals, but upon important questions of a nature altogether public. Your Excellency and Honors will at once perceive the reason and utility of this distinction, when it is considered how very important it is that to the decision of every question of a new impression, involving private rights, we should not only in fact come, but that those who are interested should have a reasonable confidence that we come, with minds entirely unshackled by preconceived opinions.

WE have therefore thought it our duty respectfully to request your excellency and your Honors to excuse us from expressing any opinion upon the first question proposed to us. Indeed, we have thought it our duty not to form any opinion, and we trust that no inference will be drawn from anything here said that our opinions incline to the one side or the other of the question proposed.

We have duly examined the second question, viz., "Have the Governor & Council of this State, by virtue of the act of June 27, 1816, authority to fill any vacancies in the Board of Trustees and Overseers happening since the 26t. of August, 1816, there not having been on that day a meeting of a quorum of either of said boards as prescribed by said act?" and we are of opinion that the authority of the Governor and Council to fill vacancies in the Board of Overseers is general, and extends to all vacancies which may already have occurred, or which may hereafter occur. But the act having given to the Governor and Council power to fill only such vacancies in the Board of Trustees as should occur previous to or during their first meeting, and the 26th of August having been fixed by law as the time of the first meeting, and no legal meeting having been held at that time, we are of opinion that the Governor and Council have not authority to fill vacancies in the Board of Trustees which may have occurred since the 26th of August last.

WM. M. RICHARDSON,
SAMUEL BELL.

Governor Plumer communicated this answer, in a special message, to the Legislature, on December 5, 1816.

In his message to the Legislature, on November 20, 1816, Governor Plumer says : —

" In obedience to the law, I summoned the trustees and overseers of Dartmouth University to meet at Hanover on the 26th of August last, the time assigned by the Legislature for their first meeting. In compliance with this request, a considerable number of respectable gentlemen of distinguished character and standing in society, from Massachusetts, Vermont, Maine, and this State, met in that town. Thirteen members of the Board of Overseers assembled on that day, and on the next fourteen were present, but they wanted one more to make a quorum. Of the Board of Trustees, on the same 26th of August, nine attended, & the next day ten, but they also wanted one to make a quorum. Although I had previous to this meeting duly summoned the trustees, who were appointed under the authority of the royal charter, to attend, yet as only one of them attended, and as there were then nine others in Hanover on the 26th of August, I again addressed a note to each of them individually, informing them of the hour and place of meeting, but neither of the nine attended on that day, or returned any answer to my request. Two days after they declared that the law of this State, passed the 27th June, 1816, to amend the charter and enlarge the corporation of Dartmouth College, was in point of precedent and principle dangerous to the best interests of society ; that it subjected the college to the arbitrary will and pleasure of the Legislature ; that it contained palpable violation of their rights ; was unconstitutional ; and that they would not recognize or act under its authority. A copy of the proceedings of the overseers and trustees acting under authority of the law, and of the trustees opposed to it, so far as they have come to my knowledge, I will lay before you for your consideration.

" There not being a quorum of either trustees or overseers

assembled on the 26th of August, and the statute giving no authority for a less number to adjourn or power to call another meeting, no further proceedings have been had.

"It is an important question, and merits your serious consideration, whether a law passed and approved by all the constituted authorities of the State shall be carried into effect; or whether *a few individuals*, not vested with *any judicial authority*, shall be permitted to declare your statutes *dangerous and arbitrary, unconstitutional and void.* Whether *a minority* of the trustees of a literary institution, formed for the education of your children, shall be encouraged to inculcate the doctrine of resistance to the law, and their example tolerated, in disseminating principles of insubordination and rebellion against government.

"Believing you cannot doubt the course proper to be adopted on this occasion, permit me to recommend the passage of a bill to amend the law respecting Dartmouth University: Give authority to some person to call a new meeting of trustees and overseers; reduce the number necessary to form a quorum in each board; authorize those who may hereafter meet, to adjourn from time to time till a quorum shall assemble; give each of the boards the same authority to transact business at their first, as they have at their annual meeting; and, to remove all doubts, give power to the executive to fill up vacancies that have or hereafter may happen in the Board of Trustees, and make such other provisions as will enable the boards to carry the law into effect and render the institution useful to the public."

Liberal and tolerant as he was in religious matters, and in the appointment of officers of the University, as we have already seen, he was equally so in other appointments.

The council consisted of five members, — three Republicans and two Federalists, each having one vote. Seventeen judges were appointed, — ten Republicans and seven decided Federalists. Of the latter, Judge Woodward accepted. All, or nearly all the others, some much against their own inclination, under a species of moral duress, declined; Webster, Thompson, and other leading Federalists, always excepting Mason, having for party purposes thrown their great influence against their acceptance.

The highest court of the State was to consist of three judges. On July 1, 1816, the governor named for that bench Mason for chief justice, and William M. Richardson and Samuel Bell for associate justices. Richardson was confirmed unanimously. The Republican councillors nominated Bell, and the Federalists opposed him on account of the transactions which culminated in the suit Bullard v. Bell; but he was confirmed. The majority of the council, in retaliation for the conduct of the Federalists towards Bell at that time, failed to confirm Mason. The governor thereupon nominated George B. Upham, an eminent Federalist, who declined for the reasons already given. Richardson in the meantime had become chief justice. The governor having brought a majority of the council to his way of thinking, and being exceedingly anxious that Mason should be placed at the head of the constitutional court, Richardson voluntarily proposed to resign that place if it could be conferred upon Mason, and to take his seat by his side as an associate.

On August 7, 1816, the governor wrote Mr. Mason as follows: "Permit me to inquire if you are appointed chief justice of that court will you accept the office? It has long been my desire that you should have that office, and I think it will be offered to you provided I have assurance you will accept it. It is an office worthy your ambition, and one I hope you will hold till you are removed to the bench of Supreme Court of the United States."

On August 18, 1816, Mason declined the office, on the ground, first, "that the salary was not a reasonable compensation;" and, second, that the law required all the judges to attend each trial term, when, as he thought, one was sufficient; — adding, "After thus stating the reasons which prevent my complying with your proposal, I trust it is unnecessary to add, that political considerations, which in these times are often supposed to determine almost everything, have with me on this subject no influence."

In relation to these appointments, Governor Plumer, in his message of November 20, 1816, from which we have already quoted, said: —

"In making, during the recess of the Legislature, the appointment of judges of the Superior Court of Judicature, and courts of Common Pleas, it was my sole object to select men of talent, of legal information, strict integrity, and such as were best qualified for those important offices, with a view to exclude, as far as practicable, the spirit of party from the temple of justice; and to inspire a general confidence in our courts of law, in which every citizen has a deep interest, I selected gentlemen of different political principles. And I regret that a number of those, who were thus appointed, declined the appointments. Whatever effect this course of proceeding may have on public opinion, I shall always enjoy the consolation that on my part it originated from a pure motive, that of the public good."

In consequence of this course of action on the part of the Federalists, on December 9, 1816, Levi Woodbury was appointed to the bench in place of Upham.

On December 19, 1816, John Harris, Moses Eastman, and Ichabod Bartlett were appointed trustees; and on the same day, Arthur Livermore, William Badger, Judah Dana, Jadutham Wilcox, Ezra Bartlett, Stephen P. Webster, all of New Hampshire, and William Bently, of Salem, Massachusetts, were appointed overseers.

The old trustees, in their memorial to the Legislature, in 1804, asserted that "*they had* no other interest than the members of the Legislature themselves." In their vindication they state their own position in stating that of the trustees of Kimball Union Academy. They say: "The Trustees of Union Academy have no private interest, either *associated* or individual, in the funds, nor even pay for their services or expenses. They are mere stake-holders, like other corporations of this kind, for the public."

Probably for this reason, though the leading trustees had

ample wealth, while the College practically had none, they took no steps by spending their own money to test these acts. But when they were in session in 1816, John B. Wheeler, of Orford, a farmer and country merchant, said to one of the professors, an old friend: "If the trustees intend to test their rights by a suit at law, and should want means, I have a *thousand* dollars at their command." The offer was transmitted to and accepted by the board. Marsh termed it "a light breaking upon blank darkness." The late Professor Adams said: "If it had not been for this unsolicited, unsuspected, unthought-of aid, the great case of Dartmouth College would not have been commenced." Adams was the one to whom Thompson wrote his famous letter (already referred to) relating to his long conversation with Webster, dated July 13, 1815. Henceforth the struggle was between the College and the University, or virtually between the old trustees and the State.

In his letter of January 3, 1817, to Judge Farrar, Mr. Brown says: "We have not yet seen any authentic copy of the act of our Legislature by which we are to be effectually put down. A copy, probably correct, has however been published in the American. According to this, it is enacted, that whoever shall presume to exercise any office in D. U. except in subordination to its Trustees, under any *name* or *pretext* whatsoever, shall forfeit and pay for every offence the sum of $500, one-half to the complainant & the other half to the U. I presume you will soon have an opportunity to see the act.

"Now what shall we do? One of these four courses must be taken. We must either keep possession & go on and instruct as usual, without any regard to the law, or withdrawing from the Coll. edifice & all the Coll. property continue to instruct as the officers of D. Coll., or relinquishing this name for the present, collect as many students as will join us and instruct them as private but associated individuals; — or else we must give up all and disperse. Will you give us your opinion what may be our duty, or what expedient, as soon as convenient. Particularly, will you give us your opinion, whether, supposing this oppressive act to be judged constitutional we should be liable to the fine, if we instruct as the *officers of D. Coll.*, relinquishing, however, the Coll. buildings, the Library, apparatus, &c.

"Whatever may become of us I trust due advantage may be taken of the Act, by which we are to be placed out of the protection of law as well as of the other acts of our Gov. & his Legislature.

"If we resolve to persevere in our duties as the officers of D. Coll., & to meet the consequences, can nothing be done for our help in Portsmouth? We must have substantial aid, or it will be impossible for us to go on.

"In your reply to this, please to give us all the advice which you think may be useful."

In his letter to Farrar, dated Washington, January 21, 1817, Thompson says: "The officers at College are very desirous to know the opinion of their friends as to the course they ought to take at the approaching crisis. I have advised Pres. Brown to call the Trustees together at Hanover, about the 4th of Feby., to compare opinions & feelings & advise such measures as the occasion demands. I have to request you to write him as soon as practicable, & give him your opinion and the opinion of our friends round you as to the measures and conduct that ought to be pursued. I have taken it into my head to write to several gentlemen in different parts of the State to do the same thing. I think it desirable to collect opinions of respectable persons, believing that a knowledge of them may be beneficial. I wish you to write him particularly on the following questions : —

'Is it expedient under existing circumstances for the Trustees and Officers to abandon their trust altogether?

"Is it expedient to amalgamate with the new order of things?

"Is it still expedient to adhere with firmness to charter rights and abide the consequences?

"Is it expedient for the Officers to attend the new boards if invited so to do?

"Can any course be pursued which will be neither an abandonment of trust nor a hindrance to the operations of the University within the meaning of the Penal Act?

"In case of an adherence to charter rights & prosecutions against us should be the consequence, is there any ground to expect pecuniary assistance, & to what extent?

"Does the subject excite any more interest amongst your folks than it did?

"I have informed President Brown that I should request you to write him after conversing with your friends, particularly Mr. Putnam & Mr. Burroughs, and he will expect to hear from you."

Olcott, in his letter of January 22, 1817, to Judge Smith, says : "I have to acknowledge the recpt. of your favor of the 4th inst., which did not reach me until the 18th. I had written you a few weeks since on college concerns, to which receiving no reply, & doubting if there may not have been a miscarriage of the letter, I am requested to address you again on the same subject, & that there may be no delay, to send a special messenger from Concord, who will bring back such communication as you may wish, in reference not only to my letter, but that of President Brown also, if you have had leisure to attend to both.

"The object of my letter was to obtain your opinion as to the best mode of instituting a suit in favor of the trustees of D. Coll. agt. Judge Woodward for refusal to deliver them the property, records, &c., of the Coll.

"The enclosed letter from Mr. Marsh to Prest. B. will show you what is desired, together with his views, and will render it unnecessary to enlarge upon the subject, — and I will thank you to let the enclosed come back to me with the package you may forward by the bearer, who will wait your convenience as to time."

This letter was received by Judge Smith on January 26, 1817, on which day he replied to Mr. Olcott in substance as follows: "A young man from Concord (express) has this moment handed me your favor of the 22d.

"Your letter of 27 Dec. came to hand 9 Jany. On the 11th I wrote you an answer, which I presume after a copy taken in the post-offices, you have recd. Till the receipt of your letter I had not heard of any intention of the trustees to institute any suits.

"Your letter mentioned that a suit was to be commenced agt. Judge W. &c., & wished for advice as to the policy of such an action, & the manner of prosecuting, &c., stating that you had opportunities of consulting with those of the trustees best able to give directions, &c. I had not then, nor have I yet seen any of the acts of the last session. Under the circumstances there was little for me to say. I could only state that I saw no well founded objection to the course proposed.

"It seemed to me proper by all means if any suit was brought, not to pass by the State courts for reasons which will readily occur to you. I had not, nor have I yet, ingenuity enough to think of any other *form of actions* but trover for the books, &c., & assumpsit for money in the name of the corporation. I do not now see any more difficulty on a writ of error in trover than in trespass, though in the former case a bill of exceptions may be necessary, but profess not to have considered the subject with any attention.

"I hope from your known candor, exemption from the suspicion of ' not entering much into *the feelings* & views of the trustees as they relate to the interests of the institution and welfare of society.'

"There will doubtless be feelings enough without my

adding anything to the mass. I can besides hardly persuade myself that feelings make any part of the qualifications of an Atty.

"The parties commonly have enough for the cause. I have always supposed that my zeal has been more manifest than legal talents or prudence. I shall be happy to find myself mistaken.

"Neither your letter nor that of Mr. Marsh seems to call for any addition to my former short letter. It will hardly be supposed that I should have made up any opinion on the various matters at issue between the Coll. and University, and I cannot think of detaining the bearer till I have done so.

"Indeed, at this time, my whole attention is engaged in the business at Dover & Portsmo. terms, &c., which commence 10 days hence.

"I can see no use in sending crude and undigested opinions, which must do hurt if any reliance is placed on them & can do no good. It will be easy to obtain abundance of such when they are *wanted*.

"Mr. M. seems to think the best form of action would be account, but understands it is not in use in this State. The common-law action of account is in use in this State, but is as tedious as a chancery suit, and I don't see its peculiar advantages in relation to error. Trespass seems to me out of the question at present. The pleadings are as at common law.

"You will not understand me as having formed any opinion as to the policy of instituting any suit. I profess to be a very incompetent judge on that subject, but if a suit had been wisely determined on I do not think from what I have heard of the acts of the last session that any reason exists for abandoning that intention."

Judge Smith, in his letter to Mr. Brown, of February 12, 1817, says: "I am just returned from Dover Court. Your letter of the 16th ult. reached this place in my absence. I have read over the act of the last session which you enclosed. The other act of the same session I have not yet seen.

"I would not undertake to give any opinion as to the true construction of the act in question. I can adopt part at least of the language of a great lawyer who when a statesman applied for his opinion on a point of law, said: ' If it be common law, I should be ashamed if I could not give you a ready answer; but if it be statute law, I should be equally ashamed if I answered you immediately.'

"There was one Parliament in those days which was called *parliamentum indoctum*

"The name would suit most of our Parliaments. Their acts are frequently difficult to construe & their legal meaning past finding out, tho' it may not sometimes be difficult to guess at what was intended. In the present it was doubtless the intention to make penal the act of assuming the office of President, Trustee, &c. of Dartmouth University — that is to subject the officers of the college under the old trustees, & the trustees themselves, to the penalty if they presume to act after they shall have been put down by the new government of the *U.* It was supposed the act of June session gave the Coll. a new name & converted it into *D. U.* The act was passed to frighten the old & and to furnish the new with weapons — when the old are removed they will incur the penalty by assuming to retain their offices — undertaking to discharge official duties — impeding the lawful, *i.e.* the new officers, in the discharge of their duties. For *every such act* the penalty will be incurred in the same manner as a person assuming to be sheriff is liable for the service of *every* precept.

"This act is predicated on the idea that the act of June session is constitutional. If it be not so then the P., trustees, &c., of D. Coll. may continue to assume these offices & discharge their duties.

"As to the question whether the officers of the college would be liable for instructing, &c., in case they should give

up the buildings & other college property.   It seems to me
unnecessary to consider it.   The act of surrendering the
property would be a clear admission that they had no right
to retain it — with it I think they ought to give up all
things — the franchise, name, &c., which are wholly insig-
nificant.   It would be no offence under the new act to
instruct, and it will be as useful without as with the name
of *D. C.*   If I were one of the trustees, at the same time I
surrendered the property I would ask Governor P.'s pardon
for my error in having treated his authority so ill.   I have
no doubt he will forgive them.

   "As to the question of the constitutionality of the last
act, I think it depends on that of June, and I suppose the
trustees and officers of the college have all made up their
minds.

   "If their confidence in the correctness of the course they
have adopted remains unimpaired, there is no occasion for
my saying anything at this time.   If they begin to feel
doubts and think of a compromise, this is a case in which
the patient must minister to himself.   I never advise.

   "I would not *advise* to an opposition even to *the letter* of
an act of the Legislature.   Whether an act of the Legislature be constitutional or not depends on the application of
general principles.   It is always (6 Cranch, 128) a question
of delicacy & there is room for an honest diversity of opinion.   No prudent lawyer will be very ready to hazard an
opinion when called on in the course of his professional
duty to maintain the affirmative.   He will of course urge
such principles & authorities as he thinks have a bearing on
the question.   But he will not be very sanguine as to the
event if he knows anything of human nature, and especially
if he has reason to believe that her judges are dependent on
a party and are indebted to that party for their appointments & perhaps their continuance in office.

   "From your letter I should conclude that the Penal Act
of the last session had produced the consequences which I

am confident it is chiefly intended to produce — a timid
spirit in those on whom it was calculated to operate.

"I write this very hastily, and not under an idea that it
will afford you any assistance. I am in the. midst of my
winter engagements and can spare no time for anything
else. It will, besides, not reach you in season."

Up to the time of the communications with counsel, etc.,
the action of the old trustees had been negative. The governor and council, armed with the supplementary acts
referred to, had summoned the trustees to meet in Concord,
on February 4, 1817. The purpose of that meeting was
well understood to be to remove the old trustees if they
failed to act, and to put the University in operation. The old
board was thus compelled to act, but were undecided as to
the course to be taken.

The old board, controlled mainly by the positive will of
the younger Farrar and the influence of Mr. Brown,
decided to institute the suit against Judge Woodward and
take the consequences.

The trustees convened in accordance with the summons,
and took action as follows: —

At a meeting of the Trustees of Dartmouth University, convened by summons from his Excellency Governor Plumer, at the
hall commonly called Mason's Hall, over the Bank, at the southerly end of the Main Street, in Concord, in the county of Rockingham, on Tuesday the fourth day of February, A. D. 1817,
and continued by adjournment to the seventh day of said February.

The committee appointed to prepare and report specifications
of charges against President Brown and other trustees, and the
professors of Dartmouth University, having reported the following articles against the Trustees hereafter named, viz. : —

1. That Nathaniel Niles, Thomas W. Thompson, Timothy Farrar, Elijah Paine, Charles Marsh, Asa McFarland, John Smith and
Seth Payson were severally, personally, and seasonably summoned, as trustees of Dartmouth University, to attend a meeting
of the Board of Trustees of said institution to be holden at Han-

over, in the county of Grafton, and State of New Hampshire, on the 26th day of August, A. D. 1816; that their attendance respectively at that time and place was necessary to constitute a quorum to transact the important business of that institution, then and there pending, of which they severally were well knowing, but they, the said Nathaniel Niles, Thomas W. Thompson, Timothy Farrar, Elijah Paine, Charles Marsh, Asa McFarland, John Smith and Seth Payson, in violation of the duties of their respective offices of Trustees as aforesaid, then and there neglected and refused to attend said board on the twenty-sixth day of August aforesaid.

2. That on the twenty-eighth day of August, A. D. 1816, the said Nathaniel Niles, Thomas W. Thompson, Timothy Farrar, Elijah Paine, Charles Marsh, Asa' McFarland, John Smith and Seth Payson, in direct violation of their respective offices, severally explicitly declared that they would not submit to a law passed by the Legislature of said State on the 27th day of June, A. D. 1816, entitled, "An act to amend the charter, and enlarge and improve the corporation of Dartmouth College," and severally explicitly refused to act under the same.

3. That on the twenty-eighth day of August, A. D. 1816, at Hanover aforesaid, the said Nathaniel Niles, Thomas W. Thompson, Timothy Farrar, Elijah Paine, Charles Marsh, Asa McFarland, John Smith and Seth Payson, did undertake and assume, in the name of this board to confer sundry literary degrees, and to manage and conduct the exercises of the last commencement at said University, without the consent, against the will, and in contempt of the authority of this board, and of the laws of this State relative thereto.

4. That the said Nathaniel Niles, Timothy Farrar, Elijah Paine, Asa McFarland, John Smith and Seth Payson, were severally, seasonably and duly summoned to attend a meeting of said trustees holden at Concord, in the county of Rockingham, in said State on the fourth day of February, A. D. 1817, agreeably to the provisions of an act of the Legislature of said State, passed December 18th, A. D. 1816, then and there to aid and assist in transacting business that was then and there important to be done to promote the interest and prosperity of said institution, and that their presence and attendance respectively were then

and there necessary, of which they were severally well knowing, but that they, the said Nathaniel Niles, Timothy Farrar, Elijah Paine, Asa McFarland, John Smith and Seth Payson, in violation of their respective duties, severally neglected and refused to attend said meeting of the trustees, at that time and place.

By means of all which the provisions of the several acts aforesaid have been contravened, and the interests of said institution injuriously affected.''

Which report being considered,—

Voted, That the said charges relative to the said Nathaniel Niles, Timothy Farrar, Elijah Paine, Asa McFarland, John Smith and Seth Payson, be taken into consideration and acted upon by this board at the hall commonly called Mason's Hall, over the Bank, in the southerly end of the Main Street, in Concord, in the county of Rockingham, on Saturday the 22d day of February instant, at ten o'clock in the forenoon; and that the secretary cause the said Nathaniel Niles, Timothy Farrar, Elijah Paine, Asa McFarland, John Smith and Seth Payson, to be severally notified and cited to appear before this board at the said time and place, to answer to the said charges, and to shew cause, if any they have, why they should not severally be displaced, discharged and removed from their respective offices as trustees of said University, by causing a copy of said charges and this vote to be delivered to each of them respectively, or left at their respective dwelling-houses, at least eight days before the said 22d day of February.

Similar, and in almost all respects identical, charges were preferred against President Brown.

The specifications against Professors Shurtleff and Adams were, in substance, —

1. The same as the third charge preferred against the trustees.

2. That they had performed certain acts as professors of the institution without taking the oaths of allegiance, etc.

3. That they conspired with Mr. Brown and others to impede, obstruct, and prevent the due execution of the act, and did so to the great injury of the University.

4. That their conduct had been in direct opposition to the law, hostile and injurious to the institution, and contrary to the duties of their respective offices.

Messrs. Brown, Shurtleff, and Adams, on February 20, 1817, made the following reply : —

We have severally received a communication from the Honorable William H. Woodward, containing specifications of charges against us, in our official capacities, and citing us to appear before your Excellency and your Honors " at the hall commonly called Mason's Hall, over the Bank, at the southerly end of the Main Street, in Concord, in the county of Rockingham, on Saturday, the twenty-second day of February, instant, to show cause, if any we have, why we should not be displaced, discharged and removed from our respective offices in Dartmouth University."

In reply, we beg leave respectfully to state that we have had and still have great doubts whether the act of the honorable Legislature of this State, approved June 27, 1816, and the act approved December 13, 1816, under which acts your Excellency and your Honors have organized by the name of the Trustees of Dartmouth University, can have validity and effect without the acceptance of the said acts by the Trustees of Dartmouth College as constituted by the charter of 1769; and the said trustees of Dartmouth College have not as yet accepted the acts aforesaid, but have expressly declined accepting the act of June, by a vote of the twenty-eighth day of August last.

Our doubts on this subject have arisen not merely from our own understanding of the Constitutions of this State and of the United States, but also from the opinion of a very large portion of the community, comprising, as we believe, a great majority of the ablest law characters in this and the neighboring States.

These doubts have received no small degree of confirmation from the arguments and reasons adduced by the minority of the House of Representatives in their protest against the act of June; from the doubts entertained on this subject by his Excellency, the Governor, and the honorable Council, as implied in their application to the judges of the Superior Court for their opinion; and from the answer of the said judges, in which they expressly state that they had not formed any opinion on the question.

With this view of the subject, therefore, we deem it our duty to wait the result of an appeal to the judicial tribunals, which has recently been made by the Charter Trustees. The judiciary we consider an essential and independent branch of the sovereignty, and that branch which alone is competent to a final determination of this question; and to their decision, whenever obtained, and whatever it may be, we shall readily conform.

None of the trustees or professors appeared to answer the charges which had been preferred against them. Mr. Brown as president and trustee, Mr. Shurtleff as professor of divinity, Mr. Adams as professor of mathematics, and Messrs. McFarland, Payson, and Farrar as trustees, were severally removed from their respective offices.

The University was duly organized. Dr. Wheelock and Judge Woodward were reinstated; but Professor Allen, the son-in-law of Wheelock, was made acting president until the restoration of Wheelock's health.

On February 20, 1817, Brown, "in behalf and at the request of the corporation," in a public address, said: —

"The trustees of Dartmouth College consider it due to the publick, and especially to the members of the institution and their friends, explicitly to make known the course they design to pursue, and their opinion relative to the state and prospects of the college.

"The trustees commenced the suit at law, which is still pending, from a full conviction that this measure was demanded of them as the constituted guardians of this valuable seminary, and as friends to the literature and the literary establishments of their country; and it is their fixed determination to prosecute it, and to avail themselves of every constitutional expedient for protecting the college, till the question in controversy shall be tried on its merits and decided by the highest judicial tribunal of this nation.

"They have an undiminished confidence that the decision will be in favor of their rights, as secured by the charter; and that they shall again be put in possession of the buildings and other property, of which they have been deprived. If, however, the decision in the last resort should be against them, they will no longer claim a corporate existence, and Dartmouth College will have been effectually destroyed. In that event, the students, should they desire it, will be recommended to either of the colleges in New England; and from what is known of the opinions and feelings of the trustees and instructors of these institutions, full confidence is entertained that the students thus recommended will be readily received. Nor is there any ground for a doubt, that the diplomas conferred by this corporation, so long as their rights remain a subject of judicial inquiry, will be recognized as valid by all literary and professional bodies throughout the country."

After their removal, the faculty published the following:

AN ADDRESS

OF THE EXECUTIVE OFFICERS OF DARTMOUTH COLLEGE TO THE PUBLICK.

As the undersigned, after the most serious and mature consideration, have determined to retain the offices which they received by the appointment of Trustees of Dartmouth College, and not voluntarily to surrender at present any property committed to them, nor to relinquish any privileges pertaining to their offices, they believe it to be a duty which they owe to the publick, no less than to themselves, to make an explicit declaration of the principles by which they are governed.

They begin by stating the two following positions, as maxims of political morality, which they deem incontrovertible: —

1. It is wrong, under any form of government, for a citizen or subject to refuse compliance with the will of the sovereign power, when that will is fully expressed, except in cases where the rights of conscience are invaded, or where oppression is practised to such an extreme degree that the great ends of civil government are defeated or highly endangered.

2. Under a free government, where the sovereignty is exercised by several distinct branches, whose respective powers are created and defined by written constitutions, cases may arise in which it will be the duty of the citizen to delay conforming to the ordinances of one branch until the other branches shall have had

opportunity to act.—IF, for example, the legislative branch should transcend its legitimate power, and assume to perform certain acts, which the Constitution had assigned to the province of the judi-cial branch, a citizen, injuriously affected by those acts, might be bound, not indeed forcibly to resist them, but in the manner pointed out by law, to make an appeal to the judiciary, and to await its decision.

THE undersigned deem it unnecessary in this place to detail the provisions of the acts of the Honorable Legislature, passed in June and December, A. D. 1816, relating to this Institution. Those acts are before the publick, and are generally understood.

THE Board of Trustees, as constituted by the charter of 1769, at their annual meeting in August last, took into consideration the act of June, and adopted a resolution " not to accept its provi-sion." In the preamble to this resolution we find a paragraph in the words following: "They (the Trustees) find the law fully settled and recognized in almost every case which has arisen wherein a corporation, or any member or officer is a party, that no man or body of men is bound to accept or act under any grant or gift of corporate powers and privileges; and that no existing corporation is bound to accept, but may decline or refuse to ac-cept, any act or grant conferring additional powers or privileges, or making any restriction or limitation of those they already pos-sess; and in case a grant is made to individuals or to a corpora-tion, without application, it is to be regarded not as an act obliga-tory or binding upon them, but as an offer or proposition to con-fer such powers and privileges, or the expression of a desire to have them accept such restrictions, which they are at liberty to accept or reject."

IF the doctrine contained in this paragraph be correct, and of its correctness the undersigned, after ascertaining the opinions of eminent jurists in most of the New England States, entertain no doubt, the act of June, and of course the acts of December, have become inoperative in consequence of the non-acceptance of them by the charter Trustees, and the provisions of these acts are not binding upon the Corporation or its officers. We take the liberty to add that, in our opinion, the reasons assigned by the Trustees in the preamble before mentioned for not accepting the act of June, are very important and amply sufficient. Indeed, it has ever appeared to us that the changes proposed to be introduced into the charter by the acts in question, would have proved highly inauspicious to the welfare of this Institution, and ultimately injurious to the interests of literature throughout our country.

THE Trustees appointed agreeably to the provisions of the act of June have, however, thought proper to organize without the concurrence of the charter Trustees, and to perform numerous decisive acts.

AT a meeting in Concord, on the fourth instant, they brought several specifications of charges against the undersigned; and at an adjourned meeting, holden on the twenty-second instant, they proceeded to displace, discharge and remove them from their respective offices in Dartmouth University. A similar procedure was adopted against four of the Trustees acting under the charter.

UNLESS we greatly mistake, in the view already expressed of the act of June, the votes of the University Trustees removing us from office are wholly unauthorized, and destitute of any legal effect; and we are still, as we have uniformly claimed to be, officers of Dartmouth College under the charter of 1769.

THE charter Trustees having resolved to assert their corporate rights, and having for this purpose recently commenced a suit against their late Secretary and Treasurer, in the issue of which it is expected the question between them and their competitors will be finally settled, the undersigned, being united with them in opinion, in principle, and in feeling, cannot consent to abandon them, or to perform any act which may prejudice their claims while this suit is pending. They must, therefore, proceed as officers of Dartmouth College to discharge their prescribed duties. They are sensible of their obligation to render submission to the laws, and their first inquiry, in the case before them, has been, what is law? The result is a full conviction in their own minds, that the course they had concluded to adopt is strictly legal, and that no other course would be consistent with their duty. If they err, their error will shortly be corrected by the decision of our highest judicial tribunals, and with this decision they will readily comply. In the meantime, while the appeal is made to the laws of their country, and to the Constitutions of this State and of the United States, which are the supreme law, they trust that none of their fellow-citizens will have the unkindness to charge them with a want of respect for the government under which they live. As soon as the will of the government shall be fairly expressed, they will render to it a prompt obedience.

THE undersigned are placed in a position singularly difficult, and highly responsible. To them it seems to be allotted in divine Providence, to perform a part, which, in 'its consequences, may deeply affect the 'interests not only of this Institution, but of all similar Institutions in this country. And although they are fully conscious of their own inability to perform this part in a manner worthy of its importance, yet they are firmly resolved, relying on divine assistance, not to shrink from any duty, or any danger, which it may involve.

THE penal act of December they cannot but regard as unnecessarily severe; nor do they see what purpose it was calculated to answer, except to influence them, by the prospect of embarrassing suits, to an abandonment of their trust. They are aware that men may be found disposed to multiply prosecutions against them, and to despoil them of the little property they possess; but they believe themselves called in Providence not to shun this hazard, as they cannot reconcile it with their obligation to the Institution under their care, to relinquish the places they occupy, until it shall be ascertained that they cannot rightfully retain them.

As the University Trustees have expressed a great regard for the laws, the undersigned have a right to expect, that neither they, nor any agents appointed by them, will resort to illegal measures to seize on the College buildings and property. Should such measures unhappily be adopted, the undersigned will make no forcible resistance, it not being a part of their policy to repel violence by violence. They will quietly withdraw where they cannot peaceably retain possession, and with the best accommodations they can procure, will continue to instruct the classes committed to them, until the prevalence of other counsels shall procure a repeal of the injurious acts, or until the decision of the law shall convince them of their error, or restore them to their rights.

FRANCIS BROWN,
EBENEZER ADAMS,
ROSWELL SHURTLEFF.

FEBRUARY 28, 1817.

On April 11, 1817, Dr. Wheelock died, having bestowed upon the University, by his last will, property amounting to about $40,000.

On June 10, 1817, Cyrus Perkins was appointed a trustee in the place of Judge Farrar, Rev. Elijah Dearborn in the place of Mr. McFarland, and Rev. Thomas Beede in the place of Seth Payson; and on the same day Roger Vose was appointed an overseer in the place of Arthur Livermore, resigned.

CHAPTER VI.

TRUSTEES *v.* WOODWARD — PROCEEDINGS IN THE SUPERIOR COURT — ARGUMENTS AT HAVERHILL — AGREEMENTS OF COUNSEL — COURT AND COUNSEL — VIEWS OF MARSH AND CHIEF JUSTICE PARSONS — THE GREAT ARGUMENTS AT EXETER—OPINION OF THE STATE COURT, BY CHIEF JUS-TICE RICHARDSON — WHAT WEBSTER AND CHANCELLOR KENT THOUGHT OF IT — DIFFICULTIES IN DRAWING THE SPECIAL VERDICT — CAUSE, WHEN AND HOW TAKEN TO THE SUPREME COURT OF THE UNITED STATES — CORRE-SPONDENCE — COUNSEL AT WASHINGTON.

AT the May term, 1817, of the Supreme Court of Judica-ture, the following plea of the defendant was filed by his counsel, Sullivan and Bartlett : —·

And the said William H. Woodward comes & defends, &c., when, &c., and prays judgment of the plaintiffs writ aforesaid,— because he says, that before the day of the purchase of the plaintiffs writ, by a statute of this State passed on the twenty-seventh day of June, in the year of our Lord 1816, entitled "An act to amend the charter & improve & enlarge the corporation of Dartmouth College," among other things is enacted, "that the cor-poration heretofore called and known by the name of the Trustees of Dartmouth College, shall ever hereafter be called and known by the name of the Trustees of Dartmouth University,"—and that the said plaintiff at the day of the purchase of his said writ was, and ever since hath been & is named & known & called by the name of the Trustees of Dartmouth University. Without this that the said plaintiff on the day of the purchase of his said writ was or since hath been or is named & known & called by the name of the Trustees of Dartmouth College as by the said writ is supposed — to wit: at Plymouth aforesaid, and this the said Woodward is ready to verify. Wherefore he prays judgment of the writ afore-said, and that the same may be quashed, &c.

(142)

The original lies before us. It bears the following indorsement of Judge Smith: " Semble, Bad.   XI MS. Rep. 179."

This plea was probably withdrawn 'by some arrangement between counsel.

Upon the motion of Judge Smith, the original declaration to which we have referred was struck out, and an amended one, in his handwriting, was " filed by leave of court, to be inserted in lieu of the original declaration." The amended declaration was " trover for two Books of Records, purporting to contain the records of all the doings and proceedings of the Trustees of Dartmouth College, from the organization of the corporation until the 7th day of October, 1816, of the value of $5,000,—the original charter of letters patent constituting the College, of the value of $10,000,—the Common Seal, of the value of $1,000,— and four volumes of Books of account, purporting to contain the charges and accounts in favor of the College, of the value of $10,000." The conversion was alleged to have been made on the 7th day of October, 1816, and the plaintiff's damages laid at $50,000.

This term of the Superior Court ended May 24, 1817. Before its close, the cause was ably argued by counsel on both sides.

Mr. Farrar, one of the counsel for the trustees, who reported the case, says that at this term " the argument was opened on the part of the plaintiffs by Mr. Mason and Mr. Smith, and on the part of the defendant by Mr. Bartlett and Mr. Sullivan."   The State report, prepared by Mr. Adams, the able and experienced clerk of this court, under the eye of the judges, says: " The cause was argued in this county, at the last [May] term of this court, by Mason and Smith for the plaintiffs, and by the attorney-general for the defendant."

No verdict had been rendered in the case, and it was apparently argued upon the declaration, the printed charter, and copies of the laws the validity of which was in question, without any written agreement or statement of facts.

The counsel for the defence drew up the following agreement : —

It is agreed by the counsel for the parties that the case be stated in a special verdict, to be drawn up (before the opinion of the court shall be delivered) by the counsel, under the direction of the court. The verdict to contain all things necessary & proper, in the opinion of the court, to raise the questions on the validity of the acts of the Legislature of June 27, 1816, entitled "An act to amend the charter & improve & enlarge the corporation of Dartmouth College "— and the act of Nov., entitled " An act in addition to an act to amend the charter," &c.

And all the facts necessary to raise the question upon the validity of those acts are admitted by the parties.

That the corporation of Dartmouth College had a charter from Governor Wentworth in 1769, which, if necessary, may make a part of this statement — that a Board of Trustees was duly organized under said charter, &c.,— that Nath'l Niles & the others claiming to be Trustees of Dartmouth College were duly appointed, &c. — that the acts of the Legislature before named, if necessary, make a part of this statement — that agreeably to the provisions of said acts a Board of Trustees was duly organized on the 4th of February, 1817, and Wm. H. Woodward chosen & qualified as Secretary & Treasurer of said Board, & had possession of the records, &c., which had belonged to Dartmo. College — that Nathl. Niles and seven others, claiming to be Trustees of Dartmo. College, refused to comply with the provisions of the Legislative acts aforesaid, or any part of them, & proceeded to remove Wm. H. Woodward from the offices of Secretary & Treasurer of Dartmo. College, which offices he had held previous to the passing of said acts — that they chose Mills Olcott, Esq., Secretary & Treasurer — who, on the sixth day of February, demanded the College books, &c., of said Woodward, who refused to give them up, claiming to hold them as Secretary and Treasurer of the Trustees of Dartmouth University.

And it is agreed that any other facts may be embraced in

such special verdict, that the court shall deem necessary to a decision on the merits.

In case the decision should be in favor of the plaintiffs, it is agreed that the court enter judgment for such sum in damages as they may think proper, which judgment shall be discharged on the delivery to the plaintiffs by the defendant of the books, &c., in his possession which are sued for.

This draft is in the handwriting of Mr. Bartlett. It bears the following indorsement in the handwriting of Judge Smith : " Statement proposed by deft., May Term, 1817, Grafton." It is obvious, for reasons deemed sufficient for them, that the astute counsel for the plaintiffs rejected this agreement, and caused one of their own to be substituted for it.

On the day after the May term, 1817, the counsel entered into the following agreement : —

Trustees of Dartmouth College *vs.* W. H. Woodward. It is agreed by the counsel for the parties that the case be stated in a special verdict, to be drawn up (before the opinion of the Court shall be delivered) by the counsel, under the direction of the Court.

The verdict to contain all things necessary and proper, in the opinion of the Court, to raise the question on the validity of the acts of the Legislature on the subject of the College or University.

	JEREMIAH SMITH,	} *For Plfs.*
25 May, 1817.	J. MASON,	
Sup. Court,	GEO. SULLIVAN,	} *For Dfts.*
Grafton.	ICHA. BARTLETT,	

Mr. Brown, in his letter to Farrar, of May 28, 1817, says : " Your obliging letter from N. Ipswich, I should have acknowledged before this time, had not ordinary & extraordinary cares occupied the whole of my attention. Immediately after receiving it we had a consultation respecting the subject to which it relates, & determined to print with-

out delay.   Spear actually begun the work.   But two difficulties arose, which made us suspend, & at length give over
the design.   In the first place, the pamphlet could not have
come out a sufficient time before the sitting of the court to
accomplish much ; in the second place, we scarcely knew
·how to defray the expense.   But what are 40 or 50 doll.
you will say?   The sum appears trifling.   But it must be
considered, that we have had & still have, a large number
of such trifling sums to raise for extraordinary purposes,
and that after these are provided for, we can scarcely live
on what remains.   This famous gentleman, the Publick,
though his liberalty has been much bruited, clenches his fist
& turns away his eye, with a most provoking indifference,
when the College begins her story of distress. — However,
I wish not to be ungateful.   We have received something :
& I trust, shall receive enough to enable us to go forward.

   " The result at Haverhill is, on the whole, the best, we
think, that could have been.   The impression on all who
were present is favourable.   We feel strengthened and
encouraged.   It will do us good to have the cause argued
at Exeter.   The merits of our side will become better
known, & the impulse given to the judges will be salutary.
Hitherto God hath helped us, & in His name we will trust.

   " The next subject in order is the Commencement.   You
must endeavour to give us a lift by helping us to numbers
& respectability.   We hope to have exercises which will not
dishonour us.   The other party (if they get forward at all)
will endeavor to make a great display — and democracy,
I suppose, will do its best.   Rumor says, that the Univ.
officers are to be the performers at their commencement, &
that they, after delivering their orations, are to be inaugurated with much pomp.   It seems to me that this will be a
pretty cold business, especially after what has taken place
at Haverhill.

"There was much of truth in Mr. Mason's remark, that 'the boys would determine this controversy.' Our graduating class will leave a large space to be supplied, & our friends through the country must do all that belongs to them to procure us a good class next autumn. The College is in an excellent state. Still, parents will fear. I wish that Mr. P. & yourself would consider whether anything can be done for us in your part of the State. Prof. Adams has procured an apparatus from Salem & Boston. Can anything favourable, *i.e.*, in proof of the permanency of the College, be made of my declining the offer at Hamilton? The prospects of that institution are highly promising, & the salary offered, $1800 — double the salary here. If you think our cause would be aided by noticing the circumstance of my declining, you may do it, as you judge proper.

"Will it still be best to publish a pamphlet? There will now be time enough; & if our friends think proper, it shall be done. Our friend P. complains a little about the manner of engaging counsel; except, however, the neglect at Washington, I have nothing to regret. The business will end well enough. Allow me, my dear Sir, to give you my unfeigned thanks for your uniform kindness, zeal, and alacrity in our behalf. We shall not repay you; but we shall be grateful & we hope you will continue to help us professionally & otherwise whenever you have an opportunity. The papers have announced the death of your kind and excellent mother. In a family bound together as strongly as yours, this separation will be most tenderly felt. May God support you all, & sanctify the dispensation to you. Your excellent Father will feel like a pilgrim & stranger indeed. Thus we fill the days allotted us & then depart. Oh how excellent that religion which surrounds the grave with light & hope, & reveals a sure immortality to the people of God."

In his letter to the same, of September 23, 1817, Mr.

Brown says : " I am more and more in favour of the print-ing, & think I can warrant you 100 subscribers in this place & the immediate vicinity. I wish you to call on the Judges without delay, that they may have knowledge of our pur-pose to lay the whole subject before the publick. This must operate as an additional motive to them to do justice. Secure the copyright.

" We came to Concord on saturday, and reached home last evening. We find 19 have been admitted ; 14 to the Freshman Class. We think the Univ. may get 4 or 5 ; per-haps more. We hope a considerable number more will join us.

" In reflecting on the argument, Prof. A. & myself have concluded it is *almost impossible* for the Judges to decide against us. — Can you not ascertain what the decision will be, soon, & communicate your opinion to us? — It is pre-sumed the *book*, in boards, will not exceed in price one dollar."

The cause was continued to the September term, 1817, at Exeter, in Rockingham County, for further argument, as the counsel for the trustees were unprepared to reply as fully as they desired.

The intellectual gifts of the court and counsel were wor-thy of the greatness of the cause. As but two of them had a national reputation, a brief sketch may not be out of place. The court consisted of William Merchant Richard-son, Samuel Bell, and Levi Woodbury.

Chief Justice Richardson was forty-four years old. He was a graduate of Harvard, a member of Congress from Massachusetts in 1812, and was subsequently reëlected ; but, being averse to political life, resigned and removed to Portsmouth, in his native State, in 1814. From his appoint-ment, in 1816, till his death, in 1838, he was chief justice of the highest court. Physically he was as imposing as he was great intellectually. Like Marshall's, his eyes were black, piercing, and brilliant ; like Marshall's, his hair was

black as a raven's wing; and like Marshall, he had refined
and simple tastes; but, unlike Marshall, he had a full, high,
and broad forehead. In learning and industry he ranked
with Chief Justice Parsons. He was a great and honest
judge. Some judges owe much of their eminence to their
subtlety in judicial fence, — a species of cuttle-fish logic.
They succeed by darkening. It is oftentimes hard to answer, because difficult to understand them. This great
attribute, though not great judicial quality, Richardson
lacked. His reasoning and his heart alike were as open
and ingenuous as the light of day. He was reverenced by
the people of the State as no other judge ever was.

Judge Bell was forty-seven years old. His was a family
famous for their talent. He was the father of the late Chief
Justice Bell; trustee of Dartmouth College (of which he
was a graduate) from 1808 to 1811; judge from 1816 to
1819; governor from 1819 to 1823, and United States senator from 1823 to 1835. He was a man of immense erudition and great business capacity, a thorough lawyer, and
possessed of great moral courage.

Judge Woodbury was twenty-eight years old. He was a
graduate of Dartmouth; was judge from 1817 to 1819;
governor in 1823; United States senator from 1825 to
1831; secretary of the navy under Jackson, from 1831 to
1834; secretary of the treasury from 1834 to 1841, under
Jackson and Van Buren; and then declined the office of
chief justice of New Hampshire. He was again senator in
Congress from 1841 to 1845, when he was appointed by
President Polk one of the justices of the Supreme Court of
the United States, which office he held until his death, in
1851. The probabilities are very strong that he would
have been president in the place of General Pierce, had his
life been spared. Of Judge Woodbury, Webster, in his letter to Judge Story, of January 4, 1824, said, speaking of
two appointments that might be made to that bench,

"There is no doubt that Judge Woodbury would be one, and he is as sound a man as I know of." Richardson was a Federalist; Bell and Woodbury were both Anti-Federalists. Mason, a competent judge, if ever any man was, said of these judges, that "three more men so well qualified as the present judges, and who would accept the office, could not be found in the State."

It is not quite clear whether Judge Woodbury participated in the decision of the cause.

The earlier volumes of the New Hampshire Reports were reported by the judges themselves. Every judge prepared for the press the head-notes, statement of case, and opinion in each cause in which the judgment of the court was pronounced by him. In every case when the full bench did not sit, the State report containing the case assumes to show the fact; but there is nothing in it to indicate that Judge Woodbury did not participate in this decision. Judge Farrar, in his report, assumes that all the judges sat, saying :

At the September Term, in Rockingham County, present all the Judges, viz. : —
　　Hon. WILLIAM M. RICHARDSON, *Chief Justice.*
　　Hon. SAMUEL BELL, ⎱ *Justices.*
　　Hon. LEVI WOODBURY, ⎰
The cause came on to be again argued.

We have before us, as we write, the printed copy of the opinion, etc., furnished by the chief justice to Governor Plumer. After entitling the cause, and stating when and where the opinion was delivered, there follows :—

PRESENT.
　　Hon. WILLIAM M. RICHARDSON, *Chief Justice.*
　　Hon. SAMUEL BELL, ⎱ *Justices.*
　　Hon. LEVY WOODBURY, ⎰

As we have before said, Justices Bell and Woodbury were graduates of Dartmouth. Webster, in the "Cæsar in the

Senate " peroration in his argument at Exeter, begged them, as alumni of the College, to forbear the fatal blow which, Brutus-like, would come so near the heart of their *alma mater*.

But, upon the other hand, the manuscript dockets of the clerk of that court show the following entries at the May and November terms, 1817 : —

Olcott, * * * Trus. Dartmouth College, *Appees.*, v. Wm. H. Woodward.

Jus. Woodbury does not sit.

Continued *nisi*.

Olcott.
May, 1817.
Jury as in
No 4,
State Trials.

29. Trustees Dartmº. College, *Apts.* v. William H. Woodward.

Honble Judge Woodbury does not sit in this case.

Verdict — Deft. not guilty.

Judgt. for Deft., his costs taxed at $11.42.

These entries were in some respects manifestly incorrect. Papers on the files show that the cause was never tried by a jury. We know that the defendant had counsel, and that Mr. Olcott was not sole counsel for the plaintiffs.

At the September term, Mason, Smith, and Webster argued the cause for the trustees, and Sullivan and Bartlett for the State. These were all members of the Rockingham bar, when it was literally "an arena of giants." Of this bar Judge Story said that it had "vast law learning and prodigious intellectual power."

At the Circuit Court for New Hampshire, October, 1812, Judge Story made the following orders : —

Whereas, the court have a full knowledge of the learning, integrity and ability of the Honorable Jeremiah Smith, and the Honorable Jeremiah Mason, and upon the most entire confidence therein, and being willing to express this opinion in the most public manner, as well as a testimony to their merits, as also a laudable example to the junior members of the bar; and the court having

taken the premises into their mature deliberation, of their own
mere motion and pleasure, have ordered, and do hereby order,
that the honorable degree of serjeant-at-law be and hereby is conferred upon them, the said Jeremiah Smith and Jeremiah Mason,
and the court do further order they be respected as such by all
the officers of this court, and all others whom the same may concern, and that this order be entered upon the records of the
court." "The court, on mature deliberation, do order that the
degree of barrister-at-law be and hereby is conferred on the following gentlemen, who are counsellors of this court, viz.: Oliver
Peabody, Daniel Humphreys, George Sullivan, and Daniel Webster, esquires; in testimony of the entire respect the court entertain for their learning, integrity and ability; and the court further
order that this order be entered among the records of the court."

At the time of the argument, Smith was fifty-eight years
old; Mason, fifty; Sullivan, forty-three; Webster, thirty-
five; and Bartlett, thirty-one. Mason was from Connecticut, but read law and commenced practice in Vermont. He
was six feet and seven inches in height, and proportionately
large in other respects. His intellectual exceeded his physical stature. Webster, with a thorough knowledge of the
man, deliberately wrote down that as a lawyer, as a jurist,
no man in the Union equalled Mason, and but one approached him, and a quarter of a century later as deliberately reaffirmed his estimate. Mason had two loves, one
desire, and one passion. He loved his family, resigning his
position as United States senator rather than be separated
from them; and next to his family, he loved the law de-
votedly. He desired a competence, and his passion was a
vitriolic contempt. The gifts and graces of the orator were
denied to this great man, but on his feet in the court-room
he was seemingly an inspired Euclid.

Smith had been four terms in Congress, judge of the
United States Circuit Court, chief justice of the Superior
Court for seven years; then governor of the State, and then
chief justice of the Supreme Court for three years. He
was of Scotch-Irish stock; possessed of great and accurate

learning, and of great natural abilities; but, like Mason, he was no orator.

Webster, in his letter to Chancellor Kent, of May 23, 1825, says: "You know Judge Smith, of New Hampshire, at least in his public and professional character. I wish to recommend him to you on the score of private worth and social qualities. There are few men in the world, I think, more to your taste.

"I entertain for him the highest regard, and true gratitude. When I came to the bar he was chief justice of the State. It was a day of 'the gladsome light' of jurisprudence. His friends, and I was one of them, thought he must be made governor.

"For this office we persuaded him to leave the bench, and that same 'gladsome light' cheered us no longer. *Ponto nox incubat astra.* I need not continue Virgil, nor say how the east wind, and the north wind, and the stormy south wind all rushed out together, and what a shipwreck they made both of law and parties.

"Judge Smith has since occasionally practised the law, but for some years has lived entirely, I believe, with his books and his friends. He knows everything about New England, having studied much its history and its institutions; and as to the law, he knows so much more of it than I do, or ever shall, that I forbear to speak on that point."

The merit of this is its truthfulness.

Of Webster, the "Great Black Giant of the East," it is only necessary to say that he was in full possession of his great powers.

Sullivan was from Irish and Revolutionary stock, — a race of soldiers, orators, and lawyers. He was attorney-general (as his father was before him, and his son after him) for twenty-one years; a classical scholar, well read in the law; an excellent special pleader; swift to perceive, prompt to act, and full of resources. He relied too little on his prep-

aration, and too much upon his oratory, his power of illustration and argument.   But neither the court, the jury, nor
the people ever grew weary of listening to his silver tones or
his arguments, that fell like music on the ear.

Bartlett, the uncle of the present president of the College,
was also of Revolutionary stock.   He and Webster were
from the same town, and theirs were the two leading families
in it.

Bartlett was a "little giant," four years younger than
Webster.   He served three terms in Congress.   He was
from a family eminent for its physicians, preachers, and
jurists.   He was indefatigable in preparation ; eloquent in
its highest sense ; ready, witty, and a popular idol.   He
was often pitted against Mason and other great lawyers.
Between Webster and Bartlett there existed a personal and
political antipathy, which continued for years.   This cropped
out in the argument of this cause, and is very apparent
from Mr. Webster's correspondence.

At the September term, 1817, the counsel for the College
met at Exeter, thoroughly prepared for the argument.

A portion of the old trustees put their case primarily upon
what may be termed the Parsons view, and the others,
upon the contract theory and the obligation clause.   The
former view was supported by Thompson, Marsh, Mason,
and Webster, though they also gave countenance to the
other theory.

It was but natural that Thompson should share the views
of Parsons.   He read law with him ; was a favorite student,
familiar with his history and opinions ; and in the remonstrance of June 19, 1816, which was undoubtedly prepared
by Thompson, and from which we have before quoted, the
Parsons view alone is reflected.

Marsh, as we have already seen, was a leading trustee,
and the one through whom Webster proposed to bring one
of the College causes in the Circuit Court.   He was plaintiff

in one of those suits, and was relied upon by Mason, Smith, and Webster to take their places, and argue these causes in the Circuit Court.

Mason, in his letter to Marsh, of April 14, 1818, says: "The counsel engaged in your first cause being pretty well exhausted, we shall expect you to come with a treasury of new things, and that you will take upon you [the] principal burden of the argument."

In his letter of September 11, 1818, to the same, Mason says: "I wrote you a few days ago. I have since received a letter from Mr. Webster, in which [he] seems to think it of *primary* importance to have one of the causes carried to the Supreme Court. Under this impression I think you had best attend the Circuit Court if possible. You will remember Judge Story said if necessary he would hold a special term for these causes."

In 1816, Marsh prepared the following "Minutes of authorities and observations in relation to the affairs of Dartmo' College," in answer to the arguments on the other side, and particularly to the message of Governor Plumer: —

"The Parliament of Great Britain, consisting of the king, lords and commons (the three estates of the kingdom), is said in the vaunting language of legal & political writers, to be omnipotent. Anciently the king was absolute — all power & authority being vested in the person of the king, he parcelled it out to the lords & commons at different periods, according as he found it necessary to flatter the one or the other, till the present Constitution became firmly established. In 1295 — 23d E 1st the first regular meeting of the commons was called by an invitation of Edward First to the different towns & boroughs in the counties, to send deputies to the Parliament. In 1296 — 24 Ed I. the king stipulated to levy no tax or impost without the consent of the lords & commons. The right of trial by jury that 'no freeman should be imprisoned or disseised of his freehold, or liberties or of free customs, &c., but by legal judgment of his peers or by law of the land,' had been enjoyed under the Saxon monarchs — & though suppressed by William the Conqueror was again revived by the claims of the people, & confirmed by his descendants Henry II. & John; & this last prince in 1215, signed the Charter of the Forrest; and at the same time that famous grant of English liberties, the *Magna Charta.*

"Thus by successive grants, & by slow degrees, the absolute power of the crown became vested in the three estates of the kingdom, the king, lords & commons. But the finishing limitation of the prerogatives of the crown was the act 13th William III. perhaps 1700, changing the terms of the commissions of the 12 judges from *durante bene placito* to *quamdiu se bene gesserint.*

"And an act in the early part of the present reign ' that the commissions of the judges shall continue in force notwithstanding the demise of the king' — the Parliament is therefore omnipotent or absolute, having derived its powers from the king, as the source of power and authority, & not from the people; and their power not being derived from the people, they are accountable to no one.

"The Constitution is made up of various grants & concessions of the crown, & acceptances by the other estates; so that even an act of Parliament, limiting the power of the respective branches, or varying the structure of the government, is a part of the Constitution. The Parliament therefore is, in its authority, paramount to the Constitution as existing at any given period.

"The Parliament of G. Britain being omnipotent, & beyond control, can pass acts of attainder; &, in this sense may be regarded as a high court of criminal jurisdiction. This power is not given to any legislative body in the United States. This may account for the expression in Blackstone, 1st B. Com. 485–512, that corporations may be dissolved by act of Parliament; & indeed is assigned as the reason though this dictum is supported by no decision   Stat. 1 Geo. 1st.

" In February 1792, the people of N. Hampshire, being then free & independent, framed, & adopted their present Constitution, giving to the respective branches of the govt their specific powers & authorities, dividing them into executive, legislative & judicial.

" The powers of each, are equally derived from the people ; & each is alike limited by the Constitution ; & neither the people, or any individual, is any more bound by any unconstitutional act of the Legislature than by any illegal act of the meanest officer of the govt. The Legislature deriving its authority from the letter of the Constitution, it is impossible that it can ever pass any act of paramount authority, or (make any law) in derogation of its provisions.

" It may now be inquired whether the act of the late General Court entitled ' an act to amend the charter & improve the corporation of Dartmouth College ' can be in any way binding upon the old corporation, upon constitutional principles, without the acceptance of the same by the corporation.

" It is remarkable that the people of N. Hampshire in the declaration of their rights have asserted, and maintained the right of trial by jury in the very words of *Magna Charta*, ' no person shall be arrested, imprisoned, despoiled or deprived of his property, immunities or privileges, put out of the protection of the law, exiled, or deprived of his life, liberty or estate, but by the judgment of his peers, or the law of the land.' (Con. N. H. Bill of Rights, sec. XV.)

" In conferring power on the Gen Court, as a Legislature, the Constitution expressly declares ' that full power & authority are hereby *given* & *granted* to the said Gen Court from time to time, to make, ordain & establish all manner of wholesome and reasonable orders, laws, statutes, ordinances, directions & instructions, either with penalties or

without, so as the same be not repugnant to or contrary to
this Constitution.'

"Usurping authority not given by the Constitution by
either branch of the govt is acting both repugnant & contrary to the Constitution. If therefore, in passing this law
(act) the Legislature has assumed powers not delegated by
the Constitution; (by) the very instrument by which the
Legislature is created, the act is void. A corporation is,
in law, a person; and as such, is invested with property,
with immunities & privileges[1] of which it cannot be divested or deprived without a due investigation in a course
of legal proceedings, in which the facts with which it is
charged, and which are supposed to work a forfeiture of
their property and privileges, shall be ascertained by the
finding of a jury, or conceded in the pleadings. The Legislature is not a competent tribunal for the trial of facts on
which a forfeiture of life, liberty, property or privileges can
be predicated; nor is it in any sense, a judicial tribunal.
If therefore, facts were ascertained, it could not pass a
judgmt of forfeiture. The Legislature can merely pass
laws for the establishment of courts of justice, & other general laws, ordinances & regulations for the orderly conduct
of the people; but have no power to carry them into effect
either as executive or judicial officers.

"But the act under consideration does, if carried into
effect, deprive the Trustees of Dartmo. College both of
their property, powers, immunities & privileges; & vest
them in another body; & this without any judgment or
forfeiture against them by any court of competent jurisdiction. The act under consideration has altered the name of
the corporation from that of Trustees of Dartmouth College
to that of Trustees of Dartmouth University; has provided
that instead of twelve, the body, shall consist of twenty-

---

[1] By incorporation it acquires *jus persona* & becomes *persona politica*, &
is capable of all civil right *habendi et agendi*. (4 Com. Dig. 255, tit. "Franchise," F.)

one — that, instead of leaving the additional number to be appointed by the trustees now in office, they shall be appointed by the Governor & Council; that all the rights, powers, authorities, property, liberties, privileges & immunities enjoyed by the Trustees of Dartmo. College, shall be holden, used & enjoyed by the Trustees of Dartmo. University. This, then, is a direct act of usurpation, taking property, rights, privileges & immunities from one body of men incorporated so as to be one person[1] in law, & giving them to another body of men : not only so, it is divesting individuals of their rights &c. It is a privilege to have a certain proportion of power, & authority & property in any body corporate ; to increase the number therefore is to divest each individual of, at least, a portion of his property, power & privileges. Now to divest any one of a part of his property, rights or privileges, or immunities, though it be but a part of what he holds in common with others, is the same in principle ; & as much against the Constitution, as to divest him of the whole.

" Depriving an individual member of a corporation of his franchise, without authority for so doing ; and without conviction in due course of law, was adjudged to be a violation of that clause of *Magna Charta*, XI Co 99 Bagg's case ; ' but when a corporation had power to remove & did remove for good cause, that will be deprivation by the law of the land.' *Idem.*

" To deprive a whole corporation of its rights ; or any portion of them must be a more gross infringement of the Constitution of N. H.

" Suppose a township granted to 60 proprietors in common, could the Legislature by an act passed before any division is made, admit 20 more persons as proprietors.

" The authorities furnish no instance where a corporation has ever been divested of its property or authority, or any portion of either without regular process, in the nature of a

---

[1] 4 Com. Dig. 255, tit. "Franchise," F.

quo warranto in which the parties have been admitted to the benefit of pleading to issue, & of trial as in other cases.

" During the tyranical reign of Charles the I & II when the corporation of the city of London, & other corporations in the kingdom were so much in the way of those ambitious princes, it was never thought practicable to deprive them of their privileges by an express act of the king or Parliament, but a *quo warranto* was always resorted to under some pretext or other.

" The case of Gresham College is relied on ; this is collected from the encyclopedia, or, perhaps, from Ree's cyclopedia ; & can, at best, be regarded only as a dictionary, or more properly, a spelling-book authority ; & is suitable only to be quoted by school-boys. It is incidentally mentioned in a biographical sketch of Sir Thomas Gresham : the particulars are not given ; yet so far as facts appear, it is not an authority in point. The property in the case by the will of Sir Thomas was vested in the corporation of the city of London in 1579 ; with other property there was given a building which was afterwards converted into a college, for the purpose of delivering certain lectures, by lecturers who should be appointed by the Mayor & Aldermen of London, & by the company ; & who should be unmarried men ; & should have fifty pounds salary, & lodging rooms in the college. It became necessary to remove this building in order to erect one for a more important purpose ; the Excise office. The Mayor and Aldermen of London petitioned Parliament for leave to remove this building ; & to have the lecturers enjoy their salaries, notwithstanding they should be married ; this was granted, by act of Parliament 8 Geo III & a stipulation made with the lecturers that in lieu of their chambers, they should receive £50 more per annum, & leave to marry ; and the lectures were afterwards delivered in a chamber of the Royal Exchange, which had been built by Sir Thomas Gresham at his own expense ; &

from the income of which he had endowed these professorships.

" This property was already vested in the corporation of the city of London unconditionally; but in trust that the avails should be paid to unmarried lecturers. If the lecturers married they would cease to be such; the Parliament dispensed with this, and enabled them to enjoy the salary notwithstanding they should marry; & all this was done at the request of the corporation, & by agreement with the lecturers. There is nothing in all this about moving the college to another place. The corporation after taking down the building, by consent of Parliament, provided another lecture room, in a building given at the same time, by the same donor, & paid the lecturers a compensation in lieu of the use of their chambers. There is no attempt here, to interfere with the property or powers of the corporation, without its consent.

" It is said ' that in this country a number of the States have passed laws which made material changes in the charters of their colleges.' It is not here said whether this was done at the request, or by the consent of their corporations. It is believed that no instance can be found where this has been attempted without such consent. The Legislature of Massachusetts some few years since, passed an act that the ministers of such & such parishes, should be, with others, overseers of Harvard College; but Chief Justice Parsons, who is said to have penned the act, inserted a proviso that the act should be obligatory when accepted by the corporation; & not till then. This was afterwards repealed & subsequently reënacted, much in the same words: this is a strong authority in our favor showing clearly the opinion of C. J. Parsons, and of the Legislature of Massachusetts that they could not interfere without the consent of the corporation. No other instance of any attempt of the kind is known, or believed to exist, in relation to Harvard College or any other institution of the kind in the Commonwealth.

" It is said that the Legislature of N. H. has often interfered in regulating and altering, charters of this kind ; &
allusion is made to acts of the Legislature in altering &
dividing towns in the State. It should be remembered that
towns are corporations of a very different nature, & for
different purposes from those for which academies and colleges are incorporated ; & though they are corporations for
certain particular, & limited purposes ; yet they are rather
to be regarded as civil divisions of the State for the purpose
of government. The charters of the respective proprie-
taries erecting the territory into towns, declares that the
inhabitants possessing them, shall have and enjoy certain
privileges ; & in general terms, all the privileges which are
enjoyed by other towns in the province : leaving it for the
Legislature to make such divisions, and confer such powers
& privileges as shall best conduce to the purposes of civil
government. It is true, that they may hold property for
certain limited purposes ; yet this is not the great object of
their incorporation ; the great end of these territorial divisions of the State into townships with limited corporate
powers, is to facilitate among the people the purposes of
self-government, & to aid in the government of the State ; &
their officers, though elected by the people of particular
districts, are yet civil officers, & properly officers of the
State ; to resist them, therefore, in the discharge of their
duties, is to resist the constituted authorities of the State ;
& it is an indictable offense. But it is not so with officers
of other corporations, they are left to their civil remedies
like other individuals — accordingly the Constitution
adopted by the people, in defining the powers of the General Court, has enabled that body ' to name and settle
annually or provide by fixed laws for the naming & settling
all civil officers within the State ; such officers excepted,
the election and appointment of whom are, hereafter, in
this form of government otherwise provided for. (See
Constitution, p. 43.)

" When we turn to the power of appointment by the governor & council (p. 51) we find that 'all judicial officers, the attorney-general, solicitors, all sheriffs, registers of probate, & all officers of the navy, & all general & field officers of the militia, shall be appointed by the governor & council,' clearly comprehending all the officers of the government except town officers, who are, therefore, the civil officers whose appointment is left to be provided for by the Legislature. Hence it is evident that towns are not, strictly speaking, corporations; but mere civil divisions of the territory of the State, for the purpose of governing themselves to a certain extent; & aiding in the government, & administration of the laws of the State — and again, though in some respects, they are corporations; yet they have not strictly speaking, perpetual succession; or, in other words, their perpetuity does not depend on any acts of their own, as electing their successors, or officers, & the like; they can neither make common nor disfranchise any member of their own body; but any person, coming to reside within their respective limits becomes, of course, a member of the corporation to every intent for which they are such; in other words, certain privileges are, by the charters of the respective towns, & by the laws of the State, granted to the persons who may come to reside on particular portions of the territory of the State; & these privileges happen in some respects, but in very few, to be such, as are incident to corporations generally; & yet, in every other respect, they are mere civil divisions of the State; &, perhaps, necessarily, liable to division, or other variations by the laws of the State, as will best answer the purposes for which they were made; & indeed are made subject to those things by their own consent in the adoption of the Constitution — all these privileges are given & regulated by statute, & are not to be regarded as grants; but as mere municipal regulations to be varied at the discretion of the Legislature, not interfering with any constitutional principles.

"The very terms of the charters of N. H. imply this, &

no more ; ' and the same be, & is hereby incorporated in a township by the name of —— & the inhabitants that do or shall hereafter inhabit the said township, are hereby declared to be enfranchised with & entitled to all & every the privileges & immunities that other towns, within our province, *by law*, exercise & enjoy.' The first essential ingredient in a corporation is ' to have perpetual succession — this is the very end of its incorporation ; for there cannot be a succession, forever, without an incorporation ; & therefore, all aggregate corporations have a power, necessarily implied, to elect members in the room of such as go off.' (1 Bla. Comm. 502.)

" Towns having no such power, are not therefore, in any strict sense corporations. (1 Roll. Abr. 514, 4th Com., F 10.)

" Again, if it were otherwise ; if they were in the strictest sense corporations ; yet, dividing the town into two, might be considered only as creating a new corporation, out of the members of an old one ; & perhaps, even then the inhabitants would not be bound to accept the privilege granted by the act making the division ; but might, if they preferred it, remain as before — certainly they might do so if they are to be regarded as corporations in these respects — and it is believed that no Legislature has ever interfered in any case of the kind, except at the request of those who were supposed to be benefitted by the alteration ; or who were to compose the new corporation. It may now be asked, in what part of the Constitution is the General Court empowered to interfere with corporations at that time existing ; or to provide for the appointment of their members or officers. The subject is nowhere mentioned ; & it is certain that the idea of confering such power never entered into the minds of the framers of that instrument. Will any one then have the boldness to say that they conferred powers, which they did not intend to confer ; & that, in relation to a subject which they have not even mentioned ; & all this in an instrument in which they were professedly defining & bestowing the powers of the respective branches of the government; & using every exertion & expression to make & keep each of them distinct.

"It is recollected that in one article of the Constitution it is expressly made 'the duty of the Legislature and magistrates, in all future periods of the government, to cherish the interests of literature & the sciences & all seminaries & public schools; to encourage public and private institutions, by reward and immunities, for the promotion of agriculture, arts, sciences, commerce, trades, manufactures, & natural history of the country,' &c.

"This seems mostly to relate to institutions then in existence, & is so far from giving countenance to rude attempts, like the present, to take away the rights, property, & privileges of those institutions, & confer them on others for personal & party purposes, that it indeed holds a very different language. It is observable that it confers the same duties on magistrates as on legislators; and it is merely to foster & encourage, & not to interfere with their internal concerns; or to vary without their consent the structure of their policy or government.

"In all the authorities which are to be found on this subject, there is not a solitary instance to be found of any interference by the government, which can, at all compare with the present attempt, either in point of principle or extent, where the government has without the consent of the corporation endeavored to change the principles, or take away the property or privileges of an institution of this kind — and if there were precedents of this kind, by the omnipotent Parliament of G. Britain, would it follow that the general court of N. H. with its derivative powers limited & restricted by the terms of the Constitution, could do the same thing?

"It seems to be a point, perfectly agreed & settled in all authorities, that the grantees in any charter of incorporation, cannot be compelled to become a corporation without their own consent — 1 Salk. 168 is in point.   S. Eyre, J., held ' that the corporation would not be divested of former rights ; but by surrender or forfeiture — G. Eyre & Holt, J., that the king cannot resume an interest he has already granted, unless the grantee concur — but in this case the corporation had concurred by accepting a new charter,' in other words, by acting under it — and accordingly in all the pleadings in cases of *quo warranto*, where the members are officers of corporations, undertake to justify acting as such under a charter, the pleadings always allege an acceptance thereof by the grantees — In Rex *v.* Richardson, 1 Bur. 517 ; King *v.* ——, 3 D Term Rep. 199.

" If therefore individuals cannot be compelled to take on themselves corporation powers, so neither can an existing corporation be compelled to accept any additional grant of powers or privileges ; nor can it be compelled for the same reason to submit to any restriction which may be imposed. The King & Queen *v.* Larwoad, 1 Salk. 168, is directly in point.

" The foregoing remarks & references were made nearly a year ago ; and are now deemed of no importance except for the purpose of facilitating a recurrence to authorities — since that time the case of Fletcher *v.* Peck, in 6th of Cranch ; & New Jersey *v.* Wilson, in 7th of Cranch, have been consulted, and are deemed to be decisions in point. — 16th May, 1817.

" Beside the authorities referred to —

" Colchester *v.* Seaber, 3d Bur. 1866 ;

" Milton *v.* Spateman, 1 Wm. Saund. 342 ;

" Lutterell's Case, 4 Co. 87, 2d vol. of octave edition, 86.

" 4 Com. Title Franchise (F. 30), *et seq.*, page 267 ;

" Baggs' Case XI. Co. 99, vol. 6, same edition 93, may be consulted with advantage.''

CHAPTER VI. — Continued.

Harvard University was chartered in 1636. The act of 1642 made the governor, deputy-governor, president of the college, magistrates, teaching elders, etc., members of the Board of Overseers. When the Constitution of the State was formed, the University was put under the protection of the State by virtue of certain provisions incorporated therein; and the grant of 1636 was "ratified and confirmed" thereby, with the proviso "that nothing herein shall be construed to prevent the Legislature of this Commonwealth from making such alterations in the government of the said University as shall be conducive to its advantage, and the interest of the republic of letters, in as full a manner as might have been done by the Legislature of the late Province of the Massachusetts Bay."

Judge Parsons became a Fellow of Harvard in 1806. Soon after, he framed a law making the alterations in the charter contemplated by the eminent jurist who penned the proviso. The bill passed, March 6, 1810; was formally accepted by the corporation, March 16, 1810, and by the Board of Overseers, April 12, 1810. This act was repealed, and the old board restored, by the act of February 29, 1812. In 1814, this repealing act was repealed, and the act of 1810 revived, with the proviso that the Senate should be added to the thirty elective members for which the act provided.

From the time he became a Fellow, till shortly before his death, Parsons was the controlling spirit; and during the troubles which followed the passage of the act of 1810, argued the cause of the University.

The counsel for the trustees in the Dartmouth College case were as familiar with the history of the troubles at Harvard, and the argument of Parsons, as Story.

We copy from the identical minutes of Marsh, and the dim, time-stained argument of Parsons, used by Judge Smith and his eminent associates in preparing their arguments in Judge Woodward's case.

The argument of Parsons " as to visitors of Harvard College," according to the filing of Judge Smith, is as follows : —

" 1. The office of Visitor.

" 2. His power & duties.

" 3. Who is the visitor of Harvard College?

" 4. The extent of the power reserved to the Legislature in the Constitution of the Commonwealth to alter the Gov't of the College in as full a manner as it could have been altered by the Legislature of the Province.

" 1. The office of Visitor is at common law arising from the lawful endowment of any charity either by the Sovereign or any private person.

" If a private person endow a charity it is inherent to his right of property to determine to what uses and in what manner the charity may be applied, and for these purposes provision may be made by his own statutes which are considered as the foundation of the endowment. He may appoint a Visitor to see that these statutes are duly executed. If the founder do not appoint a Visitor he and his heirs are of course Visitors. When the founder has made the endowment of his charity and appointed a Visitor he after that ceases to have any control over it his property having vested in the grantees, subject to the visitation of the Visitor whom he has designated & who is substituted in the room of the founder. He can therefore provide no new statutes altering the former uses of his donation, unless he has reserved such power to himself in his original foundation, nor can he revoke the visitatorial power which he has delegated; as it may affect the interest which is vested in the grantees. But the founder not having appointed a Visitor may with the assent of the grantees make what alterations may be thought proper in the appropriation of his own donation, but not in donations made to the same charity by other persons who have expressly limited their uses and alterations may also be made in the power of visitation by authority of the Legislature and by consent of the grantees and the visitor who so far stands in the place of the founder.

"2. The power and duties of the visitor are incident to him at common law, subject to the restrictions and qualifications pointed out by the statutes of the founder. It pertains to the office of visitor to see that the statutes of the founder are executed and also to exercise such powers as result from his will. If the founder instead of framing particular statutes for the management of his donation should authorize the corporation in whom the same is vested to make by laws for carrying into effect and regulating the charity with the assent of the visitor then such by laws have the force of the statutes made by the founder.

"3. The visitor of H. College. No visitor of Harvard College can be considered as existing until a donation was made by some person or public body for the purpose of founding the College and such donation cannot be made till there are proper persons to take the same. The General Court appropriated property for the purpose of founding a College; but did not grant the same to any persons whatever the property remaining the property of the colony and being managed by a Committee appointed by the General Court.

"This Committee being found an inconvenient body the Court give the trust to the Governor, Deputy Governor and magistrates & the teaching elders of the six neighbouring towns by the name of overseers, with power to manage the funds subject to the will of the donors.   In the act appointing the overseers it is ordained that the greater number present at any meeting the number necessary to constitute a meeting not being prescribed may make & establish any orders, statutes & constitutions subject however to an appeal to the whole body of overseers, who if they refuse to sustain such appeal or act thereon shall stand accountable to the next General Court.

"Soon after the Creation of the overseers on application of Mr. H. Dunster the President of the College the General Court were induced to take measures for founding a College by constituting a Corporation in whom was invested the property belonging to the College with power to manage the same agreeably to the will of the donors and for that purpose to make orders and by laws, but which were of no force until allowed by the overseers.   The last provision being supposed to be impracticable in the Government of the College the Corporation did not exercise their powers until the granting an additional Charter in 1657 (?) after this the College appears to be completely founded having a corporation in whom the funds vested with a power to make orders and by laws, so that the will of the donor was observed and subject to the control of the overseers, as a board of Visitors, who might disallow the orders and by laws made by the corporation.   The General Court of the Colony therefore were the founder of the College and instead of forming particular statutes for the college which they founded they constituted a Corporation with power to make orders and by laws for the government of the College compatible with the will of any donor & subject to the disallowance of the overseers.   And the doings of a meeting of the overseers called by notice to those members living in the six neighbouring towns are by the last Charter or appendix of 1657 finally valid without any ultimate Control being reserved to the General Court.

" The Governors or Overseers appointed to any Charitable institution by the founder are in fact the visitors thereof although they may not be designated by the name of Visitors. The College as observed now appears to be regularly founded having a Corporation to take and manage the property, subject to visitors specially appointed by the founder, who has parted not only with his property but with all control over it. What control however the General Court of the old Colony of Massachusetts Bay might in fact claim or exercise either over the funds, which they had given away or the visitatorial power which they had parted with it is not now necessary to inquire. It is sufficient to say that this foundation with this visitatorial power existed so long as that General Court — that the Court never did in fact repeal or annul this foundation or revoke the power of visitation constituted as here mentioned. The occasional interference of the Colonal General Court, after the foundation was practised either with the assent of the College or is to be considered as an assumption of power not belonging to it for in fact that Court claimed to exercise all the powers of Gov't Legislature Executive and judicial.

" Upon the repeal of the old Colony Charter & the granting of the Provincial Charter the Governor Deputy Gov. & magistrates were succeeded by the Gov'r Lieut Govr and Council as their successors in office and the power of Visitation remained in the same body until new successors were appointed by the Constitution notwithstanding several attempts to give the college a new foundation were made by the interests of its friends with the concurrence of the College.

" 4. What power the Legislature of the Province had to alter the Govt of the College requires now to be considered. The Charter that gave existence to the Provincial Legislature by confirming the property of the College necessarily

confirmed the College and confirmed the property in the
College by such tenure & on such conditions as those by
which it was before holden, one of which was to be subject
to a controul in the disposition of that property by a body
of visitors and their successors appointed by the founder.
If the Legislature had any authority to alter the Gov't of
the College without the consent of the visitors and corporation it must be either by virtue of some visitatorial power
remaining in it or by some judicial act to be passed by it or
by its Legislative authority. As to its having visitatorial
power remaining, there is no color for it, as the founder
reserved none to himself — as to a 'Judicial act the Provincial Legislature were not competent to pass any no
judicial power having been granted in the Charter. If,
therefore, the Legislature could alter the Gov't of the College it must be by virtue of its Legislative authority. The
Legislative power of every State must be such as it can lawfully exercise according to its constitution not a mere arbitrary or despotic will which may prevail because power is
not synonymous with right.

"It will not be pretended that the Legislature could divest
the Corporation of the property given it by the founder and
other donors, nor will it be contended that the Legislature
by any lawful act could alter the uses for which the property was so given or by repealing the Charter of incorporation could defeat all those donations and render them void
or could alter the constitution of the Corporation by adding
to its members or changeing its powers ; for if this were
admitted they might virtually repeal the Charter of incorporation which vests the property and the powers therein
designated in the corporation and their successors the law of
succession being established in the Charter.

"It remains to consider whether without consent the
Legislature could rightfully change the visitors of the
College and appoint new visitors not appointed by the

founder. The founder had the same power at law to appoint visitors of his Charity that he had to make the donation and prescribe the use, and the visitors have in them a vested right of visitation of which they cannot be deprived without their consent any more than of any other vested right. The Corporation also have an interest in the exercise of the right because by the exercise of it can the powers of the corporation alone be controlled. And it may be supposed that a corporation might be willing to take the management of a Charity subject to a particular visitation which they might refuse under another visitation as well as that donors might be induced from confidence in the existing visitatorial power to make donations which otherwise they might decline. The visitatorial power is therefore so connected with the Charity of its management that it seems impossible that the Legislature can have a power over the former without having it over the latter which is not contended. But if the visitors and Corporation are disposed to consent to a substitution of other persons as visitors yet it cannot be done unless authorized by the Legislature but being so authorized it may lawfully be done because it is done by the consent of all the parties interested. If however the doctrine should be admitted that the Provincial Legislature had the singular power of altering the Government of the College without consent yet if instead of exercising that power they had in fact introduced into the visitation new visitors with the consent of the former visitors and the Corporation it is extremely difficult to conceive by what legitimate authority the Legislature could afterwards deprive those new Visitors of the rights of Visitation thus lawfully vested in them. To admit this power of deprivation thus exercised would be giving to the Provincial Legislature greater power than they would have possessed if they had been founders of College & at the foundation had specially appointed as Visitors the persons thus deprived. Admitting therefore the power reserved to the Legislature of making such alteration in the Government of

the College as could have been made by the Legislature of
the late Province of Massachusetts Bay yet under this admission no alteration could be made in the Government but
with consent of the overseers & Corporation and but for
the reservation. in the proviso no alteration could ever be
made even with consent as it would have been deemed
repugnant to the Constitution which established absolutely
the Government of the College."

Two things are especially noticeable in this argument of
Parsons: From his intimate acquaintance with Dane, the
history of the times, and the great men who participated in
the Federal Convention, no man in Massachusetts was more
capable of comprehending the meaning of the obligation
clause than he; yet he passed it by in this argument as if the
thought never occurred to him that it had any application.
The other is, that, independent of the proviso, the charter
could not be altered by the Legislature, even with the consent of the overseers and corporation.

The clergymen of the " standing order," with a portion
of the old trustees and the faculty, swarmed from their General Association into the Exeter court-room. The argument
lasted two days: Mason speaking two and Smith four hours
for the trustees; Sullivan and Bartlett occupied three hours
the next day, in reply; Webster occupied less than two
hours in closing the case for the trustees. None of these
were taken down in short-hand, but, as afterwards written
out from the copious minutes and notes of counsel, or otherwise, and in some instances revised, were, except Webster's,
reported by Judge Farrar. They occupy about one hundred and eighty pages in Farrar's report, — of which forty-
three pages were assigned to Mason, who was always
comparatively brief; fifty-six pages to Smith, thirty-four
pages to Sullivan, and forty-six pages to Bartlett.

Probably in consequence of this revision, arguments on
one side were sometimes omitted, while the replies were
given. Judge Smith, in a memorandum made February

28, 1824, says that he destroyed on that day, "the minutes prepared for & used in argument at Haverhill, May, 1817, and at Exeter, September, 1817, in addition to those in this file."

"In preparing argument for T. Farrar's Vol., J. S. [Judge Smith] freely used *all his minutes* and recollection — substance same, tho' method often changed — some things omitted, &c."

In his letter to Farrar, of May 18, 1819, Webster says: "As to Ichabod's [Bartlett's] argument, I am decidedly of opinion that I would *not* publish any abuse of the Trustees, or of any of the counsel. If he has not decency enough to leave such slang out, I would not publish his argument, — and if necessary, I would state the reason in a note. As to mere *nonsense & stuff*, I w'd publish it; but nothing in any degree personal or injurious to counsel or parties. You must show the creature to Mr. Mason — & you & he must persuade Bartlett to leave out what is objectionable. He ought to see the propriety of following Mr. Sullivan's example in that respect.

"It would of course be very desirable to have his argument printed, & I think a little soft persuasion will bring him to have it put right. Ch. Jus. Richardson, I should think, would not wish that *slang* should appear as the argument in his court.

"50 to 60 pages; Good Heavens! And *all* slang. Do get it abridged.   D. W."

Those who have read the letters of Thompson to Adams, and Dunham and Wheelock to Webster, and understood the peculiar relations which subsisted between Wheelock and Webster in 1815, can hardly fail to perceive to what remarks "personal or injurious to counsel" Mr. Webster referred.

Farrar's report probably shows, fairly enough, the general course of the arguments. We have, besides, the short notes of all the arguments, as taken down by Mr. Webster with his own hand in the Exeter court-room, which lie before us as we write. No summary would do them justice, but an outline of them may be useful.

Mason's points, as stated by himself, were : "That these acts are not obligatory ; 1. Because they are not within the general scope of legislative power ; 2. Because they violate certain provisions of the Constitution of this State restraining the legislative power ; 3. Because they violate the Constitution of the United States." In Farrar's report, Mason devotes twenty-three pages to his first point, eight to the second, and six to the third.

1. He urged that "the only division of corporations material to the present enquiry, is that of civil and eleemosynary ;" that the trustees constituted an eleemosynary corporation ; that towns were civil " corporations of a peculiar kind ;" that the Legislature cannot "rightfully take from any such corporation its property, and transfer it to another ;" that " something similar to these are incorporated cities." " But where there is a special grant of peculiar privileges, the legislative power to new model or control them, if admitted at all, must be with great limitation. The Legislature cannot abolish such corporations, or do anything equivalent to it. As far as the privileges are peculiar, and such as cannot be affected by a general law, applicable to all, it is not easy to see on what principles they can be essentially changed or altered by a special act of the Legislature ;" that the College " is clearly an eleemosynary corporation, and of consequence, a private corporation."

He conceded "that the British Parliament can, as it is held, abolish corporations. So it can pass acts of attainder, and of pains and penalties. But neither can be done by virtue of the ordinary and legitimate legislative power which belongs to our Legislature. According to the theory of the British government, the Parliament is omnipotent. 'A corporation may be dissolved by act of Parliament, which is boundless in its operations.' "

" Will it now be asserted that the British Parliament or king, or both united, were competent to abolish or new model the colonial charters? If it could be done by legislative power alone, they might, for they possessed the whole legislative power over that subject-matter." " The Parliament of Great Britain had no rightful power whatever over this corporation. The Legislature of this State succeeded to all the power which the king, who granted the charter, had, and to no more."

" In England the creating of corporations appertains to the king, and he has all the legitimate power that exists for dissolving them, except what is vested in the judicial courts."

" But the king cannot abolish a corporation, or give it a new organization, or alter any of its powers or privileges, without its consent."

" As successors to the king, then, the Legislature have no power to pass the acts in question, and it may be safely asserted that before the change in the form of government, the plaintiffs could not have been rightfully deprived of their property or privileges, without a trial in due course of law."

" It is of no consequence, as it respects the right, whether the privileges granted to the plaintiffs by their charter are valuable, in a pecuniary point of view, or otherwise." He then relies upon the opinion in Calder v. Bull, 3 Dall. 383, that " the nature and ends of legislative power will limit the exercise of it."

2. That these acts were prohibited by Art. XV., the *per legem terrae* clause, Art. XXIII., which prohibits the passage of "retrospective laws," and Art. XXXVII. of the Bill of Rights of New Hampshire, which declares that the three essential powers of government ought to be kept separate.

3. That the grant was " a contract " under the clause in the Federal Constitution, and not a law. That " there can be no doubt that there were competent parties to the con-

tract, — the king, of one side, and the trustees named in the charter, of the other."

Judge Smith urged that the change of name was a violation of " chartered rights." That " here, too, the change of name seems to indicate a change in the nature of the body ; for, upon the principles of the common law, an university on the model of those at Oxford and Cambridge is a civil, while a college is an eleemosynary corporation." He enforced the same views as Mason, and commented at length upon Phillips v. Bury, and other cases relied upon in the opinion of Judge Story. He said, " It is the endowment which confers the right of visitation ; " and adds, " Let us now examine the constitution of Dartmouth College. Its original funds arose altogether from the donations of individuals, principally obtained through the agency of Dr. Wheelock. In no sense and in no way can it be said that they originated with the king or the public. Not a cent of money or an acre of land was given by the Province or any public body till after the college went into operation. * * * Though the State have given lands, they were not the real founders. They were not the *first* benefactors, who, and who only, are considered as founders. * * *

" Do the defendants' counsel contend that if a town should acquire by gift, or otherwise, a fund for the support of a school for the inhabitants of such town, that the Legislature could constitutionally annex another town, giving to all the inhabitants of the new corporation equal right to participate in this fund? * * * But still Parliament may pass many acts which our Legislature are prohibited from passing. * * *

" It is in the exercise of the same authority that Parliament can dissolve all corporations. * * *

" Here seems to be everything requisite to form a compact. The king is one party ; the donors in the first instance, and then the trustees as their *acknowledged substitutes* or representatives, are the other party. * * * It is too late for

the king to quarrel with the terms ; he never did.   *   *   *
The truth is, the trustees, as a body politic, are the legal
and equitable owners of the property and of the franchises
conferred by the charter.''

Sullivan, for the State, urged that this was '' a public
corporation ; '' that the test as to whether it was public or
private was not whether it was endowed by the bounty of
the government, or that of an individual, but, as was said
by Lord Hardwicke, '' the *extensiveness* of the objects to be
benefitted ; '' that the charter answered the '' questions,''
'' For whose benefit was this corporation erected? — for the
benefit of the persons composing it, or for that of the public ? '' by setting forth that it was '' *for the benefit of said
province;* '' that '' it appears from the charter that the corporation of Dartmouth College was established for the express, the avowed purpose of promoting the welfare of a
whole province. It was an instrument formed to attain
objects in which no individual had a particular interest, but
in which the community had a deep one. It was vested with
power to hold property in trust for the public, but it could
hold none for the use of the corporators. It was clothed
with various powers, capacities and franchises, all of which
were to be exercised for the benefit of the public, but not
one of them for the advantage of its own members, or of
any individuals whatever. In short, it was created, it
existed, only for public purposes.   *   *   *   If this corporation was a private one, I shall contend that the Legislature had a right to alter its charter, so far as the public
good required.   *   *   *

'' Suppose the lands of a private corporation are wanted
for a fortification or an arsenal ; may they not be taken?
Suppose they are wanted for a highway, or for any important public purpose ; may they not be taken?   *   *   *
Does the law guard the property of corporations with more
vigilance than that of individuals? Are the rights of the
former more sacred than those of the latter?   *   *   *

" It is alleged that these acts violate the Constitution of the United States. When a charter of incorporation is granted, there is always, it is said, an implied contract, on the part of the government, that the charter shall not be altered without the consent of the corporation.   *   *   *

" If a charter of incorporation be a contract, it certainly is not such a contract as comes within the spirit and meaning of that article in the constitution.   *   *   *   The Supreme Court in Massachusetts have said this was the design of the provision : ' The article respecting the obligation of contracts, as we all know, was provided against paper money installment laws,' etc.   *   *   *   It is remarked by Judge Johnson, in the case of Fletcher v. Peck, that the State legislatures pass laws impairing the obligation of contracts, yet that these laws appear to be within the most correct limits of legislative powers, and certainly could not have been intended to be affected by this constitutional provision.   *   *   *

" It has been asserted that Dr. Wheelock was the founder, but the assertion is supported by no evidence.   *   *   * The charter, probably in consequence of these exertions, calls him the founder. But this does not make him so. The first gift of the revenues is the foundation, and he who gives them is in law the founder. Many individuals made donations ; but who made the first? It does not appear. I am instructed to say that Dr. Wheelock made very liberal donations to Moor's Charity-School, an institution in the neighborhood of the college, though entirely distinct from it, but that he made none to the college itself.   *   *   *   In no part of the charter is it mentioned that he made any donation to the college. If he did, there is no evidence of the fact. It does not appear, then, that he was the founder, or that he had power to transfer the right of visitation to the trustees.   *   *   *

" If Dr. Wheelock was the founder and visitor of the college, he did not transfer to the trustees the right of visitation. There are no words in the charter making them visitors. * * *

" The trustees allege that the General Court attempted to compel them to act under an amended charter, and that they had no power to do it. Many cases have been cited on this point, but they only show that the king cannot compel corporations to accept or act under amended charters, not that Parliament cannot compel them. The authority of Parliament, as every one knows, is much more extensive than that of the king. The king cannot grant to a corporation exclusive privileges; Parliament may. The king cannot dissolve a corporation; Parliament possesses the power. Corporations in this State have frequently been compelled to act under amended charters. * * *

" Suppose the trustees had been guilty of great abuses of their trust, an information had been filed, and their charter had been declared forfeited. What would have been the consequences? Would the trustees have lost any thing? Not a cent. The public, and not the trustees, would have been the sufferers. * * *

" In the first place, we are told that the corporation is placed beyond the control of the Legislature. They have no authority to amend its charter; to touch its property; to take from it a single right or privilege; or to limit the exercise of any one of its powers. In the next place, we are told that the trustees are visitors of the college and of the application of its funds. This places them beyond the control of every court of law, let them do what they will with the property given to the institution. ' The sentence of a visitor, on subjects within his jurisdiction, is final and conclusive, and the king's courts cannot in any form of proceeding review the sentence.' (2 Kyd on Corp.) * * *

" It is within the jurisdiction of a visitor, it is his duty, to see that the funds given to the institution of which he is a visitor are properly applied; and when he decides, his sentence is conclusive on all courts. Suppose the trustees should appropriate the funds of the college to their own use. If they are visitors as to the application of the funds, as is contended, no court of law can make them accountable. A visitor is himself subject to no visitation, to no control. Where is the man, though possessed of the most charitable and benevolent feelings, that would give to a corporation raised so far above all responsibility? Such a corporation is a monster, that would devour all charities! The very sight of such a monster, placed beyond all legislative, all judicial control, like the terrific head of Medusa, would convert even Charity herself into stone! *   *   * That a corporation, created for the sole purpose of promoting the public interest, may be altered in such a manner as the public interest requires, is a principle as obvious to common sense as any that can be imagined."

Bartlett states the position of Mason and Smith to be, —

" 1. That the legislative acts in question are contrary to the principles of natural justice.

" 2. That corporations of this nature are independent of legislative control.

" 3. That the provisions of these acts violate the constitutions of New Hampshire and the United States."

He then argues that the first point is too indefinite ; that no court is warranted in setting aside any law because the judges may think it is contrary to natural justice ; that the provision abolishing the oath of allegiance to the king, or the section guaranteeing freedom of religious opinion, is not in violation of natural justice ; that all the authorities show that changing the name changes none of the rights, duties, powers, or privileges of the corporation ; that the State had not confiscated corporate property, but renovated the corporation, and added new members, according to the decision in King v. Pasmore, 3 Term Rep. 244 ; that Ashhurst, J., was right when he said in that case, " As to there being here a dissent of a majority of the old members, I lay no stress upon it." *   *   *

"Here the members of the old corporation have no injury or injustice to complain of, for they are all included in the new charter of incorporation, and if any of them do not become members of the new corporation, but refuse to accept, it is their own fault;" that Philips v. Bury, 4 Mod. Rep. 117, showed that "the universities in England, and institutions of a similar nature in this country," were public corporations; that the English doctrine that corporations could be dissolved by act of Parliament "had long been exercised, in practice," in Great Britain and the colonies; — citing the Land Bank and South Sea schemes; the statute declaring all corporations and licenses granted by Henry VI. void; the abolition of monopolies by Parliament; the frequent changes in the admission-fee of trading companies, in the number of their members, and their qualifications; the radical changes in the act of 5 Geo. III. in the African corporation, created by the act of 23 Geo. II.; the case of Manchester College, in which Parliament, by act of 2 Geo. II., annulled the powers of a special visitor and vested them in the crown; the abrogation of the oaths of allegiance and supremacy by the act of 1 Wm. & Mary, which provided for vacating the office of head patron in St. John's College if the incumbents refused to take the new oath.

He also referred to the act passed by Connecticut in 1723, enlarging the number of trustees of Yale College, fixing a quorum, creating new officers, and establishing other regulations without petition or consent of the corporation; to the act of Massachusetts in 1673, adding to the members of the corporation of Harvard College, "against the will of the corporation;" and to the repeal of the provision in the charter of Trinity Church, in regard to "induction," by the State of New York, by the act of 1784.

He concluded this branch of his argument with offering "to abandon the defence when one unequivocal authority shall be produced by the plaintiffs to show that the exercise of such power was ever judged illegal.   *   *   *

"But the plaintiffs have insisted that 'it is a *private eleemosynary* corporation;' and that statement is attempted to be supported, in the first place, by confounding this institution with 'Moor's Indian Charity-School,' which Dr. E. Wheelock claimed as his, and over which no other jurisdiction has been exercised but at his request. Now, no fact on record is more clearly stated than that this institution and Moor's Indian Charity-School were entirely distinct and independent of each other in their origin and establishment; were ever governed separately, without the least connection, until the school solicited the interference of the legislature and college. Their funds and property are now distinct and separate. For proof of this, we need no more time than is necessary to read the record of a vote passed by the plaintiffs, May 7, 1789, as follows: 'Representations having been made to this board, that apprehensions have arisen in the minds of some persons, that moneys collected in Great Britain by the Rev. Messrs. Whitaker and Occom, for the use of Moor's Charity-School, under the direction of Rev. Dr. Wheelock, have been applied by this board to the use and benefit of Dartmouth College;—*Resolved*, that this board have never had any control or direction of said moneys, nor have they to their knowledge, at any time received or applied any sum or sums thereof to the use and benefit of said college,' etc. A letter of instruction to Dr. Wheelock from the honorable board of trust of that school in England, April 25, 1771, states that 'the corporation of Dartmouth College in its nature and designs differs from the establishment of their school,' and forbids Dr. Wheelock from subjecting the school or its funds to the disposition of that institution."

He then replied at length to the argument that the acts in question were prohibited by the State Constitution, urging that the provisions referred to were but a reënactment of the great charter, which had not been invaded in the cases cited.

" But at last it is insisted that these are ' *laws impairing the obligation of contracts.*' Finding that the straws they have seized upon in the struggle cannot support their sinking claim, with the eagerness of desperation, they grasp at this shadow of a pretence.   *   *   * If any interpretation of that clause can be made applicable to the present case, all the benefits surely should be awarded to the plaintiffs' counsel as the first discoverers.   Most unquestionably by the survivors of the Convention who framed that instrument, such an idea would now be deemed original.   *   *   *

" In a case much stronger than the present, it was considered by the counsel as well as the court (Brown *v.* Bank, 8 Mass. 448) that 'the *notion* of a contract between the government and corporation was *too fanciful* to need any observation.   *   *   * That scholastic subtlety and ingenuity by which the plaintiffs would raise a contract in this transaction, would prove quite too much for their purpose, for in some sense even government itself is a contract, and by the same reasoning every act and every law must be considered in the nature of a *contract*, until the Legislature would find themselves in such a labyrinth of contracts, with the United States Constitution over their heads, that not a subject would be left within their jurisdiction.   *   *   *

" The plaintiffs, however, say, an express contract exists here, that they, and they alone, shall be trustees of this institution.   *   *   * By a reference to the charter it will appear that the *corporation* was created independent of the trustees ; and that they were afterwards appointed in a different clause of the charter.   *   *   *

" The provision in the charter with regard to the number, was intended as a regulation to limit the board in their appointments, and not with a view to control the Legislature.   *   *   * Who are the parties to all these contracts?   Can there be any other, either express or implied,

than the founder, the *power creating* the corporation and
those for whose benefit it is established?   As a public institution, we believe the *crown* has been shown to be the
founder.   Or even as an eleemosynary corporation, that the
rights of foundation rest in the crown, from the public
endowments.   The crown also was the *power* that created it.
The State, since the Revolution, succeeds to the rights of the
crown.   (Terrett *v.* Taylor, 9 Cranch, 50.) "

The counsel all agreed that if proceedings could be successfully instituted in the name of the State for a forfeiture,
the College funds would go back to the donors or their
heirs; and that no court of chancery existed to correct
abuses, unless the Legislature had such powers, which the
counsel for the plaintiffs denied.

More than three hundred references were made by the
various counsel, to decided cases, statutes, and standard
works of authority.

Webster was not always equally great and impressive.
Sometimes he was comparatively dry, heavy, and uninterest-
ing.   A great subject and a great occasion would always
bring out his cold, unimpassioned logic.   But when hard
pressed, or weighted down with responsibilities, as he was in
this case, he apparently became charged with volcanic fire.
His argument at Exeter was never reported; but tradition,
public prints, and old letters point to but one conclusion.   If
not the greatest, it was one of the most brilliant efforts of
his life, and produced a most extraordinary effect.   He
closed with the " Cæsar in the senate-house " peroration,
which was so much admired by Professor Goodrich and
others when he recited it at Washington (1 Life of Webster, 170), and the court adjourned in tears.

CHAPTER VI. — CONTINUED.

THE counsel for the State were overmatched; but they were able men, and, in comparison with what in other hands afterwards befell their cause in Washington, handled it with consummate skill. The counsel for the trustees differed in their views, as will hereafter appear, upon a single point, which was understood by the opposing counsel and the court to have been waived or abandoned. Upon the other points they were a unit in argument, whatever their private convictions might have been. Their strategic plan was to carry the State court with them, if possible; and failing in that, to break the force of an adverse decision by dividing the court. To accomplish this they put forth all their powers, but failed.

The judges continued the cause, for advisement, till the November term, at Plymouth, 1817. On November 6, 1817, the chief justice read the unanimous opinion of the court, adverse to the trustees, which occupies nearly thirty pages in Farrar's report. Its pith is stated in the head-notes in 1 N. H. 111, which were undoubtedly prepared by the chief justice : —

" 1. The corporation of *Dartmouth College* is a public corporation.

" 2. An act of the Legislature, adding new members to such a corporation, without the consent of the old corporation, is not repugnant to the Constitution of the State.

" 3. The charter of the king, creating the corporation of *Dartmouth College*, is not a contract within the meaning of that clause in the Constitution of the *United States* which prohibits States from passing laws impairing the obligation of contracts.''

(187)

The court say: "This cause has been argued on both sides with uncommon learning and ability, and we have witnessed with pleasure and with pride a display of talents and eloquence, upon this occasion, in the highest degree honorable to the profession of the law in this State. If the counsel of the plaintiffs have failed to convince us that the action can be maintained, it has not been owing to any want of diligence in research, or ingenuity in reasoning, but to a want of solid and substantial grounds on which to rest their arguments."

The court define at length the characteristics of private and public corporations. They do not assume, as has so often erroneously been said, but decide, that this was a public corporation, and give the reasons therefor. They say: ' Public corporations are those which are created for public purposes, and whose property is devoted to the objects for which they are created. The corporators have no private beneficial interest, either in their franchises or their property. The only private right which individuals can have in them, is the right of being and of acting as members. * * *

"A corporation, all of whose franchises are exercised for public purposes, is a public corporation. * * * Because, in both cases, all the property and franchises of the corporations would in fact be public property. A gift to a corporation created for public purposes is in reality a gift to the public. * * * Whether an incorporated college, founded and endowed by an individual who had reserved to himself a control over its affairs as a private visitor, must be viewed as a public or as a private corporation, it is not necessary now to decide, because it does not appear that Dartmouth College was subject to any private visitation whatever."

After quoting at length from the charter, the court say: " Such are the objects and such the nature of this corporation, appearing upon the face of the charter. It was created for the purpose of holding and managing property for the use of the *college*, and the *college* was founded for the purpose of ' spreading the knowledge of the Great Redeemer ' among the savages, and of furnishing ' the best means of education ' to the province of *New Hampshire*. These great purposes are surely, if any thing can be, matters of public concern. Who has any private interest either in the objects or property of this institution ! The trustees themselves have no greater interest in the spreading of Christian knowledge among the Indians, and in providing the best means of education, than any other individuals in the community. Nor have they any private interest in the property of this institution ; nothing that can be sold or transferred, that can descend to their heirs, or can be assets in the hands of their administrators. If all the property of the institution were destroyed, the loss would be exclusively public, and no private loss to them. So entirely free are they from any private interest, in this respect, that they are competent witnesses in causes where the corporation is a party, and the property of the corporation in contest. * * * They [the trustees] have no private right in the institution, except the right of office, — right of being trustees and of acting as such. It therefore seems to us that if such a corporation is not to be considered as a public corporation, it would be difficult to find one that could be so considered. * * * All private rights in this institution must belong either to those who founded or whose bounty has endowed it ; to the officers and students of the college, or to the trustees. As to those who founded or who have endowed it, no person of this description who claims any private right has been pointed out or is known to us. It is not understood that any person claims to be visitor to this college. An absolute donation of land or money to an institution of this kind creates no private right in it. Besides, if the private rights of founders or donors have been infringed by these acts, it is their business to vindicate their own rights. It is no concern of these plaintiffs. When founders and donors complain, it will be our duty to hear and decide ; but we cannot adjudicate upon their rights till they come judicially before us.   *   *   *

" But it is said that the charter of 1769 is a contract, the validity of which is impaired by these acts in violation of that clause in the tenth section of the first article of the Constitution of the United States, which declares that ' no State shall pass any law impairing the obligation of contracts.' It has probably never yet been decided that a charter of this kind is a contract within the meaning of the Constitution of the United States. None of the cases cited were like the present.   *   *   *   This clause in the Constitution of the United States was obviously intended to protect private rights of property, and embraces all contracts relating to private property, whether executed or executory, and whether between individuals, between States, or between States and individuals. The word ' contracts ' must, however, be taken in its common and ordinary acceptation as an actual agreement between parties, by which something is granted or stipulated immediately for the benefit of the actual parties. But this clause was not intended to limit the power of the States in relation to their own public officers and servants, or to their own civil institutions, and must not be construed to embrace contracts, which are, in their nature, mere matters of civil institution ; nor grants of power and authority, by a State to individuals, to be exercised for purposes merely public. Thus, marriage is a contract ; but being a mere matter of civil institution, is not within the meaning of this clause. A law, therefore, authorizing divorces, though it impairs the validity of marriage contracts, is not a violation of the Constitution of the United States.   *   *   *

"The distinction we have here endeavored to lay down, between the contracts which are and which are not intended by that instrument, seems to us to be clear and obvious. If the charter of a public institution, like that of Dartmouth College, is to be construed as a contract within the intent of the Constitution of the United States, it will, in our opinion, be difficult to say what powers, in relation to their public institutions, if any, are left to the States. It is a construction, in our view, repugnant to the very principles of all government, because it places all the public institutions of all the States beyond legislative control. For it is clear that Congress possesses no powers on the subject. We are, therefore, clearly of opinion that the charter of Dartmouth College is not a contract within the meaning of this clause in the Constitution of the United States."

"But, admitting that charter to have been such a contract, what was the contract? Can it be construed to be a contract on the part of the king with the corporators whom he appointed, and their successors, that they should forever have the control of the affairs of this institution, and be forever free from all legislative interference, and that their number should not be augmented or diminished, however strongly the public interest might require it? Such a contract in relation to a public institution would, as we conceive, be absurd, and repugnant to the principles of all government. The king had no power to make such a contract, and thus bind the sovereign authority on a subject of mere public concern. Nor does our Legislature possess the power to make such a contract. * * *

"A distinction is to be taken between particular grants, by the Legislature, of property or privileges to individuals for their own benefit, and grants of power and authority to be exercised for public purposes. The former is, in its nature, special legislation in relation to private rights ; the latter is general legislation in relation to the common

interests of all.   Chief Justice Marshall, in the case of
Fletcher v. Peck, 6 Cranch, 135, adverts to this distinction
where he says : ' The correctness of this principle, that one
legislature cannot abridge the powers of a succeeding legislature so far as respects general legislation, can never be
controverted.   But if an act be done under a law, a succeeding legislature cannot undo it.   The past cannot be
recalled by the most absolute power.   Conveyances have
been made ; those conveyances have vested legal estates ;
and if those estates may be seized by the sovereign authority, still, that they originally vested is a fact, and cannot
cease to be a fact.'   We are, therefore, of opinion that if
this charter can be construed to be a contract within the
meaning of the Constitution of the United States, yet
still it contains no contract, binding on the Legislature,
that the number of trustees shall not be augmented, and
that the validity of the contract is not impaired by these
acts."

This opinion, precisely the same as in the State report,
was published in pamphlet form in January, 1818, and
copies of it were scattered broadcast, in legal, political,
and religious circles, — Webster declining to furnish any
minutes of his argument therefor to Isaac Hill, the publisher.

Webster said of this opinion (letter to Story, September
9, 1818), " The truth is, the New Hampshire opinion is
able, ingenious, and plausible."

In July, 1818, Chancellor Kent visited Hanover.   He
called upon the president and professors of the University,
but not upon those of the College.   He purchased one of
.the pamphlet copies of the opinion referred to, examined
it, commended it in the highest terms, and concurred in the
conclusion.

Chief Justice Richardson was assailed with great virulence
for the position taken by him in his opinion, that the pur-

pose of the great barons of England, when they wrested
Magna Charta from King John, was not to tie their own
or the hands of Parliament, which they controlled, by the
per legem terrae clause, but those of the crown.   It is
worthy of note that this opinion was recently reaffirmed
by the Supreme Court, in Davidson *v.* New Orleans, 96
U. S. 102.

But in general it has received from others " scanty justice."   If the State Court erred, it did so aside from the
point referred to, and a few authorities cited upon another, with all the light that could be thrown upon it.
The private correspondence of the counsel shows, with
the exceptions named, that nothing new, as a *legal* argument, was advanced at Washington.   A comparison of the
arguments before the two courts brings us to the same
conclusion.

Thompson, in his letter of November 3, 1817, to Judge
Smith, says : " At Mr. Marsh's request, I write this line to
say that Ichabod Bartlett was heard to say they on their
part would not agree to a verdict in such form as that the
cause might be removed to the S. Court of the United
States.   This is a report.   Mr. Marsh says you must be
on your guard against chicanery.   Woodbury observed last
evening, not in my hearing, that it was doubtful whether a
decision would be had at Plymouth this term."

This letter was received by Judge Smith at Plymouth
court, November 6, 1817, the same day on which the opinion was read by the chief justice.

Trustees *v.* Woodward was, in form, taken to the Supreme
Court from the November term, 1817, of the Superior
Court of New Hampshire ; but in fact, not until late in
December, 1817, in consequence of the difficulty the counsel
for the respective parties found in agreeing upon a special
verdict.   Judge Smith drew one, Mr. Bartlett another.
No advantage could be gained for the plaintiffs over the
acute, quick-sighted, and tenacious Bartlett.

Underneath the agreement of May 25, already quoted, the following was written at the November term, 1817:

We agree that the special verdict shall be drawn up as soon as may be, and signed by the counsel on both sides, under the direction of the Chief Justice.

JEREMIAH SMITH,
GEORGE SULLIVAN.

Mason, in his letter to Smith, of December 1, 1817, says: "I have received a letter from Mr. Webster, in which he expresses a desire to have the record and writ of error in the college cause as soon as possible, to send it on and have it entered early in the docket. All that I can do in further-ance of this object is to communicate his desire to you." In his letter of December 11, 1817, to the same, Mason says: "I received your letter, and have seen Mr. Bartlett and *his verdict*. He objects to almost all yours, and we can certainly agree to little of his. He says, however, he has written to Mr. Sullivan that he drew his to match yours, and that Mr. Sullivan will not suppose that he (Mr. B.) thinks all his departures from you material, and that S. and you will probably agree. I hope you may, for I think there will [be] great trouble in any attempt to agree with B. Judge Richardson has seen both. What he thinks of them I know not. It is important they be soon completed. The bearer has both verdicts, I suppose, to deliver to Mr. Sullivan."

In his letter of December 12, 1817, Mason says to Judge Smith: "Your man came yesterday for the college verdicts, while I was reading them for the first time. I had no time to think of them. After he was gone, it occurred to me that there might be a difficulty in your verdict as to the conver-sion. If I rightly recollect, it does not state an actual con-version, but a demand and refusal. * * * Perhaps it is of no importance in our case, as the Supreme Court can reverse on one point only. And for this reason, perhaps, it would be best to have that point only presented to the court in the conclusion of the verdict rather than the general conclusion which you contemplated. I am afraid there will be a difficulty in settling the verdict. Do every thing with Mr. Sullivan if you can."

In his letter of December 22, 1817, to Smith, Mason says : "Judge Richardson got home last evening very sick, but has signed the citation and allowed writ of error without difficulty. Bartlett declined reading the special verdict; said he supposed it right, and should make no objection. I presume Sullivan will sign the agreement, etc.

"I think you had best annex the writ of error to the record & indorse a return for clerk Webster for fear he may mistake & also make the return on the citation."

This was done.

On December 25, 1817, Jeremiah Smith for " plfs.," and " Geo. Sullivan for deft," signed the following stipulation, which was sent up with the special verdict : —

It is agreed by the parties that, if the plaintiffs shall recover by the judgment of the Supreme Court of the United States, they shall accept the delivery of the articles mentioned in their declaration, in full satisfaction of the damages recovered. It is also agreed that no advantage shall be taken in the Supreme Court of the United States of any want of form in the proceedings, and that the counsel then may add any facts, documents or records to the special verdict, to be taken and deemed a part thereof, or expunge any fact therefrom which, in the opinion of the counsel or Supreme Court, may be necessary to the obtaining of a decision on the validity of the acts of the Legislature of New Hampshire, recited in the special verdict; and that, if the said acts are adjudged to be valid, the judgment is to be affirmed; otherwise, reversed. It is also agreed by the plaintiffs' counsel, in order that the same question may come fairly before the court, that the demand, refusal and conversion stated in the special verdict, shall be considered as made and done on the day preceding the commencement of this suit.

The skeleton special verdict drawn by Mr. Bartlett is as follows : —

The jurors upon their oaths say that his majesty, George the Third, king of Great Britain, &c., issued his letters patent under the public seal of the province now State of New Hampshire, in the words following.

And the said jurors upon their oath further say that afterwards upon the eighteenth day of the same December, the said letters patent were duly enrolled and recorded in the secretary's office of said province, now State of New Hampshire, and afterwards and within one year from the issuing of the same letters patent, all the persons named as trustees in the same, accepted the said letters patent and assented thereto and the corporation therein and thereby created & erected was duly organized and has, until the passing of the act by the Legislature of New Hampshire, (hereafter mentioned) of the 27th June, A. D., 1816, and ever since (unless prevented by said act and the doings under the same) continued to be a corporation.

And the said jurors upon their oath further say that said corporation at its creation and organization as aforesaid acquired & received by donation & otherwise, lands, goods, chattels and monies of great value, and from time to time since have acquired & received, in manner aforesaid, lands, goods, chattels and monies of great value, and on the same 27th day of June, A. D., 1816, the said corporation created as aforesaid, had & held and (unless prevented by said act and the doings under the same) ever since have had & held divers lands, tenements, hereditaments, goods, chattels, and monies, acquired as aforesaid, for the uses and purposes in said letters patent specified ; the yearly value of the same not exceeding the sum of $26,666.

And the said jurors on their oath further say that the greater part of said monies, & lands received and acquired by said corporation at the time of its creation and since, were received and acquired by donation and grant from the province and now State of New Hampshire — and that part of said lands holden by said corporation as aforesaid were granted by, and are situate in the State of Vermont.

And the said jurors upon their oath further say that said corporation on the same 27th day of June, A. D., 1816, was possessed of the goods & chattels in the declaration in this action mentioned, at the place therein mentioned, and for the uses and purposes in said letters patent specified, & continued so possessed until and at the time of the demand and refusal hereinafter mentioned; unless devested thereof by the said act of 27th June, A. D., 1816, and the proceedings under the same as hereinafter recited.

And the said jurors upon their oath further say that on third day of June, A. D., 1815, John Wheelock, a son and *heir* of Eleazar Wheelock, in said letters patent mentioned, and President of said Dartmouth College, duly appointed, and constituted by the last will and testament of said Eleazar Wheelock, and for thirty-five years having exercised the office of President, agreeably to the provisions of the letters patent as aforesaid, by his memorial & petition to the Legislature of New Hampshire, represented that the interests of the institution of Dartmouth College and of literature, required that the Legislature should pass an act for *the purposes* and *with the provisions* of the act of June 27, 1816, hereinafter recited.

And the said jurors upon their oaths further say that on 27th day of June, A. D., 1816, the Legislature of the said State of New Hampshire, made and passed an act entitled, "An act to amend the charter and improve the corporation of Dartmouth College," in the words following.

And the said jurors upon their oath further say that agreeably to the provisions of said act of the Legislature of June 27, 1816, the Board of Trustees as therein prescribed, was duly completed to the number of twenty-one, by the appointment of seven persons, in addition to those who at the passing of said act held the office of trustees of Dartmouth College agreeably to the provisions of the letters patent aforesaid.

And said jurors upon their oath further say, that the Board of Trustees assembled and were organized agreeably to the provisions of said act at Hanover on the twenty-sixth day of August, A. D., 1816.

And the said jurors upon their oath further say that Wm. H. Woodward, the defendant, was the secretary & treasurer the corporation of Dartmouth College at the time of the passing of said act of the Legislature of the 27. June, 1816, at the meeting of said Board of Trustees, organized agreeably to the provisions of said act of the Legislature, of June 27th, A. D., 1816, was elected and duly appointed and qualified secretary and treasurer of said corporation so organized as by said act is provided, and as secretary & treasurer as aforesaid, — at the time of the demand hereinafter mentioned and at the commencement of this action, held and still claims to hold, the articles described in the plff's. declaration.

And the said jurors upon their oath further say that Timothy Farrar, Asa McFarland, Charles Marsh, Nathaniel Niles, Seth Payson, Elijah Paine, John Smith and Thomas W. Thompson, trustees of said Dartmouth College, duly appointed under said letters patent previous to the passing by the Legislature of New Hampshire, of the said act of the 27th June, 1816, assembled at Hanover aforesaid, on the 28th day of August, A. D., 1816, and refusing to act or meet with the Board of Trustees as organized agreeably to said act of said Legislature, of the 27th June, A. D., 1816, but claiming to have authority to act as a quorum of the Board of Trustees of Dartmouth College, as organized by the letters patent as aforesaid, independent of said act of the Legislature of June 27, A. D., 1816, passed a certain declaration or resolve in words following.

And the said jurors upon their oath further say that the *said* Eight trustees above named have never accepted, assented to, or acted under the said act of the Legislature, of the 27th June A. D., 1816, but have continued to act, and still claim to act by virtue of said letters patent, independent of said act of the Legislature, of the 27 June, A. D., 1816.

And the said jurors upon their oath further say that Said Eight Trustees above named, on the 28th day of August, A. D., 1816, passed a vote purporting to remove the said Wm. H. Woodward, from the office of secretary and treasurer of the corporation of Dartmouth College, of which said votes the said Woodward had due notice, on the day last mentioned.

And the said jurors upon their oath further say, that the eight trustees above named claiming to act by virtue of said letters patent, as aforesaid, independent of said act of the Legislature, of the 27th June, A. D., 1816, on the 7th day of October, A. D.

1816, demanded of the said Wm. H.. Woodward the goods & chattels in said declaration specified, and requested the said Wm. H. Woodward to deliver the same to them, which the said Woodward then & there refused to do, & has ever since refused to do.

Upon the back is the following indorsement, in the handwriting of Judge Smith: "Spec. verdict, recd. Dec. 12, 1817, proposed by defts, not adopted."

From the indorsements on the paper, Judge Smith apparently objected to the whole, or portions of paragraphs 4, 6, 8, 9, 10, 13, and 14.

The special verdict now upon the files, aside from the copy of the charter and the acts whose validity was in question, is in the handwriting of Judge Smith, and in this form was assented to by the genial, kindly, easy, and less alert Sullivan. It is signed, "Caleb Keith, foreman; Jeremiah Smith, for Plfs.; Geo. Sullivan, for Deft."

The copy of the writ of error on file is also in the handwriting of Judge Smith. The assignment of errors on file is also in his handwriting, but is signed, "Jeremiah Smith, J. Mason."

The instructions to the clerk are in the handwriting of Judge Smith, and dated, "25 Dec., 1817."

These papers were all sent by Smith, by special messenger, and were filed with the clerk, December 29, 1817.

Subscription papers were circulated, and Webster took up a heavy collection among the Boston merchants to defray the expenses of the further litigation. All the counsel retained their connection with the cause, but none on either side were so situated as to attend to it at Washington except Webster. The trustees, the faculty, and his associates handed over the cause to him, with power to procure such assistance as he desired. The other side, for some reason which nobody seems to understand, was committed to John Holmes, of Maine, to whom Jefferson wrote his celebrated "fire-bell in the night" letter; to William Wirt, and — at too late a day — to Pinkney.

CHAPTER VII.

TRUSTEES *v.* WOODWARD AT WASHINGTON — PROGRESS OF
THE OTHER CAUSES — PINKNEY RETAINED — REARGUMENT
EXPECTED — HE PREPARES FOR IT — SUMMARILY SHUT OFF
BY A DECISION — THREE-FOURTHS OF WEBSTER'S ARGU-
MENT ON POINTS NOT BEFORE THE COURT — HIS REASONS
FOR IT — SOURCE OF HIS ARGUMENT.

ON March 10, 1818, four months and four days after the
decision adverse to the majority of the old trustees in
the State court, the first of these causes (Trustees *v.*
Woodward) came on for argument before the full bench of
the Federal Supreme Court at Washington. On March 12,
1818, the arguments closed, and the judges went into consultation. Notwithstanding the effect of the contrast
between the impotence in preparation and the weakness in
argument displayed on the part of the State, and the great
weight of the elaborated Mason-Smith-Webster argument,
and the eloquence and adroitness of Webster's great effort,
that conference revealed to the judges — an anomalous state
of things in that tribunal upon a great constitutional question — that they could agree upon nothing, that no judgment could be rendered, and that the cause must be continued to the February term, 1819, — another year.

Two of the seven judges were undecided ; Story had not
yet recanted his opinion adverse to the plaintiffs ; and the
remaining four members of the court were equally divided.
At the opening of the court on the morning of March 13,
1818, Judge Marshall announced, in general terms, the result of this conference, and that in consequence the cause
must be continued. On March 14, 1818, the court adjourned without day.

(200)

Webster's pet cases, to which we have before referred, and to which three-fourths of his legal argument as reported by Farrar was devoted, distinctly raised the point upon which he greatly relied; but they were not only not before the Supreme Court when he made that argument, but had not reached the Circuit Court. As before stated, the United States Circuit Court for New Hampshire was held at Portsmouth and Exeter, and commenced its sessions in May and October respectively. These terms were not only in Judge Story's circuit, but were held, as it were, almost within earshot of his home.

After the continuance of Trustees v. Woodward, Webster busied himself in devising means for the transfer of these causes from the May term of the Circuit Court, 1818, to Washington, in order to "give" them an "earlier standing" upon the docket of the Supreme Court. His purpose, as stated by himself, was to accomplish this by turning an agreement drawn up by counsel, like the one in Trustees v. Woodward, into a special verdict, and then inducing Judge Story, the *protégé* of Mason and great admirer of Webster, and the district judge to disagree *pro forma*, without either argument or decision, and to take the cause up at once to the Supreme Court, upon the formal certificate that the judges "were opposed in opinion."

The causes were transferred as Mr. Webster desired, but not until the October term of the Circuit Court, 1818.

From the first, the outside pressure in favor of the College upon the State and Federal judges had been very marked and persistent. Soon after Mr. Webster's argument, the requisite steps were taken to make it still more effective upon the recalcitrant judges.

In August, 1818, Webster furnished to Judge Story copies of the arguments of the counsel for the plaintiffs, delivered in March preceding, to be distributed by him to a portion of the judges. These arguments were furnished, apparently, partly in the nature of briefs, and partly as campaign documents in reply to the opinion of Chief Justice Richardson in the State court, which had been " widely circulated.''

Bad news travels fast. It was impossible for the politicians to conceal, under complimentary eulogies of the wit of Holmes and praises of the brilliant declamation of Wirt, the legal *fiasco* at Washington from those who had the honor of Wheelock and the interests of the University most at heart. This brought William Pinkney, of Maryland, — the only man at the bar of the Supreme Court who could meet Webster upon any thing like equal ground, — into these causes, invested with powers almost as absolute as those voluntarily conferred upon Webster by his great associates and clients. This fact immediately became known to Judge Story, the counsel for the plaintiffs, and their clients. No man knew the judges, their biases, and what he had to contend with, in and out of court, better than Pinkney. His first step showed the genius of a commander.

About the first of November, 1818, he notified the opposing counsel that he should move for a reargument in Trustees *v.* Woodward, and should argue it himself, if the court permitted. It is hardly possible that this was not made known to Story, his great friend and admirer, and to the other judges of the Supreme Court, at an early day. Webster and his associates and clients conferred, and took such steps at once as they could to prevent a reargument.

Pinkney never attempted to argue a cause without the most thorough preparation, and this case was no exception to the rule. In order that nothing necessary to a correct understanding of the cause might escape him, Pinkney kept Cyrus Perkins, the secretary of the University board, at his elbow for a whole week preceding the session of the Supreme Court, which nominally commenced on February 1, 1819. Dr. Perkins was professor of anatomy and surgery in the medical department of Dartmouth College. He was an able man ; the family physician of Webster, and the devoted friend of Wheelock. He had lived for years in the atmosphere of these troubles, and knew the details of their history by heart, and brought to this conference with Pinkney all the documentary evidence which it was supposed would throw any light upon the subject. On Monday, February 1, 1819, Pinkney went up by pike from Baltimore to Washington. As all the judges were not present, the court met formally on that day, and adjourned over till Tuesday, when the business of the session commenced.

As the counsel for the State had no idea that a decision would be made at that time, none of them were present at the opening of the court on Tuesday morning except Pinkney, who sat near the chief justice, watching for an opportunity to open the battle with his motion for a reargument. On the morning of February 2, 1819, the instant the judges had taken their seats the chief justice turned his " blind ear " towards Pinkney (as tradition has it, and as Mills Olcott, one of the plaintiffs, used to relate it), and shut off his motion by announcing that the judges had formed opinions during the vacation, and immediately commenced reading his opinion, which was in manuscript, in his peculiar handwriting, and on eighteen folio pages.

Judge Todd was absent from sickness ; Judge Duvall dissented ; the remaining four judges simply " concurred in the result." No opinion was ever delivered in court by any of the other judges. Some time after, Judges Washington and Story handed their opinions, which appear in the printed volume, to the reporter.

On February 3, 1819, the chief justice delivered the opinion in the case of Baptist Association v. Hart's Executors, 4 Wheat. 1, which overthrew the doctrine of charitable uses, etc., in three great States of the Union, and which has since been overturned because it reasoned history out of existence. This cause was argued at the same term with the College case. On February 8 and 9, Sturges v. Crowninshield was argued ; and on February 17, 1819, the chief justice delivered the opinion of the court in that case, Judge Livingston not concurring. On February 10 and 11, 1819, the famous New Hampshire case of Bullard v. Bell was argued by Pinkney and Webster. The defendant was one of the judges on the New Hampshire bench when the College case was decided by that court. It was one of the Hillsborough Bank cases, of which Judge Bell was president, and involved the question of his individual liability, growing out of certain transactions of the bank. Pinkney was counsel for Bullard, and Webster for Bell. It is the only instance which now occurs to us in which these two legal giants were pitted against each other in that arena. Each did his best. The cause was heard before six judges; each carried one-half the court with him, and the case was never reported.

Soon after the reading of Judge Marshall's opinion, Webster moved that judgment be entered up *nunc pro tunc*, Judge Woodward having deceased since the last term. This motion was opposed by Mr. Pinkney and Mr. Wirt, upon the ground that the other causes then upon the docket embraced additional facts, and that no final judgment should be entered until all the causes were fully heard.

On February 23, 1819, the court granted the plaintiffs' motion. On March 12, 1819, the court adjourned without day, having been in session about six weeks. Before the adjournment, Mr. Pinkney attempted to avail himself of the stipulations which came up with the special verdicts, both from the State court and the United States Circuit Court, that any facts contained in the special verdict might be expunged, and that any new facts might be added, if deemed material to a right decision of the cause. Webster, with characteristic tact, refused to allow any fact either to be expunged or added. He thus forced a judgment against Judge Woodward, and compelled Pinkney to "consent" that the other causes should be "remanded to the Circuit Court for the District of New Hampshire, for further proceedings to be had therein, according to law," without any direction from the Supreme Court.

The old trustees did not wait for the judgment in their favor, but, as soon as the news of Judge Marshall's opinion reached them, made the necessary arrangements, and on February 8, 1819, took possession, by virtue of the law of the strongest, of the College buildings, etc., which up to that time had been held by President Allen, and occupied by the officers and students of the University.

Mr. Webster followed up his judgment by serving the proper notices upon the adverse parties in the causes in the Circuit Court, to be ready for trial at the May term, which commenced on Saturday, May 1, 1819. On that day Judge Story delivered an elaborate opinion, adverse to the State, in these causes. A judgment *nisi* was then rendered for the plaintiffs, to become absolute unless the defendants, during the May term of the court held in Boston (commencing May 15, 1819), should produce such further evidence as should, in the opinion of Judge Story, be sufficient cause for further delay. On May 27, 1819, James T. Austin, one of the counsel in the interest of the University in these causes, presented the " new facts " to Judge Story. The judge took the papers and reserved his decision. Story held that none of the facts varied the case as it had been considered and decided, and that none of them contradicted the recitals of the charter, and ordered judgment and execution in these suits. Technically, this was the end of the College causes.

Webster now devoted his special attention to pushing forward the publication of Farrar's report, a work that had been for some time on his hands.

And finally, at the May term, 1820, of the Superior Court, judgment was rendered against the College, in favor of Wheelock's executor, and execution issued thereon.

Justice to all requires that we should go beneath this surface outline and enter into details.

If the construction thus given to the clause in relation to
the "obligation of contracts" is correct, it should be upheld; but if founded in error, involving, as it may, vast consequences to millions, it must be overthrown. To determine
this question, the decision, in its "inner and outer life,"
must be analyzed and weighed dispassionately in the light
which has since been thrown upon it, uninfluenced by fear
or favor, or the shadow of great names, which, like "hard
cases," so often "make shipwreck of the law."

Blocks of overruled cases, opinions swathed in confusion
and rolled in tangles, and decisions so inconsistent and contradictory that no one can reconcile them, admonish us that
other judicial tribunals, however pure, able, and learned, are
yet human, and may err. We shall assume that the judges
of the Federal Supreme Court, in their judicial earth-life,
are no exception to the rule.

Probably no litigant ever came before that court under
circumstances, entirely independent of their merits, so un-
favorable for success as the State in these causes.

Judge Wilson, who had special opportunities for knowing
the meaning of the "obligation" clause, had been in his
grave more than twenty years when the decision was made.
Apparently the history of this clause, so far as court and
counsel were concerned, was enveloped in total darkness.[1]

Judge Marshall naturally believed in a government con-

---

[1] Col. Haines, in his argument before the Supreme Court, at the February
term, 1824, in Ogden v. Saunders, said: "What were the intentions of those
who framed the Constitution when they inserted in it the provision that 'no
State should pass a law impairing the obligation of contracts?' Unhappily for
this country and for the general interests of political science, the history of the
Convention of 1787, which framed the Constitution of the United States, is
lost to the world. We are compelled to resort to contemporaneous history in
giving a construction to this Constitution; and it has already been more than
once intimated by this court, that in giving expositions to the various provisions of this great political instrument, it was well to keep in view the mischiefs
which the Convention intended to cure and prevent."

In Edwards v. Kearzey, 96 U. S. 607, Mr. Justice Swayne says: "The
point decided in Dartmouth College v. Woodward (4 Wheat. 518) had not,
it is believed, when the Constitution was adopted, occurred to any one. There
is no trace of it in the *Federalist*, nor in any other contemporaneous publication."

structed by the rules of logic, and operated upon rigid
mathematical principles.   The political aspect which had
been forced upon the case, and of which Mr. Webster availed
himself with great adroitness in his argument, in the eyes
of Marshall transformed this case into another Marbury v.
Madison (1 Cranch, 137), which was in reality a judico-
political wager of battle between John Marshall and Thomas
Jefferson, the two great Virginians whose political and
personal hate descended with them to the tomb.   The counsel for the State were new men in the cause, unfamiliar with
the local history and the arguments in the State court,
inadequately prepared, ill-assorted and inharmonious, — the
first immersed in politics, the second overloaded with business, and the third silent as a consequence of his position
in the case ; while, on the other hand, the plaintiffs not only
had corresponding advantages, but also that of the learning
and industry of Smith and Mason, and of the prodigious
intellectual power of the great triumvirate, — Mason, Smith,
and Webster, — who overtopped alike the whole court, and
Holmes and Wirt, the opposing counsel.

We have seen that but six of the forty-three pages of
Mason's argument in the State court were devoted to the
" single point " which could properly be mooted in the
Supreme Court.   Smith's great learning made him more
diffuse and discursive.   Webster's argument, etc., as carefully written out by him for Farrar, occupied forty-six
pages : six pages were devoted to a statement of the case,
ten to the question before the court, and thirty to the first
and second points taken by Mason.   In other words, at least
three-fourths of his legal argument at Washington was upon
points not before that court.

We give the admission of this fact, and his reasons for
this extraordinary course, in Mr. Webster's own words :
" It will be contended by the plaintiffs *that these acts are
not valid and binding on them without their assent*.   1. Because they are against common right and the Constitution

of New Hampshire. 2. Because they are repugnant to the Constitution of the United States.

" [I am aware of the limits which bound the jurisdiction of the court in this case, and that, on this record, nothing can be decided but the single question whether these acts are repugnant to the Constitution of the United States. Yet it may assist in forming an opinion of their true nature and character, to compare them with these fundamental principles, introduced into the State governments for the purpose of limiting the exercise of the legislative power, and which the Constitution of New Hampshire expresses with great fulness and accuracy.]

" It is not too much to assert that the Legislature of New Hampshire would not have been competent to pass the acts in question, and to make them binding on the plaintiffs without their assent, even if there had been, in the Constitution of New Hampshire, or of the United States, no special restriction on their power ; because these acts are not the exercise of a power properly legislative. Their object and effect is to take away from one rights, property, and franchises, and to grant them to another. This is not the exercise of a legislative power. To justify the taking away of vested rights, there must be a forfeiture ; to adjudge upon and declare which is the proper province of the judiciary." (Farrar's Rep. 244.)

Mr. Webster's argument was carefully written out by him, with those of Smith and Mason under his eye ; it lies before us, with its erasures and interlineations. Pages of it were suppressed. The part that was printed was substantially unchanged. The paragraph in brackets was not in the original, but was substituted for one of an entirely different character.

If he was right, if vested rights can only be divested by the courts, and the rights in question had vested in the old trustees, he had no occasion to invoke the aid of the " obligation " clause.

We have the authority of Mr. Webster for saying that, aside from a single point, and a few authorities cited in support of another, nothing as a legal argument was advanced by him at Washington which had not been urged by Smith and Mason in the State court.

Webster, in his letter to Mason, of December 8, 1817, says: "Judge Smith has written for a form of citation, etc., in the College cause, which I shall send him, & write to him for his minutes.

"My wish is to see both him & you before I go to Washington. If I should not be kept in town by the court, as I do not expect to, I intend seeing you about Christmas or New Year. Everybody will expect me at Washington to deliver the Exeter argument, therefore the Exeter argument must be drawn out before I go. I will spend a day or two on this subject at Portsmouth, or Exeter, if you incline that I should do so.

"We must have Richardson's opinion a little beforehand if we can, that we may consider its weak points, if there be any such." (Mason Papers; Harvey's Webster Papers.)

In his letter to Judge Smith, of December 8, 1817, Webster says: "If I argue this cause at Washington, every one knows I can only be the reciter of the argument made by you at Exeter. You are, therefore, principally interested, as to the matter of reputation, in the figure I make at Washington. Nothing will be expected of me but decent delivery of your matter. This seems perfectly well understood this way, and I have been frequently complimented by gentlemen saying that, if the cause goes to Washington, they shall have a chance of hearing something of Judge Smith's argument.

"I have some notion of going to Exeter for a day or two, to practice and rehearse before I go to Washington. To be serious, however, you and Mason must help me arrange the argument. The best mode will be to have it written out, or all collected in notes, so that I can write it out." (1 Webster's Priv. Cor. 268.)

In his letter to Judge Smith, of January 9, 1818, he says: " I must beg the favor of all your notes. I have not assurance enough, although not entirely destitute, to think of arguing this cause on my own strength. To argue it as you did will be more than I shall ever be able to do. I wish to present the cause fully and fairly to the court, and your notes will enable me so to do. If anybody is coming over, pray let me have them soon, and all of them. If you have no opportunity to send them direct, please forward them enclosed to Mr. Mason. I am writing to him to-day, and will ask him to take care of the packet and send it to me directly." (1 Webster's Priv. Cor. 269.) All these " notes " and " minutes " were promptly furnished to Mr. Webster, and were returned by him to Mason, March 22, 1818. In his letter of that date to Mason, Webster says: " I send you your brief and Judge Smith's ; you may both probably need those hereafter." (1 Webster's Priv. Cor. 278.)

In his letter to Judge Smith, of March 14, 1818, two days after the close of the argument, he says : " I opened the case with most of the principles and authorities on which we relied at Exeter. Your notes I found to contain the whole matter. They saved me great labor ; but that was not the best part of their service ; they put me in the right path, and conduct, as I think, to an irresistible conclusion. On some parts of the case I have varied my views a little. The rogues here in Congress complain that the cause was put on grounds not stated in the court below. There is little or nothing in this. I labored the point that it was a private corporation, a charity. Eleazer Wheelock, its founder, as such, entitled generally by law to be visitor ; all the power of visitor assigned, in law, by him to the trustees, etc. The only new aspect of the argument was produced by going into cases to prove these ideas, which

indeed lie at the very bottom of your argument." (1 Webster's Priv. Cor. 276.)

In his letter of April 23, 1818, to Mason, Webster says :
" As to the college cause, I cannot argue it any more, I
believe. I have told you very often that you and Judge
Smith argued it very greatly. If it was well argued at
Washington, it is a proof that I was right, because all that
I said at Washington was but those two arguments, clumsily
put together by me. I do not mean to hold you answerable
for any deficiencies ; but in truth I have little right to claim
the merit, if there be any, in the opening of our case."
(1 Webster's Priv. Cor. 280.) In his Sunday evening letter
to Mason, he says : " There is one point on which I have
suspected that my opinion differs from Judge Smith's ; I
think that the trustees are most clearly visitors, and that
this lies at the bottom of our case, and as visitors, I think
they are not answerable in any court, while acting within
the scope of their visitorial power. I should be glad you
would think of this a little. If I am in an error, it is a
pretty important error." (1 Webster's Priv. Cor. 311.)

In his letter to Mason, of April 10, 1819, Webster says :
" My own interest will be promoted by *preventing* the book
[Farrar's report]. I shall strut well enough in the Washington report, & if the ' book ' should not be published, the
world would not know where I borrowed my plumes. But I
am still inclined to have the book. One reason is that you
& Judge Smith may have the credit which belongs to you.
Another is, I believe Judge Story is strongly of opinion it
would be a useful work, that Wheaton's reports go only into
the hands of professional men, but that this book might be
read by other classes, &c. &c. If it should be decided at May
term that another cause should go to Washington, I should
be very unwilling to have the book published, but I have
hitherto had a strong belief we should finish the actions at
May court. I think so still, but very probably may be dis-

appointed. I should be for pressing the judge to adjourn for a short time rather than continue the causes. I think he will feel the propriety of settling the controversy as far as may be done. I shall come down, accidents excepted & very possibly Mrs. W. may attend the same court.'' (Mason Papers ; Harvey's Webster Papers.)

CHAPTER VIII.

HISTORY OF THE OBLIGATION CLAUSE—JUDGE WILSON ITS AUTHOR—MEANING OF IT—DEBATES IN THE FEDERAL CONVENTION—ARGUMENT OF COL. HAINES—VIEW OF WILSON, ELLSWORTH, LUTHER MARTIN, GOUVERNEUR MORRIS, AUSTIN, AND OTHERS.

ART. I., sect. 10, of the Constitution provides that "no State shall * * * pass any * * * law impairing the obligation of contracts." This phrase is not the language of the common law. We did not derive it from the mother country. We find its source elsewhere.

Nathan Dane, the author of "Dane's Abridgment," and to whom the Harvard Law School is so much indebted, was a Massachusetts lawyer. He was born in 1752, and was admitted to the bar when thirty years old. He was a member of the Continental Congress in 1785-6-7. In 1786 it was found necessary to establish a form of government over the vast region then known as the "North-west Territory." The task of drafting it was assigned to Dane, then thirty-four years old. On July 13, 1787, the expiring Congress, — the Convention for framing the present Constitution being then in session, — though without "the least color of constitutional authority," adopted the ordinance without a single alteration. One of its provisions (we use the italics of the author) was: "And in the just preservation of rights and property, it is understood and declared, that no law ought ever to be made, or to have force in said territory, that shall, in any manner whatever, interfere with or *affect private contracts* or engagements, *bonâ fide* and without fraud, previously formed."

That the prime purpose of this clause was to prohibit the Legislatures of the expectant States from interfering trorespectively with the enforcement of private executory contracts is obvious; that the clause adopted by the Federal Convention was intended to restrict, rather than to enlarge, the scope of the clause in the ordinance, seems clear.

That Convention nominally met on May 14, 1787. It formally concluded its labors on September 17, 1787. From time to time the "obligations of the Federal pact," the "obligations of the Confederacy," the difference between "moral obligation" and "political operation," the "obligation" of States and those of the United States, had been discussed by the leading minds in the Convention, — Judge Ellsworth, Judge Wilson, Mr. Gerry, and Dr. Johnson. On August 27, 1787, when discussing the clause conferring jurisdiction on the Federal judiciary, in answer to Gouverneur Morris (the able and adroit man who did the work of the committee on style, and gave the "finish" to the final draught of the Constitution), who proposed the question, "whether it is extended to matters of fact as well as law, and to cases of common law as well as civil law," Judge Wilson (who was even more to the committee on detail than Morris to that on style) said: "The committee, he believed, meant facts as well as law, and common as well as civil law. The jurisdiction of the Federal Court of Appeals had, he said, been so construed." On August 28, 1787, Judge Wilson and Mr. Sherman moved to insert after the words "coin money," in Art. XII. of the new Constitution, as reported by the committee on detail, of which Judge Wilson was a leading member, the words, "nor emit bills of credit, nor make anything but gold and silver coin a tender in payment of debts." After a brief debate, the amendment was adopted. Mr. King, of Massachusetts, then moved to add the clause in the ordinance of 1787 which we

have quoted from Mr. Dane. The following debate ensued : —

"Mr. Gouverneur Morris. — This would be going too far.
There are a thousand laws relating to bringing actions, limitations
of actions, etc., which affect contracts. The judicial power of
the United States will be a protection in cases within their jurisdiction; and within the State itself a majority must rule, whatever
may be the mischief done among themselves.

"Mr. Sherman. — Why then prohibit bills of credit?

"Mr. Wilson was in favor of Mr. King's motion.

"Mr. Madison admitted that inconveniences might arise from
such a prohibition; but thought, on the whole, it would be over-
balanced by the utility of it. He conceived, however, that a
negative on the State laws could alone secure the effect. Evasions
might and would be devised by the ingenuity of the Legislatures.

"Col. Mason. — This is carrying the restraint too far. Cases
will happen that cannot be foreseen, where some kind of interference will be proper and essential. He mentioned the case of
limiting the period for bringing actions on open account — that of
bonds after a certain lapse of time — asking, whether it was proper
to tie the hands of the States from making provision in such cases.

"Mr. Wilson. — The answer to these objections is, that retrospective *interferences* only are to be prohibited.

"Mr. Madison. — Is not that already done by the prohibition of
ex post facto laws, which will oblige the judges to declare such
interferences null and void?

"Mr. Rutledge moved, instead of Mr. King's motion, to insert,
' nor pass bills of attainder, nor retrospective laws.' "

On which motion seven States voted aye, and three no.

On August 29, 1787, "Mr. Dickinson mentioned to the
House that, on examining Blackstone's Commentaries, he
found that the term ' *ex post facto* ' related to criminal
cases only; that they would not consequently restrain the
States from retrospective laws in civil cases; and that some
further provision for this purpose would be requisite."

On September 12, 1787, Dr. Johnson, from the committee
on style, etc., which consisted of Johnson, Hamilton,

Gouverneur Morris, Madison, and King, reported the Constitution in a new draft. Sect. 1 of Art. X. provided: "No State shall coin money, or emit bills of credit, or make anything but gold or silver coin a tender in payment of debts, or pass any bill of attainder, or *ex post facto* laws, or laws altering or impairing the obligation of contracts, or grant letters of marque and reprisal, or enter into any treaty, alliance or confederation, or grant any title of nobility."

On September 14, 1787, "Col. Mason moved to strike out from the clause 'no bill of attainder, nor any *ex post facto* law, shall be passed,' the words 'nor any *ex post facto* law.' He thought it not sufficiently clear that the prohibition meant by this phrase was limited to cases of a criminal nature; and no legislature ever did or can altogether avoid them in civil cases.

"Mr. Gerry seconded the motion; but with a view to extend the prohibition to 'civil cases,' which he thought ought to be done.

"On the question, all the States were, no."

Later in the same day, but on whose motion does not appear, the order of the clauses in sect. 10 of Art. I., which we have quoted, was changed (the word "altering" being expunged from the "obligation" clause) so as to read, "No State * * * shall pass * * * any * * * or law impairing the obligation of contracts," etc.

"Mr. Gerry entered into observations inculcating the importance of public faith, and the propriety of the restraint put on the States from impairing the obligation of contracts, alleging that Congress ought to be laid under the like prohibitions. He made a motion to that effect. He was not seconded."

The peculiar phraseology of the "obligation" clause has for many years been ascribed to Judge Wilson.[1]

[1] Our attention has been called by Hon. Clement Hugh Hill, the author of the article on the Dartmouth College case in the January number, 1874, of

We are not aware that he ever made any public claim to it ; but it has his distinctive " ear-marks." That he moulded the phrase is hardly an open question, though it undoubtedly passed under the eye of Madison and Gouverneur Morris. Madison, manifestly referring to the evils which sect. 10, Art. I., was intended to prevent, said : " In the internal administration of the States, a violation of contracts had become familiar, in the form of depreciated paper made a legal tender, of property substituted for money, of instalment laws, and of the occlusions of the courts of justice, although evident that all such interferences affected the rights of other States, relatively creditors, as well as citizens creditors, within the State." That Mr. Madison here referred to executory contracts is too obvious for comment. The great knowledge of Mr. Madison, his experience, diplomatic tact, and judicial temper, made him the central figure in that Amphictyonic council of great men ; though he lacked the slow but powerful intellect of Ellsworth, the great legal learning of Luther Martin, and the commanding genius of Hamilton.

Chief Justice Ellsworth was a leading member of the Federal Convention. On September 26, 1787, he and his colleague, Sherman, addressed a communication in the nature of a report to the governor of Connecticut. They said : " The restraint on the Legislatures of the several States, * * * impairing the obligation of contracts by *ex post*

---

the *American Law Review*, to the following quotation from the argument of Mr. Hunter, in Sturges v. Crowninshield : " The judges of the State courts and of this court have confessed that there is in these words, 'impairing the obligation of contracts,' an inherent obscurity. Surely then, here, if anywhere, the maxim must apply, *Semper in obscuris quod minimum est sequimur.* They are not taken from the English common law, or used as a classical or technical term of our jurisprudence in any book of authority. No one will pretend that these words are drawn from any English statute, or from the States' statutes before the adoption of the Constitution. Were they, then, furnished from that great treasury and reservoir of rational jurisprudence, the Roman law? We are inclined to believe this. The tradition is that Mr. Justice Wilson, who was a member of the Convention, and a Scottish lawyer, and learned in the civil law, was the author of this phrase." (4 Wheat. 151.) Mr. Hunter was from Rhode Island, an eminent lawyer, familiar with the history of the times, and of the public men who framed the Constitution.

facto laws, was thought necessary as a security to commerce in which the interest of foreigners as well as the interests of citizens of different States may be affected."

The phraseology used shows that they understood this clause to mean in civil causes what the *ex post facto* clause meant in criminal ones.

Charles Glidden Haines, in his argument at the February term, 1824, before the Supreme Court of the United States, in Ogden *v.* Saunders, said: "In consulting the debates of the Virginia Convention, convened at Richmond in June, 1788, * * * for the purpose of deliberating on the expediency of adopting the Constitution, we find that the section which relates to the obligation of contracts was discussed by the great men of that public body. Patrick Henry, George Mason, George Nicholas, James Madison, and Governor Randolph participated in the debates to which the section gave rise, and the three former considered the expressions *ex post facto laws*, and *laws impairing the obligations of contracts* as meaning the same thing, and as relating to the redemption of Continental money and calculated to gratify the cupidity of speculation. Mr. Madison corrected these erroneous impressions ; and Governor Randolph, after he had correctly defined the legal and technical meaning of the term *ex post facto laws*, as presented by the common-law writers, also speaks of the wholesome prohibition relating to contracts. ' I am,' says he, ' a warm friend to the prohibition, because it must be promotive of virtue and justice, and preventive of injustice. and fraud. If we take a review of the calamities which have befallen our reputation as a people, we will find they have been produced by frequent interferences of the State Legislatures with *private contracts*. If you inspect the great corner-stone of Republicanism, you will find it to be justice and honor.'

" Luther Martin, whose vigor of intellect and profound researches are justly appreciated by those who knew him in the days of his pride and strength, acted a distinguished part in this country when the Constitution was framed, and he has told us what was intended by the Convention of 1787, of which he was a member from the State of Maryland, by the insertion of this prohibition. After speaking of the disability on the part of the States to emit bills of credit, he makes these remarks: ' The same section also puts it out of the power of the States to make anything but gold and silver coin a tender in payment of debts, or to pass any laws impairing the obligation of contracts.' 'I considered,' continues he, ' that there might be times of such great public calamities and distress, and of such extreme scarcity of specie as should render it the duty of a government, for the preservation of even the most valuable part of its citizens, in some measure to interfere in their favor by passing laws totally or partially stopping the courts of justice, or authorizing the debtor to pay by instalments, or by delivering up his property to his creditors, at a reasonable and honest valuation. The times have been such as to render regulations of this kind necessary in most or all of the States, to prevent the wealthy creditor and the monied man from totally destroying the poor though even industrious debtor. Such times may again arrive. I therefore voted against depriving the States of this power, — a power which I am confident they ought to possess, but which I admit ought only to be exercised on very important and urgent occasions.' So spoke this efficient member of the Convention in his communication to the Legislature of Maryland.

" With the correctness or error of his opinions the court has no concern ; but when he expressly points to the objects which it was intended to accomplish by a specific section of the Constitution, and when he makes his expositions fresh from the hall of the Convention itself, and details the evils to be remedied, great respect and deference are due to his disclosures to the Legislature of the State from which he was a delegate."

Judge Wilson was a Scotchman. He was educated at Edinburgh and Glasgow. When about twenty-five years old, he emigrated to Philadelphia, and afterwards lived in the States of Pennsylvania and Maryland. He soon became a legal celebrity. For six out of the twelve years of its existence, he was a member of the Continental Congress. He was a man of superior abilities, and possessed great learning.

He was not only a master of the civil law, but of the French and Scotch law, which had the civil law for its basis, and of the common law as well. He was in favor of a strong central government, as was his colleague, Gouverneur Morris, and Hamilton; but they differed very much in their views. Hamilton regarded the British government as the proper model, but Judge Wilson did not; he proposed to build anew from the foundation, while preserving the autonomy of the States.

In his lectures to the law school upon the " general principles of law and obligation," etc., prepared within a year after the Federal Constitution went into operation, he criticises Blackstone's definition of municipal law and its " obligation," with a severity scarcely equalled by Austin and his admirers, at a later day, upon other points. With Wilson, all forms of government and all laws were " contracts." He says: " We find that an act which, considered indistinctly and dignified by the name of law, requires the whole supreme power of a nation to give it birth, is, when viewed more closely and analyzed into the component parts of its authority, properly arranged under the class of contracts. It is a contract to which there are three parties; those who constitute one of the three parties, not acting even in public characters." " The plain and simple analysis which I have given of the nature and obligation of acts of Parliament, is evidently countenanced by the expressive legal language of my Lord Hale. It is supported and confirmed by the very respectable authority of my Lord

Hardwicke. 'The binding force,'—I use his very words
as they are reported,—'the binding force of these acts of
Parliament arises from,'" etc. "Sir William Blackstone
tells us that the original of the obligation which a compact
carries with it is different from that of a law. The original
of the obligation of a compact we know to be consent: the
original of an act of Parliament we have traced minutely to
the very same source." "In the eye of the common law,
marriage appears in no other light than that of a civil contract ; and to this contract the agreement of the parties, the
essence of every rational contract, is indispensably required." In his lectures, he says of the common law : "It
prescribes the manner and *the obligation of contracts;* it
establishes the rules by which contracts, wills, deeds, and
even acts of Parliament are interpreted." (1 Wilson's
Works, 205.) The italics are ours. Unless the contrary
clearly appeared in the context, it would be a great stretch
of imagination to say that the author, by the phrase "obligation of contracts," meant the irrevocable effect of deeds
or estates in fee-simple, vested by grant. The sharp contrast between these terms is enhanced (taking into consideration his familiarity with Justinian and Domat) by his assertion that "the common law, as it respects contracts and
personal property, discovers evident traces of the Roman
jurisprudence. * * * I suggest, merely for consideration at present, a conjecture that many of those parts were
incorporated into the common law during the long period
of near four centuries, when the Roman jurisprudence pre-
dominated in England. * * * The person to whom the
right belonged, and the person against whom it existed,
were said in Roman law to be bound by an obligation, the
notion of an obligation being that of a tie between two parties of such a nature as to confer on the one a power of
compelling by action the other to give, do, or make good
something. The obligation did not give any interest in a
thing, to get which might be the ultimate object of the proceeding, but only gave a means of acquiring it, or, under

the Prætorian system, its value." (Sandars' Justin., by Hammond, 43.) "An obligation is a tie of law which binds us according to the rules of our civil law to render something." (Sandars' Justin. 396.) "They arise *ex contractu* or *quasi ex contractu, ex maleficio* or *quasi ex maleficio.*" (Sandars' Justin. 397.)

Wilson defines a State as "an artificial person: it has its affairs and its interests; it has its rules; it has its obligations; and it has its rights. It may acquire property, distinct from that of its members; it may incur debts, to be discharged out of the public stock, not out of the private fortunes of individuals; it may be bound by contracts, and for damages arising *quasi ex contractu.*" "Smaller societies may be formed within a State by a part of its members. These societies also are deemed to be moral persons, but not in a state of natural liberty; their actions are cognizable by the superior power of the State, and are regulated by its laws. To these societies the name of corporation is generally appropriated," etc. He indorsed the common-law doctrine that "the king and the Parliament are corporations."

In his lecture upon corporations, he says: "It must be admitted, however, that in too many instances those bodies politic have, in their progress, counteracted the design of their original formation. Monopoly, superstition, and ignorance have been the unnatural offspring of literary, religious, and commercial corporations. This is not mentioned with a view to insinuate that such establishments ought to be prevented or destroyed; I mean only to intimate that they should be erected with caution, and inspected with care." (2 Sandars' Justin. 226.) Had Judge Wilson drawn his inspiration from the French jurists, it would have been with the same result.

Pothier commenced his great work when Wilson was six years old, and died in 1772. He says: "The term *obligation* has two significations. In its most extensive signification, *lato sensu*, it is synonymous with the term *duty*, and comprehends *imperfect* as well as *perfect* obligations."

"The term *obligation*, in a sense more proper and less extensive, comprehends only perfect obligations, which are called also *personal engagements*, giving to him with whom they are contracted the right of requiring the performance of them; and it is of this kind of obligation that we mean to speak in this treatise." The frequent use of this term by Judge Wilson, in both senses, shows how thoroughly he understood its meaning.

If Wilson and Morris failed to comprehend the full bearing of this clause upon the power of legislatures over corporations, it is safe to assume that no one in or outside of the Convention did.

They had special reasons for examining it with care. In 1785 they were counsel for, and argued the great cause of, the Bank of North America, then pending before the Legislature of Pennsylvania. In that argument, Wilson said: "I am far from opposing the legislative authority of the State, but it must be observed that, according to the practice of the Legislature, public acts of very different kinds are drawn and promulgated under the same form. A law to vest or confirm an estate in an individual, a law to incorporate a congregation or other society, a law respecting the rights and properties of all the citizens of the State, are all passed in the same manner, are all clothed in the same dress of legislative formality, and are all equally acts of the representatives of the freemen of the Commonwealth.

"But surely it will not be pretended that after laws of those different kinds are passed, the Legislature possesses over each the same discretionary power of repeal. * * * Still more different is the case with regard to a law by which an estate is vested or confirmed in an individual: if in this case the Legislature may, at discretion, and without any reason assigned, devest or destroy his estate, then a person seized of an estate in fee-simple, under legislative sanction, is in truth nothing more than a solemn tenant at

will! * * * To receive the legislative stamp of stability and permanency, acts of incorporation are applied for
from the Legislature. If these acts may be repealed without notice, without accusation, without hearing, without
proof, without forfeiture; where is the stamp of their
stability?" (3 Wilson's Works, 414, 415.)

Morris said: "They know that the boasted omnipotence
of legislative authority is but a jingle of words; in the literal
meaning it is impious. And whatever interpretation lawyers
may give, freemen must feel it to be absurd and unconstitutional. Absurd, because laws cannot alter the nature of
things; unconstitutional, because the Constitution is no more
if it can be changed by the Legislature. A law was once
passed in New Jersey which the judges pronounced to be unconstitutional, and therefore void. Surely no good citizen
can wish to see this point decided in the tribunals of Pennsylvania. Such power in judges is dangerous; but unless it
somewhere exists, the time employed in framing a bill of
rights and form of government was merely thrown away.

"The doubt which arises on this occasion as to the extent
of your authority is not founded on the charter granted by
Congress; but, supposing the incorporation of the bank to
have been the same in its origin as that of a church, we ask
whether the existence and the rights acquired by law can be
destroyed by law. Negroes have by law acquired the rights
of citizens; would a subsequent law take that right away?
It is not true that the right to give involves the right to
take. A father, for instance, has no power over the life of
his child; nor can a felon or traitor, pardoned by act of
grace, be by repeal of that act condemned and executed.
Should an act be passed to cancel the public debts, would
that act be valid? Where an estate has been granted by law,
can it be revoked by a subsequent law? Could the lands
forfeited and sold be resumed, and conveyed to the original
owners? Many such questions might be put, and a judicial
decision, either affirmative or negative, would be incon-

venient and dangerous. Look, then, to the end, ere you commence the labor." (3 Life of Morris, 438, 439.)

In the Convention of Virginia, of which he was a member, which ratified the Federal Constitution, Judge Marshall, upon grave consideration, informed the people of Virginia that though a State might sue upon a contract, it could not be sued; in other words, that, notwithstanding the State suability clause, the "obligation of contracts," in a constitutional sense, was a stick with but one end.

But in Chisholm v. Georgia, decided in 1793, which was *assumpsit* against a State for the recovery of money, Judge Wilson, after reasserting, in substance, the definition of a State quoted by us from his lectures, held otherwise, saying : "A State, like a merchant, makes a contract; a dishonest State, like a dishonest merchant, wilfully refuses to discharge it; the latter is amenable to a court of justice. Upon general principles of right, shall the former, when summoned to answer the fair demands of its creditor, be permitted, Proteus-like, to assume a new appearance, and to insult him and justice by declaring, 'I am a sovereign State?' Surely not."

In 1790, the law professorship was established in the College of Philadelphia, and Judge Wilson was made the first professor. In April, 1792, the Legislature fused that college in the University of Pennsylvania. Able, sensitive, and tenacious as he was, if that act had violated the Constitution which he was sworn to support, he certainly would have discovered it, and the world would have known the fact.

"A contract is a species of agreement, the accord of two wills, *conventio pactum;* and in an agreement there is, first of all, the *pollicitatio*, the offer made by one party, and then the acceptance by the other. When this accord of wills is such that the law adds a third element, the *vinculum juris*, or obligation, we have a contract." (Sandars' Justin., by Hammond, 399.)

Mr. Austin, notwithstanding his faults, had a clear knowledge of the civil law. He says: " In the proper sense of the word, a contract is a *promise*, and begets only *jus ad rem* against the promisor, — *i.e.*, a right to an act, an endurance, or a forbearance on his part." (2 Austin Jur. 239.) " Obligation regards the future. An obligation to a past act, or an obligation to a past forbearance, is a contradiction in terms." (1 Austin Jur. 458.) " In the language of the Roman law, ' *contract* ' denoted, originally, *a convention which may be enforced by action.* * * * In the language of the English law, ' *contract* ' is a term of uncertain extension. Used loosely, it is equivalent to ' *convention* ' or ' *agreement.*' Taken in the largest signification which can be given to it correctly, it denotes a convention or agreement which the courts of justice will enforce. That is to say, it bears the meaning which was attached to it originally by the Roman jurisconsults." (2 Austin Jur. 1015–16.) " The confusion of *contract* and *conveyance* by elliptical or improper expression is one of the greatest obstacles in the way of the student." (2 Austin Jur. 1006.) " I shall distinguish contracts, properly so called, from certain facts or events which are styled contracts, but which virtually are alienations or conveyances." (1 Austin Jur. 56.) " Rights *in rem* sometimes arise from an instrument which is called a contract, and are therefore said to arise from a contract ; the instrument in these cases wears a double aspect, or has a twofold effect : to one purpose it gives *jus in personam*, and is a contract ; to another purpose it gives *jus in rem*, and is a conveyance. When a so-called contract passes an estate, or, in the language of the modern civilians, a right *in rem*, to the obligor, it is to that extent not a contract, but a *conveyance*, although it may be a contract to some other extent, and considered from some other aspect. A contract is not distinguished from a conveyance by the mere consent of parties, for that consent is evidently necessary in a conveyance as well as in a contract." (1 Austin Jur. 387.)

"We must see likewise whence an action arises, and it is to be known that it arises from preceding obligations, like a daughter from a mother. But an obligation, which is the mother of an action, derives its origin and commencement from some preceding cause, either from a contract or a *quasi* contract, or a tort or a *quasi* tort. * * * And it must be known, in the first place, that an obligation is a bond of law, by which we are constrained by a necessity to give or to do something, as if one was tied and constrained to another person for a certain thing, and that other person was bound to him on the contrary for another thing. For an obligation is, as it were, a counter tie, and it has four forms under which it is contracted, and several vestments." (2 Bracton, by Twiss, 107–9.)

An interpretation which would restrict the provision to executory contracts would be much more natural and reasonable than the other.

It seems to us from the debates in the Convention, the views of Judge Wilson, and those of other eminent authorities to which we have referred, that the framers of the Constitution had this meaning in mind when they adopted the provision.

When Trustees v. Woodward, was decided, no member of the Federal Convention remained upon the bench, nor any one specially familiar with its history. Neither its journal nor the Madison Papers had been published.

It is apparent that the court regarded these as common words, and gave them the popular interpretation, when they might as well have construed the preceding words, "bill of attainder," "*ex post facto*," etc., as popular terms.

In Sturges v. Crowninshield, 4 Wheat. 197, which was under consideration at the same time with the College causes, Judge Marshall said: "In discussing the question whether a State is prohibited from passing such a law as this, our first inquiry is into the meaning of *words in common use*. What is the obligation of a contract? and what will impair it?

"It would seem difficult to substitute words which are more intelligible, or less liable to misconstruction, than those which are to be explained. * * * The words of the Constitution, then, are express, and *incapable of being misunderstood.*"   The italics are ours.

Such recklessness in assertion carries with it its own comment; and if it did not, the opinions of Livingston and Johnson, the views of all candid commentators, the wide differences in opinion in State and Federal courts, and the innumerable questions raised, most certainly would do so.

CHAPTER IX.

HOLMES, WIRT, HOPKINSON, WEBSTER—THEIR ARGUMENTS
—JUDGES DIVIDED IN OPINION—PINKNEY AND THE RE-
ARGUMENT.

WE have seen that Trustees *v*. Woodward was argued March
10, 11, and 12, 1818, by Webster, and Joseph Hopkinson of Philadelphia, for the old trustees, and by Holmes,
and Wirt of Virginia, for the State. Webster made the
opening argument for the plaintiffs, and Holmes for the defendant. Webster *was* the leading counsel on one side, and
Holmes *assumed* to be on the other. Holmes pitted himself against Webster, and Hopkinson was pitted against
Wirt. Webster spoke nearly five, and Holmes over three
hours.

John Holmes was a famous kaleidoscopic politician, and
a power in the land in his day. He was forty-five years old
when he attempted to reply to Webster. He was born in
Massachusetts, in 1773, graduated at Brown University
in 1796, with Tristam Burgess, Dr. Shurtleff, and other
celebrities. He came to the bar in 1799, and in September
of that year went into practice at Alfred, in the town of
Sanford, in the county of York, in that part of Massachusetts then known as the district and now as the State of
Maine, and which was admitted into the Union two years
after the argument in this case.

Massachusetts proper, with an area of some 7,800 square
miles, was separated from the district of Maine, which
comprised some 32,000 square miles, or about one-half the
area of all the New England States, by the south-easterly
point of New Hampshire. The York congressional district,—often termed Cyrus King's district,—bounded on

the west by New Hampshire, was represented from 1813 to 1817 by Cyrus King, a Federalist lawyer of note. Holmes took to politics as naturally as ducks to water. He was then a rank Federalist, representing that party in the Massachusetts Legislature in 1802–3, and lampooned his opponents with great virulence.

The Federalists had a strong majority in Massachusetts proper; but Holmes's own town, county, and the district of Maine being the other way, late in 1811 he suddenly went over to the enemy, and became a red-hot advocate of the national government and its war measures, was elected to the House and Senate by his new friends, and served during the war. In 1815 he was appointed commissioner by Madison, under Art. IV. of the Treaty of Ghent. He was one of the leading advocates of the separation of Maine from the old Commonwealth, which eventually became a party question. In June, 1816, the Legislature of Massachusetts submitted the question of separation to the people, with the proviso that if, upon the vote of September, 1816, "it shall appear that a majority of five to four, at least, of the votes so returned are in favor of separation, the Convention is to proceed in forming a Constitution, and not otherwise." The Convention was defeated; but Holmes, as chairman of the committee to examine the vote, etc., reported that it was carried, and that the Convention should proceed in forming a Constitution, which they did. This result was reached by an ingenious system of political arithmetic, which would have put to the blush the quota mathematics of that astute and fertile genius, Provost-Marshal-General Fry. To get their basis, the committee first rejected 173 majority against separation, upon the ground of alleged technical informalities, and then reported that 22,316 votes were cast; that there were 11,969 yeas, and 10,347 nays; that the whole aggregate majorities of yeas in towns and plantations were 6,031, and the whole aggregate majorities of nays, 4,409; that, on this construction of the act, there was a majority of five to four, at least, in favor of said district's becoming an independent State. The Legislature of Massachusetts overruled this construction, and disregarded the Constitution adopted by the Brunswick Convention ; but a Convention was carried, and a Constitution was adopted in 1819. Holmes was the chairman of the committee that framed this Constitution. He was elected to Congress from Cyrus King's district (King died in April, 1817), in 1816 was reëlected, and was in the United States Senate from 1820 to 1833.

Holmes was not without talent. He had unbounded confidence in himself, and was always cool and perfectly self-possessed ; he was a scheming, busy, restless, rollicking politician ; his broad wit, sluice-word declamation, and stinging repartee, with which he more than once silenced John Randolph and others scarcely less noted, were the delight of the crowds which gathered at the hustings and County Courts ; and his questionable stories kept every country bar-room in a roar. But he was as much out of place before Judge Marshall's court, and pitted against such a man as Webster, as it was possible to be. Caring for little else, climbing like a busy "sweep" with devious steps the dirty chimney of political preferment, he had neither taste, time, inclination, nor the mental qualities required to grasp, prepare, and argue a cause like this. The noisy eulogist and reputed *protégé* of Jefferson, he represented in politics, law, and statesmanship every thing that the soul of Marshall loathed.

Webster never made the mistake of many so-called great men, — he never underrated the power of an opponent. When he gave credit, he never erred except upon the side of generosity.

In his letter to Brown, dated at Washington, March 11, 1818, he says: "Our case came on yesterday. I opened the argument, and occupied almost the whole of the sitting in stating the burden of our complaints. Mr. Holmes fol-

232 DARTMOUTH COLLEGE CAUSES.

lowed & stated the following as his propositions. 1. This court has no jurisdiction because the parties do not live in different States (we never put the jurisdiction on that ground). 2. That the grant of 1769 was not a *contract*, but the trustees merely officers of government under the king. 3. That all corporations created by the king were dissolved by the Revolution. 4. That if the charter were a *contract*, the acts do not *impair* it. We have heard him on his three first heads. He is to take up the fourth this morning. Thus far there has nothing new or formidable developed. (All stuff.)

"Mr. Wirt is to follow Mr. Holmes. He is a man of talents, and will no doubt make the best of his case.

"Mr. Hopkinson is to reply, and will make up for all my deficiencies, which were numerous."

In his letter of March 13, 1818, to Mason, he says: "The argument in the College case terminated yesterday, having occupied nearly three days. On being inquired of by defendant's counsel whether the court would probably give a decision at this term, the chief justice answered, 'that the court would not treat lightly an act of the Legislature of a State and the decision of a State court, and that the court would not probably render any judgment at this term.' The cause was opened on our side by me. Mr. Holmes followed. His propositions, as near as I recollect, were, 1. No jurisdiction because both parties in same State. 2. Charter of 1769 not a contract; trustees, public officers, like judges, and sheriffs &c. ; College a part of government, &c. 3. All corporations abolished by Revolution. 4. If charter a contract, not impaired, a great kindness to old trustees to send them new assistants &c. Upon the whole, he gave us three hours of the merest stuff that was ever uttered in a county court. Judge Bell [one of the judges who had decided this cause in the State court, and for whom Webster was counsel in Bullard *v.* Bell, then pending before the Federal Supreme Court] was present, and had the pleasure of hearing him, but could not stay out his speech." (1 Webster's Priv. Cor. 275.)

In his letter to Judge Smith, written the next day, Webster says : "My talk occupied nearly a whole sitting. Holmes followed ; he spoke three or four hours. * * * Holmes did not make a figure. I had a malicious joy in seeing Bell [the New Hampshire judge] sit by to hear him, while everybody was grinning at the folly he uttered. Bell could not stand it. He seized his hat and went off." (1 Webster's Priv. Cor. 277.)

Judge Daggett, a member of the United States Senate from Connecticut, then fifty-four years of age, one of the foremost lawyers of his day, afterwards chief justice of the Supreme Court of that State, and one of the greatest jurists that ever honored that position, in his letter of March 18, 1818, to Mason, says : "Tom Paine, speaking, or rather writing of some one, says : ' He went up like a rocket, and came down like a stick.' That is evidently true of a certain great man from Cyrus King's district. He has attempted as a politician so much wisdom, and such a desire to be admired by *everybody*, that he has ceased for weeks to be regarded by *anybody*. His friends, however, still uphold him as a lawyer, but in the Dartmouth College Cause, he sunk lower at the bar than he had in the hall of legislature. The opinion was entirely universal that Webster rose superior even to Wirt (though it is said that *he* appeared very well), and infinitely so to Holmes." (Mason's Mem. 199.)

Webster's correspondence shows that he was promptly advised of Pinkney's connection with these causes, and the general ground to be taken by him in argument.

Hopkinson, in his letter to Webster, of November 17, 1818, says, referring to a conversation with Pinkney about this cause : "He says, ' Mr. Wirt was not strong enough for it, has not back enough.' There is a wonderful degree of harmony among our opponents in this case. You may remember how Wirt and Holmes thought and spoke of each other." (Mason's Mem. 289.) It hardly needed this letter to show the light in which Wirt regarded Holmes. If further comment were necessary upon a performance that could drive a grave and patient judge like Bell out of the court-room in disgust, it might be found in some of the legal positions taken by Holmes.

Wirt was a different man.. He was a year the senior of Holmes; possessed an ardent, social nature, and a vivid imagination; had genius and culture; was an able lawyer and a brilliant advocate of the red-baize school which went out of vogue after the advent of Webster: but he was placed second to Holmes, and could not fail to appreciate the fact; was crowded with business, unfamiliar with the local law and the history and details of the case, inadequately prepared, and had a great aversion to New England men and matters.

He had a large practice; was nominated for attorney-general of the United States on November 13, 1817, and was confirmed on December 15, 1817. He purchased an establishment at Washington, removed there and assumed the duties of his office in January, 1818, and was pushed for weeks to the very verge of endurance in attempting to give proper attention to his practice, and trying to bring order out of the chaos which he found in his new office.

In his letter of January 21, 1818, to Judge Carr, he says: "It is late at night — the fag-end of a hard day's work. My eyes, hand and mind all tired. * * * The office, I find, is no *sinecure*. I have been up till midnight, at work, every night, and still have my hands full. * * * I have much to say to you about this place, and those who are around me; but I am now worn out. We must defer all this till we meet, for I am extremely fatigued. * * * The Supreme Court is approaching. It will half kill you to hear that it will find me unprepared; but I shall contrive ways and means to keep my professional head, at least, above water. As to any great figure, I cannot promise it, in the bustle in which I am now engaged." (2 Kennedy's Mem. Wirt, 67, 68.)

In his letter of May 6, 1818, to Carr, he says: "I am, at this present, in a furious hurry. * * * Judge of the pressure on me when I tell you that I had, this •morning, to rise before five o'clock to business, and shall have so to do, I expect, till the meeting of the Supreme Court." (2 Kennedy's Mem. Wirt, 69.)

Webster, in his letter to Mason, of March 13, 1818, says: "Wirt followed. He is a good deal of a lawyer, and has very quick perceptions and handsome power of argument, but he seemed to treat this case as if his side could furnish nothing but declamation. He undertook to make out one legal point on which he rested his argument, namely, that Dr. Wheelock was not founder. In this he was, I thought, completely unsuccessful. He abandoned his first point, recited some foolish opinions of Virginians on the third. * * * He made an apology for himself, *that he had not had time to study the case, and had hardly thought of it till it was called on.*" (1 Webster's Priv. Cor. 275, 276.)

In his letter of March 14, 1818, to Judge Smith, Webster says: "Wirt has talents, is a competent lawyer, and argues a good cause well. *In this case he said more nonsensical things than became him.*" (1 Webster's Priv. Cor. 277.) The italics are ours.

No man could make a good legal argument in such a cause who "had hardly thought of it." Wirt was as guileless as a child when he made this statement; he simply told the truth. The history of the incident referred to by Webster shows this. Wirt was arguing that Wheelock was not the "founder," etc. Webster had his attention called to the clause in the charter reciting that Wheelock was the "founder," etc. Wirt had no knowledge that such a clause was in the charter, and knowing nothing of the history of Moor's Charity-School, was "dumbfounded," and, as Webster says, "abandoned" the ↔ point." Such a circumstance could not fail to leave its impress on the minds of the court, and to it we undoubtedly owe some of the language of the opinions.

Unable, from his situation, to give the judges any thing new in the way of an argument, he gave them a most brilliant and vehement declamation, arrayed in all the gorgeous colors of the rainbow. Wirt commenced his speech in the afternoon of March 11, 1818. Whether in consequence of Webster's disabling him in the tilt about the "founder," etc., or his vehemence, or, what is more probable, from both, does not distinctly appear, but contemporary accounts show that he utterly broke down, lost the control of his voice, had to apologize to the court for his inability to go on, and asked their indulgence till the next day, when he concluded. All knew that Wirt was a favorite at Monticello, that he was the right hand of Jefferson in Burr's trial, and had been his private counsel for years.

Hopkinson replied to him on March 12, 1818. He was forty-eight years of age, and an eminent lawyer. He was admitted to the bar in 1791, and was a member of Congress at the time of the argument. Webster, in his letter to Brown, of March 13, 1818, says: "Mr. Hopkinson understood every part of the cause, and in his argument did it great justice. No new view was suggested on the other side." (1 Webster's Priv. Cor. 274.) In his letter the same day to Mason, Webster says: "Mr. Hopkinson made a most satisfactory reply, keeping to the law, and not following Holmes and Wirt into the fields of declamation and fine speaking." (1 Webster's Priv. Cor. 276.) In his letter of March 14, 1818, to Judge Smith, Webster says: "Hopkinson in concluding confined himself strictly to replying, and acquitted himself with ability." (1 Webster's Priv. Cor. 277.) The most adverse critics conceded that Mr. Hopkinson argued the cause "handsomely."

And Webster, what can we say of him! In his simple and unaffected intellectual greatness, he towered as much above the mass of mankind as Mount Hood above the smiling valley of the Willamette, the foot-hills, and the snowy peaks which encircle it. He was one of those great men who are, as it were, the landmarks of ages; he was endowed with a majestic presence; those great, deep, black eyes, with their intense coal-fire glow, which had come down to him on the stream of generations from Stephen Bachiler, seemed as if they searched alike the seen and the unseen world; his wonderful voice, which has thrilled the very marrow in our bones even when the end of the mighty old man was nigh, was the attribute of one born to convince and conquer. All these were makeweights enough to be thrown into the scale on one side; but others were added.

We have seen that Mason's argument occupied forty-three, and Webster's forty-six, pages in Farrar's report. Both were slow speakers, and uttered about the same number of words in a given time. Mason spoke two hours, and Webster, at Washington, nearly five. Webster's memory was such that he could have written out his argument nearly *verbatim* had he chosen. Something must be allowed for the peroration; and something, perhaps, for condensation, though Webster generally condensed his speeches by the preparation and thought he gave them before their delivery. Making all due allowance, more than an hour was devoted to *something* which, Mr. Webster informs us, was "left out." What was it? No report of it exists.[1] We only know its drift. In adroit but cultured phrase he pressed the whole political aspect of the case upon the attention of the court. He commented with warmth and severity upon the course of the State, and the revolution which the "Jacobins" had wrought in its policy for political purposes; asserted that

[1] "While the particular institution, the fate of which was at stake in the cause, was one which the strongest sympathies of his youth and the fullest convictions of his manhood stimulated him to preserve from the control of party politics and the mischief of political legislation. Inspired by these motives, he opened the causes, in the argument of which all that is preserved is contained in the fifth volume of this work; a report which gives us only the legal reasoning of a speech that was undoubtedly as remarkable for its beauty, pathos, and eloquence, as it was for its logical power and its wealth of historical and juridical illustration." (1 Curtis's Life of Webster, 167.)

the Legislature, which was the creature of this " Jacobin " irruption, had invaded the sacred rights of property by the passage of these acts, in direct violation of the State Constitution and the fundamental principles of our government, had overturned the judiciary of the State, and created a new one to subserve its purposes ; and declared there was no protection unless afforded by the Federal tribunals.

The following extract from Mr. Webster's letter to Mason, dated June 28, 1818, shows how he felt in relation to the New Hampshire court and Legislature : " I found that the College people thought that you made a very strong impression in their cause. It would be a queer thing if Gov. P.'s court should refuse to execute his laws. I am afraid there is no great hope of their disobedience to the powers that made them." (Mason Papers ; Harvey's Webster Papers.)

We have already seen the real reason why thirty pages, three-fourths of his entire legal argument, in Farrar's report were devoted to points not before the court.

In his letter to Judge Smith of March 14, 1818, Webster says : " We finished with the third day. The next morning, yesterday, the chief justice told us the court had conferred ; that there were different opinions, and that some judges had not formed opinions ; consequently the cause must be continued." (1 Webster's Priv. Cor. 277.)

The account in the *National Intelligencer* is as follows : —

"On Friday morning, [March 13, 1818,] the chief justice observed that the judges had conferred on the cause between the Trustees of Dartmouth College and William H. Woodward. Some of the judges have not come to an opinion on the case. Those of the judges who have formed opinions do not agree. The cause must therefore be continued until the next term."

There are several accounts in private letters and public prints, but they are nearly all of the same import.

In the letter of Webster just quoted, he says : " I have no accurate knowledge of the manner in which the judges are divided. The chief and Washington, I have no doubt, are with us. Duvall and Todd perhaps against us ; *the other three holding up.* I cannot much doubt but that Story will be with us *in the end*, and I think we have much more than an even chance for one of the others.'' The italics are ours.

The guarded language of Webster, the allusion to Judges Johnson and Livingston, and the implication in the peculiar reference to Judge Story, must be read in the light of tradition and history to be fully appreciated.

Story was understood to be a Wheelock man before the passage of the act in question. He was the confidant, and apparently the adviser, of Governor Plumer, and the friend of Richardson. As before stated, Governor Plumer, at the first meeting after the passage of the act, made Story and his neighbor and confidential friend overseers of the University.

The bitterness felt towards him by the old trustees and their adherents crops out in Hopkinson's letter to Marsh, hereafter quoted. It has long been an open secret with a few that Story's first opinion was adverse to the old trustees. This gradually cropped out in lectures, addresses, and the like, and in some of the legal journals of our day. We have seen that the essential facts of the case were as well understood by the leading minds in New England two years before as two years after the decision ; and so of the general grounds taken by both sides. The question was an interesting and important one, constantly mooted in all legal, religious, and political circles. The tradition is, that Judge Story, at an early day, carefully examined the question with his characteristic zeal and indefatigable research, and arrived at the same result reached by his friend Chief Justice Richardson ; that he communicated this fact semi-confidentially to his friend Ichabod Bartlett, one of the counsel for the State, from whom in an impalpable form, in the same way, it dripped into the narrow circle of Wheelock and his special friends, — or, as Webster termed them, the ''University people.'' The authorities for this are Bartlett, Webster, and Choate. Webster, referring to this fact and the final decision, as the anecdote is related by Mr. Choate,. said to him : " Bartlett and the University people were dumbfounded, thunderstruck, when they found that Story had gone against them." It is no discredit to Story that he changed his opinion, but the contrary ; for it is the first and last, the highest and holiest, duty of ever judge to be right : but it should have made him more charitable than he sometimes seemed toward those who felt that his first opinion was the soundest.

What Mr. Webster says of Bullard *v.* Bell, etc., is an illustration of the accuracy of his knowledge of the inner workings of the Supreme Court, and the position of its individual judges. In his letter to Mason, of February 15, 1819, he says : " In Mr. Bell's case, Mr. Pinkney was near two hours in opening, and full four in the close. In that case we have no judgment yet. I think some impression was made on our side, and I have hopes of the issue, but know nothing certain." (Mason's Mem. 218.) In his letter to Mason, of February 23, 1819, he says : " In Judge Bell's case, the event is exceedingly doubtful. My belief is, there is a division on the bench. You may take it for true, at present, that Ch. J., L. and J. [Marshall, Livingston, and Johnson] are in favor of Bell ; W., D. and S., [Washington, Duvall, and Story] *contra.* It is not worth while to mention this, even to Mr. Bell. It is possible that further reflection may bring a majority to think alike, but I am fearful it must stand over and be argued again before Todd." (Mason's Mem. 221, 222.) In his letter to Mason, of February 15, 1819, he says : " The question is before the court, whether the State Bankrupt Laws [Sturges *v.* Crowninshield, 4 Wheat. 122] are valid. The general opinion is that the six judges now here will be equally divided on the point. I confess, however, I have a strong suspicion there will be an opinion, and that that opinion will be *against* the State laws." (Mason's Mem. 219.) The result in these as well as other causes which might be named shows that Webster knew whereof he spoke. Indeed, in those days, judges were not so chary as respects what transpired in consultation as they have since been reputed to be.

Wirt, in his letter to Judge Carr, of March 24, 1817, says: "In relation to the fate of the Washington cause, it is not decided. The court thought the cause with me on the evidence, on which the argument turned; but being an admirality case, they have, according to the practice of that court, indulged the opposite party with farther proof. So that it is possible we shall have another heat at it next winter. Judge Johnson, of the Supreme Court, told me here the other day that my client would certainly recover the cargo (which is infinitely the most valuable part of the subject), and as for the ship, if our adversary did not alter the cause most materially by his farther proof (which it was not believed he could do), we should get that, too." (2 Kennedy's Mem. Wirt, 21, 22.)

We have already seen that after the arguments were closed, and after he knew that the judges were divided in opinion, Webster insisted on pressing the other causes through the Circuit Court up to the Supreme Court.

From the facts already shown may be gathered some of the reasons why the personal friends of Wheelock, late in 1818, committed the fate of these causes to the great Federal lawyer, William Pinkney.

In his letter of November 9, 1818, to Mr. Brown, Webster says: "I received yours yesterday. It will not be necessary to decide on the subject of other counsel until I see you. You do not appear to apprehend my reasons exactly, and I can explain them better *ore tenus;* suffice it to say, at present, that, although if nothing should be necessary in the way of argument but a reply, Mr. Hopkinson or myself might do that, yet if it should be necessary to go over the whole ground again, some new hand must come into the cause. My own impression is to apply, in case of need, to some gentleman there on the spot. Let this rest till January. * * * I am not certain that a new argument will be ordered, and am still more doubtful whether a new opening on our side will be called for.   But this is possible, and if so, some gentleman must repeat our view, and add what he or we may have obtained new.   This event or course of things is not probable, but possible."   (1 Webster's Priv. Cor. 287, 288.)

In Mr. Hopkinson's letter to Webster, of November 17, 1818, he says: "On my arrival here [Washington] I received your letter of the 9th instant, just as I was about to write to you on the same subject.   In my passage through Baltimore, I fell in with Pinkney, who told me he was engaged in the cause by the present University, and that he is desirous to argue it, if the court will let him.   *   *   * On receiving this information from Mr. Pinkney, I seriously reflected upon the course it would be proper for us to take ; and I assure you most truly, I decided precisely in favor of that suggested by you.   It cannot be expected we shall repeat our argument merely to enable Mr. Pinkney to make a speech, or that a cause shall be reargued because, after the argument has been concluded, and the court has the case under advisement, either party may choose to employ new counsel.   I think if the court consents to hear Mr. Pinkney, it will be a great stretch of complaisance, and that we should not give our consent to any such proceeding ; but if Mr. Pinkney, on his own application, is permitted to speak we should claim our right of reply.   The court cannot want to have our argument repeated ; and they will hardly require us to do it for the accommodation of Mr. Pinkney." (1 Webster's Priv. Cor. 288, 289.)

Judge Story, in his letter to the reporter (Wheaton), of December 9, 1818, says: " The next term of the Supreme Court will probably be the most interesting ever known. Several great constitutional questions, the constitutionality of the insolvent laws, of taxing the Bank of the United States, and of the Dartmouth College new charter, will probably be splendidly argued.   Mr. Pinkney is engaged in these and in several other very important questions sent from my circuit." (Life of Story.)

Webster, in his letter to Mason, of December 12, 1818, says: " I learn that Mr. Pinkney means to put our College case on the ground that all the power of Parliament belongs to the N. H. Legislature." (Mason Papers; Harvey's Webster Papers.)

Moody Kent, in his letter to Farrar, of January 31, 1819, says: " Upon my stating to him [Thomas W. Thompson] that it was important the proposals [for publishing Farrar's report] should be opened immediately after the decision was made known, and that it would probably be made known early in Feby., he said that the cause would certainly be again argued — that the court would not refuse to hear an argument — and that the counsel recently engaged, if told that the judges had formed and drawn up their opinion, & were ready to declare it, would nevertheless argue it, and that the decision would not be published till the latter part of March." (Farrar Papers.)

Webster, in his letter to Farrar, of February 1, 1819, says: " The court met to-day, present all but Todd. Judge Johnson is here, and I suppose will sit this term notwithstanding he is nominated collector. Mr. Pinkney will be in town to-day, and I suppose will move for a new argument in the case vs. Woodward. It is most probable, perhaps, that he will succeed in that object, altho' I do not think it by any means certain. Not a word has as yet fallen from any judge on the cause. They keep their own counsel. All that I have seen, however, looks rather favorable. I hope to be relieved of further anxiety by a decision for or ag't us, in five or six days. I'd not have another such cause for the College plain and all its appurtenances." (Farrar Papers.)

In Webster's letter to Mason, of February 4, 1819, two days after the decision, he says: " On the other side, a second argument, as you know, was expected. Dr. Perkins had been a week at Baltimore conferring with Mr. Pinkney.

Mr. Pinkney came up on Monday. On Tuesday morning, he being in court, as soon as the judges had taken their seats, the chief justice said that in vacation the judges had formed opinions in the College cause. He then immediately began reading his opinion, and, of course, nothing was said of a second argument." (Mason's Mem. 213.)

Webster, in his letter to Farrar, of February 9, 1819, says: "I shall endeavor to get the judg't entered as of last term in the case of Mr. Woodward. In the other cases I hope to get a certificate which shall enable Judge Story to know what to do with them in May."

In the following private letter to Judge Smith, of February 28, 1819, which lies before us as we write, Webster says: "Judgment is entered in Trustees v. Woodward as of last Term, that the said Trustees do recover of the said Woodward the aforesaid sum of twenty thousand dollars, so found and assessed as aforesaid; & I have in my bag a mandate to the Superior Court of Judicature of the State of New Hampshire to carry this judgment into execution. So much for that cause & the *second argument* therein expected.

"As to the other causes, Messrs. Pinkney & Wirt have been very much pressed by the Agents and partizans here to argue one of these causes upon the ground of the *new facts*. By the time, however, that we approached near the causes they saw difficulties, and their zeal began to cool. It was impossible to agree on definite facts. It was hardly possible to expect any different result than had already taken place from another argument without new facts. Some of the opinions of the judges appeared to go so far as to be decisive against them, even taking the new facts for granted. At the same time we heard here the echoes of the clamor in N. H. that the cause had not been heard on its true facts. I called up the subject a day or two before we should have reached the causes, & desired to know, from the Counsel, whether it was expected to argue one of those causes. This brought on a conversation between Bench &

Bar, which finally terminated in this : that the causes should be remanded by consent ; that Defts. might, in Circuit Court, move to set aside this Verdict, if they should be so advised, when the opinions of the judges in Woodward's case should be read & known — I found this course would *be agreeable*, & adopted it at once.   In truth I did not want a second argument here upon an *assumption* of facts.   If I do not misjudge, we shall have no difficulty in the Circuit Court.   We shall not, I trust, be called on to agree on any more Special Verdicts.   If the Defts. do not acquiesce in any opinion of the judge, they must take their course by bill of exceptions.

"We are not yet thro. the Bank Question.   Martin has been *talking* 3 ds — Pinkney replies to-morrow, & that finishes.   I set out for home next day."

We have followed the italics of Webster.

Misfortunes never come singly.   It never rains but it pours.   As fate would have it, for nearly a year before the causes were sent back to the Circuit Court, Pinkney and Wirt had been on bad terms.   Pinkney had no rival, as he regarded it, at the bar of the Supreme Court before Webster appeared in the College cause ; and he spared no one who assumed to be a rival.   Oil and water would mix as soon as they, for they agreed in but one thing, and that was in their estimate of Holmes.   Early in 1818, difficulties arose between the two in a trial which took place in Baltimore.   A hostile meeting was only prevented by great exertion.   Judge Story, in his letter to Wheaton of December 9, 1818, from which we have quoted, says in relation to this matter : " I am quite persuaded, without having heard a word of the facts, that our friend Mr. Pinkney is wrong in the recent disagreement with Mr. Wirt.   The latter is a most worthy, good-humored, spirited gentleman, of eminent talents and fine accomplishments.   Mr. Pinkney should not undervalue him, nor seek to obtain a temporary glory by robbing him of a single laurel.   *   *   *   I have the highest opinion of Mr. Pinkney, who is truly *princeps inter principes*. We must talk with him on this subject, and make him feel he has much to lose, and nothing to gain, by the course he sometimes pursues. He need not fear entering into competition with any advocate. All acknowledge his talents and his learning.''

Such a state of things, to say the least, was not eminently favorable for a cordial coöperation between them. Pinkney was a great favorite with the judges, and no man stood higher with the court than he did; but it is evident they did not intend to hear him in these causes. If they had, they would not have forestalled his motion for a reargument by announcing the judgment with a single opinion when nobody expected it; or have ordered a judgment *nunc pro tunc* against the dead, when it was apparent, from the grounds upon which he resisted the motion, that the practical effect would be to drive him out of court in the other causes. The reason for this course is probably to be found in Story's letter to Mason, of October 6, 1819, — in which he says: '' I am exceedingly pleased with your argument in the Dartmouth College case. I always had a desire that the question should be put upon the broad basis you have stated; and it was matter of regret that we were so stinted in jurisdiction in the Supreme Court, that half the argument could not be met and enforced. You need not fear a comparison of your argument with any in our annals,'' — and in his opinion in Charles River Bridge *v.* Warren Bridge, 11 Pet. 584–644, which undoubtedly represented correctly, upon these points, the views of the majority of the judges who sat in the College case. See also Webster's letter to Mason, of April 13, 1819. (Mason's Mem. 223.)

We do not know what Pinkney might have done had these causes been seasonably committed to his keeping. We do know that, notwithstanding his foibles, he was a great man, — an accomplished diplomatist, a great statesman, a consummate orator and profound jurist, and one of the

purest patriots that ever breathed. He was a decided Federalist, but that never discolored his judgment of men,
measures, or parties, or obscured his sense of duty to his
country. He was about fifty-four years old when he attempted to reargue this cause. He came to the bar when
twenty-two, and was sent to the Convention which ratified
the Federal Constitution when twenty-eight. He ran the
gauntlet of the State offices, in the House, Senate, and
Council; and in 1796, Washington sent him to London as
commissioner under the Jay treaty, where he remained for
nearly eight years. In 1804, Maryland made him her
attorney-general; from 1806 to 1811, he was minister to
England, when Madison appointed him attorney-general of
the United States, which office he resigned in about two
years; in 1815, he was a member of Congress; from 1816
to 1818, he was minister to Russia and special minister to
Naples; in 1819, he was elected to the United States Senate; and died on February 22, 1822, from over-exertion in
his profession.

Even Wirt, habitually generous to others, but never just
to Pinkney, said, in his letter to Gilmer of May 9, 1822:
"Poor Pinkney! He died opportunely for his fame. It
could not have risen higher. * * * He was a great
man. On a set occasion, the greatest, I think, at our bar.
I never heard Emmet nor Wells, and therefore do not say
the American bar. He was an excellent lawyer; had very
great force of mind, great compass, nice discrimination,
strong and accurate judgment; and for copiousness and
beauty of diction, was unrivalled. He is a real loss to the
bar. No man dared to grapple with him without the most
perfect preparation, and the full possession of all his
strength. Thus he kept the bar on the alert, and every horse
with his traces tight." (2 Kennedy's Mem. Wirt. 122.)
Judge Story, in his letter to Mr. White, of March 3, 1819,
says: "Mr. Pinkney rose on Monday to conclude the argument; he spoke all that day and yesterday, and will probably

conclude to-day. I never, in my whole life, heard a greater speech; it was worth a journey from Salem to hear it; his elocution was excessively vehement, but his eloquence was overwhelming. His language, his style, his figures, his arguments, were most brilliant and sparkling. He spoke like a great statesman and patriot, and a sound constitutional lawyer. All the cobwebs of sophistry and metaphysics about State rights and State sovereignty he brushed away with a mighty besom. * * * I fear that this speech will never be before the public, but if it should be, it will attract universal admiration. Mr. Pinkney possesses, beyond any man I ever saw, the power of elegant and illustrative amplification." (Life of Story.)

The most diligent search fails to discover any trace of the great argument prepared by Pinkney in the College causes.

CHAPTER X.

WEEKS before Pinkney came into the cases, the machinery
had been devised and put in motion which was to render all
efforts on his part unavailing.

Mr. Webster had no occasion to trouble himself about the
position of Marshall and Washington, for they were with
him ; and quite as little about that of Duvall and Todd, for
they were the other way. The objective point was to control the action of two of the remaining three. Mr. Webster
knew Story's own case, Fletcher v. Peck, and that the
opinion of Mr. Justice Johnson in that case, prepared after
the most elaborate arguments and careful consideration, was
decisive against him in Trustees v. Woodward, whatever the
judge's position might be with reference to the other causes.
He knew Story's position and antecedents as well.

A full history of the movements to which we have referred
can never be written. A portion of the materials are forever lost.

Some have gone to the paper-mill, like many of Thompson's letters ; others, for obvious reasons, have been withheld from the public eye by those who have or had them in
charge. Before us, as we write, lies the written statement of
one of the great actors in this controversy, showing that on

February 28, 1824, he " destroyed " "many letters to and from F. Brown & D. Webster, & letters to & from J. Mason, T. Farrar, M. Olcott, B. J. Gilbert, T. W. Thompson, C. Marsh, A. Livermore, R. Fletcher," etc., relating to this controversy.

But enough remains to show what was done, though it does not disclose every step of the actors.

The fortunes of the old trustees were at their lowest ebb in July, 1818.   At about that time Chancellor Kent visited Windsor, as before stated.   The influence of Dunham, Jacob, Hubbard, and others had made Windsor a University stronghold.   The genial old chancellor was in the house of his friends, and unbosomed himself freely.   He read the opinion of Chief Justice Richardson, and indorsed it.   It soon came to the ears of Marsh and Webster, and the followers of Wheelock all knew it.   It roused the combative blood of Marsh; but Webster, who best understood the position of the judges in Trustees v. Woodward, was despondent.   To his chosen few he confessed that he had little hopes of success in that case.

Isaac Parker, chief justice of the Supreme Court of Massachusetts, was the devoted personal and political friend of Webster.   In his letter of April 28, 1818, to Webster, which lies before us, Judge Parker says: "The effect produced upon my mind by the argument you were good enough to send me, is such as to induce me most earnestly to wish that it may not only be printed, but published and extensively circulated.   Public sentiment has a great deal to do in affairs of this sort, and it ought to be well founded.   That sentiment may even reach and affect a court; at least, if there be any members who wish to do right, but are a little afraid, it will be a great help to know that all the world expects they will do right.   Besides, there is a natural leaning in favor of legislative power, for it is the power of the people when constitutionally exercised; but the people ought to be made to know that in certain cases their rights are above the reach of the Legislature, and thus popularity may be given to a denial of legislative power. In popular governments it is not only expedient, but wise, to get the people on the side of right principles; indeed, that is the only way effectually to prevent wrong.

" The argument of Richardson, Ch. Jus., is completely but decorously answered in your pamphlet; but, unanswered, it will have its weight, not only with the vulgar, but even with the bar and [those] who have not leisure or inclination to look into the thing themselves. It is of importance to enlist all enlightened men on your side of the question, not merely on account of Dartmouth College. Every institution in the country is liable to the same attack, and must [be] defended on the same principles. To show the importance of presenting this argument to every man's view, consider its effect upon me. When I read Richardson's opinion, although I instinctively revolted at his conclusion, yet I was unprepared to show the fallacy of his fundamental point, viz., that a literary institution was a public corporation. Now, nothing appears more weak than his position, for the contrary is demonstrated by reasoning as well as authority. You heard not Leach too, who knows almost everything, ask why a college was not a public corporation. It certainly is probable, then, that many persons, by no means ignorant, are uninstructed upon this subject, not having had occasion to consider it.

" I think, also, that every judge of the Sup. Court of U. S. ought to have a copy of this argument — for what is written, may be recurred to; what is spoken, may be lost.

" I believe the College will ultimately prevail in this suit, for I cannot well perceive how a decision against it can be maintained reputably, considering the principles already adopted by the court.

" You are aware, I suppose, that much less interest has been taken in this question by the learned public than such a great question is calculated to excite. It is because the

conduct of the trustees, previous to the assumption of
power by the Legislature, was generally thought to be unjust and founded in the narrow policy of sectarians.   The
exercise of power by the Legislature, too, has the advantage
of seeming to be favorable to more enlarged and liberal
views.

" Your pamphlet is calculated to show that something
more important than the success of a religious party is at
stake, and to awaken the attention of all who feel an
interest in the principles upon which any institution can
be supported, and this is another strong reason for publishing and circulating."

There are some singular things about this letter.   Whether
in his actual presence or not, it was undoubtedly written
after a personal conference between Marsh, the sole plaintiff
in one, one of the plaintiffs in another, and the active
counsel and a manager in all these suits, with Judge Parker,
for which purpose Marsh had apparently travelled one
hundred and forty miles from his home.

It was undoubtedly taken from the hands of its author
by Marsh to Webster, at Ipswich, where the latter was.
Whether this was done, as was suggested by Judge Smith
in relation to one of his letters, for fear copies might be
taken in the post-office, does not appear.

The letter shows for itself that it never passed through
the mail, and bears upon its back, in the handwriting of its
author, the following indorsement: " Hon. Daniel Webster.   Marsh, bearer."

The author of this letter was the one to whom Mr.
Brown afterwards referred, in his letter to Webster from
Albany, dated September 9, 1818, hereafter quoted.   The
allusion to the public sentiment in regard to the trustees,
and the necessarily more delicate one which had reference
to the position of certain judges, can hardly be misunderstood; but the framers of the Constitution never intended
to commit the guardianship and construction of that instru-

ment to a court whose decisions were controlled by the atmosphere of a manufactured public sentiment.

That Kent's opinion would have great weight with Justice Johnson, and that his opinion and influence with that of Governor Clinton were potential with Justice Livingston, was obvious to all who understood the relations of these men.

Those who managed for the College utilized this power.

Judge Woodward died, at Hanover, August 9, 1818. The death of the defendant seems to have given new life to the other side; but the legal warfare, the plottings and counter-plottings, still went on over his ashes.

Marsh, the political friend of Kent, furnished him a copy of Webster's argument, and a commentary upon the case, and the Windsor opinion referred to, in his letter to Kent, of August 22, 1818, to which the chancellor replied in his letter of August 26, 1818, hereafter quoted.

Conferences were had — mostly at Albany, New York — between Kent and Johnson, and Brown with Kent, Governor Clinton, and a *coterie* of their adherents. Kent changed his views, and agreed to draw up an opinion for Johnson in this case, who, " in the end," went with Livingston and Story. The nominal basis was, if we are to credit Kent, a political decision of the Council of Revision created by the old Constitution of New York, made when Kent, Livingston, and Clinton were members.

One of the duties of this tribunal was to see that no law passed which was in violation of the Constitution.

The Constitution of New York, of April 20, 1777, contained the following proviso: " But that nothing in this Constitution contained shall be construed to affect any grants of land within this State, made by the authority of said king or his predecessors, or to annul any charters to bodies-politic, by him or them, or any of them made prior to that day,[October 14, 1775,] and that none of the said charters shall be adjudged to be void by reason of any non-user or misuser of any of their respective rights and privileges between [April 19, 1775,] and the publication of this Constitution.''

The record is as follows : —

COUNCIL OF REVISION, ALBANY, April 4, 1804.

Present, Governor Clinton, Lewis, Chief Justice; Kent, Livingston, Thompson and Spencer, Justices. A bill entitled, ''An act relative to the election of charter officers in the city of New York,'' was before the council, which adopted the following objections reported by Justice Kent, viz.: —

Because the bill contains important alterations in the charter of the said city, and it not appearing in the bill, by recital or otherwise, that the same were made upon the application or with the consent of the parties interested, it is to be intended that they are made without such application or consent; and although it be granted that such an inference would be justified by some strong public necessity, it is not to be presumed by the council that any such necessity exists in the present case as none are recited in the bill or appear from the provisions in it; and it has been considered as a settled and salutary principle in our government that, in all cases where the ordinary process of law affords a competent remedy, charters of incorporation containing grants of personal and municipal privileges were not to be essentially affected without the consent of the parties concerned.

Notwithstanding the objections the Legislature passed the bill into a law.

Considering the well-nigh endless changes made by the Legislature in their charter, it would probably astound the people of New York, of this day, to learn that they were invalid unless made with their consent.

Though there is an apparent contradiction in the terms, Johnson was a Republican Centralist, and Kent, as his earlier decisions showed, a State Rights Federalist. They naturally gravitated towards each other.

The chancellor was a great admirer of Webster, and treated his views with extreme deference; and, though probaby not aware of the fact himself, was a strong partisan. His letters in the Bridge case, and treatment of Emmet, show this.

The question in Emmet's case was, virtually, whether the rules of court requiring three or six years' study should be suspended, so that he might be admitted to the New York bar, or whether, with his large and dependent family, he should be driven into the western wilderness. Under the advice of Governor Clinton, and DeWitt Clinton then mayor of New York, an informal application in behalf of Emmet was made to the judges of the Supreme .Court by George and DeWitt Clinton. The remainder of the story is thus told by Col. Charles G. Haines, the friend and admirer of Kent, who had it from Mr. Emmet's own lips. He says: "Chief Justice Spencer was then on the bench as a *puisne* judge. Judge Thompson and Vice-President Tompkins were also there. Chancellor Kent was the chief justice. Spencer, Tompkins, and Thompson were found friendly; Kent, peculiarly hostile. Judge Spencer was strong and decided, and Mr. Emmet always mentions the kindness, the friendship, and the effective aid of Vice-President Tompkins with many expressions of gratitude. Within two years past he argued a most important cause for the vice-president, without fee or reward, and obtained a verdict of $130,000, it being a suit with the United States. He said he did it with great pleasure, in remembrance of former friendship. Chancellor Kent was a warm, and I may almost say a violent Federalist. He execrated all republican principles in Europe, and was the disciple of Edmund Burke as to the French Revolution. He looked on Mr. Emmet with an unkind eye, and raised his voice against his appearing in the forums of our State. To the honor of the chancellor, however, let it now be said, that he' has more than once

expressed joy to Mr. Emmet that the other judges overruled
his illiberal objections." (Memoir of Emmet, by Haines,
86, 87.)

Judge Livingston was a member of the famous New York
family of that name. He was about sixty-two years old
when this case was decided by the Supreme Court of the
United States, and died some four years later. He graduated from Princeton, served upon the staff of Generals
Schuyler and Arnold in the Revolution, and was admitted
to the bar in 1783. For five years after his appointment, in
January, 1802, he occupied a seat between Kent and Thompson upon the Supreme Bench of New York. His opinions
appear in the first, and a small part of the second volume of
Johnson's Reports. They exhibit his peculiar characteristics. It was hardly necessary for Kent to tell us of Livingston's disrelish for English authorities, though he often
examined them with great care to see if they agreed with
him. His hobby was commercial law, to which fact, and
the peculiar relations which the Livingston family had held
with the political parties of New York, he was mainly
indebted for his appointment by Jefferson. He was an
accomplished scholar, an excellent advocate, and an able
judge. His peculiar organization gave him great independence. Kent had great influence with him. The shrewd old
chancellor, in his letter of October 6, 1828 (Southern Law
Review, July, 1872), says: "In February, 1798, I was
offered by Governor Jay, and accepted, the office of youngest
judge of the Supreme Court. This was the summit of my
ambition. * * * I never dreamed of volumes of reports,
and written opinions; such things were not then thought of.
* * * When I came to the bench there were no reports
or State precedents. The opinions from the bench were
delivered *ore tenus*. We had no law of our own, and nobody
knew what it was. * * * Many of the cases decided
during the sixteen years I was in the Supreme Court were

labored by me most unmercifully, but it was necessary under the circumstances to subdue opposition. We had but few American precedents ; our judges were democratic, and my brother Spencer, particularly, of a bold, vigorous, dogmatic mind, and overbearing manner. English authorities did not stand very high in these feverish times, and this led me a hundred times to attempt to bear down opposition, or shame it by exhausting research and overwhelming authority. * * * I made much use of the *corpus juris*, and as the judges (Livingston excepted) knew nothing of French or civil law, I had an immense advantage over them. I could generally put my brethren to rout and carry my point by my mysterious wand of French and civil law. The judges were republicans, and very kindly disposed to every thing that was French, and this enabled me, without exciting any alarm or jealousy, to make free use of such authorities, and thereby enrich our ' commercial law.' I gradually acquired proper directing influence with my brethren, and the volumes in Johnson, after I became judge in 1804, show it."

Col. Haines, who had for years been on terms of close intimacy with Livingston, and was as familiar with his opinions in manuscript as he was with those of Chancellor Kent, in his argument in Ogden *v.* Saunders, to which we have before referred, says: "Mr. Justice Livingston, recently one of this court, was the associate of Alexander Hamilton, Chancellor Livingston, and other able and efficient men who contributed to the establishment of the Constitution, and took a leading part himself in the events of the times."

He then quotes, in relation to the history of the obligation clause, from the opinion given by Livingston in Adams *v.* Storey. That opinion was in striking contrast with the opinion of Marshall on the same subject, in Sturges *v.* Crowninshield.

Adams *v.* Storey (Paine C. Ct. 79, 109) was decided by Judge Livingston, at the April term, 1817. It was an action brought on promissory notes made or indorsed by the defendant, then residing in Boston, to the plaintiff, who were then and at the time of the decision residents of Boston, where the notes were made payable. The notes were given, etc., prior to the passage of the statute of New York, of April 3, 1811, "for the benefit of insolvent debtors and their creditors." The plaintiff gave notice, under the general issue, that he should put in evidence a discharge by the recorder of the city of New York, granted under said statute, November 13, 1811, where the defendant then resided. A verdict was taken for the plaintiff by consent, subject to the opinion of the court on the case stated.

In summing up, Livingston says : "Upon the whole this court is of opinion, that the act of the 3d of April, 1811, is an insolvent, and not a bankrupt law — that if it be of the latter description, the several States have a right to pass bankrupt laws for themselves, until Congress shall establish a uniform system on the subject — that an insolvent act extending to past, as well as future debts, is not a law 'impairing the obligation of contracts,' within the meaning of the Constitution — and that a Federal Court, sitting within this State, is bound to support a discharge under such law, against the claim of a foreign creditor, although the debt due to him may have been contracted and made payable at his place of residence."

The opinion is about thirty pages in length, and contains an elaborate discussion of the obligation clause, and that in relation to bankruptcies. He denies that the law of the place where the contract was made enters into the contract or its obligation, and that the rule so often cited from Huberus and Casaregis has any application, and says: "When the latter speaks of contracts territorial and exterritorial, it is most manifest that he means nothing more than that a contract made in one country is not to be construed by the laws of another. Now the difficulty is to find out what the *lex loci contractus* has to do with the case of a

future insolvency, or how the law of one country can differ
from that of another in this respect. It is presumed to be
law everywhere that a man is to pay according to his contract; but if he be unable to pay any where, what then has
the *lex loci* to do with the case? * * * The power to
pass laws of this character, [bankrupt laws] it is said, is
exclusively vested in Congress, and whether they exercise
it or not, no State can have a bankrupt law of its own. As
a consolidation of the different States into one national
sovereignty was neither effected nor intended to be effected
by the Constitution, it has always been conceded that the
State governments retained so much of the power, which
they before had, as was not by that instrument exclusively
delegated to the United States. * * * It is agreed that
such exclusive alienation of State sovereignty can only exist
in three cases: where, by its terms, it is so; or where a
power is conferred on the Federal government, and the
States are prohibited from exercising a similar authority; or
where an authority is granted to the former, to which the
exercise of a like power on the part of the different States
would be absolutely and totally contradictory and repugnant.
It is not pretended that the grant of the power under consideration is exclusive in its terms, or that there is an
express prohibition on the States from exercising a like
authority, but it is supposed that such exercise would be
so totally inconsistent with the one granted to the government of. the Union, as to be necessarily comprehended in
the third class of exclusive delegation. * * * It is an
uniform rule which Congress are to prescribe. But if they
furnish none how is it an interference for each State to legislate for itself? Neither the terms nor the spirit of the
instrument are thus disturbed. It seems designedly to have
been left optional with the general government to exercise
this power, that if the embarrassments which lay in their
way were insurmountable, or very great, they might omit
to do it, and thus leave the States to take care of themselves. If it had been intended immediately to divest the

States of all power on this subject, and to compel Congress to act, the terms of the article would have been much more imperative than we find them, and probably it would have been accompanied with a prohibition on the States."

He further says: "Another constitutional objection is made to the defence which is set up in this cause. The law under which this discharge was obtained, having passed subsequent to the date of the notes on which the action is brought, is supposed to 'impair the obligation of contracts,' and therefore to be void, either in the whole or so far as it may extend to debts incurred previous to the passage of it. There is not perhaps in the Constitution any article of more ambiguous import, or which has occasioned and will continue to occasion, more discussion and disagreement, than the one under which the present difficulty arises, or the application of which to the cases which occur, will be attended with more perplexity and embarrassment. Laws may be passed which so palpably trespass on this article as to leave no doubt in the mind of any man; others again will be of so questionable a character as to render it not very easy to form a satisfactory opinion concerning them. All the other restraints upon the separate members of the Confederacy, contained in this section of the Constitution are conceived in terms so clear and intelligible, that rarely will any hesitation exist as to what will amount to violations of them; but to decide whether a law impairs the obligation of a contract, will generally be a task of some intricacy, and it will not be surprising if, in the discharge of it, great diversity of opinion should arise.   *   *   *   To arrive at the true meaning of any article of doubtful import in the Constitution, a better mode cannot be adopted than the course which is generally pursued for the interpretation and understanding of ordinary remedial statutes; that is, to recur to the situation and history of the country at the time; to its contemporaneous exposition, if it has received any; and to the general understanding of the community, especially if such understanding shall have been long acqui-

esced in by all the States and all the courts of the Union.
Keeping in view these rules, let us inquire what were the
kind of laws to which this prohibition was principally
designed to extend. There can be no doubt that by it was
intended to be corrected some, if not all, of the evils which
had crept into the system of legislation of many of the
States, and had excited a considerable alarm for the security
of *private rights*. * * * During a long and arduous
struggle for independence, much individual misery and
distress were unavoidably produced. Driven from their
homes, and cut off in many cases, from their ordinary pursuits, the resources of many were either exhausted or so
much impaired, as to induce the Legislature, on various
occasions, to listen to the pressing calls which were made
upon them to devise some mode for their relief. Various
expedients were accordingly resorted to, and the practice of
interfering between creditor and debtor became so very
extensive, and so inconsiderate, as in many instances to
place the former entirely at the mercy of the latter, and
that, too, under laws which were apparently introduced
with no other view than that of affording to the debtor a
temporary relief from the pressure occasioned by the then
situation of the country. Bills of credit, and paper money,
were issued, and by legislative sanction were substituted for
gold and silver in the discharge of debts. Creditors, in
some places, were liable, without any adverse proceeding on
their part, to be cited by their debtors, and to have the sums
due to them tendered in a currency whose depreciation at the
time produced the most glaring injustice. On their refusal
to submit to this mockery of justice, the public securities,
which had been thus offered might be deposited with some
public officer, and the creditor was forever barred from any
recovery. In other cases, payments were authorized to
be made by instalments. In some States, the interest which
had accrued during the war, or a part of it, was remitted ;
while elsewhere, not only a paper currency of no value, but

almost every species of property, was made a legal tender,
and no stipulation, however solemn, to pay in the precious
metals, afforded any security to the creditor. The courts
of justice, in many of the States, had been closed altogether,
and the creditor thus withheld, at least for a time, from
every appeal to the laws of his country, while his debtor
might be squandering the property out of which his demand
ought to have been satisfied. Geographical limits had also
been resorted to for the purpose of introducing the most
odious discriminations between creditors themselves. For
those who resided within the British lines and those who
were without these precincts, distinct remedies were prescribed, and the scales of justice so unequally graduated,
that while the latter might recover the whole of their
demands, the former, if they sued, were compelled to
receive public certificates of one description or other, of so
little value, as scarcely to indemnify them for the costs of
suit which they were obliged to pay. Very great liberties
had also been taken with British creditors, many of whom
complained, and too justly, of the impediments which continued to be thrown in their way, even after the return of
peace.''

We have the authority of Story for saying that Livingston did not recant these views in Sturges v. Crowninshield.

We copy entire the letter from Kent to Marsh, to which
we have already adverted : —

ALBANY, 26 August, 1818.

DEAR SIR, — Your letter of the 22d inst. with Mr. Webster's
argument was received this morning, & I thank you for this
mark of attention.

The argument does credit to the talents & principles of Mr.
Webster. I have been long taught by his parliamentary produc-
tions to esteem & admire him. I took a hasty journey the other
day through part of your State to recruit my spirits. Mrs K &
I started in the stage from this city and reached Brattleboro the
same day. This ride gave me abundantly what I sought, which
was jolting mountain air. The next day we went up to Hanover

& while rambling there over the beautiful green I met a gentleman I knew & this led me to an introduction to the president &
professors of the *university*. I was not so fortunate as to meet
with a similar introduction to the officers of the college though
it was equally desirable. Being on the spot & witnessing the
college sessions I was anxious to know something of the controversy though nothing was said on the subject by the gentlemen
to whom I was introduced. I had often casually heard the
subject mentioned but knew nothing of its merits. After some
search I was enabled to purchase the opinion of the Sup. Court
of N. H. as delivered by the Ch. J. and read it the next day on
my return to Windsor. That opinion furnished me with the few
scanty facts I possessed in regard to the great constitutional question and it appeared to me on a hasty perusal of it that the Legislature was competent to pass the laws in question, for I was led by the
opinion to assume the fact that Dartmouth College was a public establishment for purposes of a general nature. I knew nothing, nor
do I now know anything material in respect to the *policy or motives*
of the laws or what were the real inducements to pass them.

But I will declare to you with equal frankness that the fuller
statement of facts in Mr. W.'s argument in respect to the original
& reasons & substance of the charter of 1769 and the sources
of the gifts, gives a new *complexion to the case* and it is very
probable that if I was now to sit down and seriously study the
case with *the facts at large* before me that I should be led to a
different conclusion from the one I had at first formed. But my
hasty impressions one way or the other are not worth mentioning
for I deem them of no value. I have merely stated these inci-
dents to show how very acceptable is the argument you sent me.
I am exceedingly pleased with the settlements on Connecticut
River. We rode from Windsor to Burlington in a day and I had
only a glimpse of Woodstock where you reside as we passed
rapidly through it about sunrise. The ride that day was delightful, for I have always looked on mountain scenery and the quiet &
substantial comforts of country life with enthusiasm. I hope you
will make yourself known to me if you ever pass through Albany.

                                                JAMES KENT.
To CHARLES MARSH, Esq.

As has already been suggested, the opinion of Judge
Richardson contained a statement of facts ; and the pam-

phlet produced by Kent gave precisely the same information as the State report. Probably no person was ever
misled by the State report, — except (?) Chancellor Kent.
Strange as it may seem, Daniel Webster and Jeremiah
Mason never discovered it.

The State of New York was divided between Clinton and
Tompkins.

Unfortunately for Wheelock's adherents, the organization of the party with which they necessarily became
affiliated in New Hampshire was controlled by men bitterly
opposed to Clinton. No man knew it better than he, for
a portion of his most active supporters, like Colonel Haines,
were New Hampshire men, familiar with every phase of the
College quarrel and the political warfare in the State.

Clinton was able, strong-willed, and combative in the
highest degree. Like the petrel, he was always at home
in a storm. Governor Plumer was an anti-Clintonian.

In August, 1818, Isaac Hill, the great pillar of support
of the Wheelock cause, with whom Haines was well
acquainted, openly assailed Clinton with great bitterness
in his newspaper. It was but natural for President Brown
to " hope," under these circumstances, that Clinton " would
incline to favor us rather than our competitors."

The following remarkable letter from Brown to Webster,
dated at Albany, September 8, 1818, throws a flood of light
on this part of the inside history of these causes. He says :
" I arrived in this city three days ago on a journey under-
taken for the general purposes of the College.

" I have seen Chancellor Kent, and am to dine with him
to-day. The chancellor was in our quarter about the last
of July — saw Judge R.'s opinion — was pleased with it —
& spoke in approbation of it before the great men of Windsor. The story of course went through the country, that
Chan. K. had, after examination of the case, given a decided
opinion in favor of the Univ. Mr. Marsh sent him your
argument.

" As soon as I saw him, he began to express his regret at

what he had said at Windsor — he really had not examined the subject at all — gave a hasty perusal to Judge R.'s pamphlet — was disappointed to find in it so much legal talent — and, although he was careful to state that his opinion was not to be relied on, yet, *if the premises assumed* by the court were correct, he did not see but the conclusion would follow. This is substantially the account he gives of his remarks at Windsor. He told me he had replied to Mr. Marsh's letter accompanying the argument, and had said to him, that this argument gave a very different complexion to the case, &c.

"I think it may be of some importance to the right decision of the case, that the chancellor should not only have a correct opinion, but should be induced to declare it. Judge Johnson has been here. This the chan. mentioned, & he also said that the judge conversed on our case, & remarked that the court had a cause of 'awful' magnitude to decide &c. From what I learn from other sources the judge has formally requested the chan.'s opinion. This opinion, if given, will also have great influence on Judge Livingston. Now I think the chan. on examination of the case, cannot fail to be right. He had, he said, great pleasure in reading your argument, and spoke in terms sufficiently flattering of the legal ability & logical power displayed in it, & added he should probably, if he had time to examine all the facts, agree fully with you. But still there was some reserve, which perhaps arose altogether from an apprehension that I should imprudently report what he might say, — but possibly it may be otherwise.

"I have thought it best to communicate these facts to you, that you may consider whether any thing is to be done. Does Judge Parker know the chancellor, & would he be inclined to write him on the subject?

"*Evening.* — I have been with the chancellor. He has read the charter, and it is evident to me that he is satisfied. I asked him if the corporation of D. C. did not appear to be a private eleemosynary corporation. He smiled & said he believed he must express no more opinions till the cause should be decided.

"I have also been presented to Gov. Clinton to-day, who kindly inquired respecting our cause, & expressed a desire to see our charter & the argument. These, of course, I did not hesitate to furnish him. I shall have opportunity of calling on him again before I leave Albany, and hope he will incline to favour us rather than our competitors.

" The following statement, which I have had from the best authority, will show the *leaning* of three great men in New York : In 1803, the Leg. of this State attempted to change the charter of N. Y. City without consent of the corporation. The present gov. & chan., & Judge Livingston were of the Council of Revision (if that be the name), that year — the chan. objected to the bill, and assigned his reasons, which embrace some of the main points of your argument. The objection was overruled.[1] The next year a still further attempt was made by the Legislature, a similar objection was made, and it prevailed. Both Gov. Clinton and Judge *Livingston* sided with the chan.

" Judge Johnson expressed to Chancellor Kent a strong desire to have a copy of the printed argument. I wish you would forward one to him. I have none to spare."

This letter went from Webster into the hands of Farrar, another of the counsel. Farrar preserved it with great care, and it is now in the archives of the New Hampshire Historical Society, among the papers relating to these causes, known as the " Farrar Papers."

Whether " Judge Parker " wrote "the chancellor " or not, does not as yet appear. We have been unable to exhume the Kent-Johnson opinion, our letter-files showing that Johnson's papers, like those of Pinkney and Haines, have been scattered to the four winds.

Mr. Brown does not state who his informants, " the best

[1] See Brown's letter to Webster, of September 15, 1818, hereafter quoted.

authority," "and other sources," were. Several undoubtedly contributed, but he was probably more indebted to
Colonel Haines than any other one.

Haines was a young man of rare promise and exceptional
facilities. He was born in 1793, in Canterbury, which joins
Concord, New Hampshire, the ancient boundaries of his
native town touching the "paternal acres" of Webster.

When fourteen years of age, with Nathaniel H. Carter, who
was afterwards one of the professors in the University, and a
prominent New York Clintonian editor, politician, and man
of letters, and others, he became a clerk in the office of
Philip Carrigan, then secretary of state of New Hampshire.
He graduated at Middlebury College, Vermont, in 1816.
In 1817, for the benefit of his health, he took a trip on
horseback to Albany and Pittsburg. On this trip he became
acquainted with Surrogate Sylvanus Miller, and then with
Governor Clinton, who induced him to go to New York.
He soon returned, read law with Horatio Seymour, afterwards United States senator from Vermont, and acted as
assistant editor of a political newspaper at the same time.
Early in 1818 he removed to New York, and entered the
office of Pierre Van Wyck, became the *protégé* of Clinton,
who gave him the confidential position of private secretary, which he held till 1821. He served his patron with
a devotion which knew no bounds, till his death, July 3,
1825.

He edited *The United States Law Journal*, and wrote a
legion of essays on legal, historical, and political subjects.

It is tribute enough to his ability to say that his argument in Ogden *v.* Saunders carried with him a majority of
the Supreme Court, against Wheaton, Webster, Story, and
John Marshall, and is to-day, without a dissenting voice, the
recognized law of the Union. Webster, after his death, said
of him: "He was ten years my junior, and when he died I
think the most brilliant man in the country." Whoever
had his ear had that of Clinton.

If the daily journal which Kent kept, and his private

papers, are ever given to the public, they will probably throw additional light upon the subject.

Apparently not one word of this ever came to the ears of the counsel for the University, or any of its friends.

The statement in Brown's letter, in relation to the Council of Revision, and that of Haines in Ogden v. Saunders, on another point, are almost identical, showing that they had a common source. Colonel Haines said : " Legislative expositions are not to be relied on in determining constitutional questions ; but it may be well to state that there was formerly a peculiarity in the Constitution of the State of New York worthy of notice. The old Constitution was adopted in 1777, and established a Council of Revision, composed of the governor of the State, the chancellor, and the five judges of the Supreme Court. It was the particular duty of this Council to revise all laws before they received their last sanction, and to judge of their constitutionality. This Council was under oath to support the Constitution of the United States. One year after the adoption of the Constitution of 1777 a general bankrupt system was established in New York. In 1801 it was revised. In 1811 there was a new system ; and in 1813 the old law of 1801 was revived. Chief Justice Jay, George Clinton, Chancellor Livingston, Chancellor Kent, and Chief Justices Thompson and Spencer were members of this Council. They saw no repugnancy to the Constitution of the United States in these laws, as they came under their review.''

While en route from Albany, Brown wrote to Webster the following significant letter, which lies before us : —

REEDSBORO (GREEN MOUNTAINS), Sept. 15, 1818.

MY DEAR SIR, — I am so far on my way from Albany. After I wrote you I had repeated opportunities with the chancellor. There is no doubt that, by the argument & the charter, he is brought completely over to our side ; & he has a full impression of the importance of the question. I believe he will take every proper and prudent measure to impart correct views to others.

While I remained in Albany another copy of your argument fell
into his hands, which, he said, agreeably to the strong wish
of Judge Johnson, he should transmit to him. You will judge
of the expediency of requesting any Mass. jurist to write a line
to the chancellor, as hinted in my last. A little delay, however,
I should think advisable, should any communication be made.

I said something respecting legislative interference with the
charter of the city of N. Y. A part was correct, & a part not.
The following presents a true view of the case. With the chan.'s
permission, I copied from an appendix, in his own handwriting,
to a printed collection of the proceedings of the city corporation,
as follows: —

"IN COUNCIL OF REVISION, March 4, 1803.

"Present, the Govr.; Judges Kent, Livingston, Thompson.
The bill below mentioned was committed to me."

"IN COUNCIL, March 8, 1803.

"Present, *ut supra.*

"I reported the following objections, &c.: (The bill was entitled, 'An act to increase the number of wards in the city of New
York,' &c.)

"1. The bill contains certain alterations in the charter of said
city, not made on application, or with the consent of the mayor,
aldermen, &c.

"2. This alteration without consent is a breach of the faith
of govt. pledged to p. corporations, &c.

"3. If the alteration contained in the sd. bill can be made
without consent of the cor., others may be, &c. And any
charter or grant from govt. can be altered or rescinded at
pleasure."

(All the Council against him.)

"IN COUNCIL OF REV., March 31, 1804.

"Present, the Govr. (Clinton), George; Chf. Just. Lewis;
Judges Kent, Livingston, Thompson, Spencer.

"A bill entitled, 'An act relative to the election of charter
officers in the city of N. Y.,' was read and committed to Mr.
Justice Kent."

(From objns. I quote only the following:)

"It has been considered & treated as a settled and salutary
principle in our govt. that charters of incor. were not to be
essentially affected without due process of law, or without con-

sent of the parties concerned. Nothing but a strong *publick necessity* would justify such an interference.

(This objection was overruled by *all* the *judges*. The Govr. requested time to deliberate.)

"In Council, April 4, the Govr. reported an objection *substantially* the same" as the above; in which Judges Kent, *Livingston* & Thompson concurred; the other two non-concurred.

The chancellor sd. it was to be considered he made these objns. as a politician, not as a judge; and he was not clear that the doctrine laid down was correct, as applied to corporations for the purpose of govt., &c. Of all this a *prudent* use is to be made by us.

As to DeWitt Clinton, to whom I *lent* the argument, he went off to his canal before I called for it & carried it with him. No harm, I trust, will arise from its remaining with him.

I regard my visit to Albany as of no small importance to our cause. The Court of Errors being in session, the greatest legal talents in the State were convened there; and, so far as any impression has been given, it is unquestionably in our favor. The whole is, of course, attributable to you. Every day brings additional proofs of the propriety & even necessity of giving circulation to your argument. I ought to have added above, that Gov. Clinton said he understood the Sup. Court would sustain the action and probably decide for the College.

So much for Albany. I know not whether you will be able to decypher this; if not, please to write me, & I will endeavor to explain.   I am, my dear sir, truly yours,

                                     FRANCIS BROWN.

HON. D. WEBSTER.

Webster replied to these letters. His answers are still in existence. We have not been able to obtain them for publication, but have been courteously furnished with the following extract from Webster's letter to Brown, of September 20, 1818: "I recd. yours from Albany, & to-day that from Reedsboro'. You are probably at home by this time and will find one from me. I am particularly gratified with the state of things where you have been.

"I never doubted for a moment on which side of such a question C. K.'s mind must ultimately rest. I have studied him (in his works) many years, and I think I understand him. He has great talents, great legal learning, & greatness, *firmness*, & independence of mind. His opinion will have *weight* wherever it is known.

" I hope he may express himself as occasion may offer."

DART. COLL. Sept. 19, 1818.

MY DEAR SIR, — I have received your favor of the 6th, and have seen Mr. Marsh.

In regard to the reprinting, I have some little doubt, whether the benefit to be expected would render the measure expedient, considering how soon it may be hoped the *volume* will appear. The very scarcity of the argument, & the half-secret & cautious manner of the distribution, stimulate curiosity, & add somewhat to the *preciousness* of the document. It has already been, or shortly will be, read by all the *commanding* men of New England & New York; and so far as it has gone it has united them all, without a single exception within my knowledge, in one broad and impenetrable phalanx for our defence & support. N. E. & N. Y. *are gained.* Will not this be sufficient for our present purposes? If not, I should recommend the reprinting. And on this point you are the best judge. I prevailingly think, however, that the current [of] opinion from this part of the country is setting so strongly towards the South that we may safely trust to its force alone to accomplish whatever is necessary. I acknowledge I am sanguine, and, on that account, ought to distrust myself. I, therefore, conclude this topick by saying, if, in your opinion, any thing more *needs* to be done in enlightening the *more eminent* of the professional men of the country, let a hundred or two copies be struck off without delay. But even in that case I should recommend the principle of selection in the distribution; for I would not allow the argument to be common, until it is to be sold.

Prof. Adams has mentioned your plan for funds and I hope you will not give it up (unless a better one presents) on account of the free remarks of our excellent friend Mr. Marsh. He mentioned that he discouraged a loan — the favor must be a *gift*. I agree with him, so far as this mode can be made to succeed; so far as it cannot, the other is unquestionably to be seized with thankfulness.

It is true we shall have to struggle hard, even after we have gained the victory in the legal combat. And, therefore, it is our duty to provide, in the present exigency, which presents a tangible object to the community, for future emergencies. I do not yet despair of obtaining all that may be needed, as a gift. We can at least pull on this string for two or three months. Will it not then be best to suspend operations for a loan for the present? When January comes we shall know how we stand, & what more is necessary, and we can then act according to circumstances.

I have received an answer from Mr. Hopkinson. He consents to prepare his part of the argument for publication, and I presume it will be ready in season. The book must be out at the earliest possible day after the opinion of the court can be procured. Will it be best to print in Boston? What printers shall be employed? Will it be best to have proposals issued beforehand? What terms can be secured? — these are inquiries which have occurred to me, & which I will thank you to consider at some convenient time.

We are under obligations to Dr. Kirkland for his civilities & proffers of aid. I have no question of his sincerity; and I believe he exercises no more caution than other men in eminent stations have thought proper to observe. We will avail ourselves of his kindness at such time & in such manner as may seem best.

I am, my dear sir, as ever,

Yours,

FRANCIS BROWN.

HON. D. WEBSTER.

We have followed the italics of Mr. Brown. To him all the secrets of the counsel were committed. It is quite obvious that in this letter he personates the three judges geographically, and equally so that he regarded two of them — all that were needed — as " gained " to the side of the College, and that Johnson was favorably inclined.

In his letter, written from the College to Mr. Webster, dated September 26, 1818, Mr. Brown says: " When anything new occurs, of any importance to the common concern, I think proper to apprize you of it. I am not, however, without fear, that I shall weary you by my letters.

" Dr. Perkins has said, since his return, that he borrowed a copy of the argument, under the restriction of not allowing it to go out of his hands, of not copying it, &c., with liberty to keep it a few days or weeks. But, he observed, as some parts of it have been copied, by some of his friends at a distance, & *will be used* on their side, he thought best to return the argument to you next morning, after taking it, lest you should suspect *him* of having made the copies. He added, that he *had obtained* the abstracts. Some uncharitable individuals think it possible *the friends at a distance* were friends in Boston. What use is to be made, he did not say ; whether they are to be published in the newspaper at Concord, or only put into the hands of counsel. If parts are to be inserted & commented on in their papers, unquestionably the argument ought to be published & circulated. We shall see how this is shortly.

" At Exeter, as I learn, they are going to attempt to show from the correspondence of Dr. E. Wheelock that he considered the College to be altogether distinct from the *school;* the *school,* to be sure, being a *private charity,* — the College a *publick* institution, & on a very different foundation. I presume no such evidence will be admitted. If it should be, the trial must be long, & it is impossible to conjecture what may be shown.

" In the attempt which they will make, to prove this not to be a private elecmosynary corporation, they will probably bring in the lands & other donations given by the Leg. of N. H. May it not be of some consequence to ascertain these grants, & obtain copies from the secy's. office ?

" In the argument of the cause, I also learned, they will attempt (probably the attempt was made last March by Mr. Wirt,) to show a distinction between the *universities* in Eng. & the *colleges* founded *within* them — the latter being admitted to be charities, the former not, but designed for the purposes of regulation, government, &c., and Dart College resembles the univties. rather than the colleges in

Eng, *Ergo*, the Leg. has a right to interfere. This, I doubt not, has occurred to you. They will make it, I think, their great point.

" As to the question, 'Who shall argue the cause on our side?' I answer very decisively, yourself, unless reasons should occur against it, which I have not yet thought of. At present I think I should not be willing to trust it in any other hands.

" I have the fullest confidence in our counsel at Exeter; at the same time I should rejoice should you find it convenient to be there. They will endeavor to bring in as many things as can possibly be found to give to D. C. *the appearance* of being what it is not, an institution of a public character, such as it is admitted the govt. may control."

This letter shows that it was sent by a private messenger, Mr. Kent, directed to Webster at his old home, " Salisbury, or Concord."

The Albany conferences, as well as a portion of Judge Parker's letter, undoubtedy had their inspiration in the fertile brain of Marsh.

None knew the impropriety of the means resorted to for influencing the minds of certain judges better than Marsh; but he probably justified himself in taking such steps because of the course which he understood had been followed by Story.

We have been unable to obtain his letters, but his views in this respect appear distinctly enough in the letter to him from his associate counsel, Hopkinson, which we quote entire :—

WASHINGTON, Dec. 31, 1817.

DEAR SIR, — I received your favor of the 19th inst. enclosing a note for Mess. Gales and Seaton which I shall deliver without delay; and trust it will have the effect to induce them to keep their press silent in a matter of so much importance, and which is to come before the highest tribunal in the nation for decision. Altho. the attempts of the defts in this case to excite a prejudice in the public mind by newspapers, and party representations, is vile and unjust, it is likely they will be able to produce less effect, by these means, upon a court than a jury.

The situation in which, if you are not misinformed, Judge Story has placed himself is much more alarming to us — and so disreputable to him should he sit in the case — that I confess I am inclined to believe that your information in this respect, must be mistaken, should it however be otherwise and he is about to sit as judge in a cause in which he has been a feed counsellor, I should have no hesitation in resorting to any legal and proper means to prevent such an abuse of power and office. The influence of the judge with the court in general cases, is, I think, considerable; and will probably be very great in one like the present. If, therefore, the judge has committed himself in the way you mention, it will never do to hazard so important a case on a question of delicacy to him. As to the place the case will take on the docket and the probability of reaching it at the ensuing court, I can only say, that the clerk enters the causes as the records come to his hands, and would not feel or indeed be authorized to vary this order, and judging from past experience there will hardly be a chance of reaching, in its regular course, your cause at the coming term. The only hope arises from the nature and importance of the case, and the necessity of obtaining a speedy decision, to prevent injury, perhaps ruin *to a public institution*, if suffered to remain another year in a state of unsettled controversy. I have no doubt the court have a discretionary power over the docket, to give preference in very extraordinary cases; and it seems to me that this is one of the cases in which they might be fairly called upon to exercise it.

I fear however the consent of *both parties* would be required for such an interposition. I rejoice that the "poor droves of cattle" however improper their conduct, have been relieved from prosecutions, which would have reduced them to ruin and want, without adding much to our "overflowing treasury," or gratifying anybody but those who prosecute more for spite and profit than patriotism. We have had an unusually busy session in Congress for so early a part of the session, the new members have been very diligent in exercising themselves upon old soldiers, war-worn officers, and Revolutionary glories, and our devotion to the people has been shown by the repeal of all the internal taxes.

Jos. Hopkinson.

Soon after the decision of the College causes by Judge Story, Webster visited the chancellor, who wrote on the fly-leaf of a book, now in our possession, the following memorandum: "August 2d, 1819. A sister of the author of these volumes [Mrs. Lee], in company with *D. Webster & his wife*, was at my house in Albany and dined there."

CHAPTER XI.

THE following correspondence explains some of the perplexities of the plaintiffs in instituting the suits in the Circuit Court, and in framing the special verdicts. The abstracts of the defendant's documents (omitting the letter of Dartmouth, of April 25, 1771) were prepared by Mr. Brown. Brown, in his letter to Farrar, of February 19, 1818, says: "The trustees are together. They have resolved to commence suits without delay. Will you have the goodness to procure half a doz. blanks from Mr. Freeman, [the clerk of Story's court,] & to forward them to me immediately by mail?"

Appended to the above is the following note from Marsh to Farrar: "It is doubtfull whether the English action of ejectment will answer the object expected from it, the confession of lease, entry and ouster will not superseed the necessity of proving the Def't in possession of the premises — such was the understanding and practice in Vermont, and such is supposed to be the law in England.

"There has never been any thing in practice in Vermont analogous to the writ of entry in England. — Is anything intended by the expression in your letter " *a writ of entry,*" different from the process in use in this State vulgarly called ejectment? If so has this form of proceeding been common

(277)

in your part of the State? nothing is known of it by the lawyers here, — can you furnish a form of the writ? — I make these enquiries partly for want of time to investigate so far as would be necessary to introduce with safety a form of writ entirely new in practice in this State and the State of Vermont, and the more so as we wish to commence these suits immediately, — who is the marshall and has he any deputy in the western part of the State?"

The following, from Farrar to Brown, explains Mr. Mason's views : "Since you have left this town I have conferred with Mr. Mason concerning the actions most likely to succeed in raising the College question before the Circuit Court. He recommends the following :

" 1st. An action of trover for the College Library. To prepare the way for this action there must be an actual and *bona fide* sale for a valuable and full consideration to a citizen of Vermont. The bill of sale should be executed and the books formally delivered at some time when the library is accessible by an authorized agent of the Trustees in the manner mentioned when you were here.

" The purchaser may then offer or attempt to take possession & carry the books away, which he may do if no objection is made and then proceed in the same manner with the apparatus &c.

" But if objections are made he may then commence his action against the librarian or person or persons having the actual possession and custody of the books; as a recovery in trover will change the property and vest it in the Def't it will be best to hold in bail in a sum equal to the value of the Library. The purchaser agent and witnesses who go into the Library for the above purpose should all be citizens of another State so that if the Univ. should become Plat[s] and sue them as Trespassers the action may be removed to the Cir. Court.

" 2d. A writ of entry for some College land of the value of $2,000.00 against a tenant who has forfeited his lease by non-payment of rent. For this purpose there must be an entry and a conveyance to a citizen of Vermont on a bona fide sale for a valuable and adequate consideration.

"These are the actions which Mr. Mason thinks most likely to answer the purpose of raising the question, and which he would not have omitted for the sake of trying experiments with any other.

"But in addition to these he thinks it would be well to try some actions for the last granted township of wild land in the north part of this State, a proper conveyance to be made as in the other cases to a citizen of Vermont and the actions he would bring, are — 1st, a writ of entry directly against the Trustees of Dart Univ.y as a Corporation, and 2d, a writ of ejectment in the English form against anybody as casual ejector who would agree to be Deft & give the requisite notices to Trustees of the Univ'y. This last action he would bring on the idea that the Trustees of the University might be compelled to confess lien, entry & ouster, and take upon themselves the defence with the form of proceeding in this action. Mr. Marsh is more familiar than the gentlemen of the profession in this State and of course better able to judge of the chance of its success."

In his letter to Farrar, of February 27, 1818, Marsh says: "Your letter to Mr. Brown of the 7th instant is now before me — I wrote you a note a few days since in a letter from Mr. Brown, — since that time I have paid what attention I have been able to the subject of the letter as to the various actions Mr. Mason proposes to have bro't in order to bring our controversy properly before the court, we may perhaps succeed in planting an action of trover in the manner proposed — there is much more difficulty in instituting the actions proposed for the recovery of real property — we can scarcely find any one piece of real property which can be sold of the value of $2,000, — and of which any one is in possession in such manner that an action will lie against the tenant. A greater difficulty however at present is the form of action proposed, — the writ of entry has not been in use in this State since its existence, nor is it I believe in *common* use in any of the neighboring States. It will also be remembered that for a great number of years it has been almost unknown in the English practice, — so much so that in no book of entries within my reach is any thing like a precedent to be found. Bohun's Institutio Legalis and Lilly's Entries are the oldest books of precedents which I have it in my power to consult.

" It is proposed also to bring a writ of entry directly against the trustees of the University for the last granted township of wild land in the northern part of New Hampshire and also an Ejectment in the English form against some casual ejector for the same lands. From what opportunity I have had to examine the authorities since this subject was proposed I do not find that a writ of entry will lie to try the title to land of which no one has ever been in possession, nor will ejectments in the English form answer better in such case — the confession of lease, Entry and Ouster will neither aid the Plffs title or give him a cause of action when in fact he has none — the trespass and ejectment must still be proved against Def't and even where we proceed in ejectment *as for a vacant possession*, still it must be shown that the tenant has been *at some time* in possession, and in the State of New York it has been decided that the rules of proceeding in ejectment as for a vacant possession have no applicability in this recently settled country.

" In this last case also it is necessary to make an actual entry on the premises and there seal and deliver a lease to the plaintiff. It is unnecessary to say that this cannot be done at this season on any part of the White Hills. By *this last case* I mean when we proceed as for a vacant possession. In all other cases in ejectment a declaration must be made to each tenant in possession and affidavit of this fact must be made before the court will proceed.

" I fear, my dear sir, that we shall too much try your &

Mr. Mason's patience. I have no inclination to try 'experiments,' but want assistance to surmount real obstacles in our progress. I know that Mr. M.'s avocations are numerous 'and pressing, and wish, therefore, to make him as little trouble as possible.

" If we can prepare the conveyances after having provided purchasers, will it not be expedient that writs should be made by you or Judge Smith? Can you inform me in what way bonds are put in for costs of prosecution in the Circuit Court in your circuit? In this circuit there is a rule of court that the pl'ff in every action shall file a bond with and to the acceptance of the clerk of the court in the sum of two hundred dollars on the return of the writ for the security of cost to Def't."

The following, written by Mr. Brown, is appended: "You see what Mr. M. has written. Dr. Hatch will either hand you this, or will send it by mail, calculating to call in two or three days afterwards. He has purchased some land of Mr. Olcott, as agent for T. of D. Coll. I believe after what Mr. M. writes, it will best for you (consulting with Mr. Mason, of course) to make the writ, i. e. in this suit to be instituted by Dr. H. Other suits will be commenced in due time. In the Hall (so-called) there is no proper tenant at this time — a widow woman occupies a room or two. But Mr. Hutchinson is the Inspector. His business is to keep the keys — to let rooms — to put persons in possession — & I believe he always has the keys commanding the entrance into the house, — could the inspector be sued in ejectment? Has he the possession? Give your opinion & Mr. M.'s, if you please. I wish you to say nothing to Dr. Hatch about the Library. That business will require a little time. It is in train, but it must not take air. Mr. W. writes from Washington that the argument will be heard this term. Vacation closes to-morrow. Twenty students already on the ground, or nearly that number."

On the margin of the first page of this letter is the following, written by Mr. Brown: " As, after all, it may be expedient to sue for the lands N. of the White Hills, I wish you should write to Mr. Marsh as largely as you can."

In his letter to Farrar, of December 7, 1818, Judge Smith says: " The first leisure moment after my return from the circuit I set myself diligently to work, *as my manner is,* to revise the special verdicts in Coll. causes. I framed one for Marsh *v.* Allen *et a.* — When I was ready to submit them to Mr. Sullivan the bird had flown towards the rising of the sun, and did not revisit the western hemisphere till 10 days ago. Two days after that event I gave him the special v^s — Pierce *v.* D. U., & Marsh *v.* Allen *et a.* — with the pleas common rule form of agreement to be signed by counsel & some minutes of slight alterations in the verdicts. These you will see, no doubt, in Mr. Ich. B.'s poss'on. I requested Mr. S. to examine, & correct, & say what additions D. U. proposed, expressing with all a wish that as time pressed he would at an early day be ready to close the matter. I have not heard from him since. He has doubtless been to Portsmouth; at any rate has sent the papers to I. B., &c. He spoke of adding E. W.'s will. *Quere,* in that case would it be advisable to add any new matter on our part, as the fact that John was not, & Rodolphus, then alive, was the eldest son, & *most worthy,* &c.

" I send verdict Hatch *v.* Lang — consult with Mr. Mason, as you will in the whole matter, and send me answer to my queries.

" Hatch *v.* Lang.

" 1. Query. As to L. who is tenant for years only pleading *null disseisin* — the writ charges him with a disseisin.

" 2. Spec. v. states that L. entered under lease, and was actually possessed, & ever since hath continued in possession, &c.

" Perhaps this is well enough; the entry by D. Coll. or H. does not imply expulsion.

" 3. Should not *purpose* of entry by D. Coll. viz., to put an end to lease & extinguish all the right & title of L. under the same, &c., be stated?   See 2 A Blac 61, entry to avoid a fine.

" 4. Should not jury find entry by L. on Hatch, & expulsion as stated in the writ?   This seems necessary.

" Pierce *v.* D. U.

" The special v^t I think should state Tr. D. U. guilty, and not poor G. — the issue is so — the v. whether gen. or spec. must find the issue. — In some forms of spec. verdicts in ejectment there was no casual ejector, — the writ was served on the real tenant as it always may be.

" Marsh *v.* Allen *et a.*

" Should not entry be made before plea that Tr. D. U. at their request were admitted to defend, and they with Allen *et a.* plead A. *et a.* not guilty?

" And should not spec. v. state that A. *et a.* entered by the special order & command of Tr. of D. U. and ejected Marsh?

" And in all these spec. v^s would it not be well to state value & citizenship of parties, as in 3 Wheat. 10?

" Perhaps not essential.

" These hints are all that occur to me.   I suppose the writs, &c., are in the clerk's office; file the subpœnas. Our final deeds, records, &c., need not be filed; return me in due time those now sent.

" I am now *functus officio.* — I cannot, at any rate, go to Portsmouth; Mr. M. and you must do all there.

" Please return the verdict H. *v.* L. to me, unless you obtain R. J.'s signature at P.

" Mr. Freeman will require some time to make out papers for Washington."

In his letter of December 11, 1818, to Judge Smith, Mr. Farrar says : " Since I received your letter until this day, Mr. Mason has been out of town.   I have to-day consulted him in regard to the spe. v^s.   He thinks the one in H. *v.* L. is right in all particulars, but, if wrong in any matter of form, the easiest way to cure it is to add the broad agreement. As to it and 24th quereys he says that L. by not pleading his tenantcy for years in abatement has waived any exception on that ground, and by pleading nul dissn. he admits the disseizin if Plat. has a title. He thinks the *purpose* of entry, &c., sufficiently stated. As to L.'s continuing in the *actual possession*, &c., he thinks it is well enough unless spe. v. is altered in the 4th particular so as to find diszn. If this is alleged, the other should be left out.

"Pierce *v.* D. U. He thinks with you, that spe. v. should be agt. D. U., & not agt. G.

"Marsh *v.* Allen, &c. He has had no time to look into the authorities to see how landlord is admitted in Engd., but his impression is that it should be done as you propose — 1st, entry, that D. U. admitted, &c.; 2, then let them join in the plea that A. & al. not guilty. He thinks also that spe. v. should state that they entered by command, &c., of D. U.

"Mr. M. thinks also with you that value & citizenship need not appear in the spe. v^s.

"I have called on Ich. B. for the verdicts in the two last cases, but he has them not, & says he has not seen them. I will file the papers you have sent me, agreeably to your directions.

"If there should be anything to forward this business, which I can do after the papers are sent down, I will attend to it with all diligence.

"I wish very much to obtain a copy of the spe. v. & record in D. C. *vs.* Woodward, for the purpose which I have named to you. Will you have the goodness to loan me your manuscript when a convenient opportunity occurs of transmitting it? The argument I trust is prepared."

Upon the bottom of this letter is the following indorsement in the handwriting of Mr. Mason: —

Mr. Bartlett has called with the papers in the Coll. cases. I did not desire or expect to see anything more of them. He is very urgent to have the newly discovered papers admitted. But

I believe we shall get rid of him without making any important admissions except that his office copies are duly authenticated.

J. M.

11 DEC., 1818.

This letter was received by Judge Smith, December 16, 1818.

Farrar, in his letter to Webster, dated January 8, 1819, says: " Herewith you have the copies of the three cases certified from the Circuit Court; the copy of an agreement executed at present only by Mr. Mason; a copy of certain parts of Eleazer Wheelock's will; copy of a grant to trustees of D. Coll., June, 1807, and a copy of a memorial of Jno. Wheelock, in the name & behalf of said trustees, June, 1805. The copy of the letter of April 25, 1771, from Ld. Dartmouth & others, with Mr. Allen's affidavit, has been already forwarded. You will notice a provision in Dr. E. Wheelock's will, that, in consequence of certain property of his having gone to the benefit of the *Charity School*, it is charged with the payment of an annuity to Ralph Wheelock & C. This annuity, I understand, has always been considered as due from the College, and paid by the trustees. There is a provision in the act of June, 1807, by which the Legislature reserve to themselves the right to control the trustees in respect to the appropriation of the income of that grant. This grant remains unproductive.

" I have received a line from Pres^t Brown respecting our book, and have conversed with Mr. Mason on the subject. The Pres^t is silent in regard to the plan of it, what the introduction shall contain, &c. Mr. Mason is decidedly of the opinion that there should *be none;* that is, that the book should be *wholly* confined to the law or judicial history of the case, without any notice of the ecclesiastical or political or any other part of the preliminary dispute. His reasons are, that it is for the interest of the Institution to bury any recollection of this dispute as soon as the cause is ended, and not perpetuate the enmity of the individuals or of the party by putting into a permanent form any thing that shall compel them to look upon their own iniquity. This is a matter that you and the President must decide, and let me know how much and what matter the book should contain.

" Please to acknowledge the rec'pt of these papers."

It will be noticed that, in the abstracts made by Mr. Brown, the trustees in 1782, 1808, and in 1812 termed the institution a University; that they conferred degrees as such; that Dr. Wheelock, in his last will, recognized this " Seminary " as a University, as well as in the instances to which we have already alluded.

ABSTRACTS OF DEFT'S DOCUMENTS.

No. 1. E. Wheelock's " Narrative " &c. from 1768 to its incorporation with D. C. & removal to Han^r 1771, marked with a reference to p. 26, 30 & 35, where are passages speaking of the school as a separate Inst^n from the Col. & as connected with the Col &c.

No. 2. Extracts from ye Records of D. C. 1 vol.

" 1st. Meet'g held at Keen Oct. 1770. Whereas &c Pres't proposed that the Board should exchange 200 a^s land given by his late Exc'y B. W. to this Col for 400 a^s given to the Pres^t by the town of Hanover.

" Meet'g May 28, 1773, Vote of thanks to Gov. Coun^l & Rep's for grant of £500 for building new Col.

" Meet'g Aug. 26, 1773, Vote to receive ye 400 acr^s in lieu of the 200 patented to ye s^d Dr. E. W. under ye great seal of this Prov. by his Ex'y J. W. Esq. as by s^d patent date Dec. 19 1771, &c.

" M'g Oct. 22, 1770, Vote that Pres^t employ Surveyor &c to run the line & mark &c town of Landaff.

" M. Aug. 23, 1775. The several classes in Col & Studt^s in Moor's Charity Sch^l preferred a petition addressed to the Hon'ble Trustees of D Coll &c.

" % of Lands given to the Col. July 6, 1770, B. Wth gave 500 a^s in H. on this, Col stands. 300 a^s of which was by patent from his Ex I. Wth on 19 Dec. 1771 confirmed to the Trustees &c.

"Meet'g Sept. 20, 1782, Resolve styling this a *University* and themselves *Trustees of the University of Dartmouth*, &c.

"M'g Aug. 1812, Vote to confer Deg of A. B. on following members of this *University*.

"M'g Dec. 23, 1788, Vote app[tg] a Com[tee] to examine into the relation of Col & Sch[l] *objects of each & application of funds designated for particular objects &c.*

"(M'g May 7, 1789, consists of Preamble & Resolution to which refer.)

"Meet'g Feb. 1796, App of Josia Freeman to make division with the *Pres't of Moore's School* of the township of Wheelock & execute & receive deed of *partition.*

"M'g Aug. 1801. Pres[t] W. as Pres[t] of Moore's Ch[ty] school proposes to the Trustees to take some superintendence of the school, that they audit his %[s] &c. Voted to comply with the proposal. A Com[tee] chosen to confer with the Pres[t] on the subject & report to the next meeting.

"M'g Aug. 1805. The s[d] Com[tee] reported at the last session, that the Trustees unite with the Pres[t] in an application to the Legislature *to pass an act so far explaining & extending the act of Incorp[n] of s[d]* Inst[n] as to enable & make it the duty of the Tr with the Pres[t] for the time being to superintend Moor's School &c which rep[t] was at this session referred to a new comm[tee] who reported a draft of an act &c. Voted to accept the same.

"M'g Aug. 1807. Resolved to accept the trust created by the act of June 18, 1807, Moore's School.

"M'g March 30, 1790. Return of land granted 1789. Tract 8 m[s] square.

"M'g May 1789. Vote of thanks to Pres[t] Wheelock for his agency in obtaining the grant of 8 miles square in this State & his agencies in Ver[t] in obtaining township of 6 m[s] square for Col & Moore's Sc[l].

"M'g Jan'y 7 1808. Resolve to establish Prof[sp] of Law at *this University* as soon as adequate means shall be furnished."

No. 5. Letter of atty E. W. to Nath[l] Whitaker to receive money for the use of an Indian Ch[y] school and to supp[t] missionaries. Date May 6, 1766.

No. 6. Form of Deeds, according to which Donors in the origin of the Col. gave lands. "Whereas it has pleased his Ex[y] J.

Wth with advice of his Maj$^{y's}$ Council for the instruction of Indians began by E. W. as well as the education of others, *to erect & constitute a Col. by the name of D. C.* & by Charter under the great seal to endow the same with many noble privileges & franchises AS WELL AS TO MAKE GENEROUS DONATIONS towards a fund &c. Therefore, in consideration &c.''

No. 10. . Extract from E. W.'s will Ap. 2, 1779. " And whereas I have founded on my own tenement and at my own expense an Indian Charity School, now called Moore's Ch^y School which from small beginnings has through much labour, application & care for more than 20 years last past under a series of most signal & evident smiles of divine providence arisen to its present state of importance & appears to exhibit a fair prospect of great usefulness towards the christianizing & civilizing the natives of our Ame^{rn} wilderness which is its first object, & of conciliating establishing & perpetuating a firm & lasting friendship & peace between all the numerous tribes & the Am. colonies as well as of great edification to the ch of God among the Eng^h & is now incorporated by royal charter into and with D. C. which seminary is by s^d charter endowed with all the powers, privileges & immunities of a University, as by said charter may fully appear. And whereas it appertains unto me as founder & proprietor thereof as well as by grant in said charter to dispose of said school & all donations and grants of land & other interests any way given or granted for the benefit & use of s^d school in the best manner for the well being of the same & appoint my successor in the office of Pres^t of s^d seminary, I do therefore nominate constitute and appoint my son J. W. to be my successor in s^d office of Pres^t of my Ind Chy Sch^l & D Col with & into which s^d school is now incorporated & to him I give & grant all my right title & claim to s^d Seminary & all the appurtenances, interests jurisdictions power & authority to, in & over the same belonging to me as the founder of it or by grant in the charter to me, or by any other ways or means whatsoever.''

No. 11. Letter from Peter Gilman to E. W. Date Exeter Feb. 3, 1770. "His Ex^y Gov. W. having appointed me in the charter for D. C. one of the Trustees, I was much averse &c knowing my incapacity &c but as the Gov insisted &c I was prevailed upon &c Col. Phelps informs me the mode of fixing upon a plan for the

Col is for the trustees to write their minds to you &c. I am unacquainted & no doubt you will fix it right &c but should think Haverhill or some other river town not far distant most suitable &c.

No. 13. Grant of Landaff. Date Jan. 19, 1770. Recorded Jan. 22, 1770.

No. 14. Grant of land in Hanover, Dec. 19, 1771. "Whereas we did erect & incorporate a College &c & whereas the Tr has begun to erect buildings on a tract of 500 a. ungranted therefore give &c 300 acres part of s^d 500 a, & being the spot on which Col stands to Trustees and in consideration &c give &c the remaining 200 a. to E. W. all which on certain conditions."

No. 15. Report of Commissioners to examine a%cs of Moore's Ind Chy Sch^l June 11, 1789, finding a balance of £1,190, 10, 1 st^{lg} in favor of late & pres^t Dr. W. & that s^d expenditures have been for the use of the sch^l & not for the benefit of the Col.

No. 16. Vote of May 7, 1789. This is the same as in No. 2, disclaiming control of funds of Moor's Sch^l.

No. 17. Deed of trust E. W. to Earl Dartmouth & al, May 31, 1768. Recites that he had at his own risk and expense founded a chy sch^l — that he had by proper instrument under seal appointed his successor in the care & gov^t of the same, requiring him & his successor to make the Tr in Eng acquainted with his doings & the doings of the Tr in America; that in the same instrument he had appointed 7 other gentlemen with his successor to be Trustees here, authorizing them to confirm the appointment of his successor or choose one of their own number in his stead; fill vacancies in their own number — fix laws, rules & orders for the government &c. Therefore appoints Earl Dartmouth & 8 others to be Trustees in Eng^d & grants to them all property received or to be received in Eng^d for the use spec^{fd}. Authorizing them to disapprove of his successor & in case of a new nomination to be agreed upon by both boards & a negative on all proceedings if here — to fill vacancies in their own number. And binds himself not to alter this plan without their consent, &c.

No. 18. Grant of land, 8 m^s square, Feb. 5, 1789, and $900 June 15, 1805.

No. 19. Examination of Pres^t W.'s a%cs of Moor's School by comm^{tee} of Trustees July 21, 1805; balance in favor of the Pres^t $1,869.75.

No. 21. Letter of Earl Dartmouth & als to E. W. Ap¹ 25, 1771, warning him not to apply the funds to the use of 'D. C. but to educate Indians, & maintain missionaries &c. See whole letter.

No. 22. Letter from E W to Govr J W^th, Ap¹ 25th 1770. Hoped to meet him in Coos to fix upon a plan for the Col to his satisfaction. Gov life & sinews of the whole. Trustees in Connecticut unwilling to take any part in determining location &c.

No. 23. Memorial of Tr to Legislature, Nov. 24, 1804, praying that its financial concerns may be investigated by a com^tee and considered by the Legislature.

No. 25. Power of Att^y, E. W. to Earl of Dartmouth & others to receive in trust monies &c in his name for the use of his Indian school.

No. 26. Memorial of Tr to Legislature Dec. 1, 1803, saying among other things " as individuals they have no interest in its success & prosperity than what is common to every member of the Legislature. As visitors of the Col this responsibility is more immediate but not more real or extensive than that of the Legislators of the State." The grants collectively under the former & present government have not been ultimately beneficial to the Col to any considerable degree.

No. 29. Act of June 10, 1807. Incorporating the Pres^t of Moor's Ch^y Sch¹, and giving the Trustees of the Col certain powers in relation thereto.

No. 30. Will of John Wheelock, March 19, 1817.

As to the publication of Farrar's report, Putnam, in his letter to Farrar, dated at Pittsfield, Massachusetts, October 2, 1817, says : " Ever since I left you I have been more and more impressed with the importance of printing the arguments on the Coll. question. I have conversed much with gentlemen on this subject. The friends of the Coll. wish very much *to read* the arguments — its enemies *pretend* to desire the same. I think it important to print for many reasons — if the court should decide *against* the Coll. the public *by reading* will have an opportunity *to judge what they must be,* — if they decide *in favor* of Coll. and against the University, printing *the arguments* will make the case go off triumphantly — it will shame & confound those wise folks, those half-way friends that have *pretended to doubt.*

" I think there can be no doubt about the sale of the book. My brother, who is with me, says he should be almost willing to be responsible that every student of Coll. would take a copy.   I think a subscription paper should be passed around, — particularly *at Hanover.*

"I hope you will have it all ready for me to read by the time of my return.

" I calculate to be at Saratoga Springs about two days — whether I shall remain there will depend upon the state of things as I may find it.

" I think my health is improved — hope that God will return me prepared to engage in my great labors.   Remember me in your prayers.   I calculate to pass down to the city of New York & return thro' Conn. & Rhod. Isl^d."

In his letter to Farrar, of November 15, 1817, Brown says : " We think it more important than ever that the Exeter argument & the Plymouth decision should be printed in a book.   I mentioned the subject to Judge Smith at Plymouth, and have since named it in a letter to him.   I believe he will not object.   Have the goodness to attend to the affair without delay, & let Mr. Lamson superintend the printing.   In my opinion, the sales, if the copyright is secured, would bring a handsome profit ; and, by the way, might not this be turned to the pecuniary benefit of the College ?

" The *decision* has occasioned the defection of *one* of our students only, and an event occurred on Tuesday evening last, which, I believe, may well put all the hopes of the Univ. at rest, of an increase of their number by the diminution of ours.   This was an attempt to seize the Libraries of the private Societies in College.   Prof. D. & C., Mr. H. Hutchinson, Messrs. Cook and Bissel & fifteen or twenty more of the same stamp commenced the assault between 7 & 8 o'clock.   The Frater. were then in meeting.

They immediately adjourned, about one half repairing to the S. F.'s Lib., the other half to their own. In five minutes the whole body of the students had collected. A parley ensued. The Professors and their company surrendered themselves as prisoners and were conducted into an adjoining room until the Societies had removed all their books to a place of safety. The party were then conducted out, one by one, and attended by one or more of the students to their lodgings. The next day the Frater. proceeded to expel a member of the Univ. who aided the Prof in the attack, and in the evening the S. F.'s expelled two other members of the Univ. & summoned their brothers D. & C. to answer to certain charges brought against them. These gentlemen, I understand, are since *expelled*.

"The Univ. seems much alarmed for its credit. Mr. Allen has issued an official bulletin, which is a sort of apologetick statement, designed to sooth the feelings of one part of the community, & to increase the violence of the other. Prosecutions are threatened by the Prof. & Co. I have some fears for the consequences. In the meantime the students are perfectly regular, & attentive as usual to their studies. The Med. Stu. joined heart & hand in rescuing the Libraries from the hands of violence.

"A somewhat extensive correspondence has become necessary since the Plymouth decision, and this must excuse the hasty, broken manner in which I write."

Judge Smith, in his letter to Mr. Brown, of December 17, 1818, says: "I cannot persuade myself an argument on Coll. side will be called for. When all is over there will be time to get up a report which may be, I think, *compressed* into 1 vol

"The arguments, excepting always Mr. Webster's, may be abridged in bulk without suffering any loss in weight."

By an arrangement between Webster, Marshall, Washington, Story, and Wheaton, Trustees *v.* Woodward was first reported by Farrar ; and, as before suggested, Wheaton made up his report from Farrar's. The reasons for it will appear in the following correspondence.

Mr. Brown, in his letter to Judge Smith, of January 4, 1819, says : "Your two, letters, after going to Hanover, reached me here on Saturday, P. M., and in a few minutes afterwards Mr. Mason arrived from Portsmo. & gave us an account of what had been done. He also brought copies of the papers, which had been agreed to, furnished him by the diligent pen of Mr. Farrar.

" Anticipating the course of the Univ. in this business, I had employed a few days in investigating the history of M's school, &c., and I believe I had ascertained nearly every fact which their papers bring to light. All the 'narratives' I could obtain (seven in No.), including all except one (of 1768), I brought down to Mr. W., as also the ' Memoirs of W.' & Dr. J. W.'s ' Observations on Facts ' addressed to the Vt. Legislature in 1807. Mr. W. will take these with him. If, on my return to Hanover, I can find another nar. No. 4, it shall be sent to you.

" As to the printing, I have named the subject to Mr. Mason, & requested him to furnish his argument. He says he will think of it. I believe he will find no difficulty in consenting to the general wish. I have requested Mr. Farrar to undertake the superintendence of the printing, and to insert the matter which may be proper & necessary to make out the case, beginning with the act of the Legislature, June, 1816. Mr. Farrar will confer with you ; and I have only to desire that you will have the goodness to prepare your argument as soon as may be convenient, as it will be important to have the book ready for delivery as early as may be after the decision.

" My health has not suffered by my journey to this place. I trust, with proper care it will soon be reëstablished.

" Our controversy has been long & close, but now seems to be drawing to a close. Whatever depends on *men*, I know,

is in some degree uncertain ; but from all I can learn here
and elsewhere, I have a great degree of confidence that the
cause is gained.   Should this be the event (and indeed
whether it be or not), we shall always entertain a lively
sense of obligation to those gentlemen who have ' stood in
the gap ' & so nobly sustained the contest.   And may we
not forget our obligations to him, who has bestowed on our
wisest counsellors their talents, & by whom ' princes decree
justice.' ''

This letter was written in Boston, and received by Judge
Smith on January 9, 1819.

The reference to what had been done, and what its author
had learned in Boston '' and elsewhere,'' can hardly be mistaken.

In his letter of February 4, 1819, to Farrar, Webster
says : '' I suppose *all* the judges will give opinions to Mr.
Wheaton to be published in the College cause.   I have not
seen or heard any but the chief justice's, but I have no doubt
they will be very full and able.   I think it would be very
well to get along the *book*, but there is one difficulty in it, —
these opinions are the property of the *reporter*, his reward
for his labors is principally from the sale of his book, and
this case will make a principal part in his next volume.

'' Mr. Wheaton is an excellent lawyer and in all things
disposed to do well and act liberally, — still he might think
it not his duty to give gratuitously copies of these opinions
as the sale of your book would a little interfere with his.   I
have thought of offering him a hundred dollars for copies of
these opinions if you think it best to get them.   This will
compensate him for the loss of a sale of some of his volumes.

'' The book, if printed at all, must be printed at Boston,
& we must get Judge Story to inspect the proof-sheets of
the opinions.

'' I suppose we can get the book out by the first of June
or the middle of May, supposing the work to commence
pretty soon after my return.

"Please let me hear from you on this subject.

"If it should be necessary I could get them copied here and sent on, so as to get the book out *in April* — but I sup-pose *May* is just as well."

Thompson, in his letter to Farrar, of February, 18, 1819, says he has "a letter from Mr. Webster, saying he shall bring the written opinions of each judge."

Webster, in his letter to Farrar, of March 12, 1819, says: "I can now furnish copies of the opinions."

Webster, in his letter to Farrar, of March 29, 1819, says: "I believe Mr. Wirt & Mr. Hopkinson are both now occu-pied in writing out their respective speeches."

Brown, in his letter to Farrar, of March 31, 1819, states that $2,500 must be raised by subscription for the book; and that more than half of it was raised before he left Boston.

Webster, in his letter to Farrar, of April 3, 1819, says: "I am expecting Wirt's argument daily."

John Holmes, in his letter to Farrar, of May 10, 1819, says: "I apprehend it will be impossible to prepare my argument at length in the Dartmo. College case from very imperfect minutes. If, however, you can wait a short time, & will transmit me Mr. Wheaton's minutes, I will make the attempt. Please inform me how soon you must have it." Farrar appended a note to Holmes, saying that Wheaton's notes "are probably so brief as to afford you little or no assistance," not to be drawn from your "own notes."

Mr. Hopkinson's argument is supposed to be reported at length by Farrar. The facts are these: Hopkinson had prepared an elaborate brief before arguing the cause. He furnished it to Mr. Webster. Webster wrote out an argu-ment for him, for Farrar. It comprises the entire argument as reported, except about two pages. These were added by Hopkinson, on the topics suggested by Mr. Webster. Both the brief and the argument, as written out by Web-ster, are in our hands. It is safe to say that Mr. Webster's draft did not diminish the force of the statement made by Mr. Hopkinson in his brief.

Mr. Hopkinson, in his letter from Bordentown, New Jersey, dated May 2, 1819, to Webster, says: "I return your manuscript with many thanks for the trouble you have taken to give me a respectable position in a book whose importance I estimate as highly as you do. I have made a small addition to the argument you have prepared from my notes; and also furnish some remarks on the topicks you have suggested.

"I continue my intention to visit Boston in August; but as I shall see you on the Delaware before that time, I shall have an opportunity to fix my visit with more precision. I will soon write again; but must now put up my packet for you."

Webster, in his letter to Farrar, of June 10, 1819, says: "I have written to Judge Story enclosing your letter, and desiring him, if he thinks proper, to write a line to the clerk directing an order to issue for plea, answer or demurrer to be filed Septr. 1.

"I have now the Washington arguments, & the opinions have heretofore been forwarded to you to Exeter. I shall send the arguments the first opportunity.

"On reflexion I wish the quotation from Stillingfleet now in my argument to remain there as it is, and the additional quotation to be put into a note."

Wheaton, in his letter from New York, of August 2, 1819, to Farrar, says: "Will you have the goodness to send me by return of mail a copy of Mr. Hopkinson's argument in the Dartmouth College case. Mr. Webster desired me to write you for it, and as I am now rapidly approaching the case, I do not wish to be without it.

"I hope you had a pleasant journey home.

"I was unable to prevail on Judge Livingston to give us his opinion."

In his letter of June 19, 1819, to Farrar, Webster says: "I am placed in a very disagreeable situation in regard to this *book*, & one from which I must in some way extricate myself.

" I have become accountable for the 100 dols. to Mr. Wheaton, & have paid him also 15 or 20 dlls. for copies — all this I care nothing about. But where is the book, & when is it coming out? I have promised Mr. Wheaton a printed copy for him to publish by. He wants it; & with all my inquiries, both to you and Mr. Lamson, I can get no answer nor any information. In the meantime I hear that Mr. Mason's argument is badly printed, and that the whole thing is about as bad as it can be. What is to be done? In the first place you must send me back Holmes' & Wirt's argument as it is, for Wheaton. *He* must have it. He needs it *now* & has no copy.

" I plainly see you will not have it in print this *month*, whereas he wants it this very day, wherefore please return it by the mail carrier on Monday, that I may forward it to him. His book — at least this case — will be in print as soon as you will need it, at any rate he must have it.

" I am mortified beyond measure at the progress this printing job makes. I do not know that you are at all to blame about it, but I regret the whole undertaking. If you'd have consented that it should have been printed *here*, it wd. have been done long ago, & if gentlemen wd. not have furnished their arguments, it would have come out with't them.

" Do write to me on Monday, sendg. me back Holmes & Wirt.

" I think it but right and fair to suggest to Mr. Lamson that, unless this *book* is well printed on good paper & free from errors, the case at Washington will probably be printed *here*, in a proper manner.

In his letter to Farrar, of June 23, 1819, Webster says : " I send you a copy of the pages you mentioned beginning a little back of the third and going a little beyond the 4th, so as to show the connection. Please examine it and see if it appears to be right and to make joints.— I shall detain the arg't till you can answer this, so that if anything is wrong you can let me know ; I believe I have followed your directions.

" I enclose you also a minute furnished by Judge Story, to direct the manner of stating the opinions.

" I care less about the time when this book comes out than the *manner*. I am no great judge of these things, but if it should not be thought to be well printed, I shall wish it at the bottom of the Red Sea.

" I very much wished to see my part of it as it came out. But in this I cannot probably be gratified. It is not very material, but it is *essential* that the judges opinions be accurately printed.

" I made myself answerable for that both to the chief justice & Judge W. ; I am fearful of a thousand blunders in all these opinions. In Judge Story's particularly, the citations are so numerous, there will be errors which will not be corrected unless he sees the proof, and as the press has waited for everybody else, I think in common decency he ought to be furnished with the proofs of all the opinions. He will attend to them immediately and return the proofs in all cases the next mail. I am persuaded that in no other way will the printing of these opinions be accurate."

The directions of Story as to the form of stating the concurrence of the other judges was probably lost in the printing-office, but in his letter of July 3, 1819, to Farrar, he says : " It appears to me to be of so great importance to have the opinions of the judges of the Supreme Court of the United States printed with minute accuracy in the Dartmo. College case, that I must beg you to send me the proof sheets. You need not send the copy of the MSS. as my recollection will generally aid me.

" I will send you the proof sheets from time to time, by the return of the mail direct to Portsmouth or Exeter, as you please."

Marsh, in his letter to Farrar, of January 21, 1820, says, in relation to the suit, Allen *v.* College : " You may have

been informed that the Revd William Allen, as executor of
the last will &c of the late Dr. J. Wheelock, has commenced
a suit against the trustees of Dartmouth College for the
recovery of certain promissory notes, which have not been
hitherto questioned. We now think however that we have
suffered so much by the management of Dr. W., Mr. Allen
& their friends, that if any use can be made of the judgment for costs in the actions lately decided in the circuit
court, or any new suit for mesne profits or the like, to offset
against this demand, or for the purpose [of] effecting a
settlement on more favorable terms, it will be right to do it.
At a meeting of a committee of the trustees in Dec. last it
was agreed that Mr. Olcott should request you to procure
the cost in these suits taxed; this I presume has been done.
I have also to request you to institute a suit for the mesne
profits of the action in which I was plff and Mr. Allen and
others defendants. I think we may make some use of these
things beneficially in a settlement with Mr. Allen, and it is
certainly perfectly reasonable that he should pay us these
costs, and all damages done to the public buildings, library
and apparatus, and what injury we sustained by being deprived of their use.

"Can the trustees recover damages for the occupancy
and use of the buildings, from the time possession was taken
of them, under the University, till they were conveyed to
those by whom these three actions were instituted; if any
doubt exists in anything of this kind, will you consult Mr.
Mason, who if he is not tired of hearing of our D. C. troubles
will doubtless afford his opinion."

The writ of Allen and Wheelock against the College, to
which we have before referred, contained five counts. Three
were for promissory notes; the fourth was for an account
stated, $2,027.70; and the fifth was for $10,000, for work,
labor, care, and diligence of the second Wheelock as president of Dartmouth College, etc.

It was undoubtedly intended to cover by the latter count

certain matters about which Wheelock consulted Webster, as before stated. The trustees put the cause into the hands of Judge Smith as counsel, who, after examination, instructed them that he was unable to discover any valid defence.

We have mislaid the elaborate letter of Judge Smith containing his opinion, referred to in the following, by Thompson and cannot, therefore, insert it.

Thompson, in his letter of April 26, 1820, to his brother-in-law, Olcott, says: " I have looked at the enclosures you sent me, repeatedly, & from what I collect from them am of opinion that Mason's ideas as to the course we ought to pursue are just, & would be more to our credit & profit than any others.

" Smith writes like himself. Possibly the nature of the document or documents sent him may justify the style of his letter.

" Even in that case, a more courtly address would have answered as good a purpose. If D. U. performed the conditions precedent to which Smith alludes, & not only accepted the release, subject &c., but made the sequestration he mentions, I do not see how our court can *consistently* with their printed opinion, now say the D. U. is a nullity, or a distinct corporation from D. C. Without adopting the Washington doctrine they must pronounce the release operative. If they recognize the doctrine held by the S. C. of the U. States as the legitimate doctrine, and which ought now to be held, it might prepare the way to institute the proposed suits, if, all circumstances considered, it be deemed expedient, or what would be better still, in my opinion, it might lead to a favorable accommodation with Allen & others who are liable. Allen however I fear, is made of such unconquerable obstinacy that he would never yield. Of this you can judge better than I can.

" If D. U. did all that was necessary on their part to render the release operative, I should think it expedient, if allowable, so to plead as to try the validity of the release, and the authority of the treasurer to give promissory notes. If both points could not be tried, or rather if the pleas are inconsistent, which by the way I do not perceive, I should prefer placing the defence on the ground of the treasurer's want of authority to bind the corporation by promissory notes. But I caution you against placing reliance on my opinions, unless they accord with your own.

"It is so long since I have attended to subjects of this kind that I feel much less able to advise than I ever was. I hope Mr. Marsh will instruct you fully. If you do not hear from him at large on the subject, I hope you will without fail ride over and see him."

Marsh, in his letter to Farrar, of May 10, 1820, says: "As to the defence against the notes in suit, I hope Mr. O. and Judge Smith will profit by Mr. Mason's hint that the treasurer cannot by note bind the corporation."

Wiser counsels prevailed. This attempt on the part of the old trustees to stand upon the decision made by the State court, and to disregard that which they had obtained from the Supreme Court of the United States, failed.

At the May term, 1820, judgment was accordingly entered, by agreement, in favor of the plaintiffs, for $7,886.41 damages, and for their costs, and execution duly issued thereon May 31, 1820; but twelve years dragged their slow length along before it was cancelled by payments.

CHAPTER XII.

MARSHALL'S OPINION THE ONLY ONE READ — DUVALL DIS-
SENTS — THE OTHER JUDGES PRESENT CONCUR IN ; THE
RESULT — WASHINGTON AND STORY FILE OPINIONS WITH
THE REPORTER — LIVINGSTON AND JOHNSON — THEIR
VIEWS IN TRUSTEES v. WOODWARD, AND STURGES v.
CROWNINSHIELD — JOHNSON'S OPINIONS IN FLETCHER v.
PECK, AND OGDEN v. SAUNDERS.

THE judges who sat in Trustees v. Woodward were John
Marshall and Bushrod Washington, of Virginia; William
Johnson, of South Carolina ; Brockholst Livingston, of New
York ; Thomas Todd, of Kentucky ; Gabriel Duvall, of
Maryland ; and Joseph Story, of Massachusetts.

Webster, in his letter of February 2, 1819, to his brother,
written in court, after the reading of Marshall's opinion, says :
"All is safe. Judgment was rendered this morning reversing
the judgment in New Hampshire. Present : Marshall, Washington, Livingston, Johnson, Duval and Story. All concurring but Duval ; and he giving no reason to the contrary.
The opinion was delivered by the chief justice. It was very
able and very elaborate : it goes the whole length, and leaves
not an inch of ground for the University to stand on."
(1 Webster's Priv. Cor. 300.) In his letter, written in the
court-room at the same time, to Judge Farrar, he says :
"A judgt. has been pronounced in our favor this morning :
five judges out of the six judges present concurring. I
believe Judge Duval is the dissentient. The opinion was
pronounced by the chief justice. It was very long, and
reasoned out from step to step. It did not cite cases. I
understand an opinion has also been drawn by Judge Story,

which will probably be given to the reporter." (Note to Mem. of Farrar.)

In his letter, written the same day, to Judge Smith, he says: "I have the pleasure to tell you that the College cause has been decided in our favor. The chief justice, Washington, Livingston, Johnson, and Story, Justices, *concurrentibus;* Duval, Justice, *dissentiente; absente*, Todd. The opinion was delivered by the chief. I believe other judges also drew up opinions, which I hope to see published." (1 Webster's Priv. Cor. 299, 300.)

In his letter, written the same day, to Mr. Brown, he says: "All is safe and certain. The chief justice delivered an opinion this morning, in our favor, on all the points. In this opinion, Washington, Livingston, Johnson and Story, justices, are understood to have concurred. Duval, Justice, it is said, dissents. Mr. Justice Todd is not present. The opinion goes the whole length, and leaves nothing further to be decided. I give you my congratulations on this occasion, and assure you that I feel a load removed from my shoulders, much heavier than they have been accustomed to bear." (1 Webster's Priv. Cor. 300.)

In his letter to Mason, of February 4, 1819, from which we have already quoted, he says: "Since my arrival here I have been all the time in court, and can therefore as yet say nothing more than I have seen and heard here. Most of the judges came here with opinions drawn in the college cause. * * * Five of the judges concurred in the result, and I believe most or all of them will give their opinions to the reporter. Nothing has been said in court about the other causes. Mr. Pinkney *says* he means to argue one of them; but I think he will alter his mind. There is nothing left to argue on. The chief justice's opinion was in his own peculiar way. He reasoned along from step to step, and, not referring to the cases, adopted the principles of them, and worked the whole into a close, connected, and very able argument. Some of the other judges,

I am told, have drawn opinions with more reference to authorities." (Mem. of Mason, 213, 214.)

Mr. Hopkinson, in his letter to Mr. Brown, of February 2, 1819, — following the line of that part of Mr. Webster's argument which was "left out" of the report, — says : "Our triumph in the college cause has been complete. Five judges, only six attending, concur not only in a decision in our favor, but in placing it upon principles broad and deep, and *which secure corporations of this description from legislative despotism and party violence for the future.* The court goes *all lengths* with us, and whatever trouble these gentlemen may give us in future, in their great and pious zeal for the interests of learning, they cannot shake those principles which must and will restore Dartmouth College to its true and original owners." (1 Webster's Priv. Cor. 301.)

The italics are ours. The meaning of the words, "*all lengths,*" is to be read in the light of Webster's letter to Mason, of April 13, 1819, in which he says : "As to the college cause, you may depend on it that there will be difficulty in getting delay in that case, without reason. I flatter myself the judge will tell the defendants, *that the new facts which they talk of, were presented to the minds of the judges at Washington,* and that, if all proved, they would not have the least effect on the opinion of any judge ; that unless it can be proved that the king did not grant such a charter as the special verdict recites, or that the New Hampshire general court did not pass such acts as are therein contained, no material alteration of the case can be made." (Mason's Mem. 223.) The italics are ours. Webster here uttered, not prophecy, but fact.

Judge Livingston took his seat on the bench of the Federal Supreme Court at the February term, 1807. Story came to that bench in 1812. From that time, till Livingston's death, Story had greater influence over him, if

possible, than even Kent had.   He published no opinion in
Sturges v. Crowninshield, and we are not aware that one
exists in an accessible form.   Story was very ambitious, and
naturally desired to act as the organ of the court and to
deliver its opinion in a case of so much importance ; and
Livingston as naturally desired that his friend should have
that opportunity.   In this, as in other important cases,
Story had the good sense and tact to submit his opinion for
examination and criticism to those upon whose heads and
hearts he could rely, before it was considered by his
brethren.

Judge Prescott, in his letter of January 9, 1819, to Story,
says : " I have read your opinion with care and great
pleasure.   *   *   *   I see nothing I should wish altered
in it.   I hope it will be *adopted without diminution or sub-
traction.*"   Livingston, in his letter to Judge Story, of January 24, 1819, says : " I return your opinion in the case
of Dartmouth College, which has afforded me more pleasure
than can easily be expressed.   It was exactly what I had
expected from you, *and hope it will be adopted without
alteration*.   What you say of the contract of marriage is a
complete answer to the difficulty made on that subject, and
I am not sorry that you have taken notice of the act of the
legislature dissolving this contract, which has been passed
in this State.   As to the effect of the separation of the two
countries on the charter of this college, in addition to what
you say, it appears to me that its existence is admitted by
the very acts which are complained of."   (1 Life of Story,
by his Son, 323, 324.)   A comparison of Livingston's letter with Story's opinion, as published by Farrar, shows
that it was afterwards modified.   How radical these changes
were, we shall probably never know.

The true construction of the obligation clause was a vital
point in Sturges v. Crowninshield.   This, though it tested
the constitutionality of the New York bankrupt law, was a
Massachusetts case.   It arose in Judge Story's circuit, and

was taken from the brief term of the Circuit Court which commenced October 15, 1817, to the Supreme Court, upon the formal certificate that the judges of the Circuit Court were opposed in opinion upon the following questions : —

" 1. Whether, since the adoption of the Constitution of the United States, any State has authority to pass a bankrupt law, or whether the power is exclusively vested in the Congress of the United States.

" 2. Whether the act of New York, passed the third day of April, 1811, and stated in the plea in this case, is a bankrupt act, within the meaning of the Constitution of the United States.

" 3. Whether the act aforesaid is an act or law impairing the obligation of contracts, within the meaning of the Constitution of the United States.

" 4. Whether the plea is a good and sufficient bar of the plaintiff's action."

Sturges v. Crowninshield was transferred and reported previous to the College case ; but both were before the court and under consideration substantially the same length of time. Both were important cases, and involved the construction of the same provision of the Constitution. To be thoroughly understood, this case must be read and compared with the individual opinions of the judges in Ogden v. Saunders, Robbins v. Shaw, Mason v. Haile, 12 Wheat. 214, 383 ; Boyle v. Zacharie, 6 Pet. 348, 643 ; Rhode Island v. Massachusetts, 12 Pet. 720 ; Cook v. Moffat, 5 How. 310, 311 ; Company v. Debolt, 16 How. 416, and subsequent cases. But six judges sat in Sturges v. Crowninshield. Upon the general question, as suggested by Mr. Webster, they were well known to be equally divided. Livingston then sustained the constitutionality of these laws, in whose atmosphere he had been reared ; and we are not aware of any evidence that he ever concurred either in the adroitly framed judgment in that case, or the reasoning by which such a result was reached. As we shall hereafter see, neither Washington nor Johnson ever concurred in the reasoning of Judge Marshall in important particulars. The judgment which Webster saw was coming was the result, not of accord, but of discord, wrought into a compromise by the diplomatic skill and tact of Marshall, and his ascendancy over the wills of men, even when he could not shake their convictions.

In his revised report of Hicks *v*. Hotchkiss, 7 Johns. Ch. 296, 315, one of the last causes heard before him, Chancellor Kent felt compelled to say : —

" No objection has been raised, as far as I recollect, to the constitutionality of these insolvent laws, by the judiciary of this or of any other State, or by that of the United States until the decision in Sturges *v*. Crowninshield.

" But the case of Sturges *v*. Crowninshield is not free from difficulty as to the extent of its application. The act of 1811 was passed after the making of the contract to which the discharge under the act was pleaded as a bar, and the counsel for the plaintiff raised the distinction between the case of a contract made before and after the passing of the act; and contended, that if the act was not unconstitutional and void as to future contracts, it was clearly so as to contracts existing when it was passed. The chief justice, however, did not take notice of that distinction, and all his reasoning went to illustrate and enforce the general principle in the Constitution that contracts should be inviolable, and that any law releasing the party from his obligation to pay impaired that obligation."

Kent shrunk from the logical consequences of the reasoning of the chief justice ; but, as his opinion in Ogden *v*. Saunders shows, Marshall did not.

Judge Johnson was a South Carolinian, of English stock. He was born in 1771 ; graduated at Princeton, with the highest honors, when nineteen ; read law under the eye of C. C. Pinkney ; was admitted to the bar when twenty-two, and very soon attained eminence in his profession. When twenty-three, he became a member of the Legislature, was twice reëlected, and was speaker during his last term.

But as his tastes were judicial, rather than political, he retired from political life, and under the reorganization of the judiciary system became one of the judges of the Circuit Court.

On March 26, 1804, he was appointed by Jefferson to the bench of the Supreme Court. At the time of the decision in the College case, he was forty-eight years old. In 1822, he published the "Life, etc., of Nathaniel Greene." A portion of this work was devoted to the "history of parties." He proposed to continue the latter, and to trace how far, if at all, the Supreme Court had, by construction, "advanced beyond its constitutional limits, and trespassed on those of the State authorities;" and corresponded confidentially with Jefferson upon the subject, as their letters of April 11, 1823, and June 12, 1823, respectively show. A series of his letters to the Charleston *Courier* show that he made some progress in this work, but we are not aware that it was ever completed, or that, except in this form, any part of it was given to the world.

Judge Story, in his letter to Fay, of February 25, 1808 (1 Life of Story, 168), describing the judges, says: " I ought not to pass by Judge Johnson, though I scarcely know how to exhibit him individually. He has a strong mathematical head, and considerable soundness of erudition. He reminds me of Mr. Lincoln, [Jefferson's attorney-general when Marbury *v.* Madison arose and was decided, and the nominal successor of Judge Cushing,] and in the character of his mind he seems to me not dissimilar. He has, however, less of metaphysics and more of logic." The opinion of Story in later years was less flattering.

Soon after his accession to the bench, though politically he seems to have regarded himself as the immutable point in the universe, Story changed from a radical Republican, in the sense in which that term was used in olden time, to a Federal Imperialist of the Jay school, leaving Marshall far

behind ; and afterwards was not inclined to look with special favor upon those whose opinions were less advanced than
his own. Johnson did not grow in favor with him. He
termed Johnson's views upon certain constitutional questions " peculiar ;" and in some respects they were. Johnson's tastes were quiet, unpretentious, and scholarly. His
learning was rare, curious, and diversified ; but though his
was an important circuit, we know little of his judicial life
beyond what is disclosed by his opinions in the Supreme
Court, and they vary much. Some of them are strong and
able ; others are wanting in exactness and precision, and
indicate that the writer was confused, and unable to put his
opinion on grounds satisfactory to himself. His legal
instincts seemed to far outrun his power to make others
see, by written words, what he felt. He had little in
common with the Southern politicians of his day, with
whom he nominally affiliated. He was not only the
staunchest of Union men in the days of nullification, but
always had a strong National-Federal bias ; in a word,
though not an Imperialist, like Story, he was a Centralist
from conviction.

Before Marshall's appointment, the Supreme Court followed the English practice, under which each judge who sat
in a cause gave an opinion whenever he thought there was
occasion for it ; but, in general, those judges who presided
at the circuit declined to sit *in banc*, except in a case of equal
division. Under Marshall (who argued but a single cause
in that court before he became chief justice) this practice
was rooted out, so far as his influence extended ; the judges
reheard the causes which they had decided at the circuit ; the
practice of giving individual opinions was repressed ; the
practice became general of making one judge " the organ of
the court," of virtually assigning causes, and of taking them
home for the purpose of writing up opinions in vacation ;
and of having an opinion read by a single judge as the opinion
of the court, when the judgment received the assent of but

three, and sometimes two, of the judges, and the reasoning of a less number. This vicious practice occasioned great dissatisfaction.

The primitive court consisted of five judges. It was increased to six, and afterwards to seven. For years it was necessary for two of these judges, in general, to ride the circuit together; not infrequently, after the accession of Marshall, but four judges held the general term at Washington, and constituted the court when many important causes were decided. Two of the judges were aged and infirm, and one of them, for years before his death, was so superannuated that he practically left his circuit, a most important one, to take care of itself, and was a nonentity at Washington. The new chief had, from his acknowledged ability and force, and weight of character, and from his tact and diplomatic skill, great influence with his brethren. For years he prepared a large share of the opinions. When an occasion required, he was an adept in "patching up" compromise judgments and opinions. Confident that he was right, he sometimes entered up judgment, and read opinions as the opinion of the court, without being as careful as a discreet judge ought, to find out whether his opinion was that of a majority or minority of the court. In Rose v. Himely, 4 Cranch, 41, he delivered the leading opinion, and ordered the judgment of the Circuit Court to be reversed, etc., when in fact but a single judge agreed with him, as afterwards appeared in Hudson v. Guestier, 6 Cranch, 281. In one of the cloud of opinions delivered by Marshall at the trial of Aaron Burr, he admits that he made a mistake of a similar character in Bollman's case. In this way two judges sometimes practically became a majority of six, and three a majority of seven. The cases referred to were by no means the only instances of a similar kind, nor could they fairly be attributed to the press of business. These facts were open secrets in narrow circles. This intensified the dissatisfaction. A judiciary bill was reported to Congress by the attorney-general, which *required* the judges to deliver their opinions *seriatim* in open court, and then to give them in writing to the clerk, to be entered upon his record. This feeling lay at the bottom of the attempts in Congress (which gave Webster so much trouble, and some of the judges so much uneasiness) to prohibit the judges from setting aside a State law as unconstitutional unless a certain number of judges sat in the cause and concurred in the judgment. It was one of the causes of Jefferson's dislike of Marshall, which made him say, with a bitterness unusual to him, in his letter to Ritchie, of June 25, 1820 : "An opinion is huddled up in conclave, perhaps by a majority of one, delivered as if unanimous, and with the silent acquiescence of lazy or timid associates, by a crafty chief judge, who sophisticates the law to his mind by the turn of his own reasoning."

In such a judicial atmosphere, Johnson, keen, critical, sagacious, able, and honest, as he was, sometimes silently acquiesced in opinions and judgments contrary to his convictions ; and at others, set the example commended by Jefferson in his letter of June 12, 1823 : "I rejoice in the example you set of *seriatim* opinions. I have heard it often noticed, and always with high approbation. Some of your brethren will be encouraged to follow it occasionally, and in time it may be felt by all as a duty, and the sound practice of the primitive court be again restored. Why should not every judge be asked his opinion, and give it from the bench, if only by yea or nay? Besides ascertaining the fact of his opinion, which the public have a right to know, in order to judge whether it is impeachable or not, it would show whether the opinions were unanimous or not, and thus settle more exactly the weight of their authority."

The true construction of the obligation clause must be determined upon principle at last. In what sense did the people use these words when they adopted this provision? When we know this we know all. History, reasoning, and canons · are only pertinent as they bear upon this question.

They are intimately connected, but the words "obligation" and "contract" are no more synonymous than light and darkness. The Constitution does not prohibit legislative interference with contracts. It protects the *obligation;* but the contract is protected only so far as that results incidentally from the prohibition against impairing the obligation. That the obligation of all executory contracts, aside from those which undertake to barter away sovereignty, whether express, tacit, or otherwise inferred, or those which the law erects, as in case of absolute idiots, etc., is protected, is clear. Beyond lies the disputed territory. Marshall, in his second opinion in Fletcher v. Peck, 6 Cranch, 127, assumed that executed contracts carried with them, by implication, an obligation which the Constitution protected after the execution; in other words, that in this way the naked sale is protected. This is the foundation of the error. In that case, but five of the seven judges sat, and Johnson delivered a dissenting opinion, in the conclusion of which he says: "I have been very unwilling to proceed to the decision of this cause at all. It appears to me to bear strong evidence upon the face of it of being a mere feigned case. It is our duty to decide on the rights, but not on the speculations of parties."

His legal instincts led him, it seems to us, to the correct conclusion. He says: —

"The right of jurisdiction is essentially connected to, or rather identified with, the national sovereignty. To part with it is to commit a species of political suicide. In fact, a power to produce its own annihilation is an absurdity in terms. It is a power as utterly incommunicable to a political as to a natural person. But it is not so with the interests or property of a nation. Its possessions nationally are in nowise necessary to its political existence; they are entirely accidental, and may be parted with in every respect similarly to those of the individuals who compose

the community. * * * I have thrown out these ideas that
I may have it distinctly understood that my opinion on this point
is not founded on the provision in the Constitution of the United
States relative to laws impairing the obligation of contracts. It
is much to be regretted that words of less equivocal signification
had not been adopted in that article of the Constitution. There
is reason to believe from the letters of Publius, which are well
known to be entitled to the highest respect, that the object of the
Convention was to afford a general protection to individual rights
against the acts of the State Legislatures.''

It is obvious from the context, that in his reference to
Publius, Johnson refers, not to No. 7 of '' The Federalist,''
written by Hamilton, but to No. 44, written by Madison.
He continues : —

''Now, a grant or conveyance by no means necessarily *implies the
continuance of an obligation beyond the moment of executing it.*
It is most generally but the consummation of a contract, is
functus officio the moment it is 'executed, and *continues afterwards
to be nothing more than the evidence that a certain act was done.*''

The latter statement seems to us to contain a great and
incontrovertible legal truth. It was, in effect, what was
before said by Judge Wilson, and what was afterwards
repeated by Judge McLean.

However much we might desire to change the grounds
on which it has been assumed to rest, no honest man could
wish to disturb the judgment in this case. Taking the case
as stated in the record, it was an attempt at downright rob-
bery. Our convictions are that the judgment was sustain-
able upon other grounds than those stated.

Where the State conveys a tract of land, it does so, not as
a sovereign, but as an owner, the same as any individual,
municipal or other corporation might, and with precisely
the same effect. This was the view of Judges Johnson and
Wilson, of Morris and others, and seems now the doctrine
of the Supreme Court. Murray *v.* Charleston, 96 U. S.
445 ; Moore *v.* Robbins, 96 U. S. 533. But where it un-

dertakes to divest itself of sovereignty, it assumes to, and must, act as a sovereign.

Judge Johnson published no opinion in the College case, and gave none in Sturges *v.* Crowninshield. In Green *v.* Biddle, 8 Wheat. 96, he refused to discuss the obligation clause; but in Ogden *v.* Saunders he states what his opinion was in Sturges *v.* Crowninshield. He says: —

"The report of the case of Sturges *v.* Crowninshield needs also some explanation. The court was, in that case, *greatly divided* in their views of the doctrine, *and the judgment partakes as much of a compromise as of a legal adjudication.* The minority *thought it better to yield something than risk the whole.* And, although their course of reasoning led them to the general maintenance of the State power over the subject, controlled and limited alone by the oath administered to all their public functionaries to maintain the Constitution of the United States, yet, as denying the power to act upon anterior contracts could do no harm, but, in fact, imposed a restriction conceived in the true spirit of the Constitution, *they were satisfied to acquiesce in it, provided the decision were so guarded as to secure the power over posterior contracts as well from the positive terms of the adjudication as from inferences deducible from the reasoning of the court.* The case of Sturges *v.* Crowninshield, then, must, in its authority, be limited to the terms of the certificate, and that certificate affirms two propositions:—

"1. That a State has authority to pass a bankrupt law, provided such law does not impair the obligation of contracts within the meaning of the Constitution, and provided there be no act of Congress in force to establish an uniform system of bankruptcy, conflicting with such law.

"2. That a law of this description, acting upon prior contracts, is a law impairing the obligation of contracts within the meaning of the Constitution.

"*Whatever inferences or whatever doctrines the opinion of the court in that case may seem to support, the concluding words of that opinion were intended to control and to confine the authority of the adjudication to the limits of the certificate.*

"The first of these questions [whether a State bankrupt law, operating upon subsequent contracts, is prohibited by the obligation clause] has been so often examined and considered, in this and other courts of the United States, and so little progress has yet been made in fixing the precise meaning of the words ' obligation of a contract,' that I should turn in despair from the inquiry, were I not convinced that the difficulties the question presents are mostly factitious, and the result of refinement and technicality; or of attempts at definition, made in terms defective both in precision and comprehensiveness. Right or wrong, I come to my conclusion on their meaning, as applied to executory contracts, the subject now before us, by a simple and short-handed exposition.   Right and obligation are considered by all ethical writers as correlative terms.   Whatever I, by my contract, give another a right to require of me, I, by that act, lay myself under an obligation to yield or bestow.   The obligation of every contract will then consist of that right or power over my will or actions, which I, by my contract, confer on another.   And that right and power will be found to be measured neither by moral law alone, nor universal law alone, nor by the laws of society alone, but by a combination of the three; an operation in which the moral law is explained and applied by the law of nature, and both modified and adapted to the exigencies of society by positive law. * * * They [the parties] can enter into no contract which the laws of that community forbid, and the validity and effect of their contracts is what the existing laws give to them. * * * *If it be objected to these views of the subject, that they are as applicable to contracts prior to the law as to those posterior to it, and therefore, inconsistent with the decision in the case of Sturges v. Crowninshield, my reply is, that I think this no objection to its correctness. I entertained this opinion then, and have seen no reason to doubt it since.   But, if applicable to the case of prior debts, multo fortiori, will it be so to those contracted subsequent to such a law; the posterior date of the contract removes all doubt of its being in the fair and unexceptionable administration of justice that the discharge is awarded.''*

We regard these extracts from Johnson's opinion, a portion of which we have put in italics, as very important.

The opinions of Marshall in the College case and in Sturges *v.* Crowninshield, so far as they pertain to the construction of this clause, are virtually a single opinion. The extracts we have just quoted do not undertake to give a full history of the position of individual judges, or of the report in the latter case; but, as far as it goes, we assume that it states the facts correctly.' When the decision in Ogden v. Saunders was made, Livingston had given place to Thompson. But five of the judges, including Marshall and Story, were the ones who decided Sturges v. Crowninshield.

The dissenting opinion of Marshall in Ogden v. Saunders, if not his masterpiece, was one of the ablest efforts of his life. If Johnson had stated this history of his own views and the report incorrectly, neither Story nor Marshall could, or would, have permitted it to pass unnoticed. The simple truth is, that the dissenting opinion in Ogden v. Saunders, in its general reasoning, is identical with that in those cases; but the majority of the court, in this case, shrank from the logical consequences of that reasoning, as they did in Charles River Bridge v. Warren Bridge, 11 Pet. 420. By releasing all posterior contracts from the protection of the obligation clause, this decision changed, Judge Marshall said, " the character of the provision, and converted an inhibition to pass laws impairing the obligation of contracts into an inhibition to pass retrospective laws." Had the fathers first adopted a clause prohibiting all retrospective laws, it is impossible to believe that they would have added to it the inferior prohibition of the obligation clause.

CHAPTER XIII.

JUDGE WASHINGTON — HIS OPINION — GOLDEN v. PRINCE —
RESTS HIS DECISION ON FLETCHER v. PECK, AND PHILLIPS
v. BURY — LEGISLATIVE POWER OVER PUBLIC CORPORA-
TIONS — OGDEN v. SAUNDERS.

JUDGE WASHINGTON died November 26, 1829, some ten
years after the decision in the College case. Judge Story
says he was born June 5, 1762, but others say at an earlier
period. He was the nephew of General Washington; read
law in Philadelphia after the close of the war; was admitted
to the bar in his native county, in Virginia, and afterwards
resided at Richmond and Alexandria. In 1787 he was a
member of the lower branch of the Virginia Legislature;
and in 1788, sat with Marshall in the Convention which
ratified the Federal Constitution. At the bar he was often
pitted against Marshall, Campbell, and other prominent
lawyers. He reported the decisions of the Court of Appeals from 1792 to 1796. In these two volumes he briefly
reported his own arguments and those of Marshall, etc.
On September 29, 1798, John Adams, after hesitating for
some time as to whether Washington or Marshall should
receive the appointment, nominated him to fill the vacancy
on the Supreme Bench created by the death of Judge
Wilson. The nomination was confirmed, December 20,
1798, and he held the office till his death.

In his letter to Fay, of 1808, from which we have already
quoted, Judge Story says : " Washington is of a very short
stature, and quite boyish in his appearance. Nothing about
him indicates greatness. He converses with simplicity and
frankness. But he is highly esteemed as a profound lawyer,
and I believe not without reason. His written opinions are

(317)

composed with ability, and on the bench he exhibits great promptitude and firmness in decision. It requires intimacy to value him as he deserves."

Professor Goodrich (1 Life of Webster, 171) thus describes him in the scene which transpired during the delivery of Webster's peroration in the College case, in 1818: "Mr. Chief Justice Marshall, with his tall, gaunt figure, bent over as if to catch the slightest whisper, the deep furrows of his cheeks expanded with emotion, and his eyes suffused with tears; Mr. Justice Washington at his side, with his small and emaciated frame, and countenance more like marble than I ever saw on any other human being, leaning forward with an eager, troubled look."

His appearance was not deceptive. He was in no sense a great man or judge, but in every sense a good one. He was not an original thinker, nor a man of genius. He was neither quick, brilliant, nor profound. But he had fair abilities; his mental powers were evenly developed, harmonious, and worked in unison; he was conscious — for he expressed it in his opinions — that he was unable to convey to the minds of others the full force of his convictions, and his reasons for them; he was sometimes oppressed with Eldon's doubts, without Eldon's infirmity of procrastination; seldom able to satisfy himself; patience and painstaking became with him a religious duty, though after Story came to the bench he relied to a great extent, for authorities, on the abstracts and cases furnished by him, as did others. The fear of men and of consequences he never felt; the approbation of a "faithful few" was dear to his heart, but the praise of others fell on non-receptive ears. He had an inborn and unconquerable aversion to every form of display; in every thing he was slow, steady, and reliable. As a jurist, he was conservative, and, in general, submissive to precedent. He was an old-school Federalist, firm and decided, but tolerant of those whom he thought sincere in their support of Anti-Federalist heresies. He was the specially intimate and devoted friend of Marshall, and shared his notions relating to the " dignity of the court," and individual opinions; and in learning, he far exceeded him.

John Adams, though possessing unfortunate peculiarities of temper, was a great lawyer, and far surpassed in original genius all his gifted descendants. When he came to consider the appointment in 1798, he fixed upon Marshall or Washington as the successor of Judge Wilson, saying: " Marshall is first in rank, age, and public services, and probably not second in talents. * * * If Marshall should decline, I should think next of Washington." Jefferson, in his letter to Dr. Rush, of September 23, 1800, suggested as an illustration of the true " mode of recording merit," that " in giving, for instance, a commission of chief justice to Bushrod Washington, it should be in consideration of his integrity, and science in the laws," etc. Washington was one of the judges who concurred in the judgment in Fletcher v. Peck, though upon what precise ground, his opinions in the College case and Satterlee v. Matthewson, 2 Pet. 413–415, render uncertain. He was the only one of the seven judges who sat in the College case that is known, " upon the whole," to have " concurred in the result " at which Marshall had arrived, at the consultation, after the case was argued in 1818.

His opinion, which we have seen was never delivered, occupies about ten and one-half pages in Farrar, — about one-sixth the space taken by Marshall and Story. It differs materially from the others. To this, and its author's deep sense of duty, we are undoubtedly indebted for its publication, while we owe its brevity to the fact that he was never given to writing essays on government or etiquette, like Marshall, nor lectures or treatises on legal topics, like Story.

On the first page of his opinion he disposes summarily of the elaborate arguments of Mason and Smith upon those points before the State court, and three-fourths of that of Webster before the Supreme Court, saying: " Whether the first objection to these laws be well founded or not is a question with which this court in this case has nothing to do."

The contrast between the following opinion and that of Marshall in Sturges v. Crowninshield is very marked : — ·

Golden v. Prince (3 Wash. Cir. Ct. 313–327) was decided by Judge Washington at the April term, 1814, and published in 1827.   It was an action on a bill of exchange drawn by the defendant, May 10, 1810, at St. Bart's, for value received there, in favor of the plaintiff, on himself, and by him duly accepted, etc.   The suit was brought May 4, 1812, and the defendant pleaded his discharge under a statute of Pennsylvania for the relief of insolvent debtors, passed March, 13, 1812, under which, upon his petition, of April 20, 1812, he had provisionally obtained his certificate of discharge on April 23, and finally on May 29, 1812.   No notice of the petition had been given the plaintiff or his agents, nor had the plaintiff proved his debt under these proceedings.

The statute declared that the certificate should discharge such insolvent from all debts and demands due from him, or for which he was liable at the date of such certificate, and also from all contracts originating before that date though payable afterwards.

The court held: " The exercise of the power by the State governments, to pass bankrupt and naturalization laws, is incompatible with the grant of a power to Congress, to pass *uniform* laws upon the same subjects.

The law of Pennsylvania of 13th of March, 1812, is unconstitutional, because it impairs the obligation of a contract, and because Congress have exclusively the power to pass a bankrupt law."

In his opinion he says: " It may be proper to premise that a law may be unconstitutional, and, of course, void, in relation to particular cases ; and yet valid, to all intents and purposes, in its application to other cases within the scope of its provisions, but varying from the other in particular circumstances. Thus, a law prospective in its operation, under which a contract afterwards made may be avoided in a way different from that provided by the parties, would be clearly constitutional; because the stipulations of the parties, which are inconsistent with such a law, never had a legal existence, and of course could not be impaired by the law. But if the law act retrospectively, as to other contracts, so as to impair their obligation, the law is invalid; or, in milder terms, it affords no rule of decision in these latter cases.   *   *   *

" What is the obligation of a contract? It is to do, or not to do, a certain thing; and this may be either absolutely, or under some condition; immediately, or at some future time or times; and at some specified place, or generally. A law, therefore, which authorizes the discharge of a contract, by a smaller sum, or at a different time, or in a different manner than the parties have stipulated, impairs its obligation, by substituting for the contract of the parties one which they never entered into, and to the performance of which they of course had never consented. The old contract is completely annulled, and a legislative contract imposed upon the parties in lieu of it.   *   *   *

" But it was contended, that, if Congress shall decline to exercise the power [to pass uniform laws of bankruptcy], the right to pass such laws results to the State governments. This conclusion appears to us to beg the whole question in controversy. It resigns all claim to a *concurrent right* in the State governments, and sets up one which is to arise in a condition not to be found in the Constitution, but which is gratuitously interpolated into it.

" If, then, this claim of the State legislatures is not founded upon any express grant made to them in the Constitution, is it to be deduced from the circumstance of a *non-user* of the power by Congress? This doctrine appears to us to be as extravagant as it is novel. It has no analogy, that we know of, in legal or political science.   *   *   *

" We desire that it may be distinctly understood that we do not mean to give any opinion on the subject of insolvent laws, acts of limitation, and the like, because they are not now before us; and sufficient to the day is the evil thereof."

He seeks to show, in the next two and one-half pages of his opinion, that the charter was a contract.

His argument is, that Mr. Powell's definition is broad enough to cover executed contracts; that Fletcher v. Peck had decided " that a grant is a contract," and that the clause applies alike to executory and executed contracts; that, under Blackstone's definition of a franchise, the creation of this corporation by charter was such a contract, and extinguished the king's prerogative to bestow the same identical franchise on another corporate body, because it would prejudice his prior grant.

He then says: " It implies, therefore, a contract not to reassert the right to grant the franchise to another, or to impair it." This is the identical proposition afterwards relied upon by Story, but overturned by a majority of the court, in the great Bridge case. Its meaning is sufficiently obvious, but it seems never to have occurred to Washington that this reasoning fell far short of what was necessary. He was discussing a principle of English law in the light thrown upon it by a British author. Assuming that the king, whenever he granted a franchise, despoiled himself of the power to re-grant it, or to impair its value by a new creation under a fresh patent, he could neither expressly, nor by implication, annihilate the conceded power of Parliament to do as it pleased. Parliament had granted, and in many instances had altered and amended, charters. The king had no power to tie their hands, except by veto. Even those who believe that under a constitutional form of government the attributes of sovereignty are mere articles of merchandise, to be bartered away at pleasure, and that legislative bodies are "markets-overt" for that purpose, will hardly claim that the executive department can extinguish the veto power, present and future, by contract. If it were otherwise, the king, by contract, might extinguish the powers of the nation by thus strangling the two great estates of the realm.

He further says : "There is also an implied contract, that the founder of a private charity, or his heirs, or other persons appointed by him for that purpose, shall have the right to visit and to govern the corporation of which he is the acknowledged founder and patron, and also, that in case of its dissolution, the reversionary right of the founder to the property with which he had endowed it shall be preserved inviolate." John Wheelock, as we have seen, was the principal heir of Eleazar, who founded the charity-school. The proposition contained in the last clause quoted was, as we have seen, assumed on all hands, in the State court, to be correct. There are authorities which fully sustain it ; but, stated in these broad terms, it has, we apprehend, little foundation in principle. In general, the death of a trustee does not annihilate the trust, nor hand the fund over to the creator or his heirs. Chancery supplies a new trustee, and the blessings of the trust flow on. Corporations in England were liable to die, as well as individuals. Sometimes Parliament and sometimes the courts acted as headsmen.

He thus states the consideration of such grants : " The obligation imposed upon them [the grantees] and which forms the consideration of the grant is, that of acting up to the end or design for which they were created by their founder." And finally says : " It appears to me, *upon the whole*, [words which he afterwards repeats in relation to the judgment,] that these principles and authorities prove incontrovertibly, that a charter of incorporation is a contract."

It would seem, from this, that the naked grant is not pro-

tected; or, if it is, is so only so far as that may result from
these implied obligations.

But Mr. Webster, in his great argument in the Bridge
case, before the Supreme Court of Massachusetts (7 Pick.
437), says: "The legislature cannot grant what they do
not possess. The confusion in this case arises from considering these acts of the Legislature as laws, whereas they are
grants, which are wholly different. A law is a rule prescribed for the government of the subject; a grant is a
donation."

Of course, it would seem strange only to non-professional
eyes that absolute donations are contracts; though they
might be puzzled to understand why the gift itself was of
so little consequence, and the implied contract was of such
vast importance.

Washington devotes the remaining six pages to show
that the enactments in question did "impair this contract."
In proceeding "to mark the distinction between the different
kinds of lay aggregate corporations, in order to prevent any
implied decision by this court of any other case than the
one immediately before it," he says: "We are informed by
the case of Phillips v. Bury, which contains all the doctrines
of corporations connected with this point, that there are two
kinds of corporations aggregate, viz., such as are for public
government, and such as are for private charity. * * *
There is not a case to be found which contradicts the doctrine laid down in the case of Phillips v. Bury," — summariz-
ing the *dicta* in that case. "Such legislative interferences
[altering, etc., the charters of public corporations] cannot
be said to impair the contract by which the corporation was
formed, because there is in reality but one party to it, the
trustees or governors of the corporation being merely the
trustees for the public, the *cestui que trust* of the foundation.
The trustees or governors have no interest, no privileges or
immunities, which are violated by such interference, and can
have no more right to complain of them than an ordinary

trustee who is called upon in a court of equity to execute the trust. They accepted the charter for the public benefit alone, and there would seem to be no reason why the government, under proper limitations, should not alter or modify such a grant at pleasure. * * * In short, does not every alteration of a contract, however unimportant, even though it be manifestly for the interest of the party objecting to it, impair its obligation?"

To sustain the distinction between public and private corporations, he cites the opinion of the majority of the court in Terrett v. Taylor, saying: "In respect to public corporations which exist only for public purposes, such as towns, cities, etc., the Legislature may, under proper limitations, change, modify, enlarge or restrain them, securing, however, the property for the use of those for whom, and at whose expense, it was purchased."

We shall hereafter see what weight is to be attached to Phillips v. Bury.

In concluding, he holds that whether Dr. Wheelock was the founder or not would make no difference with the decision. He cites but few authorities, and those, aside from Phillips v. Bury, Fletcher v. Peck, and Terrett v. Taylor, etc., of no special pertinence. It may deserve consideration whether his doctrine in relation to trustees of public corporations does not, in the absence of particular constitutional provisions or special regulations, apply to all corporations.

The decisions in the American courts as to the power of the legislature over what are termed public corporations are diametrically opposed to each other. Even that great master of the law of municipal corporations, Judge Dillon, can neither reconcile them nor invent a common ground upon which they can stand. One class of cases holds that the legislature has not only absolute power over municipal corporations, but over their property; another class holds that such corporations have a dual nature, — are legal hermaphrodites; that the public side, being the creature of

legislative breath, can be annihilated by the same, but that
the private part is in effect an individual, suspended, like
Mahomet's coffin, somewhere between the heavens and
the earth, under the protection of the courts, and more
especially of the obligation clause.

The Supreme Court of New Hampshire, in a recent case
(Spaulding v. Andover, 54 N. H. 38), carried the reasoning
of Washington and the authorities on which he relied to
their logical consequences, and held, in effect, that a legislature could, through a public statute, contract by implication with a town, and that that contract was protected against
all subsequent enactments by the obligation clause, the same
as if the State had contracted with an individual.

At the February term, 1824, five years after the decision
in the College case, Ogden v. Saunders was first argued by
Webster for Saunders. This was *assumpsit* brought by
Saunders, of Kentucky, against Ogden, of Louisiana, upon
bills of exchange, drawn on September 30, 1806, by Jordan,
of Kentucky, upon Ogden, and accepted by him in New
York, of which State he was at that time a citizen. Ogden
had been discharged under the act of the New York Legislature of April 3, 1801, for the relief of insolvent debtors.
The case having been continued about three years for
advisement, was reargued by Webster at the January term,
1827. In guarded terms Washington thus states his general
position with reference to the decision, and the opinion of
Judge Marshall in Sturges v. Crowninshield: "To the
decision of this court made in the case of Sturges v. Crowninshield, and to the reasoning of the learned judge who
delivered that opinion, I entirely submit ; although I did not
then, nor can I now, bring my mind to concur in that part
of it which admits the constitutional power of the State
Legislatures to pass bankrupt laws, by which I understand
those laws which discharge the person and the future acqui-
sitions of the bankrupt from his debts. I have always
thought the power to pass such a law was exclusively vested

by the Constitution in the Legislature of the United States. But it becomes me to believe that this opinion was, and is, incorrect, since it stands condemned by the decision of a majority of this court, solemnly pronounced.'' (12 Wheat. 264, 265.) He adds: '' This leads us to a critical examination of the particular phraseology of that part of the above section which relates to contracts. It is a law which impairs the obligation of contracts, and not the contracts themselves, which is interdicted. It is not to be doubted that this term, obligation, when applied to contracts, was well considered and weighed by those who framed the Constitution, and was intended to convey a different meaning from what the prohibition would have imported without it.'' (12 Wheat. 257.) '' The universal law of all civilized nations, which declares that men shall perform that to which they have agreed, has been supposed, by the counsel who have argued this cause for the defendant in error, to be the law which is alluded to ; and I have no objection to acknowledging its obligation, whilst I must deny that it is that which exclusively governs the contract. It is upon this law that the obligation, which nations acknowledge to perform their compacts with each other, is founded, and I, therefore, feel no objection to answer the question asked by the same counsel, — what law it is which constitutes the obligation of the compact between Virginia and Kentucky, — by admitting that it is this common law of nations which requires them to perform it. I admit, further, that it is this law which creates the obligation of a contract, made upon a desert spot, where no municipal law exists, and (which was another case put by the same counsel) which contract, by the tacit assent of all nations, their tribunals are authorized to enforce.'' (12 Wheat. 258.) '' It is then the municipal law of the State, whether that be written or unwritten, which is emphatically the law of the contract made within the State, and must govern it throughout, wherever its performance is sought to be enforced.'' (12 Wheat. 259.)

CHAPTER XIV.

JUDGE STORY was about thirty-nine years of age when he
drew up his last opinion in the College case. This great
lawyer was born at Marblehead, Massachusetts, September
18, 1779. He graduated at Harvard in 1798, read law at
home with Judge Sewall from that time till January, 1801,
when he removed to Salem, and read with Judge Putnam
till he was admitted to the bar, in July of the same year.
He was a member of the lower house for the years 1805–
8; was reëlected in 1810–11; was speaker during his last
term, until he resigned, January 17, 1812, to take his place
upon the Supreme Bench, which office he held until his death,
which occurred September 10, 1845. In 1806–8 he supported the embargo with marked ability, and in 1808 was
elected to Congress, and became the most efficient instrument of its repeal. His mental and physical constitution
were both of the most elastic character. Without a stain of
impurity, he had an ardent social nature ; was open, lavish
in his kindliness to those he liked, and was a most delightful
companion, even when, in later years, he sometimes wearied
with his egotism, as he warmed with the recital of his early

(328)

combats, "shouldered his crutch, and showed how fields were won." From childhood he was ambitious beyond measure, and determined to be "the captain or nothing;" he was as proud of his plumage as any bird or woman, and as sensitive and sore as either, when it appeared to him that any attempt had been made to mar or despoil it. If such attempts were in any degree successful, though he sometimes forgave, he seldom tolerated the presence of their authors, and never forgot them, or ceased to feel the smart. Swift of apprehension, he read every thing, remembered it, put it away in order, and held it at all times at his command. In orderly industry and power of application he had no rival at the bar or on the bench. His power for the acquisition of knowledge bordered upon the marvellous; he was as busy as the "fatal sisters;" he laid all under contribution; he was the Amazon which made tributary every rill of personal anecdote or political gossip.

As a law-lecturer there never was his like; he was a full reservoir; ready, fluent, and never hesitating for a word, the flood poured at command, as zesty and sparkling as a river of champagne. He had all that New England shrewdness and practical judgment in business matters and the common affairs of life which Marshall so much lacked. No sane man was likely to tell the "sapling story" at his expense. He was a born politician and manager of men; he knew every phase of human nature, and how to deal with it. When the occasion required, he had the courage of his opinions as but few men have.

His labors were almost incredible. Besides other duties, which were enough to crush most men, he framed many of the most important acts ever adopted by Congress or pressed upon its attention, — the credit of which was usually taken by others, — and for thirty-three years turned out decisions, opinions, volumes of reports, and huge treatises upon legal topics, with the velocity of a patent machine. He was the great source of legal and political learning from which Webster, and others scarcely less noted, drew, in their debates in Congress and elsewhere. His opinions will probably stand higher, in the hereafter, than his text-books, except his works on the " Conflict of Laws " and the " Constitution."

Many of his earlier opinions in the Circuit Court are invaluable. They are replete with learning and filled with light. His opinions in the vast fields of jurisprudence, involving private rights, were generally well founded; but where some *protégé* of his was to be affected, either as counsel or suitor, where the construction of some pet statute framed by him was involved, or where certain constitutional questions were raised, he was not, from his peculiar organization and proclivities, enabled to see things as others saw them.

Whole chapters in some of his books seem to be little more than windrows of head-notes, raked together as the farmer rakes his hay in the mow-field; but when we survey the ground, the wonder is, not that they contain so many imperfections, but that his work was so well performed.

In 1801, he went into practice in Salem, less from choice than because he knew of nowhere else to go, and in a little more than ten years was elevated to the Supreme Bench. For three or four years his practice was quite limited, because branded for his political and religious views by the Federal aristocracy among whom he had cast his lot.

Few who know the New England of to-day can realize the despotic power of this autocracy in Story's youth and early manhood, unless they have felt it themselves, or been reared in the atmosphere and traditions of those who have. Its heart was in the larger places, but its influence radiated to almost every town and hamlet in New England. Webster had a vivid appreciation of its sway when he wrote to Porter, on June 4, 1802: "It [Federalism] unites in its support more than two-thirds of the talent, the character, and the property of the nation. This is too much for any administration to contend with;'' and when he cautioned his wife, the gentle and winning Grace, upon her visit to his native town, to pay due attention to "the Salisbury *quality*." It varied in its components according to localities, but in essence it was the same everywhere. It was agglomerate in its nature, but courtly, well dressed, and immensely dignified. It was a religious and political aristocracy united with one of birth, lineage, wealth, culture, and talent. A young man of genius, poor and ambitious, was received by it with imposing dignity and a lofty courtesy; and if properly submissive, in time, by its aid, might hope to be "somebody." But if he dared in religious and political matters to do his own thinking, he was tabooed in social and business life; the "freezing-out" process was resorted to; and when that failed, he was surrounded with a cordon of fire, and left to suffocate.

Even at a later day, Worcester, the favorite preacher of Judge Webster as well as Daniel, suffered martyrdom because he believed with Channing. So long as he drifted with the tide, even through the turmoils of the College controversy, all was well; but when he looked back toward Unitarianism, a fate less merciful than that of Lot's wife befel him. With exceptional cases, few natures were hardy and self-reliant enough to withstand the pressure.

Dr. Story was a man of ability, an Anti-Federalist of the most decided stamp. He took the side of Jefferson. The son, impulsive, warm-hearted, and devoted to his father, inherited the latter's views and convictions, and, in consequence, became very unpopular, was ostracised, and treated with such offensive personalities that he seriously contemplated a removal to Portsmouth, New Hampshire, or Baltimore, Maryland, to escape this persecution. In his later years, after he had taken the long stride from the school of Jefferson to that of Jay, and, in consequence, had become the idol of those who had once sought to destroy him, with his feelings mellowed by time and his associations, he gives us this portraiture of his persecution : " At the time of my admission to the bar, I was the only lawyer within its pale who was either openly or secretly a *Democrat.* Essex was, at that time, almost exclusively Federal, and party politics were inexpressibly violent. I felt many discouragements from this source. * * * To young men with my political opinions, the times were very discouraging. My father was a Republican, as contradistinguished from a Federalist, and I had naturally imbibed the same opinions. In Massachusetts, at that period, an immense majority of the people were Federalists. All the offices (with scarcely an exception, I believe) were held by Federalists. The governor, the judges, the Legislature, were ardent in the same cause. It cannot be disguised, too, that a great preponderance of the wealth, the rank, the talent, and the civil and literary character of the State was in the same scale. Almost all the profession of the law were of the party. I scarcely remember more than four or five lawyers in the whole State who *dared* avow themselves Republicans. The very name was odious, and even more offensive epithets (such as 'Jacobins') were familiarly applied to them. The great struggle was over between Mr. Jefferson and Mr. Adams, and the former had been chosen to the presidency. The contest had been carried on with great heat and bitterness; and the defeated party, strong at home, though not in the nation, was stimulated by resentment and by the hope of a future triumph. Under such circumstances, there was a dreadful spirit of persecution abroad. The intercourse of families was broken up, and the most painful feuds were generated. Salem was a marked battle-ground for political controversies, and for violent struggles of the parties. The Republican party was at first very small there; and its gradual growth and increasing strength, so far from mitigating, added fuel to the flame.

" Such was the state of things at the time when I came to the bar. All the lawyers and all the judges in the county of Essex were Federalists, and I was the first who was obtruded upon it as a political heretic. I was not a little discouraged by this circumstance, and contemplated a removal as soon as I could find a better position or prospect elsewhere. For some time I felt the coldness and estrangement resulting from this known diversity of opinion ; and taking, as I did, a firm and decided part in politics, it was not at all wonderful that I should be left somewhat solitary at the bar."

In his letter of March 30, 1803, to Duvall, afterwards the dissenting judge in the College case, declining the position of naval officer at Salem, while expressing his gratitude for the appointment, Story says : " To one just entering life, without patronage or support other than what must be derived from juridical pursuits, and at a period when persons older in the profession are so numerous as to absorb almost all lucrative business, it was a circumstance peculiarly grateful. , If the extreme degree of virulence with which I have been persecuted, in a county where all the judges and lawyers are pertinaciously Federal, and the manifest attempts to close against me the doors of professional eminence be added to these considerations, you will readily perceive that there exist great inducements for me to accept the proposed office, and thereby secure to myself a moderate independence and freedom from oppression. * * * I have long had a desire to migrate southward, in order to find a situation in which I should have only to compete with the ordinary obstacles of my profession. In your leisure, should you recollect any situation favorable to my views, the information would be grateful to me."

In his letter of June 6, 1805, to his classmate Williams, in Baltimore, he says : " Your account of Baltimore charms me. I have long had a desire to sojourn in some southern clime, more congenial with my nature than the petty prejudices and sullen coolness of New England. Bigoted in opinion, and satisfied in forms, you well know that, in ruling points, they too frequently shut the door against liberality and literature. A man who will hazard a noble action is not less exposed than certain notorious saints of old. Indeed, if I mistake not, the same spirit, under different forms, is revived, though I have good reason to believe we have no *witches* amongst us. Could I obtain any respectable situation in your pleasant climate and hospitable city, I hardly know how I could refuse it."

Notwithstanding his after-acquired dislike of "Virginia politicians" and the Southern people, he seems to have retained his kindly feelings toward Baltimore, for, at a later day, he had serious thoughts of resigning his place upon the bench and taking the cast-off sandals of great Pinkney.

In the letter from which we have just quoted, he further says: "My situation is pleasant here, so far as it respects friends. The whole Republican party are my warm advocates. Federalism has persecuted me unremittingly for my political principles; but, as my life has been sacredly pure, they do little else than accuse me of ' being a Bonaparte in modesty and ambition.' Convinced every day more and more of the purity of the Republican cause, and believing it to be founded on the immutable rights of man, I cannot and will not hesitate to make any sacrifice for its preservation. Yes, my dear friend, though I have suffered the hardness of oppression, I feel satisfied that at least I am not mistaken for a dependant or a minion." (1 Life of Story, 95, 106.) His practice steadily increased in his own State, and for some years, until its more pressing duties nearer home compelled him to relinquish it, he had a respectable business in Rockingham County, New Hampshire.

. The tide had turned; the spirit which inspired Thompson's letter to Professor Adams, from which we have already quoted, to "put down a certain man," was baffled; Story had won. Henceforth he became a leader of his party, and occupied that position until he went upon the bench. "Owing to the fact," he says, "that there were few professional men in the Commonwealth at that time belonging to the Republican party, and of those few scarcely any in the Legislature, I was soon compelled, notwithstanding my youth, to become a sort of leader in debate, and I may say that I occupied that station *de facto* during all my legislative life."

His appointment to the bench at the early age of thirty-two is not to be ascribed to his merits, marked as they were. It was due to the "accident of circumstances." Judge Cushing, a feeble old man, seventy-seven years of age, died in 1810. The position "belonged," in the phrase of the politicians, to Massachusetts proper, and to the party in political affiliation with the administration. The range for a proper selection there was exceedingly limited. Nobody thought of Story. Mr. Madison, who knew him well, on January 3, 1811, appointed Levi Lincoln, who had been the attorney-general of Jefferson, and the acting secretary of state before Madison assumed the duties of the office, to fill the vacancy, and personally pressed him to accept it. But Lincoln was compelled to decline, because of the blindness that was creeping fast upon him. John Quincy Adams was appointed in the place of Lincoln, February 22, 1811, and declined upon the ground, as is understood, that his tastes and mind were not judicial, and because he preferred to retain the position which he then held as ambassador to St. Petersburg. In this dilemma, Mr. Bacon, a member of the House of Representatives from Massachusetts, and his personal friend, suggested the name of Story. Very much to the surprise of the latter, Madison appointed him. He was confirmed November 18, 1811, and took his seat at the next term of the Supreme Court.

What was generally thought of this appointment at the time, and especially by his political opponents, is thus stated by the partial pen of his son: "The ability and learning displayed by him at the bar, as well as the spotless character with which he had passed through the fiery ordeal of politics, had won for him the respect and confidence of a large class. But there were not wanting those who looked upon his elevation with an inauspicious eye. Party animosities were then very bitter, and among his political opponents his appointment was ridiculed and condemned. Bigoted in their prejudices, some honestly thought that none but a fool or a knave could entertain Republican opinions; and others, from his youth and active political course, augured a multitude of evil consequences."

A few " leaves from life " will show better than any words of ours that this astute politician lost none of his great powers by his transfer from the caucus to the consultation-room.

An intimacy, personal and political, had subsisted for years between Story and Governor Plumer. They were both Massachusetts men; were born in the vicinity of each other; had practised at the Rockingham bar; had shared the same general views in regard to the embargo, the restrictive policy, and the great measures which preceded and arose during the war of 1812.

In September, 1815, Governor Plumer visited Story, as well as other friends, at or near his birthplace. In his journal, under the date of September 16, 1815, he says: " At Salem I spent an afternoon with Joseph Story, one of the judges of the Supreme Court of the United States. He said the judges of that court had informally considered the question whether the governor of a State was bound, on the requisition of the president, to order the militia into the service of the United States. He could, he said, discover no diversity of sentiment among them; he believed they were unanimously of opinion that the governors were bound to obey the requisition, and regretted that neither the president nor Congress had required their opinion on the subject. He complimented me on my speech to the Legislature in November, 1812, upon the question of ordering out the militia, and said that my reasoning appeared to him conclusive. He mentioned of his own accord that he had considered the law of New Hampshire of 1813, establishing the new judiciary, and was of opinion that it was unconstitutional.'' (Life of Plumer, 430, 431.)

This simple statement from the pen of a friend portrays Story's whole judicial life.

The Constitution of New Hampshire provides that the judges '' shall hold their offices during good behavior.'' The Federalists came into power in 1813, upon the anti-war issue. One of their first acts was to blot out the inferior courts, abolish the Superior Court, — the constitutional court of last resort, — turn out the old judges, by repealing the act creating these courts, and to establish a new system upon their ruins. This led to grave complications. Some of the old judges held the act void, and went on holding their terms, as did the new ones ; some sheriffs recognized the new, and some adhered to the old, court. The result was scandal and disturbances, but no bloodshed.

When the Anti-Federalists, under the lead of Plumer, came again into power, a few months after this interview with Story, they acted in accordance with his opinion, in which Plumer and other leaders coincided, repealed the act of June 24, 1813, under which the new judges held their offices, removed them by address, upon the ground that the law was unconstitutional, and restored the old system. No man knew the facts better than Webster ; but when, in his argument in the College case, he went out of his way, for a purpose, to assail with unwonted severity the State government of 1816, and especially its Legislature and the judiciary, he preserved a guarded silence as to the cause of it, which was the revolutionary proceedings of his political associates in 1813. He was careful not to suggest that the weight of his great influence had been given to make it a partisan bench. Story could have advised Marshall of the truth, had he seen fit, but the tone and coloring of the opinion of the chief shows that he did not know it.

Nothing could be more characteristic of Story than what he said to Governor Plumer about the power of the president to call out the militia, and this informal decision of the Supreme Court of the United States.

The Constitutions of Missouri, Maine, Massachusetts, New Hampshire, and perhaps other States, are substantially alike in one respect; they grant to the other departments of the State government the power to " require " the opinions of the judges of the highest court upon important questions of law, and upon solemn occasions. The opinions in 37 Mo. 193, 51 Mo. 140, 55 Mo. 498, and that of Judges Richardson and Bell, from which we have already quoted, show that no limits to this loose and ill-defined power have 'ever been fixed or established. In the Federal Convention, August 20, 1787, Pinkney submitted, among others, the following proposition : " Each branch of the legislature, as well as the supreme executive, shall have authority to require the opinions of the Supreme Judicial Court upon important questions of law, and upon solemn occasions." This project was referred to the committee on detail, and never afterward heard of. The plan for associating the judges of the Supreme Court with the executive as a " council of revision," invested with a veto power, though supported by some of the purest and ablest men in that body, was defeated by a large majority. No such provision, and none anywise akin to it, ever existed in the Constitution of the United States, and no man knew it better than Story. It has been truly said of him that he absorbed jurisdiction like a sponge. The Constitution became in his hands a most elastic instrument. He derived this power, as he did many others, by a construction so " liberal " that it was well-nigh limitless.

The Legislature of New Hampshire, in 1794, authorized the governor to call out the militia whenever required by the president. Governor Plumer, in 1812, promptly obeyed the requisitions made upon him, and was assailed with great virulence therefor. Governors Strong, of Massachusetts, and Griswold, of Connecticut, refused to obey similar requisitions, upon the ground that the governor of each State was the sole judge whether the exigency contempleted by the Federal Constitution had arisen; and it was also held in Massachusetts and Vermont, that although the president, when actually in the field, could command the militia, yet he could not put them under any but their own State officers. The opinions of Judges Parsons, Parker, and Sewall, given to Governor Strong, are to be found in the eighth volume of Massachusetts Reports, 547–550. This great question was first decided by the Supreme Court in 1827, in Martin v. Mott, 12 Wheat. 19. Story delivered the opinion of the court. It is needless to add that he adhered to the informal decision which he had announced to Plumer so many years before.

In the absence of special rules, no "indecorum," to use Webster's phrase, would be committed if counsel furnished their arguments, written or printed, to every member of the court. We commented in a previous chapter upon the fact that Webster furnished his argument, through Story, to some of the judges, and not to others.

The long struggle between Story and the Supreme Court of New Hampshire, with Joel Parker at its head, over the construction of a clause in the Bankrupt Act of 1841, is not yet entirely forgotten. The proviso in that act expressly provided that nothing in the act should be "construed to annul, destroy, or impair * * * any liens, mortgages, or other securities on property, real or personal, which may be valid by the laws of the States respectively;" and the question was, whether an attachment, made in accordance with the laws in New Hampshire, and which had, in substance, been in force since they were enacted in Massachusetts (of which New Hampshire was then a part) nearly two hundred years before, was such a lien or security. No man knew the time when it had not been denominated a lien by the courts in New Hampshire. It had been termed a

security in the statutes for many years before the existence
of the Bankrupt Act. Story, in one of his works, had
affirmed that such attachments were liens. The same view
had been taken by the highest courts of Massachusetts,
Maine, and Connecticut, by many of the most eminent lawyers in these States, and by some of the ablest Federal
judges. Story was the author of this Bankrupt Act, which
had been a pet hobby with him from the time he came to
the bench. Nearly a quarter of a century before its passage, he had importuned Webster to ask him to frame such
a law. He dinned it in the ears of his associates, and eminent and influential members of Congress, until it passed.
Grave questions arose as to the extent of the power granted
by the Constitution to Congress. The discussions at the
bar, the speeches of Mr. Benton and other eminent statesmen, and the reports of the Supreme Court, to which we
have already referred, show how greatly professional opinion
was divided. Story decided many of these questions in the
same way that he did others in his interview with Governor
Plumer. His opinion, in substance, was that the act was
uniform ; that its constitutionality must be upheld ; that it
was a good law ; that the court must supply its defects, fill
the gaps, by a " liberal " construction ; that the act gave
the district and circuit judges the power to " overhaul " and
" control " all State courts and all proceedings therein.

There is at least one member of the New Hampshire bar
still living who remembers the peculiar smile and glistening
eye of Judge Parker when he related what Story had said.
It is, perhaps, to this incident to which Parker alludes in
the close of his opinion in Kittredge v. Warren, when he
says : " We have only to remark, farther, in conclusion,
that we have been strongly impressed from the first with
the views now expressed ; and the extended examination we
have made has left no reasonable doubt upon our minds
respecting the result."

The Supreme Court of New Hampshire at the time of

this collision, to use the words of Mr. Bishop, was " one of the most able judicial tribunals in the Union."

Judge Parker was as " indefatigable " as Webster said John Wheelock was. He was a great lawyer, a great judge, and a great man. Chief Justice Bell, one of his successors, well said of him : " He was a most formidable antagonist, and combined the strength of five men with the sensitiveness and tenacity of ten women." He was a Federalist and a Whig of the iron stamp ; but such was the respect felt for him by his political opponents, that, of their own accord, they first made him judge and then chief justice of the highest court of the State, and sustained him in that position from first to last.

In April, 1842, Story gave an elaborate opinion in Ex parte Foster, 2 Story, 131. Before the filing of the petition, the property of the bankrupt had been attached on mesne process in one of the Massachusetts courts. He applied to the district judge for an injunction to restrain further proceedings in the State courts, and requiring the property to be handed over to the assignee. The District Court certified the questions to the Circuit Court. Story decided that the attachment was not protected by the saving clause, and adhered to his opinion that the State courts were but wax in the hands of the District and Circuit Courts, and that these Federal judges could " overhaul, control, or set aside " the proceedings and judgments in the State courts, just as, in Martin v. Mott, he affirmed the opinion he had given Governor Plumer eleven years before.

In Kittredge v. Warren (14 N. H. 509 — January, 1844), William H. Duncan, the son-in-law of Trustee Olcott, and the brother-in-law of Rufus Choate, who still lives, as he always has, right under the shadow of the College, was counsel for the defendant. He relied on the reasoning and authority of Ex parte Foster. This drew from Judge Parker, as the organ of the court, an able adverse opinion, nearly thirty pages in length. In July, 1844, Story, in the matter of Bellows and Peck (3 Story, 428), reaffirmed his opinion in Ex parte Foster, and replied to that of Parker in Kittredge v. Warren, in language and with an emphasis which showed how deeply his self-love had been wounded. At the July term, 1844, Parker, again speaking for the Supreme Court, responded in a masterly opinion in Kittredge v. Emerson (15 N. H. 227–280). In closing, he replied to Story's threat with the distinct notice that the State court would protect its jurisdiction and officers at all hazards, and intimated that it might not be entirely safe for those who might attempt to execute the threat. The State court ordered judgment for the plaintiff. Nobody attempted to interfere with the execution of its mandate. On June 5, 1844, the governor of New Hampshire, in his message, called the attention of the Legislature, then in session, to the controversy, and the perils that must flow from it.

On December 26, 1844, the House, sweeping away party lines, almost unanimously passed a joint resolution sustaining " the firm and decided stand " of the court " in opposition to the unwarrantable and dangerous assumptions of the Circuit Court of the United States." On December 31, 1844, Story responded to Parker and the State government with his opinion in Ex parte Christy (3 How. 292), dragging the majority of the Supreme Court of the United States into this controversy between himself and Judge Parker, in an opinion upon a point which that court could not properly consider in that case.

This was a " motion " made in the Federal Supreme Court, in behalf of the City Bank of New Orleans, that a writ of prohibition issue to the United States District Court of Louisiana, restraining it from proceeding further in Christy's case. It was so evident that no power had been conferred upon the Supreme Court to issue such a writ in such a case, that even Story decided, in five lines, without either reasoning or the citation of authorities, that the court had no jurisdiction ; but he nevertheless went on with an opinion of fourteen pages, which is a marvel for its ability and obscurity, as well as its contradictory character, in attempting to show that if the court had had jurisdiction, Judge Parker, in his opinion, was very much in error. Story has taken pains in his private correspondence to show us, beyond a doubt, what his purpose was in writing this opinion.

In his letter of January 1, 1845, to his son, he says : " Yesterday I delivered the opinion of the court in a great bankrupt case from New Orleans, embracing the question of the nature and extent of the jurisdiction of the District Court in matters of bankruptcy. It was an elaborate review of the whole statute, and we sustained the jurisdiction of the District Court over all matters whatsoever, and recognized (as, indeed, was one of the points) the right of the court to grant an injunction to proceedings and suits in the State courts. *The opinion covers the whole ground in Ex parte Foster, and also in the New Hampshire cases, which have been so stoutly contested in the State courts.* * * * I took great pains about it, and the court fully confirmed all my views. Judge Catron alone dissented."

Judge Catron, with whom Judge Daniel concurred, administered to Story a dignified but stinging rebuke for the course taken by him in this opinion. He said : " By the fourteenth section of the Judiciary Act, this court has power to issue writs proper and necessary for the exercise of its jurisdiction ; having no jurisdiction in any given case, it can issue no writ. That it has none to revise the proceedings of a bankrupt court, is our unanimous opinion. So far we adjudge, and in this I concur. For further views why the prohibition cannot issue, I refer to the conclusion of the principal opinion. But a majority of my brethren see proper to go further, and express their views at large on the jurisdiction of the bankrupt court. In this course I cannot concur ; perhaps it is the result of timidity, growing out of long-established judicial habits in courts of error elsewhere, never to hazard an opinion when no case was before the court, and when that opinion might be justly arraigned as extra-judicial, and a mere *dictum*, by courts and lawyers ; be partly disregarded while I was living, and almost certainly be denounced as undue assumption when I was no móre, — a measure of disregard awarded with an unsparing hand, here and elsewhere, to the *dicta* of State judges under similar circumstances. And it is due to the occasion and to myself to say, that I have no doubt the *dicta* of this court will only be treated with becoming respect before the court itself so long as some of the judges who concurred in them are present on the bench, and afterwards be openly rejected as of no authority, — as they are not.''

In Peck *v.* Jenness (16 N. H. 516–537 — July, 1845), Judge Parker, for obvious reasons, disregarded this opinion in Ex parte Christy. In this case (7 How. 612–626), at the December term, 1848, four years after Story read his opinion in Ex parte Christy, the Supreme Court of the United States unanimously decided that Parker was right, and Story wrong.

The written opinion to Webster, of December 25, 1833 (2 Life of Story, 155–158), upon a variety of questions, raised by certain acts of the president and Mr. Taney, in the great bank war, is another illustration of the way in which, during his whole judicial life, he sowed on every hand his written and oral opinions upon questions he was likely to be called to decide as a judge. The harvest which these dragon's teeth produced was sometimes more perilous than armed men.

STORY, "in the end," supplemented the opinion that the charter was protected by the obligation clause. This was the natural result of his new views, adopted after his elevation to the bench, under the influence of the seductive power of Marshall and the promptings of his vast ambition, that the controlling purpose of this clause, as of many others, was *not* to protect private rights, but to subserve great political ends; or, as it is put by Webster, in his celebrated argument in Ogden v. Saunders, which Story indorsed, if he did not originate : " The inquiry then recurs, whether the law in question be such a law as the Legislature of New York had authority to pass. The question is general. We differ from our learned adversaries on general principles. *We differ as to the main scope and end of this constitutional provision. They think it entirely remedial; we regard it as preventive.* They think it adopted to procure redress for violated private rights ; to us it seems intended to guard against great public mischiefs. They argue it as if it were designed as an indemnity or protection for injured private rights in individual cases of *meum* and *tuum;* we look upon it as a great political provision, favorable to the commerce and credit of the whole country. Certainly we do not deny its application to cases of violated private right. Such cases are clearly and unquestionably within its operation. Still, we think its main scope to be general and political." And in his recapitulation, Webster says : " Sixthly, that upon any other construction, one great political object of the Constitution will fail of its accomplishment."

Marshall, though firm and decided, was by nature a moderando. Circumstances, personal and political, intensified his views as he advanced in life. Jay and Jefferson were the antipodes in American politics. In 1785, Jay thus expressed his convictions: "It is my first wish to see the United States assume and merit the character of *one great nation*, whose territory is divided into different States merely for more convenient government, and the more easy and prompt administration of justice; *just as* our several States are divided into counties and townships for the like purposes." Just before the Federal Convention which framed the Constitution met, he wrote to General Washington: "What powers should be granted to the government so constituted is a question which deserves much thought. *I think the more the better;* the States retaining only so much as may be necessary for domestic purposes, and all their principal officers, civil and military, being commissioned and removable by the national government." In his opinion in Chisholm *v.* Georgia, and subsequently, Jay adhered to the same general views.

A few extracts from Story's private correspondence will show how fully, after his lurch from the school of Jefferson, he shared the views of Jay. In his letter of February 22, 1815, to Williams, Story says: "Let us extend the national authority over the whole extent of power given by the Constitution. Let us have great military and naval schools; an adequate regular army; the broad foundations laid of a permanent navy; a national bank; a national system of bankruptcy; a great navigation act; a general survey of our ports, and appointments of port-wardens and pilots; judicial courts, which shall embrace the whole constitutional powers; national notaries; public and national justices of the peace, for the commercial and national concerns of the United States. By such enlarged and liberal institutions, the government of the United States will be endeared to the people, and the factions of the great States will be rendered harmless."

In his letter of December 13, 1815, to the reporter, Wheaton, in relation to the bankrupt law, etc., he says: " I hope you will follow up the blow by vindicating the necessity of establishing other great national institutions ; the extension of the jurisdiction of the courts of the United States over the whole extent contemplated in the Constitution ; the appointment of national notaries-public and national justices of the peace ; national port-wardens and pilots for all the ports of the United States ; a national bank and national bankrupt laws. I have meditated much on all these subjects, and have the details, in a considerable degree, arranged in my mind. And, once for all, I most sincerely hope that a *national newspaper* may be established at Washington, which, for its talents and taste, shall entitle itself to the respect of the nation, and preserve the dignity of the government." (2 Life of Story, 254–271.)

We have already commented upon some of the peculiarly latitudinarian opinions given by Story to Governor Plumer. Young Story, in his life of his father, from which we have quoted, after commenting upon the case of Martin *v.* Hunter's Lessee, says : —

" This was the first great constitutional judgment delivered by my father. To this department of the law he had given little study during his practice at the bar, and, although he had always avowed himself to be a disciple of Washington, yet, as the views of the party to which he belonged were widely different from those entertained by the illustrious Chief Justice Marshall, no small curiosity was felt by his friends as to the determination his mind should take on great constitutional questions. The Republicans were strict constructionists of the Constitution, narrowing down the powers of the Federal government to the express and exact terms of that instrument, while the Federalists claimed a broader and more liberal exposition in favor of the United States. * * * Upon taking his seat on the bench, my father devoted himself to this branch of the law, and the result was a cordial adherence to the views of Marshall, whom he considered, then and ever afterwards, as the expounder of the true principles of the Constitution.

Nor did this indicate so much a *change* as a *formation* of opinion, and it is no slight indication of his independence and emancipation from the influence of party that he resigned, upon careful study and examination into the history and principles of the Constitution, his early prejudices in favor of Mr. Jefferson's abstractions for the clear and practical doctrines of Marshall. * * * His was the consistency of truth — to the living thought of the present, not to the dead opinion of the past."

The partial pen of the son has done injustice to his father. Story and Marshall sometimes rode abreast; sometimes Story, like Johnson, concurred in the opinions and judgments of Marshall from which he dissented, as in the case of United States *v.* Bevans, 3 Wheat. 336; and sometimes, as in the College causes and the case of the Cherokee Nation, he far outran the chief justice.

It is not true that this astute politician and learned lawyer was without opinions upon great constitutional questions, or that he had failed to study them before his accession to the bench. In the broils and discussions, legal and political, which grew out of the embargo, restrictive policy, etc., he had scaled the heights and measured the depths of the great powers conferred upon the general government over commerce. The same is true of the treaty-making power, and the provisions in relation to treason, as well as the great powers which give control over the purse and sword of the nation. On February 17, 1810, he argued the great Georgia case before the Supreme Court of the United States with consummate ability, and he did not do this till after he had carefully studied the obligation clause.

The nominal hearing in the causes, which had been sent up from his circuit, and remanded, was had before Story on May 27, 1819.

In his letter to Mason, of February 23, 1819, Webster says: "As to their facts, which they say are new, they will, I apprehend, be told that, if admitted, they would not alter the result; and, in the next place, that the court considers the recital of the charter as conclusive upon the facts contained in it." (Mason's Mem. 221.)

In his letter to Mason, of April 13, 1819, already quoted, he said : " I flatter myself the judge [Story] will tell the defendants that the new facts which they talk of were presented to the minds of the judges at Washington, and that, if all proved, they would not have the least effect on the opinion of any judge." (Mason's Mem. 223.) This was weeks before the facts were put in evidence before Story. If so presented to the minds of the judges, it must have been months before the formal hearing before him.

Webster in his letter to Mason, dated at Boston, May 27, 1819, says : " Mr. Austin read this morning a mass of papers about the *new facts*. The judge thought there was nothing in them, but has taken the papers for a day or two to examine them before he gives a formal decision. He says he sees nothing which contradicts any part of the recital of the charter. We had not much talk about it. Mr. A. read & stated all he chose to do, & the judge intimated that the *new facts* had no bearing on any part of the court's opinion." (Mason Papers ; Harvey's Webster Papers.)

Webster, in his letter to Brown, of May 30, 1819, says : " James T. Austin, Esq., in behalf of the University, presented the new facts to Judge Story on Thursday. They were what we expected and no more. The judge said he saw nothing to vary at all the case as it had been considered and decided. None of these ' facts ' if true changed the ground, nor did he see any the least contradiction between any of these facts and the recitals of the charter. He was willing however to take the papers and read them attentively, to the end that he might fully ascertain whether they presented any new point which could be material. He accordingly took home the papers, and to-morrow or the next day will probably announce his final decision. There is no doubt about it. These new facts whether true or false have nothing to do with the question, and you may expect judgment and execution in the causes in the Circuit Court, June 10, as by arrangement made at Portsmouth." (1 Webster's Priv. Cor. 306.)

The new facts were precisely what Webster "expected." What were they? Let Judge Smith, his associate, answer. In his letter to Mr. Brown, of December 18, 1818, Smith says: "Immediately after I sent to the post-office my letter to you of yesterday, Mr. Sullivan and Mr. Ich. Bartlett, with Mr. Upham, of the University, called on me with a bundle of papers, to be certified as authentic, and to be used in the argument of the College causes, if adjudged pertinent or proper evidence." These papers were termed by him "the Wheelock papers." We have, together with this letter, the original schedule, in the handwriting of Judge Smith. The papers are ranged in the schedule under numerous heads, commencing with the printed "narrative" of the elder Wheelock, and ending with an abstract from his will. The schedule covers numerous letters, records, and papers, including those in the matter of Landaff. The written headings alone cover nine long pages. We have referred to this evidence, and Brown's abstract of it, in previous chapters.

Aside from Story's passion, to which we have already referred, of gathering every item of legal, political, and judicial gossip, he had the amplest facilities for becoming perfectly familiar with the history of these proceedings which resulted in the College suits.

At the first hearing upon the causes in the Circuit Court, in May, 1819, Judge Story read an elaborate opinion, supposed to be substantially the same as that filed with the reporter in Trustees v. Woodward. No formal opinion is understood to have been rendered at the second hearing.

Story's views in relation to these causes are undoubtedly to be found in his opinion in Trustees v. Woodward, and Allen v. McKeen, 1 Sumn. 276–318. Story's decision in the College causes, in effect, annihilated Dartmouth Uni-

versity, handed over the munificent bequest which John
Wheelock had made to it to a New Jersey college (as is
said, to Princeton), deposed William Allen, the president,
and drove him from Hanover.

In December, 1819, the same Dr. Allen became the
president of Bowdoin College, at Brunswick, Maine, which
office he held, in legal contemplation, till 1839. This college was chartered by the Legislature of Massachusetts,
June 24, 1794. This act provided for establishing the
college; put it under the government of two bodies corporate; made the president, treasurer, and eleven others
one of these bodies, with perpetual succession; provided
for the creation of a board of overseers; gave the corporation power to declare the tenure and duties of certain
officers, with power to remove trustees, etc. The six-
teenth section gave the Legislature authority to "grant
any further powers to, or alter, limit, annul, or restrain
any of the powers by this act vested in, the corporation, as
shall be judged necessary to promote the best interests of
said college." The next section granted to the college
five townships, six miles square, to be laid out of any
unappropriated lands of the Commonwealth in the then
district of Maine, with the usual provisions that the corporation might acquire property and take donations, etc.

The lands granted vested in the corporation, and donations were given it from time to time by private individuals.
The college boards were duly organized under the charter,
and the college went into operation in the year 1801. In
July, 1801, the corporation fixed the salary of the president
at $1,000 *per annum*, payable quarterly. In 1805, this was
raised to $1,200. On November 4, 1801, the board declared
the tenure of the office of president to be "during good
behavior." The by-laws required every candidate to pay
$5 to the treasurer, for the president, and a like fee for
every medical degree.

In May, 1820, Dr. Allen assumed the duties of this office,

with this known tenure and the salary and perquisites annexed. In the same month the boards passed a vote reciting the clause in the Constitution of Maine as to endowments, and declared that their consent be given that the right to enlarge, limit, or restrain the powers given by the charter might be vested in the Legislature of Maine, and steps were taken to secure endowments. A variety of acts were subsequently passed by the Legislature, which it is unnecessary to consider. On March 31, 1831, an act passed, aimed directly at Dr. Allen, providing " that no person holding the office or place of president in any college in this State shall hold said office or place beyond the day of the next commencement of the college in which he holds the same, unless he shall be reëlected. And no person shall be elected or reëlected to the office or place of president unless he shall receive in each board two-thirds of all the votes given in the question of his election. And every person elected to said office or place after the passing of this act shall be liable to be removed *at the pleasure of the board of trustees*, or *board of trustees and overseers*, which shall elect him." " That the fees paid for any diploma, or medical or academical degree, etc., shall be paid into the treasury for the use of the college, and no part shall be received by any officer as a perquisite of office.''

The boards, in September, 1831, duly voted " that they acquiesce in said act, and will now, etc., proceed to carry the provisions thereof into effect." The Board of Trustees gave due notice to Dr. Allen, and then proceeded to elect a president; but no candidate having a majority of votes, no choice was made, and the college remained without any acknowledged president until the question was determined.

For some inscrutable reason, Dr. Allen brought *assumpsit* for money had and received, not against the corporation, but the treasurer of the college, for the salary and perquisites of office due him, as he claimed, notwithstanding his ejection from office under the vote of the boards, in September, 1831. Story decided that he could recover the perquisites in this suit, and affirmed the principle which lay at the foundation of his opinion to Plumer in relation to the Judiciary Act of 1813, and avowed by him in his opinion in the College causes,—that an office so held was a contract protected by the obligation clause; but that for the breach of that contract he must proceed, not against the treasurer, but his master, the corporation.

Dr. Allen was not only the son-in-law of John Wheelock, but his confidant and one of his principal advisers in the troubles which preceded, as well as those which followed, the removal of Wheelock by the trustees. He was familiar with the " inside history " of the causes, and Story's position in reference to them. Allen and Dr. Perkins, to whose week's conference with Pinkney we have referred, were the principal managers of the College causes on the University side after Wheelock's death. Allen went to his grave with the conviction, still shared by Wheelock's descendants, that a great wrong had been perpetrated under the color of a judicial decision. The occasion was distasteful to Allen, but he undoubtedly took pleasure in compelling Story to decide in the case between him and Bowdoin the same question which he had nominally decided in May, 1819, in the College causes. If he won, he got his perquisites and the arrears of his salary, established his right to the office, defeated the purpose of the Legislature, and emasculated the power of his personal and political enemies in the boards; if he lost, it was the vindication of himself and Wheelock and the University, and the condemnation of Story. The reluctance with which Story met this issue is but faintly shown by his " outline " and " opinion " in this case. In closing his opinion, he says : " I have now finished all that is necessary to be said for the decision of this cause. But I cannot dismiss it without expressing my regret that it has ever come before the court, and that I have been deprived of the assistance of my learned brother, the dis-

23

trict judge, in deciding it. If this court were permitted to have any choice as to the causes which should come before it, this is one of the last which it would desire to entertain. But no choice is left. This court is bound to a single duty, and that is, to decide the causes brought before it according to law, leaving the consequences to fall as they may.

" It is impossible, in any aspect of the case, not to feel that the decision is full of embarrassment. On the one hand, the importance of the vested rights and franchises of this literary institution has not been exaggerated; and, on the other hand, the extreme difficulty of successfully conducting any literary institution without the patronage and cordial support of the government, and under a head who may (however undeservedly) not enjoy its highest confidence, is not less obvious."

Allen v. McKeen was decided in May, 1833, fourteen years after the decision in the last of the College causes.

This opinion should be read as an explanation of the most important portions of the elaborate essay filed by Story with the reporter, in Trustees v. Woodward. He says: " Independent, however, of this general ground, there is another of great weight and importance, and that is, that President Allen was in office under a lawful contract made with the boards, by which contract he was to hold that office during good behavior, with a fixed salary and certain fees annexed thereto. This was a contract for a valuable consideration, the obligation of which could not, consistently with the Constitution of the United States, be impaired by the State Legislature." The general doctrine of Story, to which, so far as appears, he consistently adhered from the time of his conference with Governor Plumer till his death, that filling an office was a contract protected by the Federal Constitution, was overthrown by the Supreme Court in 1850 (Butler v. Pennsylvania, 10 How. 402), as it has been by every reputable State court that has passed upon it.

We are not aware of any body that now indorses the

theory of Story and Livingston in the College case, in which
Marshall did not concur, that the marriage contract is within
the scope of the obligation clause.   He further says : " But
if the acquiescence of the boards could be construed into an
approval of the act (as I think it ought not to be), still that
approval cannot give effect to an unconstitutional act.   The
Legislature and the boards are not the only parties in
interest upon such constitutional questions.   The people
have a deep and vested interest in maintaining all the constitutional limitations upon the exercise of legislative powers,
and no private arrangements between such parties can super-
sede them."

Taken as it reads, this would seem to be in conflict with
the opinions in the College case.

He thus states the great question of the case : " Is it [the
charter] the erection of a private corporation for objects of
a public nature, like other institutions for the general
administration of charity?   Or is it, in the *strict sense of
law*, a public corporation, solely for public purposes,
and controllable at will by the legislative power which
erected it, or which has succeeded to the like authority?"
He concedes that the College " is, in some sense, a public
institution or corporation," and that this is the popular
sense in which the language is commonly used.   He then
proceeds : " But in the sense of the law, a far more limited,
as well as more exact, meaning is intended by a public institution or corporation."

This, in effect, decides not only that all corporations, at
common law, were divided into two classes, public and private, but that the term " public corporation " is a technical
phrase of the common law, to be construed in the narrow,
strict sense usually put by courts upon the technical words
of a penal code, while precisely the opposite construction
is put upon the term " private corporation."   His subsequent
indorsement of what has often been supposed a loose statement in his opinion in the College case, shows that he meant

to assert that this rule was among "the most solid foundations of the common law."

If we may not apply to this the remark of Walpole, we
may at least that of Mr. Justice Campbell in Jackson v.
Steamboat Magnolia, in respect to another opinion of Story:
"The opinion * * * is celebrated for its research, and
remarkable, in my opinion, for its boldness in asserting
novel conclusions, and the facility with which authentic
historical evidence that contradicted them is disposed of."
(20 How. 336.)

As if fearing that some attempt might be made to relax
this rule, after quoting from his opinion in the College case,
that towns, cities, parishes, and counties, existing for public political purposes only, may in many respects be
"esteemed" public corporations, he quotes the following
passages, which, he says, "had the approbation of the
court:" "But, strictly speaking, public corporations are
such only as are founded by the government for public
purposes, *where the whole interests belong also to the government.* * * * That is, *where its whole interests and
franchises are the exclusive property and domain of the
government itself.*" He further says that a bank "whose
stock is owned partly by private persons, and partly by the
government," is a private corporation.

The first United States Bank was incorporated with a
capital of $10,000,000, and the second with a capital of
$35,000,000. The "government," under the first charter,
was allowed to hold $2,000,000, and under the second,
$7,000,000 of the stock; and yet, in McCulloch v. Mary-
land, decided in 1820, and Osborn v. The Bank, decided in
1824, Story concurred in the opinion that the Bank of the
United States was "a public corporation, created for public
and national purposes."

That Story and Marshall had, as they were wont to do,
decided the vital question upon this point, raised by these
cases, years before it came before them judicially, is well

known. The court treated the United States Bank as one of the "instrumentalities of the government," and so might a State bank be treated as one of the instrumentalities of a State government. The distinction taken was, to say the least, convenient.

The decision in Briscoe v. Bank, etc., of Kentucky (11 Pet. 257) was, "that when a State becomes a stockholder in a banking institution, it imparts none of its attributes of sovereignty to the latter, and can, as a stockholder, exercise no other power than any other holder of stock for the same amount."

Judge Story said: "When this cause was formerly argued before this court, a majority of the judges who then heard it were decidedly of opinion that the act of Kentucky establishing this bank was unconstitutional and void."

The decision in this case is especially noticeable for a reason to which no reference has been made. The corporation was a bank, created and owned entirely by the State of Kentucky. It came fully within the remarkable definition of a "public corporation" given by Story in Allen v. McKeen, to wit, one where the "whole interests and franchises are the exclusive property and domain" of the State; for he says, in his opinion in Briscoe's case: "It is clear, therefore, that the bank was a mere artificial body or corporation, created for the sole benefit of the State, and in which no other person had or could have any share or interest." He then went on to hold that the State could not confer upon such a corporation the power to issue bank-bills.

If these opinions are well founded, either the fathers must have been the most unfortunate of men in the use of language, or their great, if not paramount purpose must have been, *first*, to render it almost impossible for a State to give legal existence to a public corporation "in the strict sense;" and, *second*, if perchance such an artificial person should struggle into existence, to cut down its powers to the lowest limit; for the principle, if sound, does not stop with the prohibition against the issue of bank-bills. If such was their purpose, it is incredible that they should not have manifested it in the plainest and most unequivocal terms. There is not a shred of history or a word in the debates that affords any warrant for such an inference. The probabilities are millions to one that no such definition or distinction, or any thought of either, ever occurred to the mind of any member of the Convention.

But, in our examination of the history of these opinions in relation to the distinction between public and private corporations, we have been often forcibly reminded of what a snowy-haired chief justice — one of a family eminent for its scholars and jurists, and standing high on the roll of judicial fame, both in State and nation — once said to us about the mass of opinions upon constitutional questions: "They are filled with ingenious reasoning, ingeniously stated, for the purpose of enabling the court to reach a conclusion at which it wishes to arrive."

Story adds, in relation to Bowdoin College: "The Commonwealth of Massachusetts is its founder, having given it its original funds. But it is made capable of receiving, and has actually received, funds from the bounty of private donors."

Baron Wood, in his Institutes, upon abundant authority, says: "He who gives the first possessions is the founder of it, though they are but of small value; so that a common person may be founder, though the king shall afterwards endow it with great possessions." It is enough to say that this duplex rule, by which a "public" corporation is construed with so much strictness and a "private" one with such "liberality," was never heard of by any body before the College case. Taken in its obvious sense, and with Story's indorsement of the argument of Mason in the State court, it would transform the generality of towns, either essentially or absolutely, into private corporations. Not a few towns were chartered, under seal, upon a consideration, in the nature of a periodic rent to the throne, with an absolute grant of all the lands in the town to the persons therein named, who were endowed with "perpetual succession," with a variety of interests reserved either to the throne or for the benefit of private individuals. In others the power to divide the same, etc., was expressly reserved ; and in others the name alone was given, without any specification of other rights, powers, or privileges.

Coke, in the case of Sutton's Hospital, says : " As to the seventh objection, it is to be known that in law there are two manner of foundations : one, *fundatio incipiens;* the other, *fundatio perficiens;* and therefore, *quatenus ad capacitatem et habilitatem*, the incorporation is, *metaphorice*, called the foundation, for that is the beginning as a foundation, *quasi fundamentum capacitatis*, preceding the whole. * * * *Sed quatenus ad dotationem, the first gift of the revenues, is called the foundation, and he who gives it is the founder in law, for propria fundatio est quasi fundatio;* and the first gift is *fundamentum dotationis seu collationis, et appellatione fundi ædificium et ager continentur;* and that is proved by the statute of West. 2, c. 41. * * * And in the report I have omitted all the arguments which were made at large upon both sides, upon one common ground, where one act shall at one instant enure to divers intents distinct in time, some holding that the bargain and sale amounts not only to a dotation, but also to a foundation, and other *totis viribus e contra; for* it appears to you now, without question, that the first dotation is the foundation." (5 R. Part X., pp. *28, *32.)

If Coke and Baron Wood were right, the first donation, no matter how inconsiderable, was the foundation.

On this point, Mr. Hopkinson urged in his brief : " From this it is clear that D. W.'s original school was founded by him at great labor & expense — that Dartmouth was but an *enlargement* of that seminary, made by his own consent — & under his direction & control and so considered by all the parties. How otherwise could he [be] considered the *founder?*

"It is therefore not correct in point of fact — nor material in point of law, to say he contributed nothing to Dartmouth College if this College is but a graft on his original stock — because, the law is clear that if the original foundation of a charity is ever [so] small, & subsequent donations or additions ever so large; they are considered but additions to the first establishment, submitting to its power & coming under its government. It is seen the contributor may grant conditionally or unconditionally — if the latter he but falls into & under the first institution. If conditionally the first founder judges whether he will accept the same.   *   *   *

"We make out our claim then under D. W. by showing that his school was founded by himself at his own expense & on his own estate — that this College is but an enlargement of that charity, without any interference with his claim or right as its founder — & so considered by all the parties at the time as appears by the charter.   *   *   *

"We answer that all these contributions were to *D. W. and his school* — before the charter was granted or perhaps contemplated — that they were to his use *quoad hoc*, — and that when they afterwards passed to the College — they passed as part of his establishment — as his.   *   *   *

"We contend on behalf of the plaintiff : —

"1. That at the time, and before, this College was chartered, Dr. Wheelock had a beneficial and pecuniary interest in the funds with which it was founded ; whether it shall be considered that the charter merely incorporated the old school under a new name ; or that the College was raised on the foundation & funds of the old school."

If we are to credit Story, a majority of the court must have indorsed his own views in relation to public and private corporations, and apparently the view of Hopkinson in relation to "grafted" or "raised" foundations. If this doctrine in relation to private corporations is well founded, and if the first donor, no matter how inconsiderable the donation, is to be treated as the founder, how can any subsequent donation or addition divest the corporate body of its character as a private corporation? If it can, why does it not transform it into a public one? If the doctrine of grafted foundations is sound, why is not that of substitutionary foundations equally so?

The governor had granted Landaff to individuals. Wentworth promised Wheelock to annul the grant, and regrant it to Moor's Indian Charity-School. He, in form, annulled the prior grant without notice to the first grantees, and transferred it to the College, whose trustees were compelled to surrender it to the original grantees, whose rights had been usurped. The title failing, the State substituted another grant in place of the former, reserving the powers already referred to, and this grant was, with full knowledge, accepted by the corporation. Why was not the State the founder by substitution?

Massachusetts gave the first lands to Bowdoin, and was, therefore, the founder.

If the assumptions of the court to which we have already referred were warranted, the king first gave Landaff to Dartmouth, and was, in consequence, its founder. If a subsequent gift by the king could neither change the original foundation nor the nature of the corporation from private to public, or public to private, it is difficult to understand how like acts by private individuals could have precisely the opposite effect. It is true that the grant of Landaff was overturned, as were many other grants by the same authority, after the Revolution; but that would seem to be immaterial. If the least private interest transforms what would otherwise be a public into a private corporation, it would be a work of great difficulty to discover a public corporation in some of the States. The Federal Supreme Court and Story assume that a stream of decisions flowing

from the sources of the common law have divided all corporations into two classes, *private* and *public*. This distinction has probably become too firmly imbedded in the
body of American law to be eradicated; but on great questions which affect the vital interests of the nation, we must,
after a time, recur to first principles, or grope blindly after
justice through a bewildering labyrinth of contradictions
and absurdities.

Few judges equalled Story, either in industry or research.
Through his whole life he jotted down every authority which
he found sustaining any opinion he had advanced, and no
judge was so fond of parading his learning as he. The
only authority on this point relied upon by him, in the College cause, was Dr. Bury's case, decided in 1694. When
he came to decide Allen *v.* McKeen, in 1833, after fourteen
years more of research and investigation, he was only able
to give the additional authority of his own opinion in the
College case. It is safe to say that, if any others could
have been found, they would not have escaped him.

The contrast between the opinions of Washington and
Story upon this point is, as we have seen, very marked.
Washington simply assumes that Dr. Bury's case contains
all the "doctrine" on the subject, and that no case has
been found in conflict with it.

To fully comprehend Phillips *v.* Bury, and the cases that
followed in its train, a knowledge of the preëxisting law
and history is necessary.

College and university corporations, like others, existed
in the mother country, — (1) by the common law; (2)
prescription; (3) letters-patent from the crown; (4) grants
in the ordinary form by Parliament; and (5) by what were
in essence "charters of confirmation," granted by Parliament, where charters had been lost, or where the "jurisdiction, privileges, and statutes" of a corporation rested
in tradition.

The powers which they had, varied. In general, among

these privileges was that of the domestic forum, as it was termed, — the right to govern and correct its own members, and that of trying all civil suits, at law and in equity, in which one of the parties was a member, no matter where the other might be, before the scholars, master, steward, visitor, chancellor, vice-chancellor, or other corporate judicatories.   This was extended, in some instances, to nearly all criminal offences, including maim, felony, and treason, as well as misdemeanors.   Persons claimed these privileges who were not entitled to them, as well as those who were. Those who felt aggrieved at this claim of exclusive jurisdiction in the kingdom brought their grievances, praying for interference and relief, before the upper bench, in the time of Cromwell, upon applications for *mandamus*, prohibition, and the like.   The same course was pursued early after the Restoration.   The courts early established the rule, as a matter of sound discretion, that they would not interfere in regard to the private or domestic constitutions and statutes of such societies, but would as to the public laws of the land, for the reason that over them the founder could give the visitor no exclusive jurisdiction, — much in the same way as our courts, as regards ecclesiastical matters, remit the parties to the judicatories established by the denomination of which they are members.   The loose and inconsequential *dicta* in one of the English cases, in relation to private and public corporations, is the outgrowth of this view ; but it was never held that the king's courts had no jurisdiction where the officers of the corporation neglected or refused to take the proper oaths, as did the officers of Dartmouth College.

Phillips *v.* Bury was the famous case of Exeter College. Dr. Bury was rector in 1689.   On October 16, 1689, he deprived John Colmer, one of the fellows, for incontinency. Colmer appealed to the Bishop of Exeter, visitor of the college.   The bishop, having heard the appeal, sent his chancellor, in March, 1690, to the college to restore him ;

but Bury and the seven senior fellows refused to give him admittance. On July 26, 1690, after a variety of proceedings, the bishop deprived Dr. Bury for contumacy, and put John Painter in his place as rector, who demised to the plaintiff; whereupon the plaintiff entered and brought suit against the defendant. Justices William Gregory, Giles Eyre, and Samuel Eyre held that judgment should be given for the defendant; but Holt, C. J., held otherwise. Holt held that the court had no jurisdiction; the others, that it had. Holt's opinion, taken from his own manuscript, covers nearly thirteen pages (2 Term Rep. 346–358), and discusses a variety of questions. He held, first, that, by the particular constitution of this college, the Bishop of Exeter had power, in this case, to give sentence; and, second, that, having that power, the justice of that sentence is not to be examined in a court of law upon an action. In the course of this discussion, he says: " And that we may the better apprehend the nature of a visitor, we are to consider that there are in law two sorts of corporations aggregate, — such as are for public government, and such as are for private charity. Those that are for the public government of a town, city, mystery, or the like, being for public advantage, are to be governed according to the laws of the land; if they make any particular private laws and constitutions, the validity and justice of them is examinable in the king's courts. Of these there are no particular private founders, and consequently no particular visitor; there are no patrons of these. Therefore, if no provision be in the charter how the succession shall continue, the law supplieth the defect of that constitution, and saith it shall be by election, — as mayor, aldermen, common council, and the like. * * * But private and particular corporations for charity, founded and endowed by private persons, are subject to the private government of those who erect them; and, therefore, if there be no visitor appointed by the founder, the law appoints the founder and his heirs to be

visitors, who are to proceed and act according to the particular laws and constitutions assigned them by the founder.''

The question before the court upon this branch of the
case was, as stated by Lord Holt himself, not whether corporations were public or private, but whether the constitution, the statutes, of this particular college excluded the
jurisdiction of the courts of common law.   He held that
they did.   It is obvious that what we have quoted from him
was not only a *dictum*, but loosely worded and obscure in
meaning at that.   If taken as it reads, all banks, and the
great trading and industrial corporations, are neither public
nor private.

The House of Lords, after an argument by Bishop Stillingfleet, reversed the judgment of the three judges, holding
that the courts of common law had no jurisdiction.   We are
not aware of any evidence that that body affirmed the *dictum* of Lord Holt.   Bishop Stillingfleet based his argument
mainly upon the ground of policy.

It is quite evident that Webster had never seen Stillingfleet's report of the case, or his argument.   The MS. argument of Webster shows that he obtained all his information
on the subject from 1 Burn's Ecclesiastical Law, 439–445.
This report does not attempt to state that argument with
accuracy.   It says : —

"In the argument whereof, Bishop Stillingfleet spoke to this
effect: that this absolute and conclusive power of visitors, is no
more than the law hath appointed in other cases, upon commissions of charitable uses ; that the common law, and not any ecclesiastical canons, do place the power of visitation in the founder
and his heirs, unless he settle it upon others ; that although a corporation for public government be subject to the courts of Westminster Hall, which have no particular founders, or special visitors,
yet corporations for charity founded and endowed by private persons are subject to the rule and government of those that erect
them ; but where the persons to whom the charity is given are
not incorporated, there is no such visitatorial power, because the
interest of the revenue is not invested in them ; but where they

are, the right of visitation ariseth from the foundation, and the founder may convey it to whom and in what manner he pleaseth; and the visitor acts as founder, and by the same authority which he had, and consequently is no more accountable than he had been; that the king by his charter can make a society to be incorporated, so as to have the rights belonging to persons, as to legal capacities; that colleges, although founded by private persons, are yet incorporated by the king's charter; but although the kings by their charters made the colleges to be such in law, that is, to be legal corporations, yet they left to the particular founders authority to appoint what statutes they thought fit for the regulation of them. And not only the statutes, but the appointment of visitors was left to them, and the manner of government, and the several conditions on which any persons were to be made, or to continue, partakers of their bounty. *But that which is particularly to be observed, is, that these founders of colleges did take special care to prevent, as much as possible, all law-suits among the members of their societies, as most destructive to the peace and unity of their body, and the tranquility necessary for their studies; for they knew very well, that if any encouragements were given to suits at law, those places would in time become nurseries for attornies and solicitors, which would pervert the main design of their foundation.*

"Walter De Merton, the first founder of a college in Oxford, with revenues to support it, took such care about this, that he puts the case, in his statutes, of a warden's being deprived, and knowing that men are apt to complain when they suffer, and to endeavor in one way or other to be restored, (which causeth great heats and animosities among the contending parties,) therefore, to prevent these mischievous consequences, he puts a chapter in on purpose in his statutes, that if such a case should happen, *nulla actio, nullum juris remedium canonici vel civilis habeat.*"

Neither the crown nor Parliament had in any wise attempted to alter, amend, or repeal the charter, or the constitutions or statutes brought in question in Dr. Bury's case. The question there related entirely to the power of the courts of common law in the premises, and not to the power of the crown, Parliament, or any legislative body. The statutes and constitutions referred to were, in essence, what we term by-laws. The technical difference was, that they could not be amended or annulled except by virtue of a power reserved.

The report of this case in the House of Lords occupies about twenty-four pages in "Shower's Cases in Parliament."

The view taken by Chief Justice Holt in the court below, of course, was urged, as well as a variety of other grounds.

The argument and decision are thus summarized, at the close of the report of the case : —

"It was replied in behalf of the plaintiff much to the same effect as 't was argued before, and great weight laid upon the con. tumacy which hindered the observance of the statutes; that by allowing such a behavior in a college no will of the founder could be fulfilled, no visitation could ever be had; and all the statutes would be repealed or made void at once; that tho this crime was not mentioned 't was as great or greater than any of the rest; that here was an authority and well executed and upon a just cause and in a regular manner so far as the rector's own misbehavior did not prevent it, and therefore they prayed that the judgment might be reversed: and upon debate the same was reversed accordingly."

Notwithstanding the *dictum* of Story that the *dictum* of Holt ties the hands of the "government," it is apparent, as we have already seen, that this must refer alone to the throne, for it could not tie the hands of Parliament.

Generations to come may well marvel when they realize that this obscure and contradictory *dictum* of a single judge has been injected into the Federal Constitution, by construction, and that our whole system of government, and the vast and varied interests of our people, must be regulated in accordance with it. They might as well have expected that the mist would mould the granite.

The great case of Charles River Bridge *v.* Warren Bridge was formally decided February 14, 1837. This was virtually another college case. In 1650, Massachusetts granted to Harvard the power to dispose of a ferry between Boston and Charlestown, over Charles River, and the college held this ferry under this grant till 1785, when certain persons were incorporated as the proprietors of the Charles River Bridge, authorized to erect a bridge where the ferry was, and to take tolls for forty years, and were to pay Harvard £200 annually for thus destroying the ferry. In 1792, the charter was extended thirty years. In 1828, Massachusetts incorporated the proprietors of the Warren Bridge, with power to erect another bridge over the same river. The two bridges were sixteen rods apart on the Charlestown side, and fifty rods on the Boston side. The charter of the Warren Bridge was to expire in six years, and then be free to all.

As was obvious to the mind of every intelligent man, the effect of the second grant was to materially impair the value of the prior grant for the six years, and thereafter to render it essentially worthless. The Charles River Bridge filed a bill in equity against the Warren Bridge, at the March term of the Supreme Court of Massachusetts, 1828, praying for a temporary injunction to restrain the defendants from building a bridge under the charter, and also from suffering passengers to go over it. The court (6 Pick. 376–407) unanimously denied the motion. In 7 Pick. 344–532, the court were equally divided upon the main question. The bill was therefore dismissed, and the case went up on error from the March term, 1829, to the Federal Supreme Court. The great question, of course, was whether the second grant was prohibited by the obligation clause. It was heard before Marshall, and afterwards before Taney. The last argument was made in January, 1837. Story prepared his opinion more than five years before the decision. In his letter to Mason, of November 19, 1831, he says: " I am now engaged on the Charles River Bridge case. After it is finished I should be glad to have you read it over, if I thought it might not give you too much trouble. It is so important a constitutional question, that I am anxious that some other mind should see, what the writer rarely can in his zeal, whether there is any weak point which can be fortified, or

ought to be abandoned. The general structure of the argument, I hope, is sound; but all the details may not be."
(Mason's Mem. 335.) Mason, in his reply, of November 24,
1831, says: " I will most willingly examine your opinion on
the case you mention, and give you the result of my reflections
on it." (Mason's Mem. 336.) In his letter of December 23,
1831, to Mason, Story says: " Owing to my recent illness,
from which I am now, as I trust, entirely recovered, the preparation of my opinion in the Charles River Bridge case was
suspended. I have just completed it; and it is to be copied,
and I hope to send it to you by the middle of the next week.
If you should have examined it sufficiently to give your
opinion, I should be glad to receive it before I go to Washington, which will be by Sunday, the 2d of January. If
not, I will thank you to send it to me by mail at Washington. I wish to make some remarks to explain its great
length and the repetition of the same suggestions in different
parts of the same opinion. I have written my opinion *in
the hope of meeting the doubts of some of the brethren*,
which are various, and apply to different aspects of the
case. To accomplish my object, I felt compelled to deal
with each argument separately, and answer it in every form,
since the objections of one mind were different from those
of another. One of the most formidable objections is the
rule that royal grants, etc., are to be strictly construed;
another is against implications in legislative grants; another
is against monopolies; another is that franchises of this
sort are bounded by local limits; another, that the construction contended for will bar all public improvements. I have
been compelled, therefore, to restate the arguments in different connections. *I have done so, hoping in this way to
gain allies.* I should otherwise have compressed my opinion
within half the limits." (Mason's Mem. 336, 337.) Story
undoubtedly spoke for himself and the dead chief justice,
and his opinion was entirely consistent with those given by
him in the College causes.

The argument of Marshall on this point, in Fletcher *v.* Peck, as his reference to Blackstone shows, is that a grant by the State stands in the same place as an executed sale of a horse by A. to B. ; or, if we are to believe Webster, the gift of a sum of money from C. to D. The opinions in the College cases rest upon the same foundation. But the majority of the judges in the Bridge case evade this underlying principle by a flank movement. They say, in effect, that though a grant by the king to A. is, in a constitutional sense, as much a contract as one between B. and C., yet the grantee in the first case takes nothing by implication, while exactly the reverse is true in the second case ; and that therefore one is, in effect, protected by the Constitution, while the other is not.

While we are clear that the decision in the Bridge case was right, we are equally clear that an unsound reason was given for it. Chancellor Kent, whose view in relation to this distinction was indorsed by a large majority of the great lawyers of his day, said, in his letter to Story, of June 23, 1837 : "I abhor the doctrine that the legislature is not bound by everything that is necessarily implied in a contract, in order to give it effect and value, and by nothing that is not expressed *in hæc verba ;* that one rule of interpretation is to be applied to their engagements, and another rule to the contracts of individuals."

The decision in the Bridge case was right, for exactly the same reasons that the argument in Fletcher *v.* Peck and the opinions in the College cases were wrong.

CHAPTER XV.

CONSTITUTIONS are, in theory or in fact, a restraint upon " those in authority." They vary in form with time, place, and circumstance. The British Constitution is a mass of traditions and customs inwrought by the conservative temper of the classes which create and control the two great estates of the realm ; the constitutions of several of the colonies were royal commissions ; the constitution of Russia was a wholesome fear of assassination ; and in the United States the Constitution is, in form, a written instrument, but in fact what five or six men on the Supreme Bench see fit to make it. Gouverneur Morris, one of the greatest of its framers, called the experiment " a vain attempt to tie up the arm of government with paper bands." This is the point where our institutions touch despotism the nearest. The moss-grown rule is, that judges shall not make, but construe, laws, and interpret constitutions ; but this rule cannot remould human nature. If the judges err in their interpretation, either through mistake, inadvertence, bias, or design, the same result follows, — they alter, amend, or repeal the provisions of the Constitution. For this there is no remedy.

The influences to which we have already referred may affect the action of the court, but the judges are beyond the control of public opinion.

The fathers borrowed from Great Britain the forms of impeachment. In 1820, Jefferson termed it " an impracticable thing, a mere scare-crow ; " and the writer, not to speak of other instances, who has seen Underwood, at Richmond, occupying the seat of John Marshall, has a realizing sense of what Jefferson meant. To-day it hardly rises to the dignity of a farce. Impotent for good, these provisions must be a dead letter in the future, unless revived as an instrument of partisan vengeance, when both houses are controlled by the same party.

The Constitution provides for its amendment, but the process is slow, uncertain, and useless unless the judges favor it. In 1793, in Chisholm v. Georgia, Jay, true to his idea that States were but county corporations, sought, contrary to the opinion of Hamilton and Marshall, to bring the defendant State to the bar of his court, just as he would the members of a quoit club, or an incorporated cheese factory. The people reversed that decision, by the Eleventh Amendment.

In 1821, Judge Marshall, in Cohens v. Virginia, by a " liberal " interpretation of the original provisions and by a " strict construction " of that amendment, nullified the purpose of the people in adopting it, by holding that it did not apply where the original proceeding was instituted by the State, and that the prohibition was addressed to the Federal courts.

The Federal Constitution provides that " no State shall * * * emit bills of credit."

In Craig v. Missouri, 4 Pet. 410, and Briscoe v. Bank,

8 Pet. 118, 11 Pet. 328, 329, 350, where the State owned the bank, Marshall decided that the bank and the State were one, and were to be treated as identical, saying, in answer to the suggestion that they were not: " Is the proposition to be maintained that the Constitution meant to prohibit names, and not things? That a very important act, big with great and ruinous mischief, which is expressly forbidden by words most appropriate for its description, may be performed by the substitution of a name? That the Constitution, in one of its most important provisions, may be openly evaded by giving a new name to an old thing?"

Yet in 1824, in Osborn v. Bank, 9 Wheat. 738, which was a bill brought by the bank, in the Circuit Court, to restrain the State auditor of Ohio from collecting a tax, etc., Marshall held that, " as the State cannot be joined as a defendant, its agent may be sued alone;" and that "the prohibition to sue a State contained in the Eleventh Amendment to the Constitution does not extend to cases in which a State is not made a party on the record, *even if the State has the entire ultimate interest in the subject-matter of the suit.*"

It is obvious that a State cannot exist or act except by and through its officers, and that for such purpose they are the State.

The decision is, in effect, that the amendment did not prohibit the bringing of suits against the State, and was not so intended, but simply changed the form of the process and of the docket-entry, and provided that the *name* of the State should be struck out, and those of its officers, its other self, should be substituted for it.

This decision reduces the amendment to a quibble about forms. Whether the amendment was wise or otherwise, was one thing; what it meant was another. That Marshall thought it unwise, and cut its heart out by a judicial repeal, is evident. Taken with recent decisions on the tax power, it comes to this: The officers of a State are the State. Therefore, —

1. The State cannot be taxed [out of existence] by taxing its officers.

2. A State cannot be sued.

3. A State can be sued [out of existence] by suing its officers.

And this impotent conclusion comes from one who, before the amendment, after weeks of deliberation, announced to the Virginia Convention that a State could not be sued at all.

The same fate befell another amendment, in the Slaughter-House cases.

In 1856, in Scott v. Sandford, 19 How. 393, the court held that Congress could not prohibit slavery in territory acquired by the Federal government by treaty. This decision was reversed, a few years later, by a gigantic civil war.

Few men desire a repetition of the farce of impeachment, or the fruitless experiment of attempting to restrain the judges by constitutional amendments, or the costlier one of reversing decisions by a resort to arms.

John Marshall had no hand in forming the Federal Constitution, but for twenty-six out of the thirty-four years of his judicial life that Constitution was, through compromise or otherwise, what he saw fit to call it.

The life and acts of such a man should be scrutinized with care and weighed with candor.

Mind and body harmonized with each other, but in both Marshall was unlike other men, — an extraordinary and peculiar being. He was tall, — six feet in height, — thin, slender, angular, meagre, and emaciated, but erect and agile, while his muscles were so relaxed and joints so loose as to destroy all harmony in his movements and grace in his actions. His complexion was swarthy; his head was small, covered with shocks of thick, stout, wiry hair, raven black; his forehead was rather low, but upright, and full in the temples; his face was small, making nearly a circle in its outline; his eyes were small, twinkling, piercing, and dark as midnight;

his voice was dry and hard ; his attitudes, at best, extremely awkward, and his only gesture in speaking was a perpendicular swing of the right arm. He was of Welsh descent, and was the oldest of fifteen children. His father was a Virginia planter and surveyor, of limited means. He was born in Fauquier County, September 24, 1755, and died in Philadelphia, July 6, 1835. Previous to the Revolution, he resided most of the time near Manassas Gap and at Oak Hill. Society there was very primitive. The people lived on mush and balm tea, and the women fastened their dresses with thorns, instead of pins. The population was sparse, accessible schools were unknown, and facilities for acquiring knowledge were exceedingly limited. Until his fourteenth year, his father was his only instructor. He spent his fifteenth year with James Monroe, a hundred miles from home, in the study of Latin, under the private tutorship of a clergyman ; the next year he continued his studies, under the supervision of a Scotch parson, in his father's family ; and this was all the education he had.

Early in his eighteenth year he commenced the study of the law, but the din of the approaching conflict compelled him to abandon Blackstone and turn to other pursuits. In the spring of 1775 he was made lieutenant in a militia company, and soon after first lieutenant in one of " Minute Men ; " in December, 1775, he was in the battle of Great Bridge, about twelve miles from Norfolk ; in July, 1776, he was appointed lieutenant in the Eleventh Virginia (Continentals), and in the winter of 1776–7 joined the army at Morristown ; in May, 1777, he was made captain, and was in the engagement at Iron Hill, at Brandywine in September, at Germantown in October, and went into winter quarters at Valley Forge in December following. He was at Monmouth in June, 1778 ; with Wayne at Stony Point, and at Powle's Hook in July, 1779. In the winter of 1779–80 he attended the law lectures of Wythe, — afterwards chancellor, — at William and Mary's College, retained his con-

nection till the summer of 1780, and soon after obtained a
license to practise.   In October, 1780, he returned to the
army, and remained till 1781, when he resigned his commission, and devoted himself to the study of his profession
till after the surrender of Cornwallis, in October, 1781,
when the courts were reopened.   After the Revolution, he
became a general of the State militia, and, in consequence,
from that time till 1801, when he was made chief justice,
was almost entirely known as General Marshall.   In the
spring of 1782, he was elected a member of the lower house
from his native county ; and in the autumn, to the executive
council.   In January, 1783, he married, and removed to
Richmond, where, in spite of the flattering inducements
held out if he would remove to Philadelphia, he resided till
his death.   Early in 1784, he resigned his place in the council, and in the spring was again elected a member from Fauquier, and represented Henrico from 1787 till 1792.   In 1788,
he was one of the lieutenants of Madison, Randolph, Pen-
dleton, and Innis, in the Convention of June, which ratified
the Federal Constitution ; from 1792 till 1795, he devoted
himself almost entirely to his large and constantly increasing practice ; in 1795–6, he again represented Henrico ; in
May, 1797, he was appointed, and in July, with Pinckney
and Gerry, left the country, as envoy to France ; and on
June 17, 1798, he returned to New York.   He was elected
a member of Congress from the Richmond district by a
small majority, and took his seat at the December session,
1799.   On June 13, 1800, after the explosion in the cabinet
cabal, which had been inherited by Adams, he was made
secretary of State, and continued a controlling spirit in the
cabinet until the last hours of that administration.   On
January 20, 1801, Adams nominated him as chief justice ;
he was confirmed January 27, and commissioned on January
31, and presided at the term which ended February 9, of
the same year.

Marshall had rare gifts.   His character was the result of

a peculiar interblending of many opposites ; its power lay
in the combination.

He was simple and unpretentious, and as modest, sensitive, and averse to every form of notoriety as he was cour-
ageous ; he had an ardent social nature, a seductive personal
magnetism ; he was a delightful companion, fluent and facile
in conversation, and, aside from Andrew Johnson, the most
eloquent listener in the Union ; he was full of sly, waggish
humor, genial and convivial ; his temper was serene and
imperturbable, his patience almost inexhaustible, and his
judgment clear, cool, wary, and calculating. In youth and
early manhood he delighted in foot-races and the rough
sports of the country, and was as full of poetic longings,
aspirations, day-dreams, and romances as a school-girl.
Naturally indolent, and seldom studious, from boyhood to
the " yellow leaf" of old age his soul revelled in quoit-
pitching by day and novel-reading by night. Like Webster,
he loved a plain house and a sumptuous board, loved solid
power and the luxury of ease ; and, like Everett, loved the
old home, old scenes, old friends, and old wine. He never
sought office ; cared little for place, nothing for titles. He
was a born diplomatist, and showed himself an overmatch
for Talleyrand, with all the latter's training. He was a
natural politician, and, in general, knew thoroughly the
public men of Virginia and Maryland, with whom he was
brought in personal contact, and but little of those in the
rest of the Union. His powers of analysis, like those of
Fox, were singularly acute ; no man could be clearer, if
he chose, in statement or in reasoning ; but, when hard
pressed, his subtlety in both, equalled only by that of
Aaron Burr in practice, enabled him to ascend into the
clouds, beyond the reach of ordinary minds. He cared
little for authority, but relied mainly on his own reflections.
With Story the test was, " The policy of the law is —— ; "
with Marshall, " I have not looked much into the cases, but
I think the law ought to be —— ; " or, as Story says,

" While I am compelled to creep from point to headland, Marshall puts out to sea." Without imagination, his mind was essentially mathematical and legislative. He loved not Coke, the stern old framer of the Petition of Right, but the courtly Blackstone. He lacked the attainments of Jay, the great legal learning and the superb organizing genius of Rutledge. Great opportunities were afforded him during his long judicial life, which Ellsworth never had; but the kingly dignity, the exalted conscience, the immutability of will, and the slow but ponderous intellect of the latter were wanting.

" Never in the flow of time," to use the words of Gouverneur Morris, was there a moment so propitious for that purpose as when the work of the Federal Convention was submitted for ratification. The ablest and purest men in the Union were arrayed on the one side or the other. Talent, tact, and management carried it in New York, Massachusetts, and New Hampshire by a close vote, and in reality against the popular will.

The parties which subsequently arose were called Federal and Republican. Both were misnomers. The Federalists were not opposed to a republic, nor were the Republicans opposed to a federal government. The Constitution itself was a compromise, and, as was justly said by Ellsworth and Madison, "partly national and partly federal." Both were in favor of conferring upon the general government such powers as they deemed necessary for its preservation.

The difference was, as it were, a question of political geography, — where the boundary-line between the powers conferred upon the Federal government, and those retained by the States or people, should be located; and, as a consequence, one party became known as " liberal" and the other as " strict " constructionists. Behind each of these phrases lay a fundamental idea; but the terms themselves, as the subsequent history of parties and the country has abundantly shown, were elastic and indefinite, admirably adapted to political exigencies and the needs of politicians. There was, of course, a general accord in the views of the leaders of the respective parties, but those of Jay, Hamilton, Adams, Marshall, and Story were far from identical; and the same is true of Jefferson, Madison, and Gerry, though with them the differences were less marked. The first four favored the ratification, — part because they believed in it, and the rest as a choice of evils. Patrick Henry and Luther Martin, who afterwards became such eminent Federalists, exerted their great powers to the uttermost against it, and Gerry followed in their train. In the Virginia Convention, Madison was the great leader, — "the cloud by day and the pillar of fire by night" of its supporters. Jefferson was abroad. Had he thrown the positive weight of his great influence into the scale against it, the probabilities are very strong that no human power could have secured in its favor a majority of the Virginia Convention.

The name of Washington was undoubtedly more potent, but no one man, by his own exertions, contributed so much to secure the ratification as Hamilton; and yet, anomalous as that may seem, few, even of its opponents, had less faith in it, or disliked it more. In the Convention, on September 6, 1787, he said "that he had been restrained from entering into the discussions by his dislike of the scheme of government in general, but as he meant to support the plan recommended, as better than nothing, he wished, in his place, to make a few remarks."

In the closing hours of the Convention, September 17, 1787, he said: "No man's ideas were more remote from the plan than his were known to be; but is it possible to deliberate between anarchy and convulsion on one side, and the chance of good to be expected from the plan on the other?"

We owe to him "The Federalist." For that great work he selected for his associate his intimate personal and political friend, Gouverneur Morris. In his letter of February 24, 1815, to Hills, Morris says: "I was warmly pressed by Hamilton to assist in writing ' The Federalist,' which I declined."

There were obvious reasons for Hamilton's choice, one of which appears in the letter of Morris, of December 22, 1814, to Pickering, the discarded secretary of John Adams: "That instrument [the Constitution] was written by the fingers which write this letter." Madison — and Jay, to a limited extent — took the place of Morris. No man knew the difficulty referred to, or the views of Hamilton, better than Morris. In his letter to Walsh, of February 5, 1811, he thus states the fears of the fathers: "Fond, however, as the framers of our National Constitution were of republican government, they were not so much blinded by their attachment as not to discern the difficulty, perhaps impracticability, of raising a durable edifice from crumbling materials. History, the parent of political science, had told them that it was almost as vain to expect permanency from democracy as to construct a palace on the surface of the sea." In the letter last quoted, Morris says: "General Hamilton had little share in forming the Constitution. He disliked it, believing all republican government to be radically defective. He admired, nevertheless, the British Constitution, which I consider an aristocracy in fact, though a monarchy in name. * * * He heartily assented, nevertheless, to the Constitution, because he considered it as a band which might hold us together for some time, and he knew that national sentiment is the offspring of national existence. *He trusted, moreover, that, in the *changes and chances of time, we should be involved in some war, which might strengthen our union and nerve the executive.* He was not, as some have supposed, so blind as not to see that the president could purchase power, and shelter himself from responsibility by sacrificing the rights and duties of his office at the shrine of influence."

In his letter to Ogden, of December 28, 1804, he says:

" Our poor friend Hamilton bestrode his hobby, to the great annoyance of his friends, and not without injury to himself. More a theoretic than a practical man, he was not sufficiently convinced that a system may be good in itself and bad in relation to particular circumstances. *He well knew that his favorite form was inadmissible, unless as the result of civil war; and I suspect that his belief in that which he called an approaching crisis arose from a conviction that the kind of government most suitable, in his opinion, to this extensive country could be established in no other way.* * * * General Hamilton hated republican government *because he confounded it with democratical government, and he detested the latter because he believed it must end in despotism, and be, in the meantime, destructive to public morality. He believed that our administration would be enfeebled progressively at every new election, and become at last contemptible.*"

The Revolution brought Marshall in contact with Hamilton, then on Washington's staff, and he became so impressed with his learning and genius that he never afterwards freed himself from their influence. At a later period, he became a follower of this great leader, but, like the Taneys, and that distinguished class of Southern Federalists to whom Walcott refers, was much more moderate.

The fatigues of the camp, and the grave responsibilities which rested upon him during the war and his first administration, had their effect even upon the powerful frame of Washington; and towards the close of his last administration his energies became relaxed, and his memory, never good, seriously impaired.

Jefferson and Hamilton were pitted against each other during the first administration of Washington. On December 31, 1793, finding his situation unpleasant and his influence overweighted by that of Hamilton and circumstances, Jefferson resigned; policy and the pressure of public opinion compelled Hamilton to follow him about a year later; and Randolph, who took the place of Jefferson, was driven,

by an enforced resignation, from the cabinet in disgrace.
Washington tried in vain to fill the vacant places with men
fitted for them, but such would not accept, and he was compelled to select from an inferior class. Three out of the
four belonged to the Hamiltonian wing of the Federal party.
These men have made their own record in their private correspondence. They fastened themselves like leeches on
John Adams. Under both administrations they took their
inspiration and guidance from Hamilton. They were the
creatures through whom he moulded the policy of the government. By his election, Adams became the nominal,
while Hamilton remained the real, head of his party. The
difference between these two was almost as marked as that
between Adams and Jefferson after the French Revolution.
They differed not only in matters of detail, but as respects
first principles. Few men have been so misrepresented and
so misunderstood as Adams. Pickering, Wolcott, and
McHenry were spies in his cabinet, plotting, in the interest
of Hamilton, to defeat all his beneficent purposes and to
destroy their official head ; and the managing spirits in the
Senate, under the same control, were but little better.
Together, they made him responsible for measures which he
never originated, and to which he was at heart opposed.
Such a state of things could not last. The moderate Federalists of the South and East, under the lead of Marshall
and Dexter, rallied to the support of Adams. Pickering
refused to resign, and on June 12, 1800, Adams removed
him and put Marshall in his place.

The presidential campaign came on, with Hamilton still
plotting the defeat of Adams. The Union became an ocean
of political passion, without a parallel except that which
preceded the late civil war. Partisan fury spared nobody ;
life-long friends turned away from each other as they met ;
the furnaces of defamation, seventy-and-seven times heated,
flamed incessantly ; and more than the seven vials of vituper-
ation were poured out upon the devoted heads of Jefferson,

Adams, and their respective adherents. We can realize how such passions darken the understanding and harden the hearts of men, when we know that John Marshall, who so seldom spoke ill of any one, put his preference for Burr upon the ground that the morals and principles of even Aaron Burr were *purer* than those of Thomas Jefferson. The election went to the House of Representatives. There were sixteen States. Jefferson controlled eight, the Federalists six, and tied the other two.

From February 11 to 17, 1801, all business was paralyzed, and, in the madness of the hour, the most thoughtful and considerate men feared that the day of doom for the union of these States was at hand. More than three-fourths of the Federalists in both houses of Congress lost their heads; passion took the place of judgment. Their trusted leaders, Hamilton and Morris, lost all control over them; against their advice, they voted steadily for Burr; they determined to elect him if they could, and, if they failed in that, to put the presidency into " commission," as the British sometimes do the " great seal," by passing an act vesting its powers in Jay, Marshall, or some person to be elected by them president of the Senate. When it became reasonably certain that Burr could not be elected, Jefferson sought an interview with Adams, for the purpose of inducing him to arrest the other desperate measures. We know what that interview was, and the result of it. Jefferson was told upon what terms he could have the presidency; he refused to purchase it by capitulation. There was but one step more for the Republican leaders to take, and they acted with promptness and decision. They controlled important States, and resolved to prevent what they regarded as usurpation by a resort to arms. This shook a few of the more moderate men. The probabilities are that Jefferson never would have been president but for Hamilton, who had sought to make Pinckney president over Adams by a species of treason to the head of the ticket, and then, to defeat Burr, threw the positive weight of his great influence with certain members in favor of Jefferson. But even he was unable to secure the coöperation of Marshall.

Between Marshall and Jefferson, as before stated, there was a relentless personal and political antagonism, which had been growing for years, and which intensified as time rolled on, and colored every thought and act of each in relation to the other. The root of the political antipathy it is easy to discover, but the source of the personal hatred is unknown. There are few sadder spectacles than that of Jefferson at eighty-one, after his cordial reconciliation with Adams, and when he had forgiven every other enemy, replying to Marshall's note: "And even Judge Marshall makes history descend from its dignity, and the ermine from its sanctity, to exaggerate, to record, and to sanction this forgery;" unless it be that of the aged chief justice, eight years later, in assumed self-justification, firing a parting volley at the ashes of his dead antagonist.

In some respects these men were alike. They were of Welsh extraction, Virginians, men of eminent talents and strong convictions, simple and unaffected, and possessed of the most cordial social natures. Neither was given to enduring hatred. Jefferson forgave all but Marshall; Marshall spared the world his enmity, and lavished it upon Jefferson.

Late in 1800, Ellsworth, then in England, resigned, and Jay, who had once resigned the position of chief justice for a foreign mission, was appointed and confirmed in his place. Adams personally pressed him to accept, but he peremptorily declined. The "Ultra-Federalists" strenuously insisted that the place should be given to Justice Paterson; but Adams, partly from a dislike for that wing of his party, and partly because he desired to avoid wounding the feelings of his old friend Cushing, the senior judge, and probably because of his partiality for Marshall, who had rendered him such signal services in the case of Nash or Robbins, as well as in the cabinet, refused to make the desired appointment, and nominated the latter, who promptly accepted the position. He had abundant reasons therefor. He probably never held an office that harmonized with his tastes and diplomatic nature except that of secretary of state. He cared little for the chief justiceship itself, less for the honor, nothing for the salary. But the terms of the courts were so arranged, and the condition of the dockets such, that the position gave him what he desired, — an opportunity to remain at home, at his leisure. Previous to his accession to the bench, not only the jurisdiction of the Supreme Court was limited, but also the number of causes upon its dockets. This tribunal had been in successful operation, in general with a retinue of six judges, for eleven years, and had, so far as the reports show, including a variety of motions and matters of practice, decided sixty-four causes, an average of about six annually; and less than ten of these causes were of special importance. The position appealed to Marshall's love of power, and enabled him to keep watch and ward over Jefferson.

The appointment at first gave great dissatisfaction. The Republicans complained that Adams, because of his own personal hostility, had put the strongest opponent of their chief in Virginia as a check over him. The dominant factions of the Federal party treated the nomination of Jay as a farce, and complained that Adams had disregarded the claims of Paterson in order to reward " the favorite," who held views in relation to party policy and the construction of the Constitution more liberal than their own.

Wolcott, in his letter to Fisher Ames, states with precision what they thought of Marshall and his views: " He is, doubtless, a man of virtue and distinguished talents, *but he will think much of the State of Virginia, and is too much disposed to govern the world according to the rules of logic. He will read and expound the Constitution as if it*

*were a penal statute, and will sometimes be embarrassed with
doubts, of which his friends will not perceive the importance."*

With occasional fluctuations like that from Gibbons *v.*
Ogden (9 Wheat. 1), in which, contrary to his prior convictions, he absorbed and afterwards reiterated the argument
of Webster, to Wilson *v.* Blackbird Creek Company (2 Pet.
245), in which the reasoning and conclusion were his own,
he gradually changed his meridian toward that of Jay.

The extent of the business of the Supreme Court during
the time Marshall presided over it has been much exaggerated. Less than thirteen hundred cases were decided by it,
and, in those, Marshall delivered about five hundred opinions, or, on an average, about fifteen a year. During the
first two years after he came to the bench, but five causes
were decided, in four of which he delivered the opinion.
His first term lasted five days. The average number of
causes decided per year was less than forty. But a few
years ago, the Supreme Court of Pennsylvania, under Chief
Justice Agnew, held a term of seven weeks, and in that
time disposed of four hundred and twenty-five out of the
four hundred and fifty cases on his docket. The contrast is
apparent.

It is true that some of the decisions of the Federal
Supreme Court were of transcendant importance, but the
mass of them were of no greater consequence than those
which came before the Supreme Courts of the several States.

In December, 1801, the famous case of Marbury *v.* Madison came legitimately before the court. The facts were few
and simple.

The last part of the last session under Adams was spent
by him and his cabinet in making appointments which should
properly have gone over to the incoming administration.
The reason assigned by Adams for this step was, that he
regarded the power lodged in his hands as a great trust,

which it was his duty to exercise for the good of the Union; that his faith had been shaken in the principles of Jefferson, and particularly those relating to the judiciary; that if he did not fill the positions, and thus defeat the purposes of Jefferson, the latter would obtain control over the courts by filling them from the ranks of his political friends who shared his views, and thus endanger the government. As Jefferson phrased it: "The last day of his [Adams's] political power, the last hours, and even beyond the midnight, were employed in filling all offices, and especially permanent ones, with the bitterest Federalists, and providing for me the alternative, either to execute the government by my enemies, whose study it would be to thwart and defeat all my measures, or to incur the odium of such numerous removals from office as might bear me down." Commissions were sent to fill vacancies where no vacancies could exist, unless created by the appointee vacating one office by accepting another; others were sent through the mail to marshals, etc. Adams had signed the commissions of William Marbury, Dennis Ramsay, Robert T. Hooe, and William Harper, as justices of the peace for the District of Columbia; the secretary of state had affixed to them the seal of the United States in due form, but they had never been delivered, Adams having left before the morning light of the day on which his successor was inaugurated. They were found by Jefferson upon the table of the secretary, and he forbade their delivery.

Madison did not assume the office of secretary of state for several weeks. In the meantime, the attorney-general, Levi Lincoln, whose judicial sandals were afterwards taken by Story, was the acting secretary of state, and was cognizant of the facts. Lee, the attorney-general under Adams, moved in the Supreme Court, in each case, for a rule on Madison to show cause why a *mandamus* should not issue, commanding him to deliver the respective commissions.

Lincoln and other witnesses were examined, in the presence
of the court, upon written interrogatories.   He stated
that he was acting secretary of state when the transaction
happened ; that he did not know that the commissions ever
came to the possession of Mr. Madison, or that they were
in the office when Madison took possession of it ; he refused
to state what had become of them, the court saying if they
never came to the possession of Mr. Madison it was immaterial to the present cause what had been done with them
by others.   The rule issued; the secretary of state was
silent, but the cause was elaborately argued in behalf of the
petitioners upon the motion for a peremptory writ.   At the
February term, 1803, Judge Marshall delivered an opinion
covering nearly twenty-seven pages in the printed volume.

This was the first of that line of remarkable constitutional
opinions upon which the reputation of Marshall, as a jurist,
must mainly rest.   The issue, in a legal sense, was exceedingly narrow.   The vital and decisive question which con-
fronted the petitioners at the very threshold of their case
was, whether the court had jurisdiction ; and this depended
upon another, whether Congress could annul the Constitution, or authorize or compel the court to disregard its provisions.   This decision has often been treated as though
Marshall had discovered some new principle, as Newton did
the law of gravitation.   The question was neither new nor
difficult, nor did Marshall so regard it.   There was nothing
new in his reasoning upon that point.   He simply reiterated
what had been previously said by Hamilton, Wilson, and by
many other eminent statesmen and jurists.   In his opinion
he says : " The question, whether an act repugnant to the
Constitution can become the law of the land, is a question
deeply interesting to the United States, *but, happily, not of*
an intricacy proportioned to its interest. It seems only
necessary to recognize certain principles, supposed to have
been long and well established, to decide it.''   And in

Cohens *v*. Virginia he said : " In the case of Marbury *v*. Madison, the single question before the court, so far as that case can be applied to this, was, whether the legislature could give this court original jurisdiction in a case in which the Constitution *had clearly not given it*, and in which *no doubt* respecting the construction of the article *could possibly be raised.*"

CHAPTER XV. — CONTINUED.

IN the dark days which preceded the Revolution, the people of the Colonies had been thoroughly indoctrinated with the idea that the acts of Parliament of which they complained were unconstitutional, and therefore void, and that, in consequence, they were justified in resisting their enforcement. Judge Wilson, in a famous pamphlet, had urged with great ingenuity and force that it was the right and the duty of the courts to set aside such acts. This view was supported by many of the most eminent politicians, statesmen, and jurists of that day. This doctrine had sunk deep into the popular mind.

The judges in Rhode Island had set aside an act of the Legislature as unconstitutional. The same is true of New Jersey. In 1788 and 1793, the Court of Appeals in Virginia had done the same thing. The power of the highest court to set aside such acts was recognized in New Hampshire soon after the adoption of the written Constitution of 1784. From 1790 to 1799, they were repeatedly declared void by the highest court, and sometimes by inferior tribunals.

Jeremiah Mason began practice in New Hampshire in 1791. With characteristic humor he thus describes the manner in which two statutes of the State were set aside, one by a justice of the peace and the other " by the inferior Court of Common Pleas: " —

" At this time the Legislature was in the practice of frequently interfering with the business of the courts by granting new trials and prescribing special rules for the trial of a particular action. A ludicrous instance of the exercise of this sovereign power occurred early in my practice at Westmoreland. A poor man was accused of having stolen two small pigs of a neighbor, who

applied at my office for a prosecution for larceny. Doubting
whether the taking of the pigs, under the circumstances, amounted
to stealing, one of my students, to whom in my absence the application was made, advised to an action of trover; this was commenced, in which the two pigs were alleged to be of the value of
one dollar. The deputy sheriff, in serving the writ, finding
nobody at the defendant's cottage, left the summons safely placed
between the door and sill, which the plaintiff, living near, saw
done. As soon as the sheriff was out of sight, the plaintiff went
and stole away the summons. Unluckily for him, this was seen
by a person at a distance. The action was, of course, defaulted,
and the first news the defendant had of it was an execution. He
made a great outcry, and soon ascertained that the summons had
been stolen. He came to me with his complaint, and I offered
him to have the judgment and execution cancelled, and to let him
have a trial for the pigs. This he rejected with contempt, and
forthwith applied to the Legislature, then in session, for a remedy
for his grievance. The Legislature, without notice to the opposite
party, immediately passed an act directing the magistrate to cite
the plaintiff before him, set aside the default and try the action,
and to allow to either party an appeal. The plaintiff was cited,
and I appeared for him, and denied the power of the Legislature
to pass the act, and went into an argument on the constitutional
restraints of the legislative power. This was answered by the
opposing counsel by portraying the audaciousness of the attempt
of an inferior magistrate to question the power of the supreme
Legislature. But the justice, having been an officer in the Revolutionary army, and being desirous of sustaining his reputation for
courage, which stood high, promptly pronounced the act utterly
void, and refused to obey it. An appeal was claimed and disal-
lowed, the justice saying that, as the whole proceeding was void,
he had no rightful power to record a judgment or grant an appeal.
Thus ended the first act of the farcical drama. The defendant,
nothing discouraged by his ill-luck, obtained from the sovereign
Legislature, at its next session, an act directing the Court of Common Pleas to try the defaulted action. There the parties again
met, and, after due argumentation and deliberation had, that court
determined they would do nothing with it. By this time the pig
action had gained extensive notoriety, and tended much to bring
such special acts of the Legislature, interfering with the regular

course of the courts of law, into ridicule and deserved contempt."
(Mason's Mem. 26, 27.)

Whether the Constitution conferred upon the courts the
power to set aside, as unconstitutional, the laws passed in
violation of its provisions, was considered by the Federal
Convention. There were dissenting voices, it is true, but
the most eminent of its members treated the power as
unquestionable. Hamilton demonstrated the existence,
necessity, and propriety of this power in "The Federalist,"
and particularly in No. 78, published June 17 and 20, 1788.
Judge Wilson did the same. (1 Wilson's Works, 460,
463.) Judges of the Supreme Court, sitting at the circuit,
confirmed this view; and some of them had reiterated it in
their opinions, delivered from the Supreme Bench, without,
so far as we now recollect, a single dissenting voice, though
there were undoubtedly able men who thought otherwise.

It is no wonder, then, that Marshall regarded the point
clear and unquestionable, or that the court decided it had
no jurisdiction, and ordered the rule discharged.

The most extraordinary features of Marbury v. Madison
are, the extra-judicial character of nearly four-fifths of the
opinion, and the striking similarity in the conduct of its
author and that of Story in Ex parte Christy, to which we
have already referred. In both cases, the personal feelings
of the judges were strongly enlisted; in both, it was self-
evident that the court had no jurisdiction; in both, on that
question, the opinions were brief; and in both they went
out of their way, and attempted to decide what the law was
on a variety of the most important questions, not before the
court. Both had a purpose in adopting this censurable
course, and their eminence cannot make wrong right.

Marshall's nature was robust; he compelled argument,
listened patiently, and weighed with care, but was never
given to sentimental delicacy in the discharge of his judicial
duties. As we have already seen, he had participated in the
decision — whether at the summons of Story or of his own

motion does not appear — upon a most important question of constitutional law, when no cause was before the court; he had failed to rebuke his great friend and admirer, Wirt, who sought his opinion before he instituted his suit in favor of the Cherokee Nation. Wirt, it is true, had taken the opinion of such jurists as Chancellor Kent, Webster, Spencer, and other lesser luminaries, who were supposed to know a little something of the law; but it was, of course, infinitely more important for him to know beforehand the opinion of the chief justice, and especially when it was almost certain that his opinion upon such a question would be adopted by a majority of the court. It would simplify practice much, and lessen the labors of the profession, if all lawyers could in this way know before they instituted their causes how the court would decide them. Lord Mansfield, whom Marshall admired, had strict notions upon the subject. In Rex *v.* Earl Ferrers (1 Burr. 633), when the earl came to Westminster Hall he sent a message to the chief justice, desiring to speak with him; but Lord Mansfield bid the messenger tell his lordship, " that when an Affair was depending before the Court, he could not speak with any Body about it, *but* IN *Court.*"

In Marbury *v.* Madison, Marshall treats the case as one of " peculiar delicacy," and says, " At first view," it might " be considered by *some* as an attempt to intrude into the cabinet, and to intermeddle with the prerogatives of the executive; " and in this he was clearly right. In this case he was reviewing, as a judge, the legal effect of his own acts, and what he had omitted to do when a member of the cabinet. It puts any judge in a delicate position when he attempts to decide questions not before him, and especially where the personal relations were of such an extraordinary and peculiar character as in this case.

Marbury and Madison were the John Doe and Richard Roe of the ejectment; the real issue was between John Marshall and Thomas Jefferson, — a trial of strength in their new positions. The bulk of the opinion was a discourse upon government, addressed by one Virginia politician to another; a lecture to the new president upon the duties of his office; a horn-book for the guidance of the inferior courts in compelling the president, through his "head clerk," to obey their order, when an application for that purpose should be made to them. In Cohens v. Virginia, Judge Marshall repudiated a portion of what he termed the " *dicta* " in this opinion.

The death of Hamilton, in 1804, left Marshall the only great leader spared from the shipwreck which engulfed his political associates, and he drifted, though at first slowly, further into the Hamiltonian current. In later life, after he came under the combined influence of Pinkney, Story, and Webster, these views of Marshall were much intensified. We have before adverted to the close relations which existed between Story and Marshall, and the reciprocal influence they had over each other; that of Webster assumed a different form, and operated through another channel. Marshall did not even know Webster till after he read his speech of June 10, 1813. He regarded him as a statesman and a very able man, but never, even after the struggle between these two Titans in Bullard v. Bell, as the equal of Pinkney, whom he always declared " the greatest man and the most luminous reasoner " he had ever seen in a court of justice. Webster won upon him by his ponderous power, through Story, and by his course in relation to the court. When the attempt was made, in 1826, to repeat what transpired under Adams when the judiciary bill was passed and the appointments made, Webster, in his confidential note to Mason, of May 2, 1826, says: " In looking out for men to fill these places, a very honest and anxious desire is felt, I believe, to find men who *concur* in the leading decisions of the Supreme Court. If any error be committed on that point it will be through misinformation." (Mason's Mem. 303.) This statement carries its own comment. It is obvious what decisions Webster had in mind. We know how this sentiment pervaded the bench, and how, in consequence, Duvall endured so much discomfort, and held his place, against his own wishes, until he ascertained that he could, in effect, name his successor.

It has been suggested that Marshall dissented from the decision in Terrett v. Taylor (9 Cranch, 43). We do not so understand it.

Story, who of all men was in a situation to know the facts, in 1828, said : " Few decisions upon constitutional questions have been made in which he [Marshall] has not delivered the opinion of the court ; and in these few the duty devolved upon others to their own regret, either because he did not sit in the cause, or from motives of delicacy abstained from taking an active part.

" If we do not mistake, there is but a single case in which his judgment is known to have differed from that of the court upon any point of constitutional law. That case was Ogden v. Saunders, decided at the last term of the court, which involved the question of the constitutionality of an insolvent law which was passed antecedently to the formation of a contract and discharged its obligation."

We may remark here, that not long after the decision in Ogden v. Saunders, Mr. Webster, in a conversation with Mr. Choate in relation to that in Trustees v. Woodward, said, with his characteristic simplicity and impressive force : " There was a point which lay upon the surface of that case, neither taken by counsel nor considered by the court. If it had been properly presented, the decision would probably have been the other way." We give the statement as we have it from a member of the profession, whose personal relations with Choate and one of the leading trustees were peculiarly intimate, and to whom Choate repeated it.

Marshall adhered to the last to his opinion in the College

case. In his letter to Story, of July 31, 1833, in relation to the case of Dr. Allen against the treasurer of Bowdoin College, which we have considered in a previous chapter, he says : " I have received the paper containing your opinion in the very important case of Allen *v.* McKean. It is impossible a subject could have been brought before you on which you are more completely *au fait.* It would seem as if the State Legislatures (many of them at least) have an invincible hostility to the sacredness of charters. From this paper I should conjecture that this case will proceed no further." (2 Life of Story, 150.)

We have already shown that when this letter was written, the great Bridge case had been before the Supreme Court for years, and that Story had written out his opinion and submitted it to Mason for his inspection and revision nearly twenty months before.

We pass by the chaotic mass of contradictory opinions in relation to the powers conferred by the Constitution over admiralty causes, etc.

In Sturges *v.* Crowninshield, Marshall was compelled by the necessities of his position, as well as by his natural convictions, to adopt the middle ground between the doctrine of Johnson and Livingston on the one hand, and Washington on the other, in relation to the power of the States over bankruptcies.

In Gibbons *v.* Ogden he struck out the key-stone of the arch on which that very able constitutional lawyer, Professor Pomeroy, rests his " national " theory, by saying: " As preliminary to the very able discussions of the Constitution which we have heard from the bar, and as having some influence on its construction, reference has been made to the political situation of these States anterior to its formation. It has been said that they were sovereign, were completely independent, and were connected with each other only by a league. *This is true.*"

The doctrine of the majority of the court in Ogden *v.* Saunders, overruling Marshall, has since been affirmed (in 1872), in the following emphatic language: "The act is not an *ex post facto* law only because that phrase, in its legal sense, is confined to *crimes* and their punishment.

"The Constitution of the United States declares that no State shall pass any 'law impairing the obligation of contracts.'

"These propositions may be considered consequent axioms in our jurisprudence: —

"The laws which exist at the time and place of the making of a contract, and where it is to be performed, enter into and form a part of it. This embraces alike those which affect its validity, construction, discharge, and enforcement. * * * The ideas of validity and remedy are inseparable, and both are parts of the obligation which is guaranteed by the Constitution against impairment.

"The obligation of a contract 'is the law which binds the parties to perform their agreement.'

"Any impairment of the obligation of a contract — the degree of impairment is immaterial — is within the prohibition of the Constitution." (Walker *v.* Whitehead, 16 Wall. 314.)

But unless some limitation is imposed upon the broad terms used in these two cases from which we have quoted, a singular result might follow. The law of the place, whether statutory or otherwise, whatever it may be, by the rule stated, enters into the obligation of the contract. A., for a pecuniary consideration, might contract with B., with every possible formality of which the legal mind could conceive, to murder C. By the express terms of the contract, he might be entitled to receive his compensation. He might bring his suit, but he could not recover, because the law of the land, whether written or unwritten, stepped in at the formation of the contract and annulled the binding force of its express and positive terms.

If the College charter was a contract, it was a British contract, antedating the Constitution itself, and every principle of British law applicable to the subject, which existed at the time, entered into it or its obligation. If the proviso had been written into the charter that Parliament — the two legislative branches of the government — might alter, amend, or repeal that charter at their pleasure, this provision would have had, to say the least, as much binding force as any other in the instrument. If such a proviso had been written in, in 1769, would the adoption of the obligation clause, in 1788, have blotted it out of the charter? And yet, so far as the law of Great Britain was concerned, such a clause would have been waste paper. The legal effect of the charter was precisely the same, whether this proviso was inserted or omitted. The foundation principle upon which the whole structure of English law and government rests, is thus forcibly stated by Story: " Even in England, where the principles of civil liberty are cherished with uncommon ardor, and private justice is administered with a pure and elevated independence, the acts of Parliament are, by the very theory of the government, *in a legal sense,* omnipotent. They cannot be gainsaid or overruled.

" They form the *law of the land,* which controls the prerogative, and even the descent, of the crown itself, and may take away the life and property of the subject without trial and without appeal."

The answer, if there be any, to the supposed difficulty would seem to be that such a case or purpose never entered the minds of the framers of the Constitution, or of the people when they adopted it; but Marshall, in Trustees *v.* Woodward, concedes that this is also true in respect to the doctrine adopted by him, and holds that it is for those who deny it, or its application, to go further, and show if it had been brought to their attention they would have rejected it. How, before what tribunal, and by what evidence, can this be shown?   Such a rule makes a question of constitutional law of transcendant importance depend upon a Yankee's " guess " as to what a mere question of fact was.

But a great change in the current, prefigured by the revolt of a majority of the judges, in Ogden v. Saunders, from the domination of Marshall and Story, was to come.   The decisions in the great cases of the Mayor, etc., of New York v. Miln (11 Pet. 102), Briscoe v. The Bank of Kentucky (11 Pet. 257), and Charles River Bridge v. Warren Bridge (11 Pet. 420), were second in their importance only to the action of the Federal Convention in creating the Constitution.   They had been argued with great ability before Marshall, and had been carefully considered by him.   In his opinion, the State laws in question were in violation of the Federal Constitution, and therefore void.   The same causes were reargued before his successor, and held valid.

The decision in the case of The Mayor v. Miln, aided by that in Wilson v. Blackbird Creek Company, smoothed the way for that in Gilman v. Philadelphia (3 Wall. 713), in which a majority of the court made a dissenting opinion of Taney the law, and overturned one of the foundation principles of Gibbons v. Ogden.

We have already commented upon the great departure, in the case of Charles River Bridge v. Warren Bridge, from the construction put upon the " obligation clause " in Fletcher v. Peck and the College cases.

In 1835, the language of the Constitution was precisely what it was in 1837 ; but as names and forms cannot change substance, in these two years we lived under two materially different constitutions.   These decisions in 1837 filled Story with alarm.   The truth is thus pithily stated by his son: " The fact that, in the only three constitutional questions which came before the court this session, my father found himself compelled to deliver dissentient opinions, indicates very plainly that the constitutional views of himself and Marshall differed from those entertained by a majority of his present brethren upon the bench.   *   *   *   My father now became convinced that a new era had come, and that with the spirit which now animated the court he could not hope to agree with them upon constitutional points. His position was, therefore, rendered somewhat embarrassing, and he was very desirous to resign his office." (2 Life of Story, 271.)

Story himself says, in his letter to Harriet Martineau, of April 7, 1837 : " I am the last of the old race of judges. I stand their solitary representative, with a pained heart and a subdued confidence. Do you remember the story of the last dinner of a club who dined once a year? I am in the predicament of the last survivor." (2 Life of Story, 277.)

In his letter to Judge McLean, of May 10, 1837, Story says : " There will not, I fear, ever in our day be any case in which the law of a State or of Congress will be declared unconstitutional ; for the old constitutional doctrines are fast fading away, and a change has come over the public mind from which I augur little good. Indeed, on my return home I came to the conclusion to resign." (2 Life of Story, 272.)

In his letter of April 12, 1845, Story writes to his old friend Bacon : " I have long been convinced that the doctrines and opinions of the old court were daily losing ground, and especially those on great constitutional questions. New men and new opinions have succeeded. The doctrines of the Constitution, so vital to the country, which in former times received the support of the whole court, no longer maintain their ascendancy. I am the last member now living of the old court, and I cannot consent to remain where I can no longer hope to see those doctrines recognized and enforced.   *   *   *   I am persuaded that by remaining on the bench I could accomplish no good either for myself or for my country." (2 Life of Story, 527, 528.)

We have already referred to Fletcher v. Peck. The Legislature of Georgia, in 1795, claiming that the United

States had no title to certain Western tribal lands, that they were within the boundaries of Georgia, that Georgia held the title, subject to the unextinguished Indian title, authorized the governor, by an act for that purpose, to convey the same to James Gunn and others.   The governor made the conveyance in due form, for a valuable consideration.   A portion of these lands was conveyed by the original grantees to James Greenleaf, and from him through a chain of conveyances to the defendant, Peck.   All the conveyances after that to the original grantees were made for valuable considerations, without knowledge or notice on the part of any of these vendees that the original grantees secured the passage of this act, as was alleged, by bribery, etc.   A subsequent Legislature, alleging this corruption, passed another act rescinding the former one, annulling the deed to the original grantees, and asserting the title of the State to the lands it covered.   Peck conveyed, with covenants, to Fletcher. After the act, Fletcher brought suit for covenant broken. This, like Sturges v. Crowninshield, was a Massachusetts case.   In the one the legislation of Georgia, and in the other that of New York, was held invalid.   Whether Fletcher v. Peck was at the bottom a genuine case, or one in which important questions were mooted for the purpose of furthering in another field the interests of speculators, may be questioned, however legitimate it may have been so far as the counsel and some of the immediate actors were concerned.   This cause was argued the last time by Martin for the plaintiff, and Robert Goodloe Harper and Joseph Story for the defendant.   Few things could be more absurd than to imagine these great lawyers gravely arguing before such a court whether the solemn enactment of a great State could be set aside by the finding of a quarter-sessions judge or petit jury that its passage was procured by "undue influence," or purchase.

Judge Marshall discussed the points raised by the first count last, and seems to have held, —

1. That a State, unless restrained by its Constitution, may sell its lands.

2. There was no such prohibition in the Constitution of Georgia.

3. That the question as to the title of the United States had been settled by compact.

4. That the reservation, "for the use of the Indians," etc., "was a temporary arrangement," and did not prohibit the State from acquiring or selling these lands.

5. That somehow the Indian title either could or would not be legally invaded.

6. That a recovery might be had, notwithstanding the peculiar language of the covenants and the state of the Indian title.

7. That, as between the State and innocent purchasers, the court would not enter into an investigation of the question as to whether the original grantees obtained their title by corrupting the Legislature or not.

The fourth covenant was, that the title to the premises had been in no way constitutionally or legally impaired by any subsequent act of any subsequent Legislature of Georgia.

The third count based upon this covenant set forth the corruption of the Legislature, the annulling act at length, and averred that by reason of this act the title of Peck was constitutionally and legally impaired. The defendant again pleaded that the first purchaser under the original grantees, and all subsequent holders of the property, including himself, were purchasers without notice. There was a demurrer and joinder. Eight pages of Marshall's opinion are devoted to the discussion of the questions thus raised.

It would seem that five, at least, of the grounds upon which Marshall put the decision originated, not with him, but the counsel. The argument of the counsel for the defence upon two of these points is thus reported by Judge Cranch (p. 123): "The Legislature of Georgia could not revoke a grant once executed. It had no right to declare the law void ; that is the exercise of a judicial, not a legislative, function. It is the province of the judiciary to say what the law *is*, or what it *was*. The Legislature can only say what it *shall be*.

"The Legislature was forbidden by the Constitution of the United States to pass any law impairing the obligation of contracts. A grant is a contract executed, and it creates also an *executory* contract, which is, that the grantee shall continue to enjoy the thing granted, according to the terms of the grant."

The opinion of Marshall certainly adds nothing to the clearness and force of these positions. But he apparently originated and coupled with them the points in relation to *ex post facto* laws, bills of attainder, and estoppel.

Fletcher *v.* Peck has been commonly treated as if he put the judgment distinctly upon *the* ground that the annulling act impaired the obligation of contracts. Few things could be farther from the truth. In summing up, he puts the judgment distinctly upon the ground " that, in this case, the estate having passed into the hands of a purchaser for a valuable consideration without notice, the State of Georgia was restrained, either by *general principles* which are common to our free institutions, *or by the particular provisions* of the Constitution of the United States, from passing a law whereby the estate of the plaintiff in the premises so purchased could be constitutionally and legally impaired and rendered null and void." The italics are ours.

This is but little, if any thing, more than was said by the same judge when " delivering the opinion of the court" in Insurance Company *v.* Canter (1 Pet. 511). In that case, after discussing whether the power to govern was derived from the right to acquire territory or from a specific clause in the Constitution, he put the judgment upon the ground that, " whichever may be the source whence the power is derived, the possession of it is unquestioned." In subsequent decisions by the same court, this power has been placed first on one of those grounds and then on the other. The first proposition stated by Marshall as the foundation of the judgment in Fletcher *v.* Peck was the one, as we have seen, supported at length by Mason and Smith before the State court, and by Mr. Webster in the Supreme Court, in the College case. That this was the favorite doctrine of Story, as well as Webster, is not only well known as a fact, but is shown by Story's letter to Mason, above quoted, and in his subsequent opinions in Terrett *v.* Taylor (9 Cranch, 50) and Society *v.* Pawlet (4 Pet. 480). If this position was sound, the discussion of the obligation clause and other provisions of the Federal Constitution was unnecessary, Johnson having spoken for himself.

The second reason assigned for the judgment is, not that the annulling act was prohibited by a particular provision, — *i.e.*, the obligation clause, — but by "particular provisions" of the Constitution. Those "provisions" are sufficiently indicated in the opinion. The argument is, that the rescinding act was void because —

1. It was virtually a bill of attainder.
2. It was, in effect, an *ex post facto* law.
3. It impaired the obligation of contracts.

Marshall quotes and indorses Blackstone's definition of contracts. (2 Bla. Comm. *440, *443, chap. 30.) This chapter is entitled, "Title by gift, grant, and contract." He says: " Gifts, then, or *grants*, which are the eighth method of transferring personal property, are thus to be distinguished from each other: that *gifts* are always *gratuitous; grants* are upon some consideration or equivalent; and they may be divided, with regard to their subject-matter, into gifts or grants of chattels *real* and gifts or grants of chattels personal. * * * Grants or gifts of chattels *personal* are the act of transferring the right and the possession of them; whereby one man renounces and another immediately acquires all title and interest therein ; which may be done either in writing or by word of mouth, attested by sufficient evidence, of which the delivery of possession is the strongest and most essential. * * * A contract may also be either *executed*, as if A. agrees to change horses with B., and they do it immediately ; in which case the possession and the right are transferred together ; or it may be *executory*, as if they agree to change next week ; here the right only vests, and their reciprocal property in each other's horse is not in possession, but in action ; for a contract *executed* (which differs nothing from a grant) conveys *a chose in possession;* a contract *executory* conveys only *a chose in action.*" That the learned author did not refer to the effect of legislative enactments or the alienation of sovereignty is too obvious for comment. It is impossible to reconcile the definition of Blackstone indorsed by Marshall with Webster's argument in the Bridge case. Webster says that grants are donations ; Blackstone and Marshall, that they are not. Judge Marshall says : " The contract between Georgia and the purchasers was executed by the grant. A contract executed, as well as one which is executory, contains obligations binding on the parties. A grant, in its own nature, amounts to an extinguishment of the right of the grantor, and implies a contract not to reassert that right. A party is, therefore, always estopped by his own grant."

Precisely what is meant by this is not clear. I own a cargo of flour. About my title there is no dispute. My neighbor, knowing all about it, buys it, pays for it, and takes it away. What obligation do I owe him ; what obligation is binding on me ? I own lands, — convey them without covenants. The purchaser pays me and enters into possession. What obligation binds me ? If a legal estoppel is meant, it would seem obvious that a naked grant carries no obligation with it. The contract has been executed ; it has done its work. It is true that parties may couple executory agreements with the subject of an executed contract, but that is simply saying that parties may make executory contracts if they choose, and that the obligation of those contracts is protected.

It was not true that a grant, *ipso facto*, amounted to an extinguishment of the right of the grantor, and implied a contract not to reassert that right. It is true that this had been so held in some cases, as between the crown and its grantee, and had been applied indiscriminately to municipal as well as other corporations. For obvious reasons, no such doctrine had ever been applied as between Parliament and its grantees, or between individuals.

If a grant — which Webster, in the Charles River Bridge case, says is a donation — creates by implication a valid executory contract that the grantee shall enjoy this grant without impairment, or that the party of the first part shall not reassert the right of a grantor, the grantee is entitled to redress for the damages to which he may be put by a breach of that implied contract by the grantor. Does the phrase " implied contract " mean implied covenant? If not, what is the form of the remedy? If the title enures to the legislative grantee by estoppel, how can he recover for the loss of a title which he has not lost, and which, being vested, is so protected by the Federal Constitution that it can neither be taken away nor impaired? The idea of such a contract and estoppel is irreconcilable.

This was a suit at law, and not a proceeding on the equity side of the court. From the language used, the context, and the general drift of this branch of the opinion, it is hardly within the range of possibilities that Marshall referred, in his opinion in Fletcher *v.* Peck, to what is now known as equitable estoppel, and which was almost, if not entirely, unknown in suits at law when that case was decided.

Chief Justice Perley, in Horn *v.* Cole (51 N. H. 287), states with great force and clearness the character of, and distinction between, legal and equitable estoppels. He says :

"The ground on which a party is precluded from proving that his representations, on which another has acted, were false, is, that to permit it would be contrary to equity and good conscience. This has sometimes been called an *equitable estoppel*, because the jurisdiction of enforcing this equity belonged originally and peculiarly to courts of equity, and does not appear to have been familiarly exercised at law until within a comparatively recent date; and, so far as relates to suits at law affecting the title to land, I understand that in England, and in some of the United States, the jurisdiction is still confined to courts of equity. * * *

" So, in a writ of entry, by the technical rules of law, if the demandant proves seizin in himself, and disseizin by the tenant within the time of limitation, he is entitled to judgment; but if the demandant, having a dormant title to the land demanded, concealed his title and encouraged the tenant to purchase from another, he is not allowed, in our practice, to set up his legal title, because it would be contrary to equity and good conscience.

" It thus appears that what has been called an equitable estoppel, and sometimes less properly an estoppel *in pais*, is properly and peculiarly a doctrine of equity, originally introduced there to prevent a party from taking a dishonest and unconscientious advantage of his strict legal rights, though now with us, like many other doctrines in equity, habitually administered at law. But formerly the practice was different, and suits at law, the courts being unable to give effect to this equity, were often enjoined where the party insisted on his rights at law, contrary to the equitable doctrine.

" It would have a tendency to mislead us in the present inquiry, as there is reason to suspect that it has sometimes misled others, if we should confound this doctrine of equity with the *legal estoppel by matter in pais*. The equitable estoppel and legal estoppel agree, indeed, in this: that they both preclude from showing the truth in the individual case.

The grounds, however, on which they do it are not only different, but directly opposite. * * *

"Legal estoppels exclude evidence of the truth and the equity of the particular case, to support a strict rule of law, on grounds of public policy.

"Equitable estoppels are admitted on exactly the opposite ground, of promoting the equity and justice of the individual case by preventing a party from asserting his rights, under a general technical rule of law, when he has so conducted himself that it would be contrary to equity and good conscience for him to allege and prove the truth."

The probabilities are but little stronger that Marshall referred to the technical estoppels of the law. They were universally recognized at that time as odious, were strictly construed, and never favored. A seal does not necessarily estop him who seals. That a grantor may estop himself by a solemn admission of fact, or bind himself by an executory agreement embodied in a sealed instrument, was as well known then as now, and it is entirely immaterial whether the deed was a warranty, release, or quitclaim; but the naked grant had no such effect. Some have supposed that Marshall meant to assert the principle that there was an implied warranty of title alike in sales of personal and real estate. It is the generally recognized American rule, at the present time, that the seller of a chattel, *if in possession, but not otherwise*, warrants, by implication, that the title is in him. It is unnecessary to consider the numerous exceptions to this rule, and limitations upon it. Even in this qualified form it was not the settled rule, either in this country or Great Britain, when Marshall wrote his opinion; and even this rule, to use the emphatic language of Professor Parsons, "must be confined to sales of *chattels.* In the sale of *real estate* by deed there are no implied warranties."

Taken in connection with the position of counsel, already stated, the only simple and natural explanation of the lan-

guage of the chief justice, which we have quoted, is that he
saw that it was impossible to construe the obligation clause
to apply to any but executory contracts; that he thought
its framers ought to have protected grants and conveyances
as well; that he felt they were within the mischiefs against
which they should have guarded, and he, therefore, invented
the "legal fiction" that an executory contract was always
inside the body of an executed one, in order to bring it
within the protection of the obligation clause.

A comparison of the opinions and the position of the
judges who sat in Fletcher v. Peck and Trustees v. Woodward shows a marked change in nine years. Marshall did
not, in the College case, as in the former, put the decision
upon several, but a single provision of the Constitution.
The positions that the acts were void because they were
virtually bills of attainder, or *ex post facto* laws, the argument
in support of which occupies so conspicuous a place in the
opinion in Fletcher v. Peck, were apparently abandoned, —
at all events, they disappeared, — with the position that
the State was estopped. But the implied contract, to which
the question of estoppel was mistletoed in some mysterious
way, still appears. Singular as it may seem, Mr. Justice
Johnson, after the somewhat remarkable conference at
Albany, descends from the pedestal of his "higher law," —
the highest ever heard of, that "which will impose laws
even on the Deity," — abandons his stout dissent from Marshall, in Fletcher v. Peck, in relation to the obligation
clause, and concurs in the judgment in the College case
"for the reasons stated by the chief justice." Whether
this was the result of the compromise in Sturges v. Crowninshield, or in some other case, and, if so, how much was
saved because "the minority thought it better to yield
something than risk the whole," we have no means of
knowing.

We need not search far for Marshall's real reasons. He
feared the people and the States. He felt that there should

be a restraining power somewhere.   He thought it would be
exercised with more safety and consideration by the court —
i.e., himself — than by any other department of the government.   He seized the elastic words of the obligation clause
and gave them the construction which he thought would
best accomplish that end.

CHAPTER XVI.

THE opinion of the chief justice in Trustees v. Woodward
is very able. Less could not have been expected from such
a man, in such a cause, under such circumstances. He had
decided the case in March, 1818, and knew how nearly alone
he stood, for Judge Washington had restricted his reasoning so as to "prevent any implied decision by this court
of any other case than the one immediately before it."
He knew the views of the doubting as well as the recalcitrant judges, and he had abundant leisure in which to adapt
his opinion to the exigencies of the case. To these considerations we undoubtedly owe the fact that, in clearness
and massive strength, this opinion falls far short of those
given in Gibbons v. Ogden, Brown v. Maryland, McCul-
loch v. Maryland, Ogden v. Saunders, and other cases that
might be named. It is as remarkable for its omissions, for
the coloring with which he invested and the fog-bank in
which he enveloped the facts, as it is for the skill and subtle

(411)

force of statement which enabled him to transfer it to the domain of abstract reasoning.

He opens the discussion with the following characteristic, but remarkable statement. He says: "It can require no argument to prove that the circumstances of this case constitute a contract. An application is made to the crown for a charter to incorporate a religious and literary institution. In the application it is stated that large contributions have been made for the object, which will be conferred upon the corporation as soon as it shall be created. The charter is granted, and on its faith the property is conveyed. Surely, in this transaction, every ingredient of a complete and legitimate contract is to be found."

Few men admired Marshall as much as Wirt, who says: "In a bad cause his art consisted in laying his premises so remotely from the point directly in debate, or else in terms so general and so specious, that the hearer, seeing no consequence which could be drawn from them, was just as willing to admit them as not." Nothing could be more applicable than this to portions of the paragraph we have quoted from the opinion.

The vital question was not, as Judge Marshall has put it, whether the charter was a "contract" in a common-law sense, or some other sense, but whether it was a contract in a *constitutional* sense.

The chief justice had abundant opportunity for knowing the most essential facts. His opinion as reported, as well as that in Baptist Association v. Hart's Executors, and the most essential part of another to which we have already referred, was wrought out by him, at his leisure, during the long vacation between March 14, 1818, and February 1, 1819. He had before him, before his opinion was reported, the special verdicts in these causes, and the stipulations sent up with them; he had heard all that was said by Webster, Hopkinson, Holmes, and Wirt in the first case, and had Webster's brief; he had heard the arguments of Wirt,

Pinkney, and Webster in relation to the facts in the other causes, upon the latter's motion for a judgment *nunc pro tunc* in Trustees *v.* Woodward, and had participated in the informal conferences between court and counsel which followed.

The proposition quoted is, in effect, that it was self-evident that the charter was a contract. Marshall apparently treats the remainder of the paragraph as conclusive evidence of the truth of this proposition. If so, its terms, " so general and so specious," could hardly have been better calculated to confuse and mislead.

The internal evidence afforded by the charter itself shows that, though the substance may have been furnished by Wheelock, its legal verbiage and framework were the work of lawyers ; and, were it otherwise, history would bring us to the same conclusion, for we know who did it. These terms must be presumed to have been used in the sense in which they were used by skilled lawyers of that day.

The paragraph quoted in relation to " an application," etc., is manifestly an inference drawn by Marshall from the recitals in the charter and the finding in the special verdict, that the trustees accepted and assented to the letters-patent ; that the College corporation was duly organized ; and that, " immediately after its erection and organization as aforesaid, the said corporation had, took, acquired, and received, by gift, donation, devise, and otherwise, lands, goods, chattels, and monies of great value," etc.

Marshall says " an application " was " made to the crown, " reciting what he says " is stated " " in *the* application." In this he follows Webster's brief, instead of the language of the preamble in the charter itself. If at all, this was true only in a specially narrow and exceptional sense. No application was, in fact, made to the king ; nor did he, in fact, grant the charter ; nor did he know of either ; and the same is true of the Home Office. An application, in its normal legal sense, is a petition in writing ; and we are compelled to believe from the context that Marshall used the term in this sense.

If, by a fiction of law, Governor Wentworth could be treated as the crown, it is equally clear that no such " application " was made to him.

After Wheelock had ascertained, through Cleveland, that the governor would grant the charter for the Indian Charity-School, like a sensible man, he put his papers, etc., into the hands of his legal advisers, and had them put in form, not an " application " for a charter, but a draught of a charter itself. This draught, which was placed by Wheelock in the hands of Governor Wentworth, neither was nor assumed to be a charter of the College. Wentworth, under the advice of his counsel, amended the charter in important particulars, and, thus amended, he issued it under the great seal of the province.

Webster and Marshall substituted for the word " represented," which is used in the preamble, the word " application." No one can read the charter without appreciating the marked difference in the meaning of these terms

Marshall says the application was " for a charter to incorporate a literary and religious institution." What " religious and literary institution? " Few would gather what the truth was from the seemingly studied ambiguity of this phrase.

The representation referred to is incorporated in the preamble in these words : " And the said Wheelock has further represented a necessity of a legal incorporation in order to the safety and well-being of said seminary, and its being capable of the tenure and disposal of lands and bequests for the use of the same." The representations set forth in the preamble, and which precede the one we have quoted, remove every possibility of doubt as to what was intended by the term " seminary." They refer, with the utmost distinctness, not to what, in fact, had no existence, but to Moor's Indian Charity-School, which had existed for years. Marshall's statement confounds the two, makes them one, and treats them as identical.

We have shown — and might at far greater length — by the whole course of proceedings before the granting of the charter; by the action of the trustees of the College at their first meeting under it; by the emphatic declarations and the life-long conduct of the elder Wheelock in relation to the separation of the funds, and otherwise; by the early legislation in relation to Moor's Charity-School, which has gone unquestioned to this day; and by the conduct of the second Wheelock and his successors until the charity-school virtually expired, that this attempted confounding of the two was directly in the teeth of the plans, purposes, and intentions, not only of those who procured the charter, but of those to whom it was secured.

Marshall next says: " In the application it is stated that large contributions have been made for the object, which will be conferred on the corporation as soon as it shall be created."

It is clear, though Webster had too much sagacity and circumspection to put it in that peculiar form, that he here again alludes to the representations referred to in the preamble.

It is impossible to set forth in detail each gift, donation, subscription, and grant, with the circumstances attending it, and we shall not attempt it. An examination of the history already given, and of the preamble, will be sufficient.

The representations in the preamble are: —

1. That Dr. Wheelock, on or about 1754, in Connecticut, " at his own expense, on his own estate and plantation, set on foot an Indian Charity-School;" that he, " for several years, through the assistance of well-disposed persons in America, clothed, maintained, and educated a number of the children of the Indian natives, with a view to their carrying the gospel in their own language, and spreading the knowledge of the Great Redeemer, among their savage tribes, and

hath actually employed a number of them as missionaries and
school-masters in the wilderness for that purpose ; '' '' that
the design became reputable among the Indians, insomuch
that a larger number desired the education of their children
in said *school*, and were also disposed to receive missionaries
and school-masters in the wilderness, more than could be
supported by the charitable contributions in these American
colonies ; '' that '' Wheelock thought it expedient that endeavors should be used to raise contributions from well-
disposed persons in England for the carrying on and
extending said undertaking,'' and sent Whitaker and Occom
to England '' for that purpose ; '' that, to enable Whitaker
the more successfully to perform his work, Wheelock gave
him a full power of attorney, by which Whitaker solicited
the Earl of Dartmouth and eight other '' contributors to the
charity '' '' to receive the several sums of money which
should be contributed to such charity, which they cheerfully
agreed to do ; '' that these nine were duly appointed '' trustees of the money which had then been contributed, and
which should, by his means, be contributed for said purpose ; '' that the trustees had '' accepted '' this '' trust ''
'' under their hands and seals,'' and that the same had
been duly '' ratified by a deed of trust '' duly executed by
Wheelock.

The purpose of Wheelock in this is perfectly obvious.
He desired to raise funds in Great Britain to build up his
school in Connecticut. He knew that he was unknown to the
mass of those who would naturally be disposed to favor his
design, and that they would be likely to contribute much
more freely if they knew that their funds were to be placed
in the hands of some of the most eminent men in the kingdom as trustees, who would keep the expenditures within
the scope of the trust. Nine thousand four hundred and
ninety-four pounds, seven shillings, and seven and one-
half pence were thus raised in England, and placed in
the hands of these trustees. This, with the Scotch fund, —

likewise a trust-fund, — made about £12,000. In those days this was a large sum to be applied for such a purpose in the primitive regions of the New World. Not a penny of this sum was contributed for a college, or any other purpose, in New Hampshire. Wheelock had bestowed funds of his own upon his Connecticut school. He was not the owner of this £12,000 in his own right. At best, he was not the owner in any sense, other than any trustee is the owner of trust-funds conveyed to him by a trust-deed for a specified purpose. The English funds were collected and paid into the hands of these trustees, and held by them under a deed of trust. This was confirmed by Wheelock by his deed. These funds could in no sense be considered the funds of Wheelock; and the same is, in general, true of the Scotch fund. The trustees had no authority to expend these funds in building a college in New Hampshire; and their agent, Dr. Wheelock, had less, if such a thing is possible. The stream could not rise higher than the fountain. But, as we have seen, the trustees were opposed to an incorporation of the School even; they knew nothing about the incorporation of the College; they were not consulted about it; it was done behind their backs; and when they ascertained the fact, they were exceedingly indignant about it, and regarded it as an attempt to pervert the trust and annihilate their powers.

To do Wheelock justice, he did not claim that these funds could be used for College purposes; he conceded that they could not. He erected the first buildings with Charity-School funds, etc.; but he justified this expenditure distinctly upon the ground that it was made, not for the College, but for the Charity-School, for which the funds were contributed.

Assuming that he understood the facts, the implication from Marshall's statement would seem to be that the governor of the province, upon whom the crown had never conferred the power to create such a corporation, had the lawful authority to take from the trustees in the mother country, without their consent and against their will, the funds committed to their keeping, and thereon lay the foundation of another institution, which none of the donors had in mind when they made their contributions, and that such taking was protected by the obligation clause. There is no such blemish from Wheelock's standpoint that the School and College were distinct.

It is sufficiently obvious that these contributions were not made "for the object" of establishing Dartmouth College, or that these funds were to "be conferred" on that "corporation as soon as it shall be created."

2. That Wheelock had "given full power to said trustees to fix upon and determine the place of said *school* most subservient to the great end in view; and, to enable them understandingly to give the preference, the said Wheelock has laid before the said trustees the *several offers which have been generously made in the several governments in America,* to encourage and invite the settlement of said *school among them* for their own private Emolument and the increase of learning in their respective places, as well as for the furtherance of the general design in view;" "that a large number of the proprietors of lands in the western part of this our Province of New Hampshire, animated and excited thereto by the generous example of his Excellency, their Governor, and by the liberal contributions of many noblemen and gentlemen in England, and especially by the consideration that such a situation would be as convenient as any for carrying on the great design among the Indians; and also considering that, without the least impediment to the said design, the same school may be enlarged and improved to promote learning among the English, and be a means to supply a great number of churches and congregations, which are likely soon to be formed in that new country, with a learned and orthodox ministry, they, the said proprietors, have promised large tracts of land for the uses aforesaid, provided the *school* shall be settled in the western

part of our said Province ;" that the trustees had "given the preference to the western part of our said Province, lying on the Connecticut river, as a situation most convenient for said *school*." Then follow the representations in relation to a charter, which we have already quoted. The preamble then sets forth that Wheelock had represented that, in the infancy of the institution, the gentlemen nominated by him in his last will as "trustees in America should be of the corporation now proposed ;" "that also, as there are already large collections for said *school* in the hands of the aforesaid gentlemen of the trust in England," etc., "said Wheelock desires that the trustees aforesaid may be vested with all that power therein which can consist with their distance from the same."

Few things are clearer than that all this refers to the Charity-School and the trust funds collected for it.

This is made almost self-evident from the fact that the preamble to the charter and the preamble to the Wheelock draft are precisely alike, with the exception of a dozen verbal changes which in nowise affect the sense. This draft was incontestably framed months before any suggestion was made, even in the postscript of a letter, that Wheelock, or those he represented, desired a charter for a college, or that the Indian Charity-School or its funds should be swallowed up in it.

We have already adverted to the pointed terms in which a variety of donations and conveyances, as well as the subscriptions of 1755, were made to the School, not to the College.

Marshall says : "The charter is granted, and on its faith the property is conveyed." A few pages further on, he says : "From this brief review of the most essential parts of the charter it is apparent that the funds of the College consisted entirely of private donations. It is, perhaps, not very important who were the donors. The probability is that the Earl of Dartmouth and the other trustees in England were, in fact, the largest contributors.   *   *   *

" It is not too much to say, that the funds were obtained by him, in trust, to be applied by him to the purposes of his enlarged school."

The *fact* was, that when the charter was granted, and for months afterwards, the College had no funds whatever, aside from the Landaff grant, and not a penny had been pledged to it, so far as appears. The Charity-School, at this time, was an existing institution. About $60,000 had been raised in the mother country for it, besides several thousand dollars in this country, and, besides, the Landaff grant of twenty-four thousand acres, which had been pledged, not to the College, but to the School, and without which the one would never have been removed to New Hampshire, or the other created. The Earl of Dartmouth and the trustees contributed nothing to the College, but to the School.

The only inference to be drawn from the language of the chief justice is, that the crown promised to grant a charter, not for the Charity-School, but for the College, and that upon the faith of this promise all the "funds" to which we have referred were raised for the College, and were given and conveyed to it as soon as it was chartered.

This subtle statement evades the question of royal foundation, on the one hand, as Story's definition of a public corporation did upon the other. As we have already seen, Governor Wentworth made the promise of the Landaff grant at the same time he promised to grant the charter. The promise was in terms made " to the use of the School," and the School was to have " the quit-rents " " free."

The first donations given to the School had been eaten up years before the project of any foundation in New Hampshire had been thought of, while the Landaff grant was undoubtedly the first conveyance to the College.

If the date of this conveyance is to be disregarded, and the " promise " is to be relied on for the purpose of fixing the " foundation," it does not change the result whether the conveyance to the College was a breach of the promise and a perversion of the donative trust, or otherwise; for this "promise" was made in 1768, at the same time as the promise for a charter for Moor's School, was indissolubly linked therewith, and was not only the first in the province, but the pivot promise which brought the institution here.

If the promise made by the governor is to be treated as made by the crown, it would be a royal foundation, and Marshall concedes, in his opinion, that the Revolution put the State in the place of the crown and Parliament; and this would make the State the visitor, as suggested by Mason.

Whether the distinctive character and legal efficacy of a royal grant can be drowned out because other gifts were made by individuals, and the grant itself transformed thereby into "private donations," is at least questionable.

This fundamental error embraced in Marshall's statement is repeated in a great variety of forms, and pervades the entire opinion. As we have already shown, this proposition is contrary to the facts, and unwarranted by the findings in the special verdict.

The conjecture in relation to the Earl of Dartmouth is but little nearer the truth than this opinion, based upon the assumption. Whether we say, with Webster, that "the recitals in the charter were conclusive," or, with Story, that there is not the "least contradiction." between the "new facts and the recitals," we arrive at the same conclusion, — that these "funds" were the funds of the School, and not of the College.

Upon his assumption — having decided in less than two lines, without reference to any authority whatever, that this charter was a contract — he concedes, in the next paragraph, that the question before the court was, not whether it was *a* contract, but whether it was a contract in a *constitutional sense*.

We have already noted some of the changes in the drift since the opinion in Fletcher *v.* Peck. In that case, Marshall based the vital portion of his argument in relation to contracts upon the definition of a grant quoted from Blackstone. In his opinion in the College case he makes no allusion to that or any other definition or authority upon that point. Indeed, he does not assume to base it upon authority. He simply refers twice to Blackstone upon a point not decided, and, in summing up on another point, says: " This opinion appears to us to be equally supported by reason and by the former decisions of this court."

In Fletcher v. Peck, Marshall put his decision, so far as the obligation clause is concerned, upon the ground that it covered both executory and executed contracts, because " they [the words] are general, and are applicable to contracts of every description."

In Ogden v. Saunders, Webster simply reëchoes this when he says: " The words are general. The States can pass no law impairing contracts, — that is, *any* contract."

The chief justice was not allowed to forget this, for Mr. Hopkinson, in his argument, said: " Then it is said this is not such a contract as is intended in the Constitution. *Why not?* The Constitution speaks of contracts *generally*. No discrimination or limitation. Who then shall make one?" — and cited as authority, Fletcher v. Peck. But Marshall, in Trustees v. Woodward, found it necessary to disregard this argument, and the authority of his own opinion, to impose important " limitations " upon this doctrine, and to concede that there were many contracts not protected by the Constitution.

We have seen that the author of the obligation clause regarded all our constitutions and laws as contracts, in a general sense.

On account of his location, Hopkinson was familiar with Wilson's Works, if the court were not, and in his argument cited them as authority to this point.

If they were contracts in a constitutional sense, no law or Constitution could be altered or amended unless that power was reserved therein. Webster, in one of his most important arguments, brought Marshall and his court face to face with the fact that none of the constitutions of the original thirteen States, save that of New Hampshire, contained any provisions for their amendment.

To avoid the effect of this argument, Marshall, in Trustees *v.* Woodward, says : " On the first point it has been argued that the word ' contract,' in its broadest sense, would comprehend the political relations between the government and its citizens ; would extend to offices held within a State for State purposes, and to many of those laws concerning civil institutions which must change with circumstances, and be modified by ordinary legislation, which deeply concern the publick, and which, to preserve good government, the publick judgment must controul.   That even marriage is a contract, and its obligations are affected by the laws respecting divorces.   That the clause in the Constitution, if construed in its greatest latitude, would prohibit these laws.   Taken in its broad, unlimited sense, the clause would be an unprofitable and vexatious interference with the internal concerns of a State ; would unnecessarily and unwisely embarrass its legislation, and render immutable those civil institutions which are established for purposes of internal government, and which, to subserve those purposes, ought to vary with varying circumstances.   That as the framers of the Constitution could never have intended to insert in that instrument a provision so unnecessary, so mischievous, and so repugnant to its general spirit, the term ' *contract* ' must be understood in a more limited sense.   That it must be understood as intended to guard against a power of at least doubtful utility, the abuse of which had been extensively felt, and to restrain the legislature in future from violating the right to property.   That anterior to the formation of the Constitution a course of legislation had prevailed in many, if not in all, of the States, which weakened the confidence of man in man, and embarrassed all transactions between individuals, by dispensing with a faithful performance of engagements. To correct this mischief, by restraining the power which

produced it, the State legislatures were forbidden ' to pass
any law impairing the obligation of contracts,' —that is, of
contracts respecting property, under which some individual
could claim a right to something beneficial to himself; and
that since the clause in the Constitution must, in construction,
receive some limitation, it may be confined, and ought to be
confined, to cases of this description; to cases within the
mischief it was intended to remedy.

"The general correctness of these observations cannot be
controverted.   That the framers of the Constitution did not
intend to restrain the States in the regulation of their civil
institutions, adopted for internal government, and that the
instrument they have given us is not to be so construed, may
be admitted.   The provision of the Constitution never has
been understood to embrace other contracts *than those which
respect property, or some object of value, and confer rights
which may be asserted in a court of justice.*   It never has been
understood to restrict the general right of the legislature
to legislate on the subject of divorces."

The short of all this is, that the term " contracts " is used
in the Constitution, not in a general, but in a limited sense ;
that that instrument is to be read as though the word *pecuniary*, or some essentially equivalent word or phrase, was
written in before the word " contracts."   And Ogden *v.*
Saunders substantially incorporates the word *retrospective*
before the word " law " in the obligation clause.

The term " contracts," in its normal sense, refers to
executory contracts.   We have already referred, at length, to
Dr. Hammond's edition of Sandars's Justinian, and other
authorities, on this point; and have also quoted the statement of Mr. Austin (which was, in effect, the opinion of
Judge Johnson in Fletcher *v.* Peck), that " where a so-
called contract passes an estate,   *   *   *   it is to that
extent not a contract, but a *conveyance*, though it may be a
contract to some other extent, and considered from some
other aspect."

No matter what the chief justice might think about it,

the true and unmistakable American doctrine is, that the respective States did not take their powers, by inheritance or otherwise, from the crown or Parliament, but from the people. The States have such powers, and such only, as the people by their respective State Constitutions have given them. The Supreme Court, in Lane County v. Oregon (7 Wall. 76), and Texas v. White (7 Wall. 700), have decided, ' as the foundation idea of this government,' that " the Constitution, in all its provisions, looks to an indestructible union composed of indestructible States ; " and that " without the States in union there could be no such political body as the United States." If so, how can a State constitutionally snuff out both its own existence and that of the United States by bartering away, by legislative enactments, sovereign powers, which are indispensable to existence?

There were abundant reasons why the prohibition should be levelled at the interference with executory contracts. Marshall limits the clause to contracts which respect property. Looking at the matter from the standpoint which he undoubtedly occupied in Fletcher v. Peck, and following his own reasoning in relation to executory and executed contracts, why should he? Marriage is a contract. At common law, like other contracts, it could not exist without the consent of the parties. A valid marriage merges the promise to marry in the contract. Marriage embraces both an executed and an executory contract, — one party proposes, and the other accepts. When consummated, it is an executed contract. The parties have become man and wife. The " implied " continuing contract is that they are to live together in that relation, in conformity to all the laws of the land which may be thereafter enacted. To this extent like that invented by Marshall, it is purely an executory contract. If one party breaks this executory contract, the courts can release the other party. The legislature cannot authorize divorce for a past act. Marriage is not a matter of mere civil institution. It might as well be said that a conveyance, or that the mass of commercial transactions are matters of civil institution.

Marriage is a contract, subject to such prospective legislation as may provide what subsequent breaches of the executory contract shall be sufficient grounds for discharging the parties from its obligation ; but this is for special reasons of State policy touching the great interests of society, in maintaining the power of regulating the terms upon which so peculiar and important a contract may be rescinded or annulled.

It seems to us, from the debates in the Convention, the views of Judge Wilson, and those of other eminent authorities to which we have referred, that the framers of the Constitution had in mind the meaning given by the civil law when they adopted the provision. An interpretation which would restrict the provision to executory contracts would be much more natural and reasonable than the other. A comparison of the passages quoted with those from Story, to which we have already adverted, shows how Marshall shrank from the logical consequences of his position and reasoning.

Prior to the adoption of the Constitution of 1784, in New Hampshire, decrees for divorce, etc., had always been granted by the Legislature. That Constitution provided that " ALL causes of marriage, divorce, and alimony, and all appeals from the respective judges of probate, shall be heard and tried by the Superior Court, until the Legislature shall, by law, make other provision."

The natural inference would seem to be that such decrees, taking into consideration the then existing law as to property rights of men and their wives, might affect " contracts " " which respect property, or some object of value," etc.

Marshall further says : " The case being within the *words* of the rule, must be within its operation likewise, unless there be something in the literal construction so obviously absurd, or mischievous, or repugnant to the general spirit of the instrument, as to justify those who expound the Constitution in making it an exception." Placing these passages beside those already quoted, but one construction can be put upon them. His canon of constitutional interpretation was, that the term "contracts" was used in a limited and not in a general sense; but, presumptively, was used in a general and not in a limited sense until the contrary was shown "beyond a doubt."

We have already commented on his practical test, that those who claim that a given case does not come within the limited sense of the term must show that, if such case had been brought to the attention of the fathers, they would have "varied" "the language" "so" "as to exclude it, or it would have been made a special exception." How is it possible to show such an exception, or, indeed, any other, when the Supreme Court itself concedes that the point raised in this case had never occurred to any human being when the Constitution was adopted? A grave question of constitutional law reduced to a question of fact, and that decided upon conjecture!

One year after the decision in Trustees v. Woodward, Marshall delivered the opinion of the court in Owings v. Speed (5 Wheat. 420). The case was simple enough. In 1785, Virginia issued a patent to Bard and Owings for one thousand acres of land in Bardstown. In 1788, the Legislature of Virginia passed an act vesting one hundred acres of this tract "in trustees, to be laid off in lots, some of them to be given to settlers, and others to be sold for the benefit of the proprietors." This suit was brought in the Circuit Court of the United States, as was Fletcher v. Peck, and three of the College causes, and involved, as Marshall claimed, in one form, the same question as Trustees v. Woodward. That question was, whether the act impaired the obligation of contracts. It was held that it did not.

Marshall, in Trustees v. Woodward, says: "According to the theory of the British Constitution, their Parliament is omnipotent. To annul corporate rights might give a shock to publick opinion, which that government has chosen to avoid; but its power is not questioned. Had Parliament immediately after the emanation of this charter, and the execution of those conveyances which followed it, annulled the instrument, so that the living donors would have witnessed the disappointment of their hopes, the perfidy of the transaction would have been universally acknowledged. Yet then, as now, the donors would have had no interest in the property; then, as now, those who might be students would have had no rights to be violated; then, as now, it might be said that the trustees, in whom the rights of all were combined, possessed no private, individual, beneficial interest in the property confided to their protection. *Yet the contract would at that time have been deemed sacred by all. What has since occurred to strip it of its inviolability? Circumstances have not changed it. In reason, in justice, and in law it is now what it was in 1769.* * * *

"By the Revolution, the duties, as well as the powers, of government devolved on the people of New Hampshire. *It is admitted that among the latter was comprehended the transcendant power of Parliament, as well as that of the executive department. It is too clear to require the support of argument that all contracts and rights respecting property remained unchanged by the Revolution. The obligations, then, which were created by the charter of Dartmouth College, were the same in the new that they had been in the old government. The power of the government was also the same.* A repeal of this charter at any time prior to the adoption of the present Constitution of the United States would have been an extraordinary and unprecedented act of power, but one which could have been contested only by the restrictions upon the Legislature to be found in the Constitution of the State. But the Constitution of the United States has imposed this additional limitation: that the legislature of a State shall pass no act 'impairing the obligation of contracts.'"

It is clear, from this, that at some time after the Revolution the Legislature of New Hampshire had the power to pass the acts in question or to annul this charter.   When and how was it lost?

Whether or not Marshall, with the rest of the people of Virginia, lived for more than half a century under a Constitution which discarded what he, in Fletcher *v.* Peck, termed the " general principles which are common to our free institutions," we have no occasion to inquire.   If this act was the exercise of a "judicial" power, the decision in Owings *v.* Speed cannot be reconciled with the reasoning in Fletcher *v.* Peck.

We are not aware of any difference in the moral quality of robbing a man of his real estate, whether done by the Virginia or any other Legislature.   The act the constitutionality of which was in question in Owings *v.* Speed took the land of A. from him and vested it in B.   The acts of the Legislature of New Hampshire, the constitutionality of which was brought in review in Trustees *v.* Woodward, ousted no trustee, and took away none of *their* property. They were left as they stood before, but others were added to their number.   We are unable to see any greater "perfidy" in this act than there was in the act of the Virginia Legislature, which despoiled the owners of their real estate, and of all right, title, and interest therein.

Precisely what is meant by the passages last quoted from Marshall's opinion in Trustees *v.* Woodward, taken together, is not in all respects clear.   Some of the propositions, it seems to us, are in flat contradiction of each other.   Apparently, they can only be reconciled upon the assumption that Marshall intended to adopt in fact, while avoiding it in name, the first proposition of Mason at Exeter, — afterwards enforced by Webster at Washington, — that, laying the State and Federal Constitutions out of the case, the acts in question were void because judicial, and not legislative, in their nature.   If this were so, we are unable to see how a reservation in a charter, that it might be altered, amended, or repealed at pleasure, could change the nature of the power, transform what was in essence judicial into that which was legislative, and thereby, in effect, confer upon Congress and the State Legislatures judicial powers which the respective Constitutions have denied to them.

In Crease v. Babcock (23 Pick. 334), the Supreme Court of Massachusetts held that " a reservation by the Legislature of the right to repeal an act of incorporation for a violation of the charter, or other default, is not unconstitutional on the ground of being a reservation of judicial powers."

The distinction suggested is not warranted by any of the later decisions of the Supreme Court, ending with the so-called Granger cases.

In the turn-table Legal Tender cases (Hepburn v. Griswold, 8 Wall. 603; Legal Tender cases, 12 Wall. 457), the majority of the Federal Supreme Court first held that Congress had no general power, under the Constitution, to pass a law "impairing the obligation of contracts;" but afterwards, the minority, now transformed into a majority, held that Congress had the power. It seems never to have occurred to any of the judges that this power was judicial, and not legislative; and the same is true of the subsequent decisions upon the effect of the reservation clause.

The superstructure falls with the foundation. Wherever the power exists, — and the principle is the same whether the reservation is written in or implied, — the exercise of that power is everywhere deemed an act of legislation.

If we assume that a charter is not a contract, the power to alter, amend, or repeal — it being legislative — must, as a fundamental principle of British law, be deemed, by implication, to exist in every charter. This charter, then, in legal effect, was precisely what it would have been had the reservation clause been written in. If the charter was a contract, the same result follows from the principles underlying the decision in Ogden v. Saunders. Parliament, then, as an act of legislation, had the power to alter, amend, or repeal the charter at pleasure, and the people of New Hampshire had the same right after the Revolution, unless they had divested themselves of that power by the State or Federal Constitution. The decision of the State court was conclusive in this action that the State Constitution had no such effect. The only remaining question, then, was whether the Federal Constitution, by the obligation clause, had blotted out this integral part of the charter or contract.

If, as Marshall says, the charter was a contract, and " circumstances have not changed it," and, " in reason, in justice, and in law, it is now what it was in 1769," it is simply impossible that the Federal Constitution should annul such an important provision in the contract.

It would, indeed, be singular if a provision of the Constitution, adopted for the very purpose of preventing interference with contracts, should subvert the purpose of its originators by striking out, in effect, a vital part of them.

Those who believe that charters are not contracts in the sense of the Constitution, or that the purpose of its framers was inconsistent with the retention of the reserved power, look at the question from a different standpoint. A pointed illustration of the latter view may be found in the effect of the adoption of the Constitution on the following provision of the charter : "And we do further will, ordain, and direct that the President, Trustees, Professors, Tutors, and all such officers as shall be appointed, for the *public instruction and government* of said college, shall, before they undertake the execution of their offices or trusts, or within one year after, take the oaths and subscribe the declaration provided by an act of Parliament, made in the first year of King George the First, entitled 'An act for the further security of his Majesty's person and government, and the succession of the crown in the heirs of the late Princess Sophia, being protestants, and for the extinguishing the hopes of the pre-

tended Prince of Wales, and his open and secret abettors,' —
that is to say, the President before the Governor of our
said Province for the time being, or by one by him empowered to that service, or by the President of our said Council,
and the Trustees, Professors, Tutors, and other officers,
before the President of said College for the time being,
who is hereby empowered to administer the same ; an entry
of all which shall be made in the records of said College."

The Legislature of New Hampshire, by the act of June
27, 1816, — one of the acts complained of, — attempted to
abrogate this oath of allegiance to the British king and to
substitute another for it.   The seventh section of that act
provided, " that the president and professors of the University, before entering upon the duties of their offices, shall
take the oath to support the Constitution of the United
States and of this State, certificates of which shall be filed in
the office of the secretary of this State within sixty days
from their entering on their offices respectively."

This, we have seen, in the mother country, was a public
law which the courts were bound to enforce, and which was
nowhere deemed any infringement upon the rights, powers,
and privileges of such corporations.   Why should it not be
so here?   Why should Dartmouth College be more private, have more rights, than any so-called private eleemosynary corporation in Great Britain?

This is one of the acts set aside by Marshall in this case,
as unconstitutional.

The chief justice, in his opinion, makes no allusion to the
oath of allegiance required by the charter, though the broad
terms used by him would seem to cover it.   If the charter
was in 1816–19 precisely what it was in 1769, " in law,"
the officers were still bound to take the oath of allegiance
to the British crown.   It is hardly possible, however, that
Marshall could have meant this.   The oath required was
inconsistent with the Constitution, and, therefore, by implication, was annulled by it.

Did the power to alter, amend, and repeal occupy essentially the same position? And was that also annulled?

Marshall lays some stress upon the term "forever," etc. These are merely formal words, like those common alike in all instruments of this character, both where the power is expressly reserved and where it is not. It might as well be argued that the words, "of our special grace," "mere motion," etc., made the grant a "gratuity," and thus put it beyond the protection of the obligation clause. They can no more annul the power where it is a part of the contract or charter by implication, than where it is expressed.

We have previously shown that the distinction between public and private corporations, in the sense in which those terms were used by Story and his compeers, was unknown before the decision in Trustees v. Woodward.

Unless we are to look, contrary to the view of Marshall in Craig v. Missouri, at "names, not things," this was a university. The governor who granted the charter so regarded it, and proposed, of his own accord, to hedge it about with the jurisdiction of universities in England with which he was acquainted. Dr. Wheelock, the founder of the school and the master-spirit of the whole undertaking, so regarded it, and acted in accordance with that view until his death. The trustees, who were the corporation, acted upon this understanding almost down to the time when the controversy broke out. They voted to establish professorships, examined students, and conferred upon them degrees as officers of the University, and in a variety of ways held the institution out to the world as such. To-day it embraces in its fold the agricultural and medical colleges, and the academic, scientific, and civil-engineering departments, which are, in fact, colleges, simply bearing a "new name for an old thing."

Even the charter itself, in a variety of forms, uses the universities in the mother country as the measure or standard of the "power and authority" conferred by it. It puts the

" degrees " on the same footing " as are usually granted in
either of the universities or any other college in our realm
of Great Britain." When the charter speaks of " either
of the universities," it refers directly to the Universities
of Cambridge and Oxford. Of this there is no doubt.

Moor's Indian Charity-School had " alms, free bounty, to
be distributed," and so have some, and perhaps all, of these
colleges ; but the University, as such, none. Judge Smith,
in his argument, conceded that, if a university, it was " upon
the principles of the common law a civil, and not an ' eleemosynary, corporation.' * * *

" But there is another division, proper to be stated at
greater length, I mean of civil and eleemosynary corporations. We have both sorts. Our civil corporations are
created for government, and for ' the carrying on of divers
special purposes.' Our counties, towns, parishes, school-
districts, &c., are civil corporations for government, and our
banking, insurance and turnpike companies are civil corporations for particular purposes — in no way connected with
charity. In England the general corporate bodies of the
Universities of Oxford and Cambridge fall under the head of
civil corporations ; *because merely for government;* not for
dispensing alms, but *for governing the particular colleges
which dispense* them." Even President Brown, who had
lived for years in the atmosphere of these great lawyers,
and absorbed their views of the legal phases of the case as
a sponge does water, says this was the " great point of the
defence," " the latter [colleges] being admitted to be
charities, and the former [universities] not, but designed for
the purposes of regulation, government, &c." He questioned the fact, but not that the law followed the fact. If
the corporation was a university, why could not the State
provide for its " regulation, government, &c."

Marshall makes no allusion to these provisions in relation
to the universities. There were obvious reasons for this
omission. Each of the universities was little else than a

plexus of political privileges, — an empire within an empire, — including the right to seats in Parliament.   If they were not "public corporations," if such things existed, it was next to impossible to find them.   The attempt to do so might have taxed even the marvellous inventive genius of Marshall till the strain stranded its thews.

The Granger cases mark an era in the judicial history of the Union.

The precise points actually decided in these cases are of little importance, as compared with the significance of the reasoning on which they rest, and the consequences which must flow from them in the future.

They show that the domination of the East in the Supreme Court, as well as in other departments of the government, has become a matter of history, and that the great West and South-west hold the future destinies of the country.   Eastern people are proverbially slow about some things.   They learn slowly what they do not wish to know.   Any other people would have appreciated at once the significance of late decisions of the Supreme Court, in a class of municipal-bond tax cases, to the effect that the judgments of the whole retinue of Federal courts, with the Supreme Court at their head, in causes in which they had jurisdiction, were not binding, but merely advisory to a meeting of municipal voters, and that the last was practically the tribunal of *dernier ressort*.

If the Supreme Court erred in the Granger cases, they did so having all the light that could be thrown upon the subject by the ablest men in the profession, for before them were the opinions and arguments of Benjamin R. Curtis, William M. Evarts, E. Rockwood Hoar, Matt. H. Carpenter, Judge Lawrence, Judge Dixon, the Sloans, Mr. Cook, Mr. Stoughton, Mr. Carey, Judge Ryan, and others.

In these cases, Chief Justice Waite, speaking for the majority of the court, nominally recognizes the authority of Trustees *v.* Woodward.   Chief Justice Taney tacitly did the same in Charles River Bridge *v.* Warren Bridge ; but no lawyer ever doubted that Justice Grier — speaking for himself, Mr. Justice Field, and Chief Justice Chase — reaffirmed the opinion of Taney, when he said, in his opinion in the Binghampton Bridge case : "But, assuming a power for one legislature to restrain the power of future legislatures, those who assert that it has been exercised should prove their assertion *beyond a doubt.* Such intention must be clearly expressed in the letter of the statute, and not left to be discovered by astute construction and inferences. Although an act of incorporation may be *called* a contract, the rules of construction applied to it *are admitted to be the reverse* of those applied to other contracts."

The opinion of Taney in the Bridge case was, as Story felt, a great departure from the principles underlying the opinion of Marshall in Fletcher *v.* Peck and in the College case. But the opinions in the Granger cases (94 U. S. 113–187) are in effect a far greater one. No considerate man can believe for a moment that such decisions could have been rendered by Judge Marshall's court after the decision in the College case. It is simply impossible to reconcile the two, unless the decision in Trustees *v.* Woodward is to be limited to "eleemosynary corporations," — a distinction ignored by all the cases.

Some of the opinions of the present chief justice are brief, terse, and compact in fibre, while others are diffuse and discursive, but marked with originality. The originality of the use made by him of the sayings of Lord Hale and others, though reminding one of a speech of Colonel Barre, is worthy the genius of Marshall in his best estate. That the "use was public" was conceded by the counsel for the plaintiffs, in a variety of forms, in the College case. Mr. Hopkinson said, in his brief: "We must also look to its *origin.* It is not enough that it is in fact beneficial to the public — a *manufactory — canal — road* — made by an individual for public use, with express stipulations.

"The public have an interest in everything done by the citizens. King can't *touch* a college charter."

In Planters' Bank *v.* Sharp (6 How. 327), the Supreme Court says : "One of the tests that a contract has been impaired is, that its value has, by legislation, been diminished. It is not, by the Constitution, to be impaired at all. This is not a question of degree, or manner, or cause, but of encroaching in any respect upon its obligation, — dispensing with any part of its force."

The chief justice makes no attempt to attack the judgment or to demolish the opinions in the College case, but to undermine them, and pulverize their foundation as with dualin, by adopting the theory of "public use," etc., pressed upon the judges but discarded by them in that case. If the decisions in Trustees *v.* Woodward and Bank *v.* Sharp are to be deemed correct expositions of the Constitution, Judges Field and Strong may well say, as they did in their dissenting opinions, "If this be sound law, if there be no protection, either in the principles upon which our republican government is founded, or in the prohibitions of the Constitution against such invasion of private rights, all property and all business in the State are held at the mercy of a majority of its Legislature. The public has no greater interest in the use of buildings for the storage of grain, than it has in the use of buildings for the residences of families, nor, indeed, any thing like so great an interest ; and, according to the doctrine announced, the Legislature may fix the rent of all tenements used for residences, without reference to the cost of their erection. If the owner does not like the rates prescribed, he may cease renting his houses. He has granted to the public, says the court, an interest in the use of the buildings, and ' he may withdraw his grant by discontinuing the use ; but so long as he maintains the use, he must submit to the control:' The public is interested in the manufacture of cotton, woollen, and silken fabrics, in the construction of machinery, in the printing and publication of books and periodicals, and in the making of utensils of every variety, useful and ornamental ; indeed there is hardly an enterprise or business engaging the attention and labor of any considerable portion of the community, in which the public has not an interest in the sense in which that term is used by the court in its opinion ; and the doctrine which allows the legislature to interfere with and regulate the charges which the owners of property thus employed shall make for its use, that is, the rates at which all these different kinds of business shall be carried on, has never before been asserted, so far as I am aware, by any judicial tribunal in the United States.

" The doctrine of the State court, that no one is deprived of his property, within the meaning of the constitutional inhibition, so long as he retains its title and possession, and the doctrine of this court, that whenever one's property is used in such a manner as to affect the community at large, it becomes by that fact clothed with a public interest, and ceases to be *juris privati* only, appear to me to destroy, for all useful purposes, the efficacy of the constitutional guaranty. All that is beneficial in property arises from its use, and the fruits of that use ; and whatever deprives a person of them, deprives him of all that is desirable or valuable in the title and possession. If the constitutional guaranty extends no further than to prevent a deprivation of title and possession, and allows a deprivation of use, and the fruits of that use, it does not merit the encomiums it has received.'' (Munn *v.* Illinois, 94 U. S. 141.)

" So long as that decision remains, it will be a waste of words to discuss the questions argued by counsel in these cases. That decision, in its wide sweep, practically destroys all the guaranties of the Constitution and of the common law invoked by counsel for the protection of the rights of the railroad companies. Of what avail is the constitutional provision that no State shall deprive any person of his property except by due process of law, if the State can, by fixing the compensation which he may receive for its use, take from him all that is valuable in the property? To what purpose can the constitutional prohibition upon the State against impairing the obligation of contracts be invoked, if the State can, in the face of a charter authorizing a company to charge reasonable rates, prescribe what rates shall be deemed reasonable for services rendered? That decision will justify the legislature in fixing the price of all articles and the compensation for all services. It sanctions intermeddling with all business and pursuits and property in the community, leaving the use and enjoyment of property, and the compensation for its use, to the discretion of the legislature." (Stone *v.* Wisconsin, 94 U. S. 186, 187.)

This decision was not put upon the ground that the owners of the elevators, as private individuals, stand as they would if, in the same capacity, they had owned the Suspension Bridge, — the connecting link between two great public thoroughfares.

That artificial — in the respects now under discussion — have, at most, no greater rights than natural persons, is one of the principles underlying this decision.

If the court can look at the facts in the case of private individuals, take judicial notice of them, in order to determine whether any " employment " or " business " has been " clothed with a public interest," it can do so in the case of corporations. If they could do it in Munn *v.* Illinois and Stone *v.* Wisconsin, they could do it in Trustees *v.* Woodward.

What were the purposes for which Dartmouth College was incorporated, and what were the facts? The charter thus sets forth the purposes : —

" KNOW YE THEREFORE, That We, considering the premises, and being willing to encourage the laudable and charitable design of spreading Christian knowledge among the savages of our American wilderness, and also that the best means of education be established in our Province of New Hampshire, for the benefit of said Province, do * * * will, ordain, grant, and constitute that there be a College erected in our said Province of New Hampshire, by the name of DARTMOUTH COLLEGE, for the education and instruction of youth of the Indian tribes in this land in reading, writing, and all parts of learning which shall appear necessary and expedient for civilizing and christianizing children of pagans, as well as in all liberal arts and sciences, and also of English youth and any others.''

The doors of the College have been open for more than a hundred years to all who sought its facilities. The College prescribed the terms on which they were admitted, fixed the compensation, and gave notice thereof to the world. Its graduates have gone forth by thousands to take their places in all the professions and walks of life ; the artificial power acquired by them there has been so much capital ; the influence of the institution has been felt in every department and throughout the Union. In view of these facts, well might Chief Justice Richardson say in this cause, as he did (1 N. H. 119), '' These great purposes are surely, if any thing can be, matters of public concern.'' Judge Marshall goes further. He says : '' The particular interests of New Hampshire never entered into the mind of the donors, never constituted a motive for their donation. The propagation of the Christian religion among the savages, and the dissemination of useful knowledge among the youth of the country, were the avowed and sole objects of their contributions. In these New Hampshire would participate ; but nothing particular or exclusive was intended for her. Even the site of the College was selected, not for the sake of New Hampshire, but because it was ' most subservient to the great ends in view,' and because liberal donations of land were offered by the proprietors on condition that the institution should be there established. The real advantages from the location of the College are, perhaps, not less considerable to those on the west than to those on the east side of Connecticut river. The clause which constitutes the incorporation and expresses the object for which it was made declares those objects to be the instruction of the Indians, ' and also of English youth and any others.' So that the objects of the contributors and the incorporating act were the same — the promotion of Christianity and of education generally ; not the interests of New Hampshire particularly."

As we have already seen, even Mr. Hopkinson, counsel for the College, declared it to be a "*public institution.*"

The College was located on the borders of two States ; on the banks of what was, to some extent, a natural highway, and where, at the time of its location, it was supposed that the great artificial lines of travel would converge, and where it was hoped would be located the future capital of a State.

The elevators were located at Chicago, which, partially in consequence of natural facilities, but to a far greater extent in consequence of artificial ones, has become a great focal point for the reception and transhipment of grain. The doors of these warehouses have been open for the transaction of this business, in its present form, only about twenty years.

The College has received students, and sent forth educated men with their diplomas ; the warehouses have received grain, and issued it under certificates of deposit. The College takes toll in the nature of pay for services rendered ; so do the warehouses. If " avoirdupois " is to be the test, the warehouses have the advantage ; if brain sweat is to be the test, the College leads.

The use in one case is public ; how can any man say it is not so in the other? It seems to us that Chief Justice Waite reëchoes the proposition of Lord Hardwicke, enforced by Sullivan in his argument, and enlarges its scope. He says : " Property does become clothed with a public interest when used in a manner to make it of public consequence and affect the community at large. *When, therefore, one devotes his property to a use in which the public has an interest, he, in effect, grants to the public an interest in that use, and must submit to be controlled by the public, for the common good, to the extent of the interest he has thus created.* * * * But we need not go further. Enough has already been said, to show that when private property is devoted to a public use it is subject to public regulation. It remains only to ascertain whether the warehouses of these plaintiffs in error, and the business which is carried on there, come within the operation of this principle. *For this purpose we accept, as true, the statements of fact contained in the elaborate brief* of one of the counsel of the plaintiffs in error." The brief referred to summarized the magnitude of the warehouse business at Chicago.

These principles are far-reaching in their consequences. As applied to corporations, in the absence of a positive prohibition, the nature of the business or employment " as public," or as affecting public interests, enters into and permeates the charter, leavens the lump, and, in effect, transforms it *pro hac vice*, into what, since Trustees *v.* Woodward, is commonly termed a public corporation. As we have already shown, the ablest courts and jurists have differed widely as to the extent of the power which legislative bodies may exercise over such corporations. We have before suggested what we regard as the true rule.

To carry out the principles laid down by them, it seems to us that the Supreme Court must hold that legislatures may, in general, authorize the taking of the private property of individuals for grain-elevators, hack-stands, bakers' ovens, and whatever else the court may regard as " public " employments. The test of a public use seems to be what is beneficial to the public, or what legislative bodies may deem advantageous to many people.

The Constitution imposes a restraint upon the exercise of this power. What the real or constructive public may take in this way, they must pay for.

But what is termed the power of " regulation" is far more important than that of eminent domain, and especially when applied to corporations.

Whenever the nature of the employment or business enters into a charter, the power of regulation goes with it. So far as the court has yet gone, the real or constructive public may not take the property itself without paying for it; but, under the guise of "regulation," this public may take the beneficial use of it by paying a nominal price, such as the public, through its legislative bodies, see fit to say is reasonable.

In The Boston Beer Company *v.* Massachusetts (115 Mass. 153), the plaintiffs claimed that, under their charter of February 1, 1827, incorporating them " for the purpose of manufacturing malt liquors in all their varieties, etc., in Boston," etc., which the Legislature had no power to alter, modify, or repeal, they had the right to keep for sale the products of their manufacture, notwithstanding the provisions of the statute of 1869 prohibiting the manufacture of malt liquors to be sold in the State, and brewing and keeping them for sale, under the penalties of fine, imprisonment, and forfeiture of the liquors to the State, because, if otherwise, the State could prohibit them from carrying on the very business for which they were chartered. The State court held that the Legislature had the constitutional right " to destroy the uses which were previously enjoyed, or the property so made the subject of legislation ;" and that this would in nowise impair the obligation of the contract.

The Supreme Court of the United States has recently affirmed this judgment, as it also has the constitutionality of the Thurman bill.

Since the decision in the Granger cases, in New Jersey *v.* Yard (95 U. S. 104), Farrington *v.* Tennessee (95 U. S. 679), Murray *v.* Charleston (96 U. S. 432), Edward *v.* Kearzey (96 U. S. 595), and other cases, a portion of the judges have attempted to bolster up some of the most objectionable features in the decision in the College case.

The Supreme Court has, however, made some progress, so that we are not entirely without hope that the right will ultimately prevail. In New Jersey *v.* Yard, Mr. Justice Miller says: "The writer of this opinion has always believed, and believes now, that one legislature of a State has no power to bargain away the right of any succeeding legislature to levy taxes in as full a manner as the Constitution will permit." This is refreshing. Why does not the same principle apply to the power of the State over its judicial process; to the right of eminent domain; to the police power, which has suddenly assumed such enormous proportions; and, in short, to every act whereby the legislature attempts to divest the State of any attribute of sovereignty?

In Fletcher *v.* Peck, the court decided that the States were prohibited by the obligation clause from "impairing" *any* contract, including legislative grants; in Trustees *v.* Woodward, that the clause referred only to contracts in respect to property; in the Bridge case, that, presumptively, it did not refer to royal or legislative grants; in Ogden *v.* Saunders, that it had no reference to prospective contracts; in the Granger cases, that the legislature was only prohibited from interfering with the formal title and nominal use of the grantees under these charters; and in the Beer case, if we are correctly advised as to its import, that the legislature may extinguish the charter and the rights of the grantees by prohibiting or destroying that use, if deemed detrimental to the public morals.

This zigzag line is the natural result of pushing the interpretation of the clause at first beyond its normal meaning, in disregard of the principles of legal gravitation.

The Supreme Court may, for the time being, hesitate and fluctuate as in the South Ottawa Bond case, but these rules must govern until, as it has already done in relation to admiralty jurisdiction, it turns its eye to the pole-star of legal truth, and, in spite of adverse winds and baffling currents, sails out into deep water and ignores the pernicious principles supposed to have been established in Trustees *v.* Woodward.

INDEX.

OVERSEERS,
>board of, created, 109.
>names of, for university, 111.
>members of board of, appointed; meeting of, at Hanover; meeting fails for want of a quorum, 112.
>action taken by, 114, 115.
>vacancies in board of, filled, 124, 141.

PAINE, ELIJAH,
>sketch of, 82, 83.
>>(See REMONSTRANCE; TRUSTEES.)

PARKER, WILLIAM,
>sole legal adviser of Gov. Wentworth, 34.
>sketch of, 35.

PARSONS, THEOPHILUS,
>sketch of, 167, 168.
>argument of, 168–174.
>does not allude to obligation clause, 174.
>>(See PARSONS VIEW.)

PARSONS VIEW,
>the, 108, 168–174.
>part of trustees, with Webster and Mason, rely on, 154.
>considered charter unalterable by Legislature, 174.

PARTIES,
>Federal and Republican; difference between, 378.

PHILLIPS v. BURY,
>history of, 363–367.
>opinion of Holt, 364, 365.
>in the House of Lords, 365.
>argument of Stillingfleet, 365–367.
>question in issue in, 366.
>*dictum* of Holt in, relied on by Story, 367.

PIERCE v. GILBERT,
>writ; university vouched in; verdict; taken to United States Supreme Court, 3.

PINKNEY, WILLIAM,
>brought into the college causes, 202, 241.
>gives notice of motion for reargument; closeted with Dr. Perkins, 202.
>the chief justice shuts off reargument by, 203.
>meets Webster in Bullard v. Bell, 204.
>Wirt and, on bad terms, 245, 246.
>sketch of, 246–248.
>machinery in motion that was to render efforts of, in colleges causes unavailing, 249.
>estimate of, by Marshall, 394.
>>(See COLLEGE CAUSES; TRUSTEES v. WOODWARD.)

PLYMOUTH,
>half shire town of Grafton County, 1.

STORY, JOSEPH — *Continued.*
  industry of; authorities relied on by, in College cases, 362.
  writes opinion in Charles River Bridge case five years before it was decided, 368.
  object of, 369.
  is alarmed by decisions of Supreme Court, and contemplates resigning, 399, 400.
  (See LETTERS; WILLIAM PLUMER; JOHN MARSHALL; TRUSTEES *v.* WOOD-WARD.)

SUBSCRIPTIONS,
  for carrying on controversy raised by Webster, 199.
      (See MOOR'S INDIAN CHARITY-SCHOOL.)

SULLIVAN, GEORGE,
  made barrister-at-law, 152.
  sketch of, 153, 154.
  argument at Exeter, 179–182.

SUPREME COURT OF THE UNITED STATES,
  attainments of the present judges; lacks unity of old bench, 17.
  drifting back into the doubt and uncertainty of the earlier years of its existence; a bivouac for politicans in early days; the country has outgrown the, and the inevitable result; defects in its organization, 18.
  Trustees *v.* Woodward carried to, 193.
  argument before, 200.
  judges of, unable to agree, 200.
  human, like other tribunals, 206.
  position of judges of, in Trustees *v.* Woodward, 249.
  framers of the Constitution did not intend that the construction of that instrument should be made by; controlled by a manufactured public sentiment, 252.
  practice of delivering opinions in, before and after Marshall's appointment to the bench, 309, 310.
  primitive, 310.
  opinions of, on constitutional questions, 358.
  fruitless experiment of imposing restraints upon, by constitutional amendments, 374.
  decision of, reversed by a resort to arms, 374.
  business of, 385, 386.
  doctrine of Marshall and his court modified by, 399.
  progress of, 443, 444.
  "in the end," must be governed by true principles, 444.
      (See TRUSTEES *v.* WOODWARD; OBLIGATION CLAUSE.)

TAXATION,
  legislation in relation to, 70, 72, 79, 80.
  decisions of court, 71, 73, 74, 77.
  of State, 373, 374.
      (See RELIGIOUS PHASE, ETC.)

THOMPSON, THOMAS W.,
  sketch of, 83, 84.

TABLE OF CASES.

(467)

www.ingramcontent.com/pod-product-compliance
Lightning Source LLC
Chambersburg PA
CBHW020522270326
41927CB00006B/410